The hidden musicians

The hidden musicians

Music-making in an English town

Ruth Finnegan

WESLEYAN UNIVERSITY PRESS
Middletown, Connecticut

Published by Wesleyan University Press, Middletown, CT 06459
www.wesleyan.edu/wespress

First Wesleyan edition 2007

Originally published in cloth by Cambridge University Press in 1989

Printed in the United States of America

Library of Congress Control Number 2007929707

ISBNs for the paperback edition:
   ISBN-13: 978-0-8195-6853-3
   ISBN-10: 0-8195-6853-8

The Library of Congress has cataloged the original edition as follows:

LIBRARY OF CONGRESS CATALOGING-IN-PUBLICATION DATA

Finnegan, Ruth H.
The hidden musicians: music-making in an English town / Ruth
Finnegan.
     p.   cm.
Bibliography.
Includes index.
ISBN 0-521-36066-8
1. Music—England—Milton Keynes—20th century—History and
criticism. 2. Musicians—England—Milton Keynes. I. Title.
ML286.8.M54F5   1989   2007
780'.9425'91-dc 19   88-30031

To my parents
AGNES and TOM FINNEGAN
music-makers in that other fair city,
Derry

Contents

Contents

Illustrations

Illustrations

Preface to the 2007 edition

People are always complaining that things aren't the same as in some golden age in the past – which for some is now the period twenty years ago when I first carried out this study of the amateur musicians in the English city of Milton Keynes. It is true that the local choir I sing in has dwindled drastically since its earlier heyday. It's now down to a small core of mostly rather ageing members, and we sometimes worry about its continuance. On the other hand it has just appointed a new conductor – and an excellent one too. So, as it has done continuously since 1973, the Sherwood Choral Society goes on singing devotedly at its Wednesday evening practices and performing at its regular local concerts. Then again, new choirs have been founded in the meantime and are going strong, and another choir I sing in is getting almost too big for its long-time rehearsal place. The ebb and flow of specific groups is after all nothing new. Now, in the twenty-first century, the cyclical celebrations of the year are still supported by enthusiastic volunteer musicians, invisible to some but bringing their expertise to bear on the expected occasions. Brass bands are still performing in public places around the city, new rock bands emerge with their flamboyant names, and the old as well as the new styles are played across the wide spectrum from classical and brass band music to folk, jazz, country and western, and rock.

Of course there have been many changes in the city of Milton Keynes during those twenty intervening years, but what strikes me now are the continuities in its music-making, not just the changes. The town has grown bigger in both population and area. New migrants, both national and (far more than before) international, have settled in, providing additional resources for music and raising new issues for social and political debate both within and outside the city. New musical styles and fashions have flourished. The range of music shops has changed, and with the expansion of the city glamorous new venues for music have been erected and are patronised by visiting professionals. There are new technologies too, which many musicians have turned to avidly. In short, music in its varying guises seems to have remained as strong a commitment as ever for those thousands of people engaged in the musical pathways charted out in this study, and Milton Keynes still hosts a profusion of diverse musical worlds.

Many of the musical organisations noted in the 1980s still in one way or another function today, with their continually renewing cycles of members and innovations, not least the larger-scale and more formalised associations like the brass bands, operatic societies, classical orchestras, and the leading country-and-western club. Among the small bands only a sparse handful have survived since the 1980s (among them the Fenny Stompers of chapter 8), but just as before, new bands arise to fill the places of the old, themselves no doubt destined to dissolve in the coming years, following the same pattern of dissolution and renewal as in earlier years.

The wondrous new technological devices for music-making and -listening and the opportunities of the web in one way make for striking changes in the musical environment. But at the same time much of what musicians exploit them for seems to be an extension of what they were doing already – for publicity, for recording and distributing their music, for experimenting, for listening and interchanging with others. Amidst all the changes, the pubs, schools, churches and homes still provide venues and occasions for music-making, and the rituals of urban living still give a meaning and a call for the services of local musicians.

When I was first contemplating this study of amateur music-making nearly thirty years ago – for it took far longer than I could ever have believed at the outset – my basic questions were essentially ethnographic. Rereading the material now reminds me of the queries I started out with, when I was eager simply just to discover what kinds of musicians and music-making operated in the town where I lived. Other questions soon emerged. Certainly individuals and their diverse preferences and commitments were central – but in the numerous music-making options in the town, were there also some systematic patterns and conventions? And how was it that the rich musical traditions that are taken to be a valued a part of English culture (and not just English I suspect) were actualised and sustained, and by whom? Did the practices at the local level accord with more generally held beliefs about music or about city life? Perhaps many of the answers will by now seem fairly obvious, but on several of those points I had some surprises at the time.

The music-making activities in this one smallish English town at this one period of time were certainly extensive enough to fill a book, and I remain happy that they did. But another result of my recent rereading is to renew my awareness of its gaps. It confined itself primarily to the amateur musicians (or, more accurately, to the amateur end of the complex amateur-professional continuum) and said little about the professionals or the music industry more generally. Not that I apologise for that focus, for the book is long enough already, but it did mean that this study of music in the city of Milton Keynes is only about certain dimensions and not about *all* its musical activities, either then or now. Nor did the study really get into the role of the mass media – again a deliberate decision given the over-emphasis on that angle at the time (or so I thought) at the expense of local creativity. If I was embarking on a new study now I might try to come to grips with the many-sided and elusive ways in which people use the variety of contemporary media (and, currently, the developing electronic technologies and the internet) and how these options interrelate with local artistries and interpretations. It is a subject of growing interest, not least for the ways in which such technologies may be reviving our grasp of the multisensory and performance qualities of much music-making – not just as a matter of audition but often also as visual, corporeal and material.

One gap that troubled me from the start came from my inability to go further into the musical practices of what might now be termed 'minorities,' whether defined in cultural, religious or ethnic terms. More specifically I was aware that a small number of individuals (and to some extent groups) had, for example, Vietnamese, Pakistani, Polish, Irish and Italian backgrounds or Islamic, Hindu or Sikh affiliations. I would have found it appealing to have undertaken a proper study of all or any such groups, especially those with non-European traditions, and, to be candid, I felt quite badly that as an anthropologist I was not including some in-depth material on the specificities of their activities, language and, of course, music. Given several more years or an army of research assistants (none of which I had), perhaps I could have gone some way in that direction. As it was, I had to face the fact that the city of Milton Keynes at the time had only a small number of such residents, and in order to produce a balanced local study I needed to focus on the predominant musical pathways being followed at that time and in that place. Although I did wish to note the presence of additional traditions and the issues raised in trying to handle them (subjects touched on in the chapter on 'Plural worlds'), I was unfortunately unable to elaborate further on the wider range of musics.

Another factor also was at work, for such musics were not necessarily associated with distinctive or, as it were, sustained communities within the city. In fact many (though not all) of the people who could in some sense be regarded as being of 'non-English origin' – which in itself is an elusive and controversial concept – had lived in the area for many years, had been born there and/or had children in local schools. A number were in fact participants in one or more of the musical worlds that *are* portrayed here. I should also add that at that time there seemed little evidence of anything that could be identified as a distinctive 'black' culture in Milton Keynes. There were scattered exceptions, true, chiefly in the abstractions of university-centred debates and in a very few bands where colour was possibly of some relevance. But in general one of the surprises, at least to contemporary readers, was the relative lack of what might now be called 'ethnic consciousness' in Milton Keynes musical practices – a difference no doubt from a number of cities, including certain other British cities even at that time. By now things have probably changed. With the expansion of Milton Keynes and the increase in international migration, the city has in some respects become more heterogeneous – it now has an extensive Somali community for example. Both for that reason and because of the more overt public debates over race, ethnicity and religion that have in some ways been raising consciousness in the interim, a contemporary study might need to approach things somewhat differently.

If I was starting off anew, I would also want to take account of the many advances in the study of music and culture in the years since I conducted the earlier study. Many wonderfully detailed and sensitive ethnographies of musical practices have been completed since then, leading to challenging new insights and perspectives, some of which confirm that I was correct in attaching importance to music. Expanding work exists on experience and lived meaning; on audiences; on the sounds of the city, recorded and 'background' as well as live; on 'world music'; on the interaction of the global and local; on music and place; and on the overarching social and economic powers and constraints and opportunities that I touched on only lightly but that perhaps carry more weight than I was alive to at the time. Musicological analysis – something of which I may have been over-suspicious for its imbuement with narrow-minded, elitist analyses – also has started to come into its own as an illuminating route into the further understanding of the 'popular,' not just of high-art western musics. There is much to learn from the many perceptive studies conducted over recent years, quite a few of them associated with this very Music/Culture series in which I am honoured to be included. If I were writing now I hope I would be more informed by this developing work on a subject that, too little regarded in earlier years, is now being understood so much more deeply.

That said, I believe a place still exists for a study of the kind represented by this book – an ethnography specific to its place and time both in the content of what it documents and in its historically situated approach, struggling to expand into a greater understanding of the pluralism of multiple musics, of musical practices not just works, and of the active pathways trod by practising musicians in a local setting. Such ethnographies, I believe, can retain their value. As well as resonating with experiences elsewhere, these individual musicians and their arts are unique to a time and place, realising their complex and imaginative musical action in a specific and multifaceted setting.

I suspect that many authors secretly like some of their books more than others. Perhaps I may be allowed to end with my personal feelings about this one. Returning to it has made me recognise that amongst my various offerings over the last forty years or so *The Hidden Musicians,* with all it shortcomings, is indubitably one of my favourites. Trying to work out why has been interesting. It's no doubt partly that the book came out of a huge amount of work (it was all vastly more complicated and extensive than I really had been prepared for), that it enlarged and challenged my own preconceptions, that it tied in to an activity to which I attached real value and presented me with some complex intellectual, methodological and moral challenges. There were hard patches, needless to say, and the work went on a very long time, but it was also fun to do because I was dealing with something that I personally enjoyed and found inspiring. Most of all it involved human beings, not just abstractions or generalisations, and the complex and diverse pathways they so impressively both trod and created irrespective of the ways the scholars thought they ought to be behaving. In the end, I still like this study because it is about real people in a real, not a pseudonymous, place that existed and exists: about people actively engaging in intensely human practices in which they took trouble and pains, in which they experienced disputes and sociabil- ity – and, rightly, delight.

Milton Keynes, England   R.F.
December 2006

Preface

This book began from my own unquestioning participation in local music, which only later turned into active curiosity. I had been involved in amateur music as both consumer and participant for many years, particularly in the town I had lived in since 1969 – Bletchley, later part of the 'new city' of Milton Keynes. Dwellers elsewhere were quick to label this area a 'cultural desert', but I myself found plenty of music going on locally.

At first, I just took this local music for granted and, beyond a vague expectation that the necessary arrangements would just be there for me and mine, did not think much about it. In any case my academic attention was in typically anthropological fashion mainly concentrated on comparative issues about oral literature and performance outside Britain. Rather late in the day I realised that what was going on around me was an equally interesting subject, linking with many of the traditional scholarly questions about the social contexts and processes of artistic activity and human relationships. There turned out too to be even more local music-making than I had at first appreciated from my own limited experience. My sensitivity to the artistic activities on my own doorstep was not much aroused by the standard works on British popular culture with their focus on sport or the mass media rather than the local arts, or by press discussion of music in terms of national professional activities or centralised funding and its problems. But eventually I began to wonder just how music was practised locally and what was the taken-for-granted system which under-pinned the amateur operatic societies, brass bands, rock groups, church choirs or classical orchestras. These apparently simple questions turned out not to be much thought about or as yet the subject of very much systematic research. This study attempts to provide some answers.

The book focusses on local music in one English town – Milton Keynes in Buckinghamshire in the early 1980s – in order to uncover the structure of the often-unrecognised practices of local music-making. Milton Keynes is not of course typical of all English towns, but it is in any event a *real* place which contains real people experiencing and creating musical forms which they themselves value and to which they are prepared to commit a great deal of their lives. I believe that it is a better test case for exploring the significance of local music as it is actually practised than the usual abstract or evaluative theorising.

It is easy to underestimate these grass-roots musical activities given the accepted emphasis in academic and political circles on great musical masterpieces, professional music, or famed national achievements. But for the great majority of people it is the local amateur scene that forms the setting for their active musical experience, and it is these 'ordinary' musicians and their activities that form the centre-piece of the study. Among them I include the untrained as well as the highly accomplished, the 'bad' as well as the 'good' performers. This partly comes from my own experience, shared with many others, that even a poor executant can take a genuine part in local music – in my case as a none-too-competent choral singer, lapsed cello player, recorder dabbler, mother of musically inclined children, and enthusiastic but musicologically unsophisticated audience member. It is also based on my conviction that amateur practitioners are just as worth investigation as professional performers, and that their cultural practices are as real and interesting as the economic or class facets of their lives to which so much attention is usually devoted.

This study is not just about Milton Keynes but also has implications for our understanding of musical – and social – practice in general, and what this means both for its participants and for wider relationships in our society. It also touches on controversial issues about the nature of popular culture, the anthropology and sociology of music, and the quality of people's pathways in modern urban life. I hope it can lead to greater appreciation and study of what are, after all, among the most valued pursuits of our culture: the musical practices and experiences of ordinary people in their own locality, an invisible system which we usually take for granted but which upholds one vulnerable but living element of our cultural heritage.

Acknowledgments

I have much gratitude to express. Among my more formal thanks – but no less sincere for that – are those to the Faculty of Social Sciences at the Open University for research funding and other support, to the Milton Keynes Development Corporation (MKDC) for a generous grant towards the cost of the illustrations and to the staff of the Open University Library for their unstinting response to my continual requests. I am also most grateful to Eric Gates and the MKDC Recreation Unit for allowing me to consult their files; to Paul Smith (the County Music Adviser) and the Rev. Gethin Abraham-Williams for help and advice on the school and church surveys respectively; and to the many groups and individuals who gave permission for the reproduction of the illustrations or helped me to locate them.

For more personal thanks I must mention first my assistant Liz Close, who did the interviewing that provided much of the quantitative stiffening in this study. Her energy, cheerfulness, and knowledge were invaluable, and I and all readers of this book are greatly indebted to her. I have also been wonderfully fortunate in the cooperation of those at the Open University who over the years helped to organise me and the ever-changing manuscript, particularly Gloria Channing, Joan Smart and Margaret Allot: I could not have done without them.

No study of this kind would be possible without the help of large numbers of local people – musicians and others – who shared their time and insight so freely not only in formal 'interviews' but in friendly conversations and tolerant understanding of my own musical inadequacies. I can never fully repay what they gave or write as complete an account as each would deserve, but I hope they will feel that what is written here gives at least some idea of the valued part they play in our musical pathways. Because it is impossible to name all who contributed it seems wrong to single out any; but I cannot refrain from mentioning the particular kindnesses and help given by Matt and Jane Armour, Doreen Beacham, John Close, Malcolm Crane, John and Lila Drinkwater, Rod Hall, Sue Jarvis, Arnold Jones, Clive Keech, Gordon Ratnage, David Stevenson, Anita Tedder, Pauline Thomp-

Acknowledgments

son, Peter Waterman, Ralph and Cora Willcox, and – let me remember them with particular warmth and gratitude – Ella and Franklin Cheyne. I would also thank my three daughters Rachel, Kathleen and Brigid and their teachers (helpful, if partly unwitting, participants in the research) and – in a very personal tone – Sherwood Choir members for putting up with me over the years, before, during and after this research. To all of these, and to the many others who shared so much with me, my admiration and thanks.

Because this is an unusual study, drawing on many academic areas but not quite orthodox in any of them, I have particularly appreciated friends and colleagues outside the locality who have encouraged me, listened patiently, read part of the typescript, or – maybe without realising it – suggested some new line of thought. Once again they are too many to name, but let me at least acknowledge the great stimulus I received from the participants (critical as well as sympathetic) in the various seminars and workshops where I tried out earlier versions, and, among individuals, from John Blacking, Dieter Christensen, John Davis, Mary Douglas, Jerry Eades, Steven Feld, Simon Frith, Ralph Grillo, Mark Hustwitt, Bernice and David Martin, the McCaugheys of Melbourne, Alan Macfarlane, Jim Obelkvich, Leo Treitler, Elizabeth Whitcombe and Tokumaru Yosihiko (not that any of them will necessarily agree with what I say here). Four friends did their best to delay this too-slowly maturing book by capturing my time for other tasks: Jean La Fontaine, the unstoppable combination of Peter Zorkoczy and Nick Heap, and, most of all, Raymond Illsley; but I find that I am unexpectedly grateful to them too, since the detachment and wider experience they forced on me ultimately helped its completion.

My more general academic debts will probably be obvious from the text of the book. Among them I would particularly pick out the work of Howard Becker, John Blacking, Ulf Hannerz, Richard Bauman and Roger Abrahams. Finally Sue Allen-Mills and her colleagues at Cambridge University Press provided invaluable help, my husband David Murray gave his usual unequalled academic stimulus and moral support, and my mother, as all through my life, started it all off and kept me going.

Sources for illustrations

Figures 1, 2, 4, 5, 6: Milton Keynes Development Corporation; 3: Charlie Wooding; 7: Mrs Betty Pacey; 8, 9, 10, 11, 12, 14, 19(b) and (c), 20, 22, 24, 25, 26, 27 and 31: Lionel Grech Milton Keynes Photo Services; 13: Rod Hall; 15: Dennis Vick; 16: the T-Bone Boogie Band and Trevor Jeavons; 18: G. Vulliamy and E. Lee, *Popular music: a teacher's guide* (Routledge, 1982), p. 8; 19(a): Roger Hawes and the Void; 19(d): Pat Collins and Static Blue; 21: Mrs Trude Bedford; 23: John Close and Basically Brian; 29: Betty Black, Brackley

Abbreviations

BMK   Borough of Milton Keynes (boundaries somewhat wider than the new city 'designated area' – see figures 1 and 2)

MKDC   Milton Keynes Development Corporation (responsible for the development of the 'new city', and in the early 1980s gradually handing over some of its earlier functions to BMK)

MU   Musicians' Union

WAP   Wavendon Allmusic Plan (professional organisation based at Wavendon just outside the new city area but within the BMK boundaries, directed by John Dankworth and Cleo Laine, popularly referred to as 'WAP')

CRMK   Community Radio Milton Keynes

I

Introductory

1

The existence and study of local music

A choir of local residents – men, women and children – file in special costume on to the platform for their annual concert accompanied by visiting soloists and an orchestra of local amateurs. A jazz and blues group play to enthusiastic fans over Sunday lunchtime in the foyer of a local leisure centre. A brass band of players from their teens to their seventies thunder out Christmas carols beside the local shops, making a bright show as well as resounding harmony with their military-style uniforms and gleaming instruments, and one member rattling the collection box. An inexperienced but ambitious band of teenagers set up their instruments in a pub for their first gig, nervous about performing in public but supported by friends sitting round the tables, and deeply enthusiastic about the new songs they have spent months working on. Or a part-time church organist extricates herself from her other commitments to come again and yet again to provide the musical framework for another Saturday wedding or Sunday service.

Most readers will have encountered at least some of these events – or of the many similar activities that take place in one form or another in English towns today.[1] It is to such events and their background that this book is devoted: grass-roots music-making as it is practised by amateur musicians in a local context.

It is of course widely accepted that musical activities of this kind are part of modern English culture. But the organisation behind them is seldom thought about or investigated. In fact we regularly take them so for granted that we fail to really *see* the unacclaimed work put in by hundreds and thousands of amateur musicians up and down the country. Yet it is this work, in a sense invisible, that upholds this in other ways well-known element of our cultural heritage.

Despite its familiarity there are real questions to be investigated about local music in this country. What exactly does it consist of? How is it sustained and by whom? Are the kinds of events mentioned earlier one-off affairs or are there consistent patterns or a predictable structure into which

3

they fall? Are they still robust or by now fading away? Who are these local musicians – a marginal minority or substantial body? – and who are their patrons today? And what, finally, is the significance of local music-making for the ways people manage and make sense of modern urban life or, more widely, for our experience as active and creative human beings?

It will emerge from the account in this book that the work of local amateur musicians is not just haphazard or formless, the result of individual whim or circumstance. On the contrary, a consistent – if sometimes changing – structure lies behind these surface activities. The public events described above, and all the others that in their various forms are so typical a feature of modern English life, are part of an invisible but organised system through which individuals make their contribution to both the changes and the continuities of English music today.

I think of this set of practices as 'hidden' in two ways. One is that it has been so little drawn to our attention by systematic research or writing. There has been little work in this country on the 'micro-sociology' of amateur music; and, incredibly, questions on active music-making as such (as distinct from attendance at professional events or participation in artistic groups generally) seldom or never appear in official surveys – almost as if local music-making did not exist at all. Thus academics and planners alike have somehow found it easy to ignore something which is in other ways so remarkably obvious.

Second and perhaps even more important, the system of local music-making is partially veiled not just from outsiders but even from the musicians themselves and their supporters. Of course in one sense they know it well – these are not *secret* practices. But in another it seems so natural and given to the participants that they are often unaware both of its extent and of the structured work they themselves are putting into sustaining it. We all know about it – but fail to notice it for what it is.

The purpose of this book, then, is to uncover and reflect on some of these little-questioned but fundamental dimensions of local music-making, and their place in both urban life and our cultural traditions more generally.

The example I focus on to illustrate these themes is the town of Milton Keynes in Buckinghamshire. Clearly this town, like any other, has its own unique qualities, described more fully in chapter 3 and, more indirectly, throughout the book. Suffice it to say here that I am not claiming that Milton Keynes is in every way representative of all modern English towns – clearly it is not – but that I am following one well-established tradition in social and historical research, that of using specific case studies to lead to the kind of illumination in depth not provided by more thinly spread and generalized accounts.[2] Having lived in the area for a dozen years or more I have been able to draw on lengthy experience of local music practices as well as on the more systematic observation I undertook in the early 1980s, supplemented by local documentary sources and surveys (more fully described in the appendix on sources and methods), so as to reach an understanding in some depth of the patterns of local music-making. The main research was during the period 1980–4, so in describing the specific findings I have mostly used the past tense. As will emerge, the *detailed* groups and events were sometimes ephemeral and so are not appropriately described in the present, unlike many of the continuing and more general patterns (analysed later in the book) to which this local case study contributes.

One point of the book is thus merely to provide an empirically based ethnography of amateur music in one modern English town at a particular period. What kind of music-making actually went on there? This might seem a simple matter on which the answers must surely already be known. But in fact it is a question surprisingly neglected by researchers. There are of course some excellent historical accounts,[3] illuminating research on specific topics,[4] and a plethora of variegated work on the mass media and the nationally known bands and their procedures.[5] All these make their own contribution to our understanding of English music. There is also plenty of writing by ethnomusicologists and others on musical practices far away or long ago, as well as nostalgia for the 'rich amateur world' of earlier days, for New Orleans in the 'jazz era' or for Liverpool in the 1960s. But there is little indeed on modern grass-roots musicians and music-making across the board in a specific town: its local choirs, for example, Gilbert and Sullivan societies, brass bands, ceilidh dance groups or the small popular bands who, week in and week out, form an essential local backing to our national musical achievements.[6] I hope therefore that this first detailed book on local music in a contemporary English town – for there is no comparable study – will provoke further investigation of a subject so important for our understanding both of music and of the practices of modern urban life.

The picture that emerges from this ethnography is not quite what one might expect from some of the more general and theoretical writing about English culture. Let me foreshadow briefly some of the approaches and findings that will be elaborated later.

Perhaps the most striking point is how far the evidence here runs counter to the influential 'mass society' interpretations, particularly the extreme view which envisages a passive and deluded population lulled by the mass media and generating nothing themselves.[7] Nor can music be explained (or explained away) as the creature of class divisions or manipulation, or in any simple way predictable from people's social and economic backgrounds or even, in most cases, their age (as will emerge in chapter 10, the theory of a 'working-class-youth sub-culture' has little to support it). And far from music-making taking a peripheral role for individuals and society – a view propagated in the kind of theoretical stance that marginalises 'leisure' or 'culture' as somehow less real than 'work' or 'society' – music can equally well be seen as playing a central part not just in urban networks but also more generally in the social structure and processes of our life today. It is true that local music-making in the sense of direct participation in performance is the pursuit of a minority. But this minority turns out to be a more serious and energetic one than is often imagined, whose musical practices not only involve a whole host of other people than just the performers, but also have many implications for urban and national culture more generally.

Given this importance, why has the existence and significance of these local musical practices been so little noticed? In addition to the difficulty of explicitly noticing the taken-for-granted conventions which invisibly structure our activities, reasons can be found in current and earlier approaches to the study of music. These have often rested on assumptions which conceal rather than illuminate the kind of evidence revealed in this research. Among such assumptions challenged in this book, let me briefly highlight three.

First, and perhaps most important, musicological analyses have been concerned either to establish what kinds of music (or music-making) are 'best' or 'highest' – or, if not to establish them, then to assume implicitly that this is known already with the direction for one's gaze already laid down. This book accepts neither of these paths. Once one starts thinking not about 'the best' but about what people actually *do* – about 'is' not 'ought' – then it becomes evident that there are in fact *several* musics, not just one, and that no one of them is self-evidently superior to the others. In Milton Keynes, as in so many other towns, there are several *different* musical worlds, often little understood by each other yet each having its own contrasting conventions about the proper modes of learning, transmission, composition or performance. Because the pre-eminent position of classical music so often goes without saying, the existence of these differing musics has often simply been ignored.

Or again – to look at the same problem but from a different viewpoint – the common social science emphasis on 'popular' or 'lower-class' activities has led to particular research concentrations. Rock (and sometimes brass band music) has been particularly picked out as if only it, and not classical 'elite' music, were somehow worth serious consideration. But what became very clear in this study is that *each* musical tradition – classical, rock, jazz or whatever – can be studied in its own right. When no longer judged by the criteria of others, each emerges as in principle equally authentic and equally influential in shaping the practices of local music.

This study, therefore – unlike most others – does not concentrate on just *one* musical tradition but tries to consider all those important in the locality: an 'obvious' thing to do, of course – except that few scholars do it. Thus part 2 presents several musical worlds in turn through both general summaries and short case studies of particular groups and clubs – detailed ethnographic description that forms the necessary foundation for the later analyses. Part 3 then picks out some of the contrasting conventions which both differentiate and to some extent unite these differing worlds as a basis for the more general reflections in parts 4 and 5.

The discussion of each tradition is thus inevitably quite short, and some might argue that I should instead have concentrated on understanding just one world in depth. But despite its costs this comparative approach is essential to discover the interaction of traditions in the local area, and provide the perspective for a more detached view of their differences and similarities. The existence of this varied and structured interplay of differing and interacting worlds is something that simply does not surface at all in studies focussing exclusively on just a single tradition.

To some it may seem perverse to treat all these forms of music as on a par. But I take the view that music is neither something self-evidently *there* in the natural world nor fully defined in the musical practices of any one group; rather what is heard as 'music' is characterised not by its formal properties but by people's view of it, by the special frame drawn round particular forms of sound and their overt social enactment. Music is thus defined in different ways among different groups, each of whom have their own conventions supported by existing practices and ideas about the right way in which music should be realised.[8] My own musical appreciations were of course enlarged by this study (though I continue to have my own preferences), but as a researcher I consider the only valid approach is not to air my own ethnocentric evaluations as if they had universal validity but to treat the many different forms of music as equally worthy of study on their own terms.

I have thus quite deliberately not confined this study to classical music, or indeed to so-called 'popular' music,[9] but have tried to give some description of the practice of music across the whole spectrum to be found in the locality. It therefore covers music-making in the classical tradition, jazz, brass bands, musical theatre, country and western, folk, pop and rock as well as some of the more common contexts and institutions associated with music-making more generally. If this seems to draw the book out to inordinate lengths and include over-simplified or 'obvious' descriptions of traditions familiar to particular readers, remember that each world and context was to its participants a full and richly creative one – for them *the* most truly musical one, certainly not to be omitted in any fair account of local musics – and that at least some readers will be unfamiliar with any given tradition and will need some straightforward introduction. And looking at one's 'own' in the setting of comparisons with others can (as I discovered) throw new light on taken-for-granted conventions.

A second reason why the extent of local music-making and its underlying structure has been little noticed is that it is relatively unusual to concentrate on the *practice* of music: on what people actually *do* on the ground. That there are of course many other valid and illuminating approaches to music I do not wish to dispute. But for the purposes of uncovering the local activities, the standard analyses in terms of traditional musicological theory or of the intellectual content or texts of music cannot take us very far. These are the second set of assumptions, then, that I question in this study. Most misleading of all in this context is the powerful definition of music in terms not of performance but of finalised musical *works*. This is the more so when it is accompanied – as it so frequently is – with the implication that these works have some kind of asocial and continuing existence, almost as if independent of human performances or social processes, and that it is in musical 'works' that one finds aesthetic value (see, for example, Sparshott 1980, p. 120). This is a view of music that may have some limited validity in the classical tradition, but even there obscures the significance of its active realisation by real human practitioners on the ground; and for many other musical traditions it is altogether inappropriate for elucidating how music is created and transmitted. Such an approach would uncover few of the activities described in this book.

The concentration here, then, is on musical *practices* (what people do), not musical works (the 'texts' of music). This is admittedly partly due to my own inadequacies. I am unqualified to undertake the musicological analysis of musical texts either by training or from the kind of data I collected, and should therefore make clear that this study is *not* intended as a work of musicology – or at any rate not musicology in the commonly used formalist sense of the term (see, for instance, Treitler's useful critique in Holoman and Palisca 1982). More positively significant for the approach of this study, however, I discovered that looking closely at people's *actions* really was a route to discovering a local system that, even to me, was quite unexpected in its complexity and richness.

Looking at practice rather than formalised texts or mental structures, at processes rather than products, at informal grass-roots activities rather than formal structure has always been one strand in social science research (perhaps particularly in anthropology); sometimes too in the humanities. Recently this emphasis has come more to the fore in a number of areas, a trend with which I would wish to associate my own work.[10] This kind of focus is one that, unlike more 'formalistic' analyses, leads to a greater appreciation of how individuals and groups organise and perceive their activities at the local level, whether in music-making or any other active pursuit.

Most studies of music and musicians are of professionals. This is the third major reason why amidst the concentration on central institutions, 'great artists' and professional musicians, local music has been so little noticed. But musical practice can equally be found among amateur and local practitioners.[11] Why should we assume that music-making is the monopoly of full-time specialists or the prime responsibility of state-supported institutions like the national orchestras or opera houses? Once we ask the question and start looking it becomes clear that it is also the pursuit of thousands upon thousands of grass-roots musicians, the not very expert as well as expert, still learning as well as accomplished, quarrelling as well as harmonious – a whole cross-section, in other words, of ordinary people engaged in music in the course of their lives. This book, then, is not on central institutions or the professionals, but about amateur music-making in a local setting.

With the partial exception of brass bands, there has been little study of amateurs in England: indeed, as Muriel Nissel sums it up in her authoritative *Facts about the arts*, 'very little information at present exists on the varied and widespread activities of the many people involved in the arts as amateurs' (1983, p. 1). Given this lack of research it is perhaps not surprising that the role of local musicians should be so little appreciated, but their contribution becomes very obvious once attention is focussed on the actual practices of these part-time amateurs. Not that the concept of 'amateur musicians' is unambiguous – some of the complexities and qualifications surrounding the term are explored in the next chapter – but it can be said that the findings of this study reveal how serious a gap in our knowledge has resulted from the existing concentration on the professionals.

The main points I have been making can best be summed up by saying that we should not assume – as many past studies and approaches have implicitly done – that we already *know* what in fact should still remain as a question for investigation. It is easy to think that we already know or agree on what is most 'important' about music, how it should be defined and judged, how people value and experience different aspects of our culture, or how far people's lives are determined by, say, governmental decisions, the mass media, socio-economic class – or the practice of music. But these questions need both further thought and empirical investigation on the ground before we can accept the sometimes unquestioned conclusions of, say, the mass society theorists or the class-dominated visions of some social scientists, at least as far as local music goes; for when these and similar assumptions are investigated at the local level, the reality turns out to be rather different.

This study therefore is not intended to contribute to some great Theory of music, but rather to be a more modest social study based in the first instance in the local ethnography but also moving out to wider questions and drawing inspiration from a broad if somewhat unsystematic range of sources across several disciplines, in particular anthropology, sociology, urban and community studies, folklore, the study of 'popular culture', the more anthropological side of ethnomusicology, and social history. These ethnographic findings and the theoretical approaches which I found useful to elucidate them illuminate some central questions in the social study of both urban life and musical practice. These to some extent underlie the exposition throughout (specially in parts 4 and 5) and are taken up for more explicit discussion in the two final chapters. Their end result is sometimes to build on but also often to reject the emphasis and conclusions evident in a number of other studies of music by the test of the facts as discovered in this case study of musical practice.

The approach in this book thus follows a rather different line from that of the majority of studies of music.[12] A focus on the existence and interaction of different musics, on musical practice rather than musical *works*, and on the amateur rather than professional side of music-making reveals the hitherto unsuspected scope of music-making, with far-reaching implications for our lives today. One revelation was the sheer amount and variety of local music: far richer, more creative and of more significance for people's lives than is recognised even in the participants' own consciousness, far less in much conventional social science wisdom about English culture. Many of our valued institutions are pictured as just floating on invisibly and without effort. On the contrary, as will become clear, a great deal of work and commitment have to be put into their continuance: they do not just 'happen' naturally.[13] Local music, furthermore – the kind of activity so often omitted in many approaches to urban study[14] – turns out to be neither formless nor, as we might suppose, just the product of individual endeavour, but to be structured according to a series of cultural conventions and organised practices, to be explained in this book, in which both social continuity *and* individual choices play a part. The patterns within this system may not always be within our conscious awareness, but nonetheless play a crucial part in our cultural processes.

This study will therefore, I hope, enhance our understanding of British *cultural* institutions, a subject on which social science writing is relatively sparse compared to the huge number of treatments of, for example, social stratification, industrial employment, or macro-studies of society or state. Artistic expression and enactment are also important to people, perhaps as significant for their lives as the traditional concerns of social theorists – or, at any rate, it seems often to be a matter of mere assumption rather than objective evidence that they are not. I hope my treatment may help to redress the balance of social science work on Britain as well as lead to greater understanding of the nature and implications of local music.

One final point. It is hard to write at once with the social scientist's detachment and at the same time with a full personal appreciation of the human creativity involved in artistic expression and performance.[15] The constant temptations are either to fall into the reductionist trap of, say, seeing music as just the epiphenomenon of social structure or alternatively to be swept away by the facile romanticising of 'art'. By considering mainly musical *practice* and its conventions rather than musical *works*, I hope to some extent to have avoided the second of these temptations. As for the first, a written academic account can probably never totally avoid giving a faceless and reducing impression of what to the participants themselves is rich and engrossing artistic experience; I am also aware that by comparing the many different musics in the area I am depriving myself and my readers of the full understanding that a deeper search into just one musical group or tradition might have provided. I hope, though, that despite all this my genuine appreciation for the *real* (not merely 'reflective' or 'secondary') musical achievements of local musicians will still shine through the attempt at objectivity and reveal something of a reality that has too often remained unnoticed.

2

'Amateur' and 'professional' musicians

Before the more detailed account of local musical practice I must comment briefly on one key term in this book: 'amateur musicians'. The word 'amateur' is of course widely used and, more or less, understood. But it is also surprisingly elusive, and some discussion of the complexities involved is a necessary preliminary to the later description.

Many different kinds of musicians operate in localities up and down Britain. Some can be described – and would describe themselves – as professionals in that they make their living from music. In Milton Keynes, for example, there was the music professor who commuted daily to his London music college and performed with players outside the area, or the singer-guitarist who belonged to a nationally famous rock band but did not perform locally. There were also the members of bands and ensembles who regarded themselves as locally based but were prepared to travel through the region or beyond to perform for a fee; or again, the musicians who earned only small fees but played on in the hope of more and better bookings or just for the love of music. In addition there were the music teachers who lived and taught locally, thus depending on music for their main livelihood but sometimes also performing from time to time for a fee. There were also local residents for whom musical activity meant just one or two evenings out a week at the local choir or in the local band or orchestra – the kind of activity that people perhaps associate most readily with the term 'amateur music'. And there were those who in the past had lived from their music – singing in cabaret, for instance, or round the working men's clubs – or had been 'professionally trained', but now just engaged in it for a pleasurable leisure pursuit or the occasional engagement. Among the various musicians, then, some regard music as their only real employment (with varying success in terms of monetary return), some value it as an enjoyable but serious recreation outside work, and some treat it as a part-time occupation for the occasional fee.

Among all these variations, which are the 'amateur' musicians and groups on which this study claims to focus? Unfortunately there is no simple answer, nor are the 'amateur' always unambiguously separated from the 'professional' musicians. The reasons for this as well as the complexities surrounding these at first sight simple concepts need to be explained not just to clarify my own presentation but also because the complex amateur/ professional interrelations form one essential element in the work of local musicians. This point is worth stressing because most studies of modern musicians either confine their interest to the more professional practitioners (though often without saying so) or else take the amateur/professional distinction as given and so not worth exploring.[1] In local music, however, the interrelationship and overlap between these two is both highly significant for local practice and also of central interest for the wider functioning of music as it is in fact practised today.

The term 'professional' – to start with that one – at first appears unambiguous. A 'professional' musician earns his or her living by working full time in some musical role, in contrast to the 'amateur', who does it 'for love' and whose source of livelihood lies elsewhere. But complications arise as soon as one tries to apply this to actual cases on the ground. Some lie in ambiguities in the concept of 'earning one's living', others in differing interpretations about what is meant by working in 'music', and others again – perhaps the most powerful of all – in the emotive overtones of the term 'professional' as used by the participants themselves.

Taking music as 'the main source of livelihood' does not always provide as clear a dividing line as might be supposed. In the local area, for example, there was the classically trained vocalist who decided not to pursue her full-time career after the birth of her daughter but picked up the odd local engagement for a moderate fee, often accompanied by a local guitar teacher: professional or amateur? Again, local bands sometimes contained some players in full-time (non-musical) jobs and others whose only regular occupation was their music; yet in giving performances, practising, sharing out the fees and identification with the group, the members were treated exactly alike (except for the inconvenience that those in jobs had to plead illness or take time off work if they travelled to distant bookings). A number of band members regarded their playing as their only employment (perhaps also drawing unemployment or other benefits), but how far they actually made money from it was a moot point: as will emerge later, even if they earned quite substantial fees and spent most of their time on activities related to their music, they could still end up out of pocket and perhaps engaged in musical performance as much for the enjoyment and the status of 'musician' it gave them as for money. Some players had part-time jobs (voluntary as well as paid), or made a certain amount in cash or kind through informal transactions such as dress-making, giving lifts or mending a friend's car in return for comparable favours, all without really affecting the status of their continuing musical activities. Others again worked in full-time non-musical jobs but still received fees for their playing on such occasions as, for example, providing the instrumental accompaniment for a local Gilbert and Sullivan performance, often on equal terms with more full-time musicians. In all such cases (typical rather than unusual ones) neither payment nor amount of time provides an unambiguous basis for differentiating 'professionals' from 'amateurs'; the difference is at best only a relative one.

Membership or otherwise of the Musicians' Union might seem a more easily identifiable criterion of professional status. In the local context, however, this was usually of only minor importance as a marker. According to locally circulated MU literature, membership was open to musicians of all kinds – bands, groups, orchestral musicians, chamber musicians, folk and jazz – and was for 'everyone ... who makes their living, or part of their living, from performing music': i.e. not just the *full-time* performers. It therefore covered wide variations in the amount of time spent on, and financial return from, musical activity. In practice union membership among local musicians was unpredictable. Established performers who regularly played in large halls up and down the country (venues that regarded themselves as 'professional' or – equally relevant – had agreements with the MU) were quite often members; but otherwise membership seemed to be related as much to chance – having on some past occasion (perhaps only once) played in a place which demanded it or having friends who pressed it – as to the economic significance, number of performances, or artistic quality of most players' musical activities. Indeed, despite official MU policy, several bands contained both union and non-union players. The MU did attempt a special recruiting drive among Milton Keynes musicians in early 1982, but the overall picture remained very patchy – certainly no yardstick for a clear amateur/professional divide. In general, players took pride in the label 'musician', and were mostly not too concerned whether or not this was 'full time' or 'part time' or validated by union membership.

In local music, then, the at first sight 'obvious' amateur/professional distinction turns out to be a complex continuum with many different possible variations. Indeed, even the same people could be placed at different points along this line in different contexts or different stages of their lives. Some *were* clearly at one or other end of the continuum, but the grey area in the middle in practice made up a large proportion – perhaps the majority – of local musicians. My initial statement, therefore, that this book is about amateur musicians needs some modification. It would be more accurate to say that it focusses mainly on the amateur rather than professional end of an overlapping and complex spectrum, taking account of the variations along this continuum. This can also be stated more positively, for the 'problem' of distinguishing these apparently key terms is not just a matter of terminology. It alerts us to the somewhat startling fact that one of the interesting characteristics of local music organization is precisely the *absence* of an absolute distinction between 'the amateur' and 'the professional'.[2]

In this context, then, all the practitioners studied in this volume can be called 'musicians', and I have followed local practice in using this term (confusing though this may be at first to those for whom the immediate sense of 'musician' is a full-time professional). There is also a sense (more fully explored in chapter 12) in which audiences can be said to take a necessary part in successful musical performances,[3] so though 'audience behaviour' as such is not the main focus audiences too are treated as in a sense active and skilled participants – even themselves 'musicians' of a kind.

Another interesting feature of the 'amateur'/'professional' contrast lies in differing interpretations by the participants themselves. When local musicians use the term 'professional' they often refer to evaluative rather than economic aspects: the 'high standard' of a player, his or her specialist qualifications, teachers, musical role, or appearance as a regular performer with musicians themselves regarded as 'professional'. The term is an elusive one, the more so in that someone can be regarded as 'professional' in different senses of the term or according to some but not other criteria. I heard one player described as 'a professional, really, even though he earns his living from something else' and another as 'maybe not recognised as professional by the East Midland Arts Association scheme, but he *really* is, you know'. It is a term readily used to describe others (or oneself) with great conviction and certainty, but in practice rests on underlying and disputed ambiguities.

One specific incident can demonstrate the relativity and conflicts within the 'amateur' versus 'professional' distinction as locally experienced. This arose from the formation of the high-status Milton Keynes Chamber Orchestra. It was started up in 1975 under the auspices of the 'new city' Development Corporation and at first included many local music teachers and students. But by 1980 most of these had been eased out. There was heated controversy over whether they should be members and on what grounds, and emotive interchanges in the local press and elsewhere. The conductor on the one side argued that 'we are looking for an absolute professional standard. If we get a local professional who is equal to an outsider obviously we would prefer him. But we are not in business for semi-professionals. There is plenty of opportunity for them at the Sherwood Sinfonia' (the leading 'amateur' orchestra). In his view and that of the organisers, local teachers were 'semi-professionals', in contrast to the full 'professional' performers. He was strongly supported by some of his colleagues, as well as by enthusiasts for the high standard of the Milton

Keynes Chamber Orchestra's local concerts. Other local musicians, how-ever, especially the teachers and part-time performers, retorted that the early publicity by the orchestra had been seriously misleading when it stated that 'the proportion of players drawn from the area will increase' and 'that it will become almost entirely derived from its own geographical base': 'it seems we were good enough to get the orchestra off the ground and then be discarded, to be replaced by London professionals'. Some letters dropped dark hints about personal links ('why are some local semi-professionals still playing if the orchestra is not intended for them?' 'is it a question of "if the face fits" and not the playing standard?'), and there were complaints that the orchestra had virtually become 'London based' after the conductor moved to a prestigious music post in a leading London school. The terms 'professional', 'semi-professional' and 'amateur' were flung around with increasing bitterness and the correspondence raged on for two months, turning in part on such questions as when a 'semi-professional' is a 'professional' and when an 'amateur', and relating this among other things to the rate of fees or the conductor's own status. The orchestra continued, but the underlying issues were never settled to the satisfaction of all the parties and many hurt feelings remained.

As this dispute illustrates, the problematics of the terms 'amateur', 'professional' and 'semi-professional' are not just of academic interest but can enter into the perceptions and actions of those involved in local music. The label 'professional' is used – and not only in this case – as an apparently objective, but in practice tendentious, description to suggest social status and local affiliation rather than just financial, or even purely musical, evaluation. From one viewpoint, it connotes high-standard or serious performance as against 'mere amateur playing', and from another, outsiders coming in from elsewhere to take prestige or fees from local players, or entertainers who try to charge more than those paying them would like. Thus the emotional claim – or accusation – of being either 'amateur' or 'professional' can become a political statement rather than an indicator of economic status.

This adds yet a further dimension of ambiguity to the difficulty of isolating the 'amateur' side of music-making. If one pays attention to local perceptions, then it is difficult to be more definite than saying once again that this study focusses on the amateur end of the continuum – for that there was some such continuum, however elusive, was generally accepted locally. Even this vague statement, however, does have some meaning, for it thereby excludes any detailed description of the explicitly 'professional' Wavendon Allmusic Plan (WAP) run by John Dankworth and Cleo Laine, the Milton Keynes Chamber Orchestra, or BMK–MKDC Promotions, which organised large-scale concerts by professional orchestras and other outside performers. But it also has to be accepted that there were many ambiguities between the 'professional' and 'amateur' spheres and it is impossible, therefore, to keep them entirely distinct.

These overlaps and interactions between the (relatively) 'amateur' and (relatively) 'professional' are also of interest in themselves. For the world of professional music in Britain, with its famous orchestras, opera centres, and pool of high-status performers, is often pictured as an autonomous and separate one. Yet when one looks more closely, it quickly becomes obvious not only that – as just indicated – there are *degrees* of 'professionalism', but also that professional music feeds directly on local amateur activities and would be impossible to sustain without them.

Thus, whatever may be the case in other countries, in Britain in the 1980s the budding professional musician regularly gets started through local non-professional opportunities. This is particularly noticeable in classical music when it is based on encouragement through schools, churches, friends and parents, as well as on the system of local teachers and national music examinations. One important stage for many is to try out their wings in local amateur groups – a school bassoonist, for instance, playing in a scratch orchestra to accompany a local operatic performance, or an aspiring violinist acting as leader or soloist for local youth orchestras before going off to music college. This apprenticeship in performing skills is an essential preparation for the would-be full-time musician. Every year a handful of young players go on from their localities to further professional training in music, a reservoir of already partly trained talent brought up through the local amateur organisations.

A similar interaction is also involved in the next stage of a young professional's career. A musician's home area is often his or her first resource for recruiting the first pupils or trying out public performance. This is where the musician is already known and has the necessary contacts. In Milton Keynes, for example, students away at music college tried to keep some pupils at home and to appear as soloists with local amateur groups or at local music events. If they are fortunate, they gradually build up their contacts more widely (making prominent use in their publicity of sympathetic reviews from local newspapers) and start practising farther afield.

Even beyond these personal career stages, the general interaction between amateur and professional worlds is very perceptible at the local level. Amateur groups like to put on grand performances from time to time with soloists who appear for a fee (how large the fee and how well-known the artist depending partly on the available money, though personal links on the soloist's side also sometimes play a part). This is particularly common in choirs, who often need solo singers to appear with them or instrumentalists to supplement local players accompanying their big concerts, but local orchestras too like to stage some concerts with outside soloists. Local music societies too engage performers – both individuals and small ensembles – to appear at local concerts for their members, selecting their chosen artists in part from the brochures or letters with which secretaries of local music groups are deluged. This continuing interdependence is essential to both sides: to the individual artists on the one side who, whether just starting out on their careers or already established professional players, have the opportunity to perform for a fee before an audience; and to the local groups on the other, who both want the prestige and need the services of experts to assist them in performing admired works in the classical canon.

This interdependence of performers at different points along the amateur/professional continuum is particularly strong in the classical music world, where the accepted repertoire includes many works based on solo–group interaction. But it also comes out, if in rather different forms, in other types of music. Local brass, folk, and country and western bands form both the training ground and the reservoir from which the players and bands who eventually 'make it' in terms of fame and finance are ultimately recruited. This is particularly important for rock players, who typically learn 'on the job' by becoming members of local groups, sometimes with practically no previous musical experience at all but developing their skills through local practising and performing. The largely 'amateur' activities at the local level – the 'hidden' practice of local music described in this book – provide the essential background for the more 'professional' musical world.

The local situation, then, is a complex one. Rather than the presence of any absolute divide between 'amateur' and 'professional' there are instead a large number of people and groups who, from at least some viewpoints and in some situations, can be – and are, both by themselves and in this book – described as 'musicians'. And this is despite their having a whole range of different economic, occupational, social and musical characteristics in other respects. Though this book concentrates mainly on the amateur end of this multi-faceted continuum, in view of the many overlaps and interrelationships the spheres cannot be totally separated: the concept of 'amateur' music is a relative, partly arbitrary, and sometimes disputed label rather than a settled division. In this context the difficulty of making any absolute divide is more than just a problem of presentation; it also tells us something about the characteristics of contemporary English music-making and forms the background to the people and music described in this book.

3

Introduction to Milton Keynes and its music

In Milton Keynes local music was unquestionably flourishing. A quick preview of the music-making going on between 1980 and 1984 can give a preliminary indication of its extent.

Here, then, is a summary list of the main groups and activities in and around Milton Keynes in the early 1980s, each the subject of fuller exploration in later chapters: three to four classical orchestras and several dozen youth and school orchestras; five to eight main brass bands and several smaller ones; nine or ten independent four-part choirs in the classical tradition together with many small groups, and choirs in most schools and churches; around six operatic or musical drama societies, including two Gilbert and Sullivan societies; over a dozen jazz groups playing in regular jazz venues known to their devotees; five or six folk clubs, a dozen folk groups, and about four 'ceilidh' dance bands; two leading country and western bands plus other more fluid groups and an extremely successful club; and a hundred or more small rock and pop bands. Live music was being heard and performed not just in public halls but also in churches, schools, open air festivals, social clubs and pubs, and the local newspapers were teeming with advertisements about local musical gatherings.

Definitive numbers are impossible, if only because groups typically formed, disappeared and re-formed during the four years of the research, and because of varying definitions of 'music' or of 'group' as well as the problem of just how one draws the boundaries of 'Milton Keynes' or of 'Milton Keynes music'.[1] But in all there must have been several hundred functioning musical groups based and performing in and around the locality, and hundreds of live performances each year.

How can this striking efflorescence of the musical arts be explained, and how was it sustained? One crucial factor might at first sight seem to lie in the special position of Milton Keynes as one of Britain's 'new towns' with consequential financial and social benefits. Let me start therefore by explaining this background.

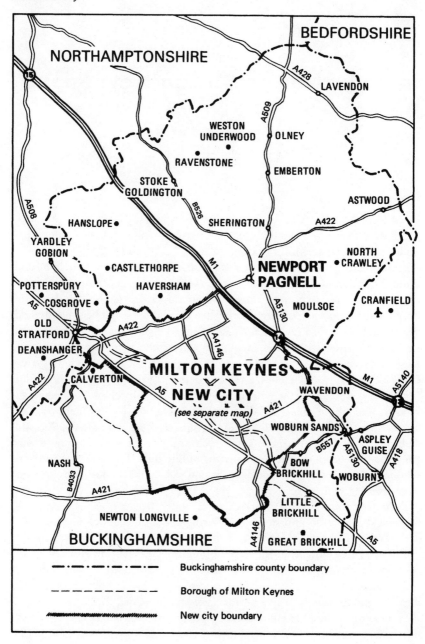

Figure 1 Borough of Milton Keynes and surrounding area

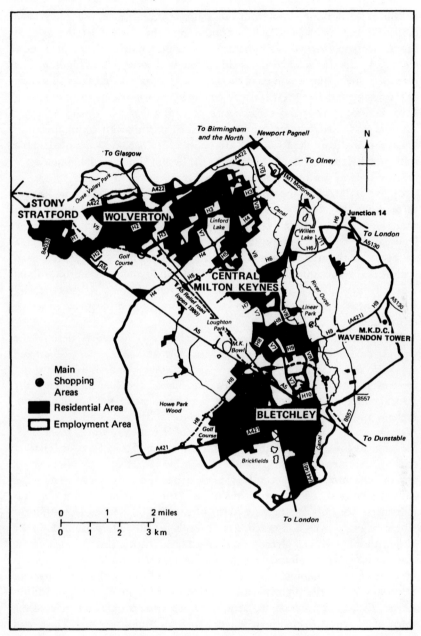

Figure 2 The new city of Milton Keynes (designated area) at the time of the research

Milton Keynes originated from 1960s plans to create new towns to relieve industrial and social pressures in London and the South-East. An area of 22,000 acres in North Buckinghamshire was designated in 1967 as a 'new city'[2] and a development corporation created with government funding. The plans were being implemented in the 1970s and 1980s, so that the population of the designated area grew from 40,000 in 1967 to 77,000 in 1977, 95,000 in 1980, 112,000 in 1983 and 122,000 in 1985 with a target of 200,000 in 1990. The site was partly chosen for its established north–south communication links: starting from the Roman Watling Street (to become a main coaching route north, later still the A5) as well as the Grand Union Canal, nineteenth-century railway and, more recently, the M1.

By the early 1980s 'the new city of Milton Keynes' had become known throughout the country for its glamorous advertising, its large covered shopping centre (reputedly the largest in Europe) and its imaginative landscaping with its millions of trees. It had also managed to attract a variety of both large and small firms, mostly light industries, distribution centres and offices offering a wide spread of employment. The promotional literature describes it, in typically glowing language, as 'a growing city which is providing people with an attractive and prosperous place in which to live and work'.

The town thus built up was not totally new, however, despite the impression sometimes given to outsiders. The Milton Keynes 'designated area' also incorporated thirteen or so existing villages and, more important, three established towns of some substance. These were Bletchley, originally a local market town, then, from the establishment of the London–Birmingham railway, a thriving industrial centre and later London overspill; Wolverton, once itself a 'new' town, home of the railway works from 1848, for long the largest single employer in the area; and Stony Stratford, dating back to the thirteenth century and still notable for its Georgian high street and old coaching inns. As can be seen clearly in the aerial views in figure 3, Milton Keynes was a mixture of the old and the new. The locality was thus influenced not only by the new plans of the Milton Keynes Development Corporation (MKDC) interacting with both private enterprise and public authorities, but also by already-established local institutions. Because of the existing links which already ran across the area, Milton Keynes was often thought of as not confined just to the 'designated' site of the 'new city' but also as taking in the slightly wider area covered by the Borough of Milton Keynes (BMK). BMK included around 20,000 more people and covered the town of Newport Pagnell and villages such as Woburn Sands. These had long been part of the local connections in this part of North Buckinghamshire and were also increasingly associated with Milton Keynes. Indeed for certain purposes such as educational or church organisation it was such links and not the 'designated area' boundaries which were applied (figures

Figure 3 New and old in Milton Keynes
(a) The crowded village of Stony Stratford with its long High Street (the old Roman Watling Street), old inns, churches, market and Horsefair Green
(b) New city housing estate (Fishermead), showing the more spacious new layout with the typical Milton Keynes grid pattern, roundabouts, and green tree-planted areas separating the estates

COMPARISON WITH NATIONAL AGE STRUCTURE   CHANGE IN AGE STRUCTURE SINCE 1976

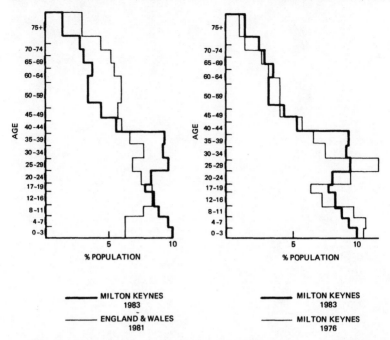

Figure 4 The changing age structure in Milton Keynes and its comparison with national patterns. By 1983 the population of Milton Keynes was still very much younger than in the country as a whole, but less so than in 1976. There was still a higher proportion of those aged 0–11 and 20–40, but there had been a significant increase in the proportions of teenagers, middle-aged and older people in the population. Based on *Milton Keynes House-hold Survey*, 1983

1–2, and also the discussion in the appendix, p. 346); much of the analysis here assumes this wider sense of 'Milton Keynes'.

During my research in 1980–4 there was thus a rapidly growing population, drawn mainly from London and the South-East. New houses and halls were being built, schools, pubs and churches opened, and new industries established. The population structure was fairly characteristic of a developing area: more in the 0–11 and 20–40 age groups and more families with young children than in the British population as a whole (a difference gradually decreasing as the town became established). Similarly the socio-economic structure had its own particular features, with a relatively, though not strikingly, high proportion engaged in skilled manual (and perhaps later non-manual) work (see figures 4–6). The owner-occupier rate for housing was low, if rising, by national standards (41 per cent in 1979, 49 per cent in 1983 as against the 1983 national average of 57 per cent). This was hardly

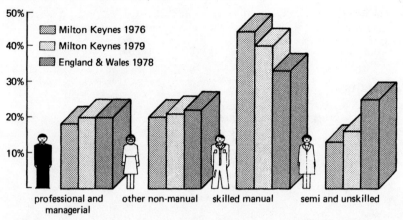

Figure 5 Socio-economic profile of Milton Keynes in 1979. Based on Postal Survey, 1979

surprising given the numbers of houses for rent built in the early days of the city, but the high proportion of what was – in effect – council housing may be unexpected to those who think of the Milton Keynes population as all 'middle class' or unusually well-to-do.

Milton Keynes thus represented a complex interaction between old and new and was in some ways gradually moving nearer to the national average. In certain respects it could indeed claim to be a 'new city' – an image effectively propagated by the vision (and lavish advertising) of the development corporation and its officials – and was certainly characterised by an influx of new population and government funding in the 1970s and early 1980s.

It could be, therefore, that the proliferation of music in Milton Keynes should be related to this recent development. One could point to the gathering of a young and mobile population in carefully planned urban locations and to the enlightened policy of MKDC, who from the start emphasised the development of recreational facilities and the encouragement of the arts. The patterns of local music could thus be viewed as a successful response to these development policies in the favourable context of a new city.

This clearly *was* one dimension. But it would be over-simple to see it purely in these terms. The evidence for this assertion will emerge from the later description, but one point is worth making at once. This is that amidst the effective advertising, it is easy for outsiders to forget that Milton Keynes did not begin from a *tabula rasa*. There was already an extensive population in the area, particularly in the established town of Bletchley (which long continued to be the single largest centre of population within Milton Keynes) but also in Stony Stratford and Wolverton, each with further links

Introductory

POPULATION

Designated Area

At designation (January 1967)	40,000
At time of Survey	112,000
Now (March 1985)	122,000

AGE GROUPS

0–4	10,970	40–44	6,080
5–8	8,470	45–49	4,690
9–12	7,820	50–54	3,640
13–15	5,290	55–59	3,570
16–19	7,050	60–64	4,090
20–24	8,960	65–69	3,250
25–29	10,510	70–74	2,950
30–34	10,050	75+	3,050
35–39	10,260	Not answered	1,950

HOUSEHOLD TENURE

Total households 39,780

Rent		Sale	
Corporation	33%	New Town	16%
Borough	15%	Sitting tenant purchased	4%
Other	3%	Other	26%
		Shared ownership	3%

SOCIO-ECONOMIC GROUP

Base: those in work 46,404

Professional/managerial	16%
Other non-manual	36%
skilled manual	28%
semi-skilled manual	12%
unskilled manual	5%
self-employed (non-professional)	3%

ECONOMIC ACTIVITY

Base: 16 + years 79,250

Full-time work	50%
Part-time work	
16–29 hrs	6%
16 or fewer	3%
Seeking work	8%
Permanently sick	2%
Retired	13%
Student	3%
Keeping house	15%

Figure 6 Milton Keynes facts and figures (1983). Based on *Milton Keynes Household Survey*, 1983

to such other nearby centres as Woburn Sands, Newport Pagnell, Buckingham and the intervening villages. These towns and villages had their own active and continuing cultures – different, no doubt, from the larger-scale and more 'nationally' oriented institutions later encouraged by the MKDC but each with its own validity. The later developments in the 1970s and 1980s can only be fully understood as involving some interaction – often congenial, sometimes abrasive – with already established local institutions.

A detailed account of the earlier history of local music would be a subject on its own, but some illustrations can put the later situation into perspective. One was the long choral tradition in the locality. This went back to the last century, particularly in the established association between choirs and local churches and organists, and continued strongly in more recent times. Between the wars, for example, there was the flourishing Co-operative Choral Society in Bletchley under its lively railway conductor, still well remembered by older Bletchley inhabitants, followed by the Bletchley Ladies Choir, which lasted for over twenty years from the 1940s on, as well as regular choral performances in the local churches, and a well-attended Free Church Choir Festival in the 1950s. Many of the surrounding villages had their own choral societies and competed with the Women's Institute choirs in the Buckingham music festival. Newport Pagnell's choral society, still flourishing in the 1980s, had been putting on performances and inviting outside artists to sing with them since 1910 (with a few interruptions), and people still talked of the wartime occasion at the Electra Cinema when Owen Brannigan sang and was paid with £10 and two dozen eggs. These earlier traditions formed the base for later developments like the still-existing Bletchley-based Sherwood Choir, drawing many of its members from the older Bletchley Ladies Choir. This and many other recent groups were able to build on the established choral tradition not only for their singers but also for ready audiences, instrumental support, and recognised performance venues like the old churches.

The same interaction between the new and the already established was also to be found in other musical forms. Brass bands played an important role in the 'new city', merely the most recent manifestation of an already strong local tradition which included several brass bands dating back to the turn of the century or earlier. Similarly there were earlier orchestras such as the inter-war Apollo Orchestra in Bletchley, church concert parties like the Spurgeon Baptist Chapel's Busy Bees, and dance bands like the Papworth Trio (figure 7) who were performing all through the war for parents' association dances in the school halls – a role now more usually fulfilled by the 'ceilidh' folk bands – and continued to play for Bletchco Players (a drama group still in existence) till the 1950s. The newer musical groups thus fitted easily into the local situation, sharing in the same tradition of performance for local events and societies.

There was also the already-existing base of individual performers and local music teachers, some of whom had been putting on regular recitals by their pupils in the inter-war years, and of schools and other groups producing operas and musical plays. To this was added the foundation of

27

Figure 7 The Papworth Trio, a popular dance band in the Bletchley area from the 1930s to the 1950s, led by the local greengrocer, pianist and organist Tom Papworth

the LEA's North Bucks Music Centre in Bletchley in 1964. This provided a focus both for school music and for local groups founded in the seventies to practise on its premises off Sherwood Drive, among them the Sherwood Sinfonia, Sherwood Choir and re-formed Bletchley Band.

Many other 1980s groups too had their roots in earlier societies: for example the flourishing Milton Keynes Amateur Operatic Society (founded 1952 as the Bletchley Amateur Operatic Society following the tradition of the pre-war Bletchley and Fenny Stratford Amateur Operatic Society), the Milton Keynes and District Pipe Band (founded from Bletchley, 1971/2) and the Bletchley Organ Society with its regular monthly meetings since 1971. Similarly many of the earlier local festivals continued into the 1970s and 1980s, sometimes the models for parallel festivals in the 'new city'. Among these were the annual Bletchley Middle School Music Festival, the Bletchley and District First Schools Folk Dance Festival, the Boys' Brigade annual procession, and the Spurgeon's Church 'Carols for Everybody', a yearly event since 1961. The Milton Keynes Festival of Arts was founded as the Bletchley Festival of the Arts in 1968 and by the 1980s was attracting thousands of entries each year from throughout the city and beyond. The tradition of music in the schools was important too, and ex-scholars of the (earlier) Bletchley Grammar School and Radcliffe School in Wolverton were formative influences in local folk and rock music, and together with newcomers were still making an active contribution to the local music scene in the 1980s.

To explain the musical character of Milton Keynes solely in terms of the new city or initiatives from above would thus be an over-simplification. It is understandable that some of the officials planning the arts should take the view that cultural development had to be initiated from the top – even half-believe that without their support grass-roots music could not really flourish. This, after all, is an approach in keeping with the accepted planning philosophy that 'in all types of new community the basic responsibility for recreational provision lies with the local authority' (Veal 1975, p. 79). An early arts manager in the city explained the process of 'bringing art into the lives of those living in a new city' from the viewpoint of planners: 'It is a slow but rewarding process. One digs, fertilises, plants, prunes and tends – with a great deal of love. After many years the roses will have developed and the prize blooms will be ready for show.'[3] Certainly this central encouragement *was* one real element. Without the initial sponsorship by the MKDC and BMK many of the larger-scale and more 'nationally' oriented and 'professional' musical institutions like the Wavendon Allmusic Plan, the Milton Keynes Chamber Orchestra, or the 'February Festival' would never have been set up; and MKDC in particular had an impressive record in tapping both private enterprise and local initiative to encourage a wide variety of local recreational opportunities. But concentrating only on a top–down model would be to miss the essential contribution of the *existing* musical traditions which not only often continued as important foci for local interest but also laid the base for later additional activities. Indeed some MKDC administrators explicitly recognised this, notably certain leading individuals in the 'Social Development' programme who made a point of working with existing musical groups and responding to the initiatives of local residents. The informal processes and expectations underlying the local practice of music and the people who maintained the local clubs and groups over the years thus also played a crucial role, one that cannot be understood by considering the official institutions alone.

Probably no city is 'typical', and it will be obvious from the above that Milton Keynes in the early 1980s certainly was not. It was a 'new city' growing in population by some tens of thousands during the research and characterized by lavish publicity, demographic and social structure divergent from the national 'average', and the special impetus of new challenges and new developments in a new environment. In the absence of comparable studies, we do not yet know what *is* 'typical' of musical practice in contemporary English towns. This study does not therefore claim to present a detailed representation of all English towns, but to give an ethnographic account of just one at one particular period.

Hence I have no doubt that the details of the extent and nature of the musical activities presented here or the personalities who helped to create them are indeed unique. But equally I feel certain from the informal evidence discussed later, from the existing foundations in the area, and from the very mix of people from different origins in Milton Keynes, that many of the broad patterns described in later chapters are to be found fairly widely in England – an invisible system structuring and maintaining local music up and down the country.

2

Musical worlds in Milton Keynes

This part gives some account of the differing musics in Milton Keynes in the early 1980s. It is difficult to know how to present the inevitably overlapping and heterogeneous material of so complex a study as that of the musical activities of a whole town. I finally decided to begin with a plain description of the main 'musical worlds' into which local music-making seemed broadly to be divided (in part 2) and then (in part 3) consider some of the contrasts and comparisons between them before going on to the further analysis in parts 4 and 5.

The idea of a musical 'world' partly arises from local participants' own descriptions. Brass band involvement was 'a world on its own', and classical art music seen as a 'quite different world' from that of rock music. The term has also been used by anthropologists and others to refer to people's 'world view' or to different 'social worlds', emphasising the differing and complex cultures of ideas and practice within which people variously live.[1]

This has been taken further in Howard Becker's illuminating study of 'art worlds' (1982). Since the concept of musical 'worlds' has structured my presentation in this part, it is worth quoting Becker's exposition:

Art worlds consist of all the people whose activities are necessary to the production of the characteristic works which that world, and perhaps others as well, define as art. Members of art worlds coordinate the activities by which work is produced by referring to a body of conventional understandings embodied in common practice and in frequently used artifacts...

The interaction of all the involved parties produces a shared sense of the worth of what they collectively produce. Their mutual appreciation of the conventions they share, and the support they mutually afford one another, convince them that what they are doing is worth doing. If they act under the definition of "art", their interaction convinces them that what they produce are valid works of art. (Becker 1982, pp. 34, 39)

The 'musical worlds' of Milton Keynes were instances of such 'art worlds'.[2] They were distinguishable not just by their differing musical styles but also by other social conventions: in the people who took part, their values, their shared understandings and practices, modes of production and distribution, and the social organisation of their collective musical activities.

Part 2 therefore presents in turn some description of the various musical worlds of classical, brass band, folk, musical theatre, jazz, country and western, and rock or pop music which could with varying degrees of distinctiveness be found in Milton Keynes. Each is treated here as valid in itself, presented at least in part from the viewpoint of its participants. This approach is necessary for understanding the conventions in these differing worlds in their own terms, but it is also one that, surprisingly, cannot be taken for granted. 'Music' tends to be at once a word of approval and one that means different things to different people; what one group unam-biguously define as 'music' may be rejected by others as not 'really' music, or as 'mere noise' or 'childish' or 'just a boring series of notes'. It thus takes some detachment as well as self-education to envisage music right across the spectrum from 'pop' to 'classical' as equally valid, for this means refusing to accept any one set of assumptions about the 'true' nature of music and instead exploring each 'world' as of equal authenticity with others.

4

The classical music world at the local level

Classical or 'serious' music is what many readers will first think of when music is mentioned. For its participants this is *the* world of music, the type of music which in its repertoire, teachers, and performance is music *par excellence*, validated through state and church patronage and by its acceptance as part of the artistic heritage of European Christian civilisation. As one of the central cultural traditions of our society perhaps it seems too familiar to need explication. But one aspect that is often overlooked is the role of the amateur musicians and their local activities. This chapter describes some of the local practices and practitioners within classical music, the way these relate to the wider classical model, and the essential contribution they make to the continuance of classical music as a performed art form.[1]

The local activities and groups within this classical music world took various forms. There were the occasional visits of famous professional orchestras and soloists to give performances in one or other of the local halls, and concerts by local orchestras and choirs with visiting professional soloists. Local pupils from time to time went on to professional music training at one of the specialist music colleges outside the area after initial instruction by local teachers. But these more spectacular events were only part of the picture, for there were also the 'lesser' local activities that on a day-to-day basis both reflected the ideal classical model and, ultimately, enabled its realisation in practice.

School music was one important element. In addition to formal music lessons, children's ensembles played regularly outside lessons, and schools put on concerts for parents and friends (described further in chapter 15). The Buckinghamshire Education Authority also ran two music centres (one in Bletchley – the North Bucks Music Centre – and one at the Stantonbury Education Campus) which organized peripatetic instrumental teachers for local schools and 'Junior Music Schools' on Saturday mornings where local children played in groups or gave regular termly concerts (see figure 8). Like

Figure 8 The North Bucks Youth Orchestra (one of the many junior orchestras at the North Bucks Music Centre) perform *Swan Lake* at their termly concert accompanied by local dancers

the schools, these centres were predominantly in the classical (and to a lesser extent brass) tradition, and also encouraged classical musical activity by teaching and by providing rehearsal facilities and other services for classical groups. They formed one local nucleus of musicians, many also functioning as private teachers or members of local orchestras, choirs and other ensembles.

There were also the many private music teachers and their pupils. They too played a part not just in socialisation *into* music but in the actual music-making of the locality, hundreds of hours of playing every week. There were scores of instrumental and singing teachers with varying qualifications, above all in piano teaching, and each year about a thousand practical music examinations for the national examining schools were held in local centres – some indication of the extent of classical music. Private music teaching, especially to children, was a flourishing industry with pupils of varying levels of proficiency playing musical instruments not only to their teachers but also at school or church, in local groups and in the home.

The churches were another context for the local enactment of classical music. Many had their own choirs, together with one or more organists who played from the recognised classical repertoire on church occasions, including the life-cycle ceremonies so often held in church – christenings, weddings, funerals. It was thus through the churches as much as through formal concert halls that many people came to appreciate the large proportion of the classical musical heritage that is so closely associated with the Christian tradition, and themselves actively participated in it (see further in chapter 16).

A further essential part in the local enactment of classical music was played by the local groups formed to promote or perform music. The extent and scope of these active musical groupings, and the systematic conventions by which they organised their music, may well surprise those who bemoan the disappearance of active music-making today, or the 'cultural desert' in our cities. Let me illustrate this by some description of the local orchestras, instrumental ensembles, and choirs.

First, the orchestras. The best known was the Milton Keynes Chamber Orchestra, founded 'to provide a regular series of high quality professional concerts in the new city' as part of MKDC's strategy for making the city a centre for artistic excellence. As described in chapter 2, this soon became recognised as a professional orchestra, with national as well as regional connections, and many of its players lived outside Milton Keynes. As such it does not really come within the scope of this study, but did have some relevance in that its regular local rehearsals and performances provided one model for younger instrumentalists as well as a focus for local audiences keen on hearing professional playing.

Among the other orchestras the highest in the classical hierarchy was the Sherwood Sinfonia (figure 9). This was founded in 1973 as a high-standard amateur orchestra for the area and by the 1980s was playing regularly under a professional conductor. Local music teachers made up a substantial proportion of its members and recruited their advanced pupils from local schools, supplemented by other experienced players from the area, playing the typical classical orchestral instruments: strings (violins, violas, cellos, double bass), wind (flutes, oboes, clarinets, bassoons, trumpets, horns, trombone and tuba) and percussion – about 55 players in all. Membership was restricted to those with the appropriately high-level qualifications, the accepted criteria being high grades reached in the nationally recognised examinations, personal recommendation by an existing member (especially the music teachers) or in some cases audition. In keeping with the classical music tradition, the orchestra had enlisted a nationally known and highly

Figure 9 Christmas concert by the Sherwood Sinfonia. The leading amateur orchestra rehearse for their concert with the St Thomas Aquinas school choir at Stantonbury Theatre

qualified musician as their President, his name printed in its full glory on the orchestra's letterhead: Sir Thomas Armstrong, MA, D. Mus. (Oxon.), Hon. FRAM, Hon. FRCO, Hon. FTCL.

The Sherwood Sinfonia were a serious and committed orchestra which took justifiable pride in their high standards, and at the same time remained very local in their playing, membership, audiences, rehearsals and performances. They gave about four concerts a year in local halls, mostly playing works from the accepted classical repertoire by composers like Mozart, Dvořák and Brahms, though for their light-hearted Christmas family concert, they chose lighter pieces together with joke items, quizzes, or audience-sung carols. As with most groups of this kind, they moved through a repeated annual cycle: the weekly rehearsals were climaxed by the intensive activity leading up to the regular concerts, each preceded by its three-hour afternoon rehearsal and culminating in the evening performance in front of an audience largely made up of friends and relations. In the early 1970s the Sherwood Sinfonia was described as '*the* classical musical activity in the town', and even ten years later, despite the founding of the Milton Keynes Chamber Orchestra, it had not wholly lost this position.

When orchestras and ensembles were graded in typical classical fashion by their playing and performing standards, other orchestral groups were reckoned lower in both expertise and aspirations. There were the Newport Pagnell Concert Orchestra (founded in 1980) and the older Wolverton Light Orchestra, both expecting to recruit players who were of reasonably high standard (the national Grade VII examination was mentioned as desirable for the former, for example) but were perhaps not experienced enough for the Sherwood Sinfonia or just preferred a different kind of musical expression and atmosphere. Some individuals played in more than one orchestra, often choosing to go to the Wolverton Light Orchestra with their second instrument 'for fun'. These orchestras had the same general range of instruments but were smaller and more locally orientated than the Sherwood Sinfonia. They relied on local soloists and conductors rather than professionals from outside, and appeared at smaller local venues like churches and community centres, often with a special emphasis on raising money for local charities. But they too were definitely part of the classical music world, playing with no small degree of lengthily acquired proficiency on classical instruments. It was through them, and those like them, that this classical tradition was in practice maintained at the grass roots, part of the long-flourishing continuity of British amateur music-making.

There were also other more fluid instrumental groups. Some were initially scratch groups who had joined up for some festive occasion or to accompany a local choral performance, like the North Bucks Music Centre Orchestra (accompanying the Sherwood Choir), the Simon Halsey Orchestra (with the Milton Keynes Chorale), or smaller ensembles like the Wavendon Festival Strings, Walton Festival Strings or Cavatina Strings. There were also 25–30 school orchestras, together with three or four 'Saturday music school' orchestras in each of the two music centres, with their gradually changing membership as children worked through the various grades.

Each of these musical groups – which may sound uninteresting in a bare list – was made up of active and cooperating individuals. Each involved an immense amount of commitment and skill, and the co-ordination of quite large numbers of people (even the Saturday junior orchestras could contain 30 or 40 children/teenagers). All depended on voluntary participation by the players, time that could equally well have been spent on other activities.

There were also smaller classical instrumental groups, though their numbers and importance seemed to be nowhere near those of the more 'popular' bands discussed in later chapters. Classical groups did not have the same recognised public outlets as rock, jazz or folk groups, they tended to play in private – thus unknown to others – and perhaps instrumentalists in the classical tradition found individual or orchestral playing more satisfying than chamber groups. However, there were some small groups, not all long-lasting. These included the Bernwood Trio, the Milton Keynes Baroque Ensemble, the Syrinx Wind Quartet, the Syrinx Wind Octet, the Baroque

Brass Ensemble, the Seckloe Brass Ensemble and – in slightly different vein – the Milton Keynes Society of Recorder Players, who played monthly in Walton Church. Most of these were amateur (though some were mixed or 'semi-professional', i.e. with local music teachers) and, being small, had no need for the formal conductor expected in the larger groups. In addition there were fluid private arrangements by which people met in each other's houses – preferably one with a piano – to sing or play together.

To many English readers, the existence of these orchestral and instrumental groups may in a way seem scarcely worth remark – a natural part of local classical music and of English urban life. But this active instrumental activity at the grass roots is not found everywhere. It has sometimes been claimed that the success of English players in European youth orchestras is due to the distinctive English development of local- (not just national-) level playing, with school, youth and adult amateur orchestras in just about every English town. The orchestral and other instrumental groups in Milton Keynes both followed out this taken-for-granted pattern and played an active part in its continuance.

The local choirs made up the other main strand in the classical music world, a natural outgrowth of the strong choral tradition in the area. Besides the many church and school choirs there were also independent choirs, each with their own conductor or musical director (usually male and with formal classical training), which often contained at least a scattering of music teachers and of experienced choral singers. The leading choirs in this mould were the Milton Keynes Chorale and Danesborough Chorus (each with 80-plus members, and often appearing on large city occasions like the prestigious February Festival) and the smaller Sherwood Choral Society (30–40 members: see figure 29 and further discussion in chapter 18). Some continued the tradition of the older locally based choral societies, like the Newport Pagnell Singers, with their roots in the Wolverton Choral Society, dating back to early in the century; the Stratford Singers at Stony Stratford (see figure 20), 'one of the most popular choirs in Milton Keynes', according to the local newspaper, formed in 1974 'to sing together for our pleasure and that of the audience'; and, until it ended in 1980, the Bletchley Ladies Choir, dating from the 1940s.

Most larger choirs were (like the orchestras) based on the accepted British 'voluntary association' model, with written constitution, elected officers and committee, formalised membership subscriptions and accounts, and Annual General Meeting. They normally rehearsed one evening a week throughout the year with a break in the summer, meeting in one or other of the local halls or in village, school or community meeting-places. They had broadly similar yearly cycles. A Christmas concert was usually one high point – so much so that a city-wide committee tried (not altogether successfully) to arbitrate between choirs' claims for the same Saturday evenings in

December. There was also often a major concert in the spring or summer, with occasional smaller performances at other times in the year.

Each was worked for according to an accepted routine of rehearsals and performance. It started with detailed practisings of isolated parts of the works under the conductor (and perhaps his or her assistant), singing to piano accompaniment, then moved gradually towards consolidating the piece as a whole, culminating in the intensity of the later rehearsals when the work began to 'come together', then the great but sometimes traumatic rehearsal on the afternoon of the concert (often a revelation to the choir as for the first time they heard the whole work complete with solos and full accompaniment). Last came the experience of the full evening performance before an audience.

This cycle of rehearsal–performance was a recurrent one, especially when, as commonly with the large choirs, the music came from the renowned classical repertoire of oratorio and church music. These were mostly four-part works, ideally with orchestral accompaniment and visiting soloists, by such composers as Handel (*Messiah* was still one of the great popular pieces, the music known to most singers), together with Haydn, Mendelssohn, Brahms, Bach, Vivaldi, Fauré, and others in the recognised classical canon whose works were over the years sung alternately by the various local choirs. These formed the core of the expected choral reper-toire, but there were also concerts of more modern works, especially English compositions by, say, Vaughan Williams or Britten, 'light classics' by Bizet or Sullivan, and arrangements of both popular and esoteric carols. Many choir members were already acquainted with much of the classical reper-toire (some had been choral singers for 30, 40 or even 50 years). At the least, they had long-practised skills in sight-reading from written music (an essential requirement for every choir) and in recognising familiar cadences and styles. The classical ideal in terms of repertoire, highly graded direction, and aspirations to a 'high-standard' performance was very much to the fore, expressed through the actual singers on the ground who had gained their expertise through a process of informal learning and practising in the amateur tradition.

The same general patterns were also followed by the many smaller choirs like the Orphean Singers, Fellowship Choir, Guild Singers, Canzonetta Singers, Miscellany, St Martin Singers, Woburn Sands Band Madrigal Group and the all-female Erin Singers. Many of these continued over the years, but there were also shorter-lived groups like the New City Choral Society, the Bletchley Further Education College Choir and some who appeared under fluctuating names (the Senior Citizens' Choir developing into the Melody Group, for example). There were also temporary groups who sang together just for a particular occasion, whether large, like the 180-strong Festival Choir (the joint Danesborough Chorus and Milton Keynes

Chorale) at the 1982 Milton Keynes February Festival, or small, like the Village Maidens from the local Women's Institute, who sang after a Christmas pantomime at Stoke Hammond School, and, finally, the various madrigal groups that formed from time to time. Many smaller choirs put on several small events during the year rather than working up one or two main works on the model of the rehearsal–performance cycles of the larger choirs, and sang frequently at churches, fêtes or clubs to raise money for some local good cause or provide entertainment at hospitals or old people's homes. But here too there was still a stress on rehearsing to reach as high a standard as possible, almost always with a piano accompaniment and under the direction of a conductor. The different categories shaded into each other, of course, and some small choirs had highly qualified conductors or practitioners in classical music terms (the Open University Choir, for example, or the Tadige Singers), but in general the smaller choirs laid less emphasis on specialist classical training and (unlike the larger, more ambitious choirs) quite often had female conductors.

The number of choirs in the area was thus great. There were perhaps 100 in all, with membership ranging from 90 or so down to around 12–15 (a not uncommon number for the smaller groups), or as few as 5 or 6 in some church choirs. The total number of choral singers in the area was thus probably well over 1,000, though it is hard to calculate exact numbers because of the amount of multiple membership – another notable feature of the choral tradition.

These many choirs and instrumental groups practised through the year without always being especially noticeable except to those most directly involved. However, there were points in the year when their activities became more prominent. At Christmas practically every choir and orchestra gave performances, and there were also a great many concerts towards the end of the summer term in the school year. Easter too had its performances, together with other key festivals in the Christian year (especially, but not only, by the church groups). Another high point was February. The annual 'February Festival', initially promoted by the MKDC arts division, included both nationally and internationally known professional artists from outside the area, and a few of the leading local groups.

February was also the month of the Milton Keynes (earlier Bletchley) Festival of Arts, a more modest and locally generated event, which followed the established music festival tradition of competitive classes in music, dance and speech for both children and adults in a wide range of ages and standards, judged by visiting adjudicators. It included classes for solo singers and performers on just about every classical instrument, band, recorder groups, small ensembles, and church choirs. The largest choirs and orchestras did not enter, but the festival still provided a showpiece of the classical music world in Milton Keynes. Over the days of the festival, many hundreds of entrants came forward and performed in two Bletchley halls, from piano classes for tiny tots to 'recital classes' by young aspirants for music college entrance. The festival had grown from one day in 1968 to an event of more than a week and over 3,000 entrants (almost 80 per cent of them local) by the mid 1980s.

But a mere catalogue gives no real taste of what these many musical activities meant to the participants. This was something over and above the time and work they put into them or the incidental results (sociability or friendship or status) that certainly also often flowed from them. The rewards for those committed to the classical music world are hard to capture in precise words, but they certainly included a sense of beauty and fundamental value, of intense and profoundly felt artistic experience which could reach to the depths of one's nature. For participants in this world there was perhaps nothing to equal the experience of engaging in a beautiful and co-ordinated performance of some favoured classical work, whether in practice or (at a heightened level) in public concert: the expectant thrill of players or singers entering a hall in their special dress ready for performance, the familiar and evocative sounds of tuning up in front of the audience, the hushed moment as the performers gathered themselves to start or the conductor called all eyes by lifting his baton, and the split second of silence (more of symbolic quality than measured time) at the end before performers and audience returned alike to the everyday world. For those steeped in the classical tradition these richly symbolic moments were experienced as somehow implicating the deep core of people's being.

This experience was not, ultimately, dependent on the super-high professional standards insisted on in the elite national music world. It was something within the compass and imagination of the quite ordinary part-time musicians in the local halls and schools and churches.

These locally practising musicians were of course influenced by many things, social as well as musical, and it would not do to give either too purist or too generalized a picture of what drew each to his or her musical engagements or the views each held of these. One aspect, however, which to some degree or other set them within an overall common background was the general evaluation of the place of classical music in our culture and the model most people had of this. These shared assumptions were usually implicit only, but some brief (if simplified) comments on this model of classical music are relevant for understanding the local scene, even though to many readers they may seem too obvious and 'natural' to need stating.

The musical organisation, artistic forms, and personnel associated with classical music in the broad sense of that term[2] were widely, if rather vaguely, assumed to be bound up with many privileged institutions and values of our society: the educational system, church and state functions, and the generally accorded status of a 'high art'. This status was further supported by the existence of specialised musicians who had managed to establish themselves as a recognised profession with control over recruitment and evaluation. The performances and high-level teaching provided by these experts formed the most visible element in what was accepted as the classical music world. The model of classical music in English society was explicitly defined by the specialists in terms both of the kind of music played – most typically performed in a formal public concert – and its historical and theoretical basis.

There were many detailed differences within this overall world, not least the changing historical styles as analysed in advanced musical studies, but in general terms the current idea of the European classical music tradition, as distinct both from non-European music and from 'popular' forms, centred round transmitting the works of influential musicians from the past – the 'great composers'. Musical genres have of course varied at different historical periods, but those commonly cultivated in local (as in national) performances included orchestral symphonies, suites and concertos, instrumental sonatas, oratorios and classical operas, and vocal music of various kinds, usually with instrumental accompaniment and with the underlying idea that their central essence could be – and was – represented in written scores. There were also classical compositions for particular instrumental combinations from recorder groups to string quartets and instrumental duets, following accepted conventions about both the instruments (specific types of strings, wind and keyboard together with the voice and to some extent percussion), and about how they should be played.

In practice what was classified as within this classical tradition depended not so much on an objective set of criteria as on cultural conventions about the appropriate forms and contexts of music – ones which those outside this world regarded as uninspiring but which classical musicians could justify both in terms of particular patternings of melody, harmony and thematic structures and by the accepted classifications by music specialists, further authorised by the strongly held image of this music as an artistic heritage coming down in written form from the past. Just what was included changed from time to time, and the whole concept of classical music was certainly fuzzy at the edges; what was clear was that it was based not just on musicological content but on definitions and validations by particular groups of people.

This socially defined canon of classical music was what present-day musicians largely worked with. A few themselves composed, but in general their central responsibility was the perpetuation of this heritage, teaching others the skills to appreciate it or to realise it in their own playing. They thus transmitted the musical works written by earlier composers and did so in a context in which this was considered a high, indeed revered, form of artistic expression supported by widely accepted values about high art and (in some cases) direct state patronage. Concerts by nationally and internationally known soloists and orchestras and by varying combinations of professional players, both live and broadcast, epitomised what most people envisaged as the classical music tradition of this country, backed up by the system of specialised music training, national music colleges and professional musicians.

These activities by elite musicians perpetuating the musical heritage of the past in public concerts made up the most visible manifestation of classical music. But they did not constitute the whole of the classical musical world as it was realised in practice. Certainly this particular model deeply influenced even those on the face of it far removed from the specialist performances of highly qualified professionals. But, as will be clear, there was also a whole grass-roots sub-structure of *local* classical music. Though perhaps 'invisible' to most scholars, in practice this was the essential local manifestation of the national music system, and also (as emerged in chapter 2) both interacted with it and formed its foundation. One aspect was the provision of audiences with the necessary skills of appreciation for professionals coming to give concerts locally, but it extended far beyond this to the whole system of local training, playing, actively practising musical groups and public performances by local musicians.

This ideal classical model was a powerful one which, however vague at the edges, implicitly moulded people's views of music and of their own participation in it at the local level. They were taking part, it was assumed, in a high art form validated by an authorised historical tradition and a structure of professional specialisation in which experts had to undergo rigorously assessed training ultimately controlled by the highest members of the profession. Of course not everyone who went to a classical concert, learnt the piano or played the violin in a local orchestra had formulated this explicitly or expected his or her own performance to measure up to the highest level of this ideal. Nevertheless, the model had a profound influence throughout the musical groups and activities that were widely seen as part of the world of classical music.

The local awareness of links with the wider classical world and its authorised canon from the past came out in many contexts. One concrete form was the printed scores and music 'parts' which were a necessary channel for transmission and performance among local classical groups, both instrumental and vocal. These were often borrowed rather than bought and when a local choir, say, found itself, as so often, singing from old and well-marked copies, it was easy to picture the earlier choirs 20, 30, even 50 years ago singing from the self-same copies – and repertoire – of classical choral music in the days when, perhaps, those parts cost just one penny. Local performers could also regard themselves as the amateur counterparts of the specialist professionals, their reflection at the local level, playing however imperfectly from the same classical canon. It was this pervasive model of the lengthy and highly valued classical tradition which ultimately set the definitions of the musical activities in which local amateurs were engaged.

Amidst these many locally based classical musical activities, what kind of people were the main participants? Is the prevalent assumption justified that classical music is primarily a 'middle-class pursuit' or confined to the 'elite' rather than the 'common people'? Judging by Milton Keynes there was certainly one sense in which this was true: if one focusses primarily on highly trained *specialist* musicians and the national institutions in which they participate, this is almost by definition an elite and select world; and insofar as *this* model influenced people's interpretations, classical music was indeed pictured as, in its fullest and best form, a high-art pursuit for the few. But, as becomes clear by examining the local situation, the actual practice which upholds and perpetuates the classical music world consists of more than just these elite musicians. The local amateurs and small-scale events also play an essential part. In *their* case it is by no means so evident that an elite or a 'middle class' label is correct. Indeed my main conclusion – however banal – was that local musicians and participants in local musical activities varied enormously in terms of educational qualifications, specialist expertise, occupation, wealth and general ethos.

Some musical groups did approach more nearly than others to the ideal of the expert professionals in terms of specialist musical qualifications, and this often – though not always – went along with the kinds of jobs or back-grounds loosely referred to as middle class. The leading amateur orchestra, the Sherwood Sinfonia, was a good example. Players had gone through the formal examinations of the national music institutions, and there was a high proportion of local music teachers and of individuals in high-status occupa-tions among their members. But even here there were exceptions, like the young sausage-maker, later music shop assistant, who besides being a Sherwood Sinfonia violinist was a keyboard player and composer with a local rock group, or pupils from local comprehensive schools not all in the 'best' areas. The amateur and widely based emphasis within English music was particularly noticeable in the choirs, with their long tradition of extensive local participation without formalised musical expertise or selec-tive background. It was true that the older pattern of local choral societies made up of a cross-section from one locality was – with the change in transport arrangements perhaps – being replaced in the 1980s by choirs recruited on a city-wide rather than neighbourhood basis; but both local ties and a wide mix of backgrounds were still evident in the church and school choirs (see chapters 15 and 16). In such cases generalisation about classical music practitioners coming from just one social background or set of occupations does not stand up: many (though not all) choirs were very mixed.

The same applied to instrumental players, despite the elite nature of some smaller ensembles. Piano and organ playing were widespread, sometimes still learnt on a self-taught basis (especially in church contexts), and even instrumental groups were not all highly select. The Wolverton Light Orchestra, for example, went back far into the local history of Wolverton, the town long dominated by the local railway works. It was first founded as the Frank Brooks Orchestra after the First World War by a bandmaster of the Bucks. Volunteers who also conducted the local brass band, and was later renamed the Wolverton Orchestral Society. Between the wars it played light music with a First World War flavour, the thirty or so players giving regular winter concerts in local cinemas. It was revived after the Second World War, but later took the title Wolverton Light Orchestra to make clear that in contrast to the newly founded Sherwood Sinfonia their policy was to play smaller-scale works rather than symphonies. This they were still doing very effectively in the 1980s, giving six or seven concerts a year, mainly around the Wolverton area, with a playing membership of about thirty. By then there was a fair proportion of local schoolteachers in the orchestra, but over the years – and to some extent still – it had been strongly rooted in the local community and still had a mainly self-taught conductor from the local railway works. It would be hard to regard this as a select elite or middle-class activity in the sense often attached to those terms.

All in all, the picture was a varied one. The high-culture model of classical music should not lead us to conclude without further question that the musicians who *in practice* made up the classical music world at the local level were themselves members of some clear elite or drawn predominantly from some single class. For Milton Keynes, at least, the evidence points to a weighting towards teachers and fairly high-status occupations in several of the more aspiring instrumental groups, but otherwise – and particularly in the choirs – great heterogeneity of background, education and occupation.

The power of the specialist model, then, which focusses attention on professional concerts and national performing organisations, should not be allowed to obscure the equally real practices of local performance, training and appreciation. This classical ideal – misleading though it can be – is nevertheless of great relevance for the local scene. It provides a framework for the local practice, and without it one justification and measure for the many local orchestras, choirs and instrumental ensembles would be lacking. The recognised tradition of the classical repertoire and the currently accepted styles of presentation also provide local groups with a rationale which they both draw on and help to perpetuate. All in all the over-arching classical music model on the one hand and the local performers and enactors of the tradition on the other interact together in a complex and varied way to transmit and sustain, carry and form, the national and enduring world of classical music so characteristic of this country as a whole and so richly practised at the local level

5

The brass band world

Given the well-known association of brass bands with the North, the strength and continuity of the local brass band tradition came as something of a surprise. For there were five to eight main brass bands in and around Milton Keynes in the early 1980s (the exact numbers depending on just where one draws the boundaries): the Wolverton Town and British Rail Band, the Woburn Sands Band, and the Bradwell Band (all going back many decades), and the more recent Stantonbury Brass, the re-formed Bletchley Band and (from 1984) the Broseley Brass; also regarded as in a sense local were the century-old Great Horwood Band and the Heath and Reach Band, in villages about five miles from the city boundary. There were also youth bands, bands connected with the Boys' Brigades and similar groups, and Salvation Army bands in Bletchley and Bradwell. Brass band gatherings like the Bletchley spring festivals had been a local tradition for some time, and were currently concentrated in two annual events, with 50 or so brass bands coming from all over the country to the February 'entertainment contest', and a massed concert by local bands every autumn.[1]

The main bands contained 15 to 30 amateur players each, fluctuating according to the fortunes of the band at any one time, the regulation 'competition band' being 25 plus conductor. Their instruments were the standard brass combination of cornets, trombones, baritone and tenor horns, euphoniums, B♭ and E♭ basses, and percussion, played by members of many different ages and, in most of the bands, of both sexes. They made frequent public appearances (far more often than the choirs and orchestras) – highly visible performances, because of the loudness of brass instruments, the tradition of playing in the open, and their distinctive uniforms.

Brass band players were exceptionally articulate about their traditions; 'it's a world on its own', I was constantly told, 'a whole world'. Among all the musical spheres in Milton Keynes, it was the brass bands and their players that most emphatically made up a self-conscious 'world' with its own specific and separate traditions.

This perception was partly moulded by the popular publications about brass bands, the activities of national brass associations and the strong if unwritten traditions that have grown up round brass bands since the last century. This too was how outsiders often regarded them. The image was of bands as essentially working class, following their own autonomous musical style and repertoire separate from the elitist high culture, and composed of (male) players who were either self-taught or had learnt within the family or the band itself. In the past, so went the tradition, it was the heavy manual workers like miners who formed the brass bands: their work-hardened hands could not cope with stringed instruments, but they had one sensitive part left to them – their mouths and tongues. The brass bands were also assumed to be closely linked to their local community, which they supported both through local performances and through carrying the band's name forward in the glamorous brass competitions.

Band members in Milton Keynes were well aware – indeed proud – of this long brass band tradition which itself shaped their understanding of present-day activities, as well as influencing their repertoire and mode of performance. What is more, several of the brass bands in the area did indeed date back to the turn of the century or earlier, a continuity which added to their sense of historic tradition. The Wolverton Town and British Rail Band was started in 1908 and had even earlier antecedents, the Great Horwood Band was formed in the 1880s, and the Woburn Sands Band in 1867 (though it had lapsed for many years until its refounding in 1957), while the Bradwell Band dated its foundation precisely to 15 January 1901, since when it had had a continuous existence as the Bradwell Silver Prize Band, Bradwell United Prize Band, United Brass Band, then Bradwell Silver Band. Even the younger Boys' Brigade Bugle Band in Bletchley had continued without break since 1928, while the Heath and Reach Band was approaching its fiftieth anniversary. Others, like the old Bletchley Brass Band or the Newport Pagnell Town Band, had not survived but still left their traces in personal memories and in the music stamped with their name now used by other local bands. Inherited band resources like instruments inscribed with earlier players' names or the music library, as well as memories of glorious exploits in competition or of contacts with leading local families, also brought home the length of tradition. Some bands had documentary records going back fifty years or more, with newspaper cuttings recording their festivities and successes; these often documented the strong family tradition characteristic of brass bands, fathers being followed over the generations by sons, grandsons and nephews. No other named local musical groups (with the possible exception of a few church choirs) had as long a continuous existence, so that though there had been both demises and new foundings, brass band members were in fact correct to see their tradition as a long-established and vigorous one.

Awareness of their proud history thus played a part in local activities, and to some extent this continuity was striking. The tradition of informal learning was also still influential, and there were still many family links and loyalties within the bands. The competition world was sometimes another continuing context for performances and aspirations, while the tradition of service to 'the community' and appearances at local events remained a valued one, and at least some players still spoke of the ideal of bands as essentially made up of 'ordinary working lads'.

This traditional image of the 'brass band movement' was thus of real relevance, influencing repertoire, mode of training, self-image and family and community links. However, as even some players themselves admitted, the picture was also changing, and local brass band practice often did not fit with the traditional image.

For one thing the playing of brass instruments was becoming more assimilated to the 'classical' music model, and the modes of learning and performance were changing. Brass instruments were energetically taught in the schools by peripatetic teachers on the same basis as other classical instruments, supplementing the bands' own youth training schemes and informal teaching. Partly as a result, more girls were learning. Milton Keynes brass bands included female players, and in some of the younger bands girls were actually in the majority – very different from the past. New groups were founded which, unlike the older bands, drew their models not just from inherited tradition but from televised performances and classical instrumentalists.

Brass bands were also part of the high-profile cultural developments promoted by the MKDC. One of the first ensembles off the ground in the show-piece Stantonbury Education Campus was Stantonbury Brass, a youth band run by the Stantonbury Music Centre – an effective choice given the shorter lead time for training up a viable brass than string group. This successful young band was invited to perform at MKDC and BMK-sponsored events and to represent Milton Keynes abroad. Again, the Milton Keynes brass band festival, though building on established local bands, was directly encouraged by the new city's administration (which happened to include some influential brass enthusiasts). For many, therefore, brass bands were not a separate world of lower-class or 'popular' as against 'high' culture, but a recognised part of official cultural events in the city. The links with classical music were also increasingly accepted by players and audiences generally, not just because of school brass teaching but through the widely watched BBC 'Young Musician of the Year' competition, in which brass instrumentalists always formed one section. One recent winner was claimed as a 'local boy' (he came from Bedford and had played as soloist with local brass bands); this added new prestige to brass band playing, and the number of children (or rather parents) interested in brass lessons immediately jumped. There was thus contact between brass band and the classical music worlds, with some overlapping membership between brass bands and classical ensembles (like the Woburn Sands Band and the Sherwood Sinfonia).[2]

Another way the older image no longer really applied was in band membership. The 'working-class' picture may have influenced people's perceptions, but by the 1980s hardly fitted the Milton Keynes bands. The new bands (the Bletchley Band and the Stantonbury Brass) were mostly young people of very mixed backgrounds, many still at school, and had girl players as well as boys; and even the older bands included a fair mix. This, furthermore, was how at least some bands in practice saw themselves, even if they also relished the nostalgic flavour of the earlier image. One long-established band, I was told by its secretary, included political commitments 'across the whole spectrum' and a cross-section typical of local brass bands generally: postmen, teachers, telephone engineers, a motor mechanic, personnel manager, master butcher, university teacher, train driver, and schoolchildren from state and independent schools. Another band (partially overlapping in membership with the first) was less varied, with a larger proportion of jobs like clerk, labourer, storeman, or shopworker, but also including computer engineers, a building inspector, a midwife and several schoolchildren; as their musical director summed it up, 'the old cloth cap and horny hand image is dying out'.

The bands also contained players who had learnt their craft in several different modes. Some had indeed learnt in the traditional way from brass players within their own families or bands, then perfecting their skill through actual band playing. Others had been taught in the formal classical mode which stressed reading music and being able to play in classical music ensembles. Others had combined the two. This mixed experience did not seem to undermine the communal loyalty of the bands, and was indeed exploited by the bands, who used a variety of methods in their own youth sections. But it was yet another way in which the model of one homogeneous brass band tradition was being modified in the light of actual practice.

The day-to-day commitment of players to their band was apparently as strong as ever. The common pattern was of one or, more often, two weekly practices of several hours – two weekday evenings or one plus a weekend meeting. Some bands ran training sections on yet another evening, when experienced players joined in teaching the younger members.

Despite the strong family and personal link in local brass bands, the organisation was quite formal, on the 'voluntary association' pattern so common in English society. Bands were formally constituted, had the same kind of committee structure as choirs and orchestras, functioned on the basis of membership fees and audited accounts, and held an Annual General

Meeting with formally conducted proceedings. They were also hierarchically organised under a permanent conductor (sometimes with assistant) who directed the practices and the public performances, assisted by a committee. Unlike some earlier brass bands they were not sponsored (apart from the launch money for the new Broseley Brass) and with the partial exception of the Wolverton Town and British Rail Band, who still held meetings in the British Rail Engineering canteen, they were not attached to particular works, but supported themselves as independent bands from their own contributions.

A great deal of authority lay with the conductor (sometimes entitled musical director), backed up by the committee. The Bradwell Band constitution, redrawn in 1978, stated that the conductor or his deputy had full control of band personnel during engagements with the right to report any irregularity to the committee, who would 'deal with the offending playing member'. Similarly he was to report any playing member frequently absent from practices or performances without his permission (a more stringent rule than for many other types of local musical group), and in general 'when in uniform, playing members must uphold the dignity of the Band at all times, and engage in no activity that would bring the Band, Trustees and Patrons into disrepute. The conductor shall refer to the committee any breach of this rule by any member.' The actual conduct of affairs is of course often less formalised than constitutions suggest, and an atmosphere of camaraderie and enjoyment was one noticeable characteristic of local brass bands. Nevertheless there was also a definite air of authority at band events, and practices were hierarchically directed sessions when people worked at the conductor's bidding in a highly disciplined setting which players felt strongly obligated to attend.

In addition to routine practices, the bands all took on performing commitments, especially in the summer and at Christmas (see below). Some also competed, and new local and regional competitions had been developing which several local bands entered. The Woburn Sands Band, for example, after being out of the competition world for a time, had begun competing again about ten years before and was advancing up the national grading system. Stantonbury Brass and the Bletchley Band also entered competitions regionally and the new Broseley Brass were already having success. Other bands concentrated more on local appearances, but the tradition of competitiveness was still a powerful one even for currently non-contesting bands, coupled with an awareness of the distinctiveness and pride of each separate band.

The competition world also had its own rituals. This made heavy demands on band members, for it meant not only playing at as high a standard as they could possibly achieve, but also the necessary travel and assessment of their own and other performances. The sense of occasion in these highly structured and intensive competitions had much to do with the enthusiasm of brass band players both for the 'brass band movement' as a whole and for their strong identification with their own bands.

Competitions were not the only occasions for band loyalty and sense of performance. Local brass bands had an accepted obligation to play at local events and in the community that they regarded as, in some sense, 'their own'. Local fêtes, carnivals, outdoor carol services, charity occasions, the big events at Christmas and the Remembrance Day rituals all regularly involved appearances by one or another of the local bands.

Indeed at some times of the year, they had little respite from playing. Take, for example, the Bradwell Band's 1980 Christmas events as listed in the local newspaper's notice (not their only Christmas engagements): Thursday 18 December, Eaglestone Hospital, 7.0 p.m.; Sunday 21st, The Green, Newport, 10.30 a.m.; Monday 22nd, New Bradwell streets, 7.0 p.m.; Tuesday 23rd, Bradville streets, 7.0 p.m.; Wednesday 24th, New Bradwell streets, 7.0 p.m.; Christmas morning, New Bradwell streets, 6.0 a.m. Their very similar programme in the Christmas season in 1982 (out 'carolling' every day from 11–25 December inclusive) followed a long tradition in the area culminating in the famous 'Christians Awake' at six on Christmas morning in New Bradwell, a tradition which had not been broken for well over fifty years. It caused amusement as well as pleasure – who really wanted to be woken up or out at that time in the dark and freezing cold? – but was close to the hearts of band and New Bradwell residents alike, and players spoke warmly of going out before dawn, being greeted with drinks or gifts or, by the children, friendly abuse, and finding glasses of whisky waiting on the best doorsteps. Similarly, the Woburn Sands Band year's events in 1982 covered over twenty performances – at local brass band festivals in February and October, the Regional Round of the National Brass Band Championship in March, then the Finals in London in October, local concerts in April and May, appearances at a dozen fêtes, carnivals, fairs and shows in local towns and villages throughout the summer, hymn-singing under the tree at Simpson village in July, Remembrance Day ceremonies in November, and OAP and Women's Institute parties in December; in addition nearly three weeks in December were committed to carolling around the local areas.

Given the intensity of such commitments on top of the regular band practices which timetabled their weekly activities throughout the year, it is not surprising that players spoke of the band 'taking over their whole lives', with consequences for all their other obligations; but they added that this was well compensated for by the 'good humour and fun' of band life. For some, brass playing took a dominant role in planning their lives; at least one player had settled in a particular village because of its band. For others, band commitments had become almost 'like a job' – except that they felt less guilty taking a holiday from their paid employment than from the band –

and a high proportion of their 'free' time was taken up by band obligations: performing and practising, travelling, organising uniforms and music, fund-raising, or preparing and transporting instruments.

The band could be a source of more than just musical co-operation, for several bands had associated groups, and performed social as well as musical functions. The Wolverton Town and British Rail Band had a Ladies Supporters Club which met once a month at the BR Canteen at Wolverton to raise money for the band, while the Woburn Sands Band had its own madrigal society led by a horn player who was also a singer; members met in turn at each other's houses after Sunday morning band practice. Bands took some social responsibility for their members, marking events like weddings, deaths, departures, successes, and also sometimes co-operating in baby sitting, arranging transport, and other less directly band-related exchanges such as sharing skills or information.

Participating in a brass band was more than just 'going along for a blow'. Quite apart from the intensity of the musical commitment, band members – and above all the organising committee – inevitably became involved in a host of social and financial arrangements. Some of these practical aspects are explored further in part 4, but for brass bands particularly there was the heavy cost of instruments and uniforms and the importance of the music library. Brass instruments were not cheap, especially the larger ones, and brass players might find themselves using instruments worth £600, £1,000, £2,000 or more. Bands sometimes undertook to lend out instruments to players, a heavy drain on their resources, for £1,000 or more might have to be expended annually on purchases and repairs with all the fund-raising and background work that entailed. Uniforms too were expensive, and fitting out a band with a new uniform at the cost of many hundreds of pounds often had to be paid for through local fund-raising events and gifts – another way in which a band was bound into the locality in which it both played and raised money. Local people helped the Wolverton Town and British Rail Band to raise £3,000 for thirty-three new uniforms in 1981, for example, and were thanked by a free charity concert. The result was a highly visible group, clearly marked out by their military-style costume, clearly distinguished from other groups in the area (see figure 10).

The music library was an important band possession. This contained the multiple music parts played by the band and its predecessors, a mark not only of tradition through time but, as the players themselves put it, a 'priceless' resource for them. Of course bands experimented from time to time with 'newer' music, but given the availability of their own library of the classic band repertoire there were economic as well as sentimental reasons for bands to make good use of the (literally) well-worn music that had come down to them. This was yet another sign of their unity as one named band, and (together with their other heavy investment in instruments and uniform)

Figure 10 The eighty-year-old Wolverton Town and British Rail Band. The current members pose in their band uniform

one factor in the long life of brass bands compared to other musical groupings.

Most bands were also bound by additional links of kinship and friend-ship. The local brass bands seemed to be full of relatives – at first sight, quite remarkably so until one recalls the common tendency for music in general and brass banding in particular to run in families and the long history of many of the local bands. It was common for several members of one family to play in a band, both within and across the generations, made easier by the lack of interest in *age* so long as members could *play* (in local bands the age range was from 9 to 70). Playing together forged intense relationships and provided a sphere in which more links could be formed which in turn bound the members together yet further. This was especially so in the longer-established bands, but it also extended to the more recent ones, some of which had been helped by friends or relatives in the others (the Bletchley Band, for example, was founded by players from the Woburn Sands Band and the Bradwell Band). These links were not always and in every respect harmonious, of course – but this was perhaps all the more evidence of the bands' close-knit quasi-family nature.

It was not just the number of hours, social ties or amount of trouble that for participants constituted their affiliation to the brass band world, but the qualitative experience and the meaning this held for them. They were

Figure 11 An informal photograph of the Woburn Sands Band shortly after competing in the National Brass Band Finals, showing the age range typical of many music groups (here 11 to 70)

creating and transmitting music known to be part of the brass band repertoire, music coming down to them from the past as visibly enshrined in their own library and store of instruments or, if embarking on innovative ventures, doing this within the traditional brass conventions and in this sense making it their own. They were engaged in the joint act of making and receiving music in a known and valued tradition with its evocative visual as well as acoustic associations: the glittering polished instruments, band insignia, proud display of uniforms, and quasi-military and tradition-hallowed bearing.

The music above all was central, with its burst of sound filling the surroundings, arising from not just hours but years of skilled work and enacted by two dozen or so people participating as both individuals and a collectivity in a context in which age and background were of no account for 'you're pursuing an activity and in pursuit of that activity one loses oneself'. Building on their hours of practice, they were taking part in a performance to the highest standard the band could produce, an event unique to them yet tradition-drenched, of both public acclaim and rich aesthetic meaning. Small wonder that one player summed up banding as 'a way of life' which, despite the grumbles, 'I wouldn't be without'.

This sense of belonging to an integrated distinctive world, the inheritors of a proud and independent tradition, was further enhanced by the continuation of the long tradition of brass bands performing a public function for the local community. Of course such a statement needs qualification. What was seen as 'local' or 'the community' varied according to the speaker(s), the situation, even the time of year. And in some respects brass bands were just like any other musical groups performing in and around their own local base at both small and large events, not necessarily admired by or (probably unlike nineteenth-century bands) even known to all the local residents. What was striking, however, was the explicit ideology that brass bands had a direct relationship to their 'own' locality. The band was expected to turn out on 'public' occasions and to play a part in rituals of the musical, religious and official year, while in return members of the locality should support them not only in musical events but also in fund-raising, particularly in street donations to band funds during the 'Christmas carolling'. The local band's public appearances at Christmas festivities, local carnivals and shows, ceremonies like the public opening of some new institution, or (as representatives of their own locality) in competitions or visits outside were seen as a necessary part of such events and an expected function of the band. The sense of let-down when there was once a mix-up and the local brass band did not play at the local Remembrance Day brought home the importance many people attached to this function – even those who did not particularly like brass band music.

One of the images associated with local brass bands in the 1980s (as earlier) was of a group performing an integrating and public role for their locality. Even though by the 1980s band players did not necessarily live in the immediate neighbourhood at all, local brass bands could still see themselves as somehow representing and enhancing the whole 'community' at public events – whatever that 'community' might be in different circumstances: the local village for the Woburn Sands Band; the town of Wolverton and its workers for the Wolverton Town and British Rail Band; or, in some situations, the whole developing new city of Milton Keynes. This aspect was no doubt facilitated by the ability of brass bands to perform so visibly and audibly in the open air, but even so it was remarkable that a musical tradition which was also seen as separate from others and was certainly not to everyone's taste should nevertheless have been accepted as being somehow 'above the battle' and, despite its basis in the world of privately organised voluntary associations, as providing mutually beneficial support for the large 'community' occasions.

Up to a point, just about all the voluntary musical groups performed something of this public function, but it was in the case of brass bands that this idea was most prominent. Brass bands both constituted a quite explicitly perceived 'world of their own' and, at the same time, were called on most directly of all the groups considered here to support the public celebrations of the communities in which they practised.

6

The folk music world

Active performers of the music known as 'folk' were a select minority in Milton Keynes, in contrast to the wider distribution of many other local forms. But for the performers their participation in the folk music world was a source of the greatest satisfaction, often taking up just about the whole of their non-working time and playing a large part in their self-definition. Their numbers were not negligible either. In the Milton Keynes area in the early 1980s, there were at any one time about a dozen 'folk groups', four or more 'ceilidh' dance bands and five or six 'folk clubs', the latter dependent on a pool of local performers. 'Folk music' was also heard and danced to by a much wider circle through the established custom of local associations hiring a folk dance band to play for their annual socials.

Understanding the folk music world can best start from some description of the 'folk clubs'. These were independent clubs with their own clientele and organisation, meeting regularly in local pubs: the Song Loft (earlier the Stony Stratford Folk Club) at the Cock Hotel in Stony Stratford on every other Friday; the Hogsty Folk Club (later the Hogsty Music Club) weekly or fortnightly on Mondays, then Tuesdays, at the Holt, Aspley Guise; Folk-at-the-Stables at WAP, usually monthly on Saturdays (a more professionally oriented club than most, though with an amateur resident band, the Gaberlunzies); the Fox and Hounds Folk Club at Whittlebury (earlier the Whittlebury Folk Club) on the alternate Fridays from the Song Loft; and the slightly different Lowndes Arms Ceilidh Club at Whaddon on the last Thursday of the month, a folk dance club similar to the folk clubs in atmosphere, music, personnel and resident band. It will be clear from the list both that the club network was extensive and that clubs went through different locations, names and timing. This immediately points to one characteristic of local folk clubs – their relative transience under a given title. There were others too, even less long-lasting, which for a time engaged people's enthusiasm but faded out after a few years or months, among them the Black Horse Folk Club, the Bull and Butcher Singers' Club, the Cannon

Blues and Folk Club, and the Concrete Cow Folk Club; and how the new Merlin's Roost Folk Music Club would do (founded autumn 1984) still remained to be seen. There were also gatherings on a regular but less formal basis, like the Sunday lunch sing-songs that drew 50–100 people at the Bull Hotel in Stony Stratford, then shifted to the Black Horse at Great Linford, where (as one leading singer put it) 'anybody's welcome to join in, play along, sing a song, add some harmony to a chorus, or simply have a beer and listen'.

Amidst all these changes there were always some five or six clubs which devotees could attend. The accepted system was that club meetings were arranged on a periodic cycle, avoiding mutual competition by functioning on different nights throughout the week or month. A real enthusiast could spend almost every night each week at one or other of the nearby clubs.

There were detailed differences between clubs, for, as one experienced performer commented, 'each club goes its own way, does it how it works for *them*'; but there were also recognisable patterns. Almost all were associated with a local pub, meeting weekly or fortnightly in its 'special function' room. They were open to casual visitors, but also normally had membership subscriptions, and the entrance fee of around £1.00–£1.50 was lower for members. Around 40–70 typically came on any one night, roughly half men and half women, with 120 or 150 for a well-known artist. Clubs usually ran both 'singers' nights', at which the club members provided free entertainment, and evenings with visiting 'guests'. The visitors were paid a fee, the amount varying according to reputation and distance: a local musician might get £10–£20, a well-known non-local artist up to £100. The balance between singers' and visitors' nights partly depended on club size (and hence funds). A well-off club aimed to have three or four guest nights to one 'singers' night', but this was not always easy since even with an entrance charge of £1.50 the room (and audience) might not be big enough to recoup the cost of an expensive guest.

An evening session involved a high level of participation from those present, and even where there were invited performers local members often performed too as 'floor singers'. The general atmosphere was relaxed, with people sitting around tables drinking as they listened or joined in the songs, but there were elements of formality too. Starting and finishing times were fairly strictly kept to, there were accepted conventions about introducing and applauding performers, and the organisers tried to stop too much moving around during the performance of a song – in contrast to some other musical performances in pubs. Since finance was always a problem the evening often included a fund-raising raffle, sometimes with a recording by the visiting performer as the prize.

The clubs were run by local organisers and committees (with the partial exception of the Folk-at-the-Stables, backed by the professional organisation of WAP – though even there the artistic side was organised by a local teacher and folk musician). The work involved was extensive – arranging with the local pub, booking guests, ensuring a supply of floor singers, organising publicity, and entertaining visiting artists. Above all the organisers had to worry about funding – and for most folk clubs this was precarious. True, a certain amount came in from club fees, entrance charges, and raffles, but against this there were the constant expenses: rent of the hall, publicity, entertaining, and guest artists' fees. Most clubs just could not afford high fees. This was probably one reason why they had few professional artists – in the sense, that is, of full-time musicians; for in the other sense of accepted standards many folk performers *were* regarded as 'professional', combining full-time jobs with regular appearances in the clubs. The fees remained low from the performers' viewpoint, but clubs still found it hard to make ends meet and for this reason local guests often agreed to take minimal fees or to perform 'free'. They might still be entertained to food and drinks, and a token of, say, £10 might be pressed on them in the form of a gift. The organisers usually found they were 'dipping into their own pockets' for stamps, phone calls, petrol, entertaining guests, providing the tickets or prizes for the raffle, having visiting artists to stay or just putting money 'into the kitty'. Regular members too joined in, not least through the pressure to make generous contributions via the fund-raising raffles. Given these constraints, it is scarcely surprising that some clubs were ephemeral, rather that there were always *some* folk clubs flourishing, several having lasted for years.

Folk clubs were to be found not only in the immediate area, but also in a circle around it. There were folk clubs at, for example, Nether Heyford, Daventry, Aylesbury, Luton and Dunstable, all on occasion patronised by Milton Keynes residents. How far people were prepared to travel depended on both commitment and mode of transport (most in fact had access to cars). Some devotees spent just about every night of the week at some folk club or other in what they classified as the vicinity, up to twenty-five miles or so away. One husband-and-wife pair, for example, keen folk enthusiasts and performers, regularly spent their evenings (after work) as follows: Sundays, Daventry Folk Club (the oldest in the area, going since 1965); Mondays, Hogsty Folk Club, Aspley Guise; Tuesdays, either the Nether Heyford Club or the Black Horse Folk Club at Great Linford; Wednesdays and Thursdays, 'not so good because people had no money', but sometimes playing at home; Fridays, alternately the Cock at Stony Stratford or the Whittlebury Folk Club; Saturdays, Folk-at-the-Stables, Wavendon. This weekly cycle was not unique. Another example, typical of several, was someone in a demanding, full-time job who nevertheless 'lived for folk': Sundays, Daventry; Mondays, Hogsty; Tuesdays, Old Sun Folk Club at Nether Heyford; Wednesdays, teaching German (his one non-folk evening);

Thursdays, practising; Fridays, the Cock, Stony Stratford or Whittlebury; Saturdays, live performance locally or further afield.

There was also the wider network of folk clubs that had been growing up throughout the country from the late 1950s, each with their own local cycles. Folk enthusiasts who had to travel to other parts of the UK could (and did) consult the English Folk Dance and Song Society directory of clubs and made a point of attending them. As one much-travelled folk participant put it, 'they're all the same – and, different. You can go into any and know they'll be friendly.' Women might feel self-conscious in a strange pub, but in a folk club 'you feel quite comfortable'. It was accepted form to walk into an unfamiliar club anywhere, perhaps asking 'Any chance to sing?' or perhaps waiting to be persuaded the first time, but then recognised in later visits; names and personal contacts were not needed, for the system was open and familiar. One experienced folk attender summed it up: 'you just feel at home straight away – a home from home'.

The folk club world was thus country-wide, and in contrast to some other forms of music the national network of clubs was known and accessible to all enthusiasts. This wide perspective among folk music devotees also came out in the regional or national folk festivals, and Loughborough, Reading, Norwich and Cambridge were among large folk events attended by local enthusiasts and performers. Folk news-sheets (like *Shire Folk* and *Unicorn*) were also springing up in certain regions, and these too encouraged wider awareness of the folk music world, as did the English Folk Dance and Song Society and Perform (a national society to encourage live music, with strong links to the Milton Keynes folk world), and the established practice of folk performers circulating as guest artists among folk clubs and festivals up and down the country. For Milton Keynes dwellers their local clubs were what they were most regularly involved in, but they were also very aware of the country-wide 'folk world' of which they were a part.

Many of those who attended the folk clubs went as receptive and participating audience or provided 'floor' performance from time to time. The clubs also thus rested on a pool of informal local talent in the form of floor singers or instrumentalists and – not least – chorus participants, apparently so readily available in Milton Keynes folk settings. But there were also the actively performing groups, together with a few individuals who themselves travelled the 'folk club circuit'. Of these categories, the most important locally were the bands, for though some well-known performers (like Matt Armour or Beryl Marriott) lived locally, they made relatively few local solo appearances and even then mostly performed in virtue of their membership of a local band or club.

In the early 1980s, there were about a dozen folk bands of one kind or another in and around Milton Keynes. Some were ephemeral, but all had put on at least some performances. They included the Cock and Bull Band (mixed amateur and professional); the Boodlum Jug Stompers; the Hogsty-men; the Hole in the Head Gang; Merlin's Isle; Pennyroyal; the Whittlebury Residents; the Green Grass Band; Streets Ahead (folk rock); Threepenny Bit (a school group); the short-lived and part classical England's Lane; and various school and church groups. In addition there were the barn dance or 'ceilidh' bands: Music Folk; the Gaberlunzies (and its stretched version, the Gaberlunzies Elastic Band); the Banana Barn Dance Band; and Sunday Suits and Muddy Boots.

These bands performed in the local folk clubs just described, and for local fêtes, weddings or dances. Some also appeared on an occasional or regular basis at pubs and social clubs. Outdoor events and local folk festivals were also popular occasions for performance. Some of these, like the Cock and Bull Festival, were short-lived only, but there were also annual events like the one-day Black Horse Folk Festival. The largest regular gathering was the 'Folk on the Green' festival in Stony Stratford (figure 12). This had taken place yearly in June since 1973 and by the early 1980s was attracting 2,000–3,000 people a time, having become accepted, as a local newspaper rightly expressed it, 'as one of the great family events of the year, now an established tradition'. It was the brain-child of a local primary teacher and a low-cost event dependent on local performers rather than imported pro-fessionals. The 1982 'Folk on the Green', for example, included seven named local artists performing as individuals, plus the local groups Pennyroyal, the Hole in the Head Gang, the Stony Stratford Morris Men, Old Mother Redcaps and Mentil and the Lentils, and other years followed the same pattern – a magnificent show-piece of local folk talent.

The dance or 'ceilidh' bands (as they were usually referred to) formed another category, specialising in playing for country-type dancing. Such bands had been growing enormously in popularity and there was scarcely a PTA dance or sports club social for which the organisers did not at least consider the option of hiring one of the local folk dance bands for a 'barn dance'. Since the band came complete with a caller to instruct the dancers the whole event was ready-organised, with little for the committee to do but provide the food and enjoy themselves. These bands were in great demand and able to charge high fees.

Music Folk can serve as an example of one such ceilidh band. It was founded in 1980, growing out of an earlier Open University folk club, then becoming associated with a local folk dance club when the caller joined. It consisted of six players on melodeon/harmonica, double bass, piano-accordion, recorder, acoustic guitar and fiddle plus a dance caller. Most of the players had academic connections: a couple worked at the Open University as editors, one had a Ph.D. in physics, and another was an FE computer lecturer who also brought along her son – still at school but already an effective double bass player (family links within bands were

Figure 12 (a) and (b) 'Folk on the Green' in 1981: the annual folk event on Horsefair Green in Stony Stratford, attended by hundreds of participants and scores of active performers

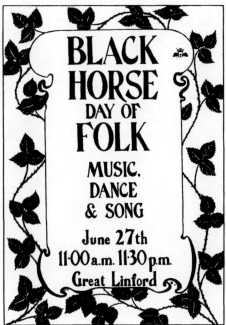

Figure 13 Publicity for local folk events: posters by the local teacher and musician Rod Hall

common in local folk music). The fiddler alone had a different background, working with the Water Board and joining through a personal motor cycling connection. Some of the players were self-taught, two were classically trained but had had to adapt to folk style, one had previously learnt the piano formally but had taught herself the piano-accordion for the group, and two had passed A level music – a mixture of learning styles and musical backgrounds characteristic of the folk music world. They played lively and melodic music and clearly derived the greatest enjoyment from the various medleys of familiar tunes which they played as 'so many yards of music'. Their own preference and the view they had of their music was to emphasise 'traditional' forms, some based on manuscript collections, others on newer compositions by other folk musicians which were classified as 'within the tradition' – pieces like 'The boys of blue hill', 'Orange and blue', 'Oh Eliza' and 'The king of the fairies'. They had begun to establish themselves as one of the recognised local ceilidh bands in the area, performing every two or three weeks at barn dances for local PTAs or social clubs, folk dance events, folk clubs and various private occasions, concentrating on the nearby area to avoid too much travelling. Their fees scarcely covered expenses, and were in any case sometimes handed back when they played for a local charity like Willen Hospice. They thus had some way to go before they reached the popularity of older bands like the Gaberlunzies or the Cock and Bull Band, and were still trying to expand their clientele by pressing their telephone number on all likely contacts. But they were already experienced enough to need only the occasional rehearsal in each other's homes and to be very aware of the satisfactions of joint playing: '2 + 2 = 5', as one put it, for 'by playing with other people you get another dimension to performance'.

A related set of activities were those of the Morris dancing groups. The best known were the Stony Stratford Morris Men with their female counterparts Old Mother Redcaps (named after a historic local hostelry), but there were also the more recently founded Garland Dancers, and, further afield but still with Milton Keynes links, the Akeley Morris Men and Brackley Morris Men. These were not primarily music groups but did include the kind of music that overlapped with that of the folk bands. There was overlap of personnel too, and Morris dancers frequently appeared at folk festivals and fêtes, accepted by local folk musicians as belonging to the same folk world.

It is not easy to define precisely the kind of music played in the folk clubs and groups. It varied not only between different groups and clubs, but even at the same clubs on different nights; and it was not fully agreed exactly where the boundaries of 'folk' should be drawn. Generally the music known locally as 'folk' tended to be melodic, relatively quiet and intimate in presentation (in contrast, for example, to much rock or country and western music), with particular emphasis on song and often an explicitly regional flavour, from Ireland, Scotland or particular English counties. The range of instruments was wide. In Milton Keynes folk groups these included: mandolin, banjo, guitar (often but not always acoustic), fiddle, melodeon, concertina, string bass, ukelele, harmonica, recorders, flute, euphonium, and, in a few cases, dulcimer, psaltery, pipes and tabor, crumhorn or washboards; also occasionally piano and percussion (drums, cowbells, wood blocks); and, very important, the voice. There was thus no one set combination of instruments or number of players, so groups of from three up to six or eight (the latter especially in dance bands) were quite normal, with a whole variety of instruments being played by their often multi-instrumental members.

The 'folk'ness was indicated not so much by the instruments or musical works as by playing style and the musicians' approach to it. This was often different from classical tradition even when the instrument was the same. For example there was a marked contrast between classical violin playing and the short-bowing, largely one-position, and loosely held form of folk 'fiddling'. The pattern of learning and transmission was also distinctive. The main emphasis was on memory and playing by ear rather than the characteristically classical reliance on written forms. On the other hand there was less opportunity for extensive improvisation than in jazz and more attention to fairly exact reproduction of songs and tunes in broad outline (there could be detailed variation in performance). Given the repetitive stanzaic form of much of the music, learning an item was quick and bands often had enormous repertoires without much need for frequent rehearsal. Paralleling this, learning to play or sing folk music was commonly (though not always) learnt 'on the job', inspired by recordings or live performance instead of or as well as written music.

Above all the 'folkness' of the music was assured for the participants by its enactment within a setting locally or nationally defined as 'folk', and by a strongly held, if not always articulated, set of ideas about the kind of enterprise in which they were engaged. Understanding this needs a short excursion into the scholarship and development of folk music.[1] Briefly, popular views of 'folk music' are still much influenced by ideas developed with particular explicitness in the nineteenth century according to which folk tradition was handed down over the ages, primarily by little-educated country-dwellers. The lore of this 'folk' was held to be simple and spontaneous, owing more to 'nature' than conscious art, more to communally held tradition than individual innovation, with each nation and, to an extent, each region having its own 'folklore' implanted deep in the soil and soul of its people. These general ideas were reinforced in the late-nineteenth- and early-twentieth-century collections by Cecil Sharp and similar collectors of 'folk songs' and 'folk music' which were seen as springing from national or regional roots over the ages, remembered especially by the older people, and pertaining essentially to unlettered country folk.

The views of these earlier scholars and collectors fundamentally influence the whole concept of what it means (still) to classify something as 'folk'. During this century the concept has been widened to include urban and industrial forms like mineworkers' or political songs, expressing 'the people' against authority. The British 'Folk Revival' in the 1950s introduced yet another twist, together with the popularity of the acoustic guitar and the beginning of the present system of 'folk clubs' from the mid 1950s, but these new forms too became assimilated within an overall 'folk' ideology and the staple repertoire continued to be validated by reference to regional rural roots or drawn from the collections and styles authorised by such bodies as the English Folk Dance and Song Society or books like *The Penguin book of English folk song* or A. L. Lloyd's *Folk song in England*.

This series of assumptions is not just a matter of intellectual history, for it still influenced how contemporary folk music performers in Milton Keynes interpreted their activities. In practice their music came from varied sources (i.e. *not* just oral and regional tradition 'through the ages'), it was played on a variety of instruments (guitars and drums, as well as the 'older' fiddles, pipes or vocals), it contained new compositions as well as older songs, and was carried on by players both with and without formal musical training. They saw themselves nevertheless as carrying on a tradition from the past – and in a sense, of course, they were right. For the music and modes they cultivated, changing though they were, were indeed broadly set within recognised conventions of what was to be counted as 'folk music' – even though the images of the modern executants may have been set not so much by 'rural tradition' as by the intellectual perceptions of certain scholars and collectors. It may be questionable whether there really ever was a distinctive corpus of music produced by a definable 'folk' in the rural setting envisaged by the purists, but this belief, conjoined with socially recognised definitions and practices, provided an implicit authorisation for 'folk music' as it was being performed and enjoyed in urban settings in the 1980s.

This complex of ideas was part of a more general philosophy, operating nationally, about the nature of 'folk music' and 'folk musicians'. At the local level, these ideas were largely implicit rather than an articulated ideology, but the underlying assumptions emerged when people were challenged to explain the nature of their activity, as well as in the vocabulary used in discussing music and music-making. Local musicians spoke of the 'pastoral' or 'traditional' nature of their music and regarded the test for whether a song (even a new song) really was 'folk' as being whether it passed into the 'oral tradition': 'if it's still valid after twenty years then it's folk'. Some valued contact with 'the regional roots' of their music (one band, for example, arranged a tour of Scotland 'to find more tunes'), and musicians liked to stress their own links with particular English or Celtic origins. They associated their music, and hence themselves, with 'the folk' – ordinary people – in the past and the present.

When one looks at how 'folk music' was actually organised in Milton Keynes, however, it is striking how far it was at variance with many of the tenets of this implicit ideology.

First, the social background of the local folk music participants was far from the rural unlettered 'folk' of the ideal model. They were a highly literate group, most of them in professional jobs and with higher education; many had degrees, even postgraduate qualifications. There was a high proportion of teachers, and other jobs (to give some typical examples) included banker, accountant, medical researcher, pharmaceutical chemist, civil engineer, business director, personnel manager, and social worker. Members of the folk music world liked to think of themselves as in some sense 'the folk' or at any rate as 'classless'. In a way they were justified: once within a folk club or band their jobs or education became irrelevant. They were thus themselves startled if made to notice the typical educational profile of folk enthusiasts. If any of the local music worlds could be regarded as 'middle class' it was that of folk music, for all that this ran so clearly counter to the image its practitioners wished to hold of themselves.

A further complication was the variety of learning and transmission modes. There was a tradition of self-learning and playing by ear, and it was unusual to see written music used in performance, but in practice many folk performers could *also* read music or had learnt an instrument within the classical mode. This was hardly surprising considering the typical educational background, but it certainly made the picture more complex than it first appeared. Similarly, in spite of the emphasis on *oral* transmission, writing in fact played an important part. Many songs in the recognised folk corpus derived from published collections, and printed or manuscript songbooks were also used (several local players had consulted manuscript archives in Cecil Sharp House in London). Certainly there was also oral transmission and singers often learnt songs from each other and from recordings, but the highly literate background of antiquarian scholarship was one prominent strand in the folklore movement and its local practice.

Despite the broadly agreed parameters of the 'folk' model there was also controversy about exactly where in practice the boundaries of folk music should lie. At the local level this was expressed in two opposed camps. There were those operating mainly on the folk club and folk festival circuit, regarded by many as *the* context of 'folk music' today – often well educated, professional and middle-aged with few if any teenage adherents. This wing was judged by the other side to be stuffy and 'narrow', opposed to innovation. Others favoured the more experimental and – in their eyes – creative mode of trying out new forms and combinations, in particular blending with rock, using electric guitars, amplification and a greater emphasis on percussion, even sometimes referring to their music as 'folk-rock'. Several musicians also played blue grass or jazz along with 'folk' or were co-operating with orchestral players in the classical mode. Some wanted to break away from the 'traditional folk club' paradigm and tried out clubs for a wide range of music (as in the short-lived Cannon Blues and Folk Club or Muzaks), not surprisingly regarded as 'fringe' by the more purist enthusiasts. Bands in this mode – Merlin's Isle, for example – could not always find a ready niche for their performances: not 'folk' enough for the folk clubs (to which in any case they did not wish to confine themselves), not close enough to rock to be welcome in many pubs. Folk music of this innovative kind was having quite an influence. A blend of various types of music centred round, or at least including, accepted 'folk' genres helped to make the annual 'Folk on the Green' day so popular, and the musical plays on local historical themes such as *All Change* or *Days of Pride* also owed much to the talents of a local teacher who combined his primary devotion to 'folk' music with a classical interest (further details in chapter 13, p. 164).

The controversy between the folk club purists and the (mostly younger) experimenters was unlikely to have any quick resolution. *Both* sides in fact accepted innovation in instruments, presentation and composition, and even some of the established clubs were trying to transform a narrow 'folk' image into a more open one, as in the Stony Stratford Folk Club's change of name to the Song Loft, and the Hogsty Folk Club to Hogsty Music. The difference was thus partly just in emphasis, but it also lay in the performance settings (folk clubs and festivals on the one side and the less specialised pubs, clubs and halls on the other) and in differing personnel and social groups. In the end both sides shared something of the same basic model of 'folk music' as well as a remarkable commitment not only to shared experience in the beauty of their music but also, in an obscure but deeply felt way, to the ethical and imaginative values somehow enshrined in the notion of 'folk'.

Perhaps, then, when one comes down to its actual realisation in the local context, there can be no real definition of local 'folk music' beyond saying that it was the kind of music played by those who called themselves 'folk' performers. The classification was ultimately forged through current social institutions and how these were imaged by the participants rather than in purely musicological terms or because of any *actual* historical pedigree (handed down orally through the ages, for example). 'Folk music' was just that currently performed within, or in association with, the local 'folk world' described here.

For those involved in that world – complicated and contentious as it sometimes was – the sense of identity and value it brought seemed some-times to be the most meaningful experience of their lives. Just about all the local folk enthusiasts were people in highly regarded and satisfying jobs. Yet for many of them, it was the 'after hours' folk music activities that they seemed to live for. Indeed for some, beyond the bare hours spent at work, there appeared to be literally no time for anything else but folk music anyway – out just about every night at one or other of the local folk clubs as either audience or performer, or, on the few free evenings, practising at home; and if travelling away from home, then visiting folk clubs there. Others drove themselves less hard, but for many of them too the weekly or twice-weekly visit to a folk club or performance with their own folk group took up much of their spare time and interest. As one local performer said, confessing that he knew nothing about any other local music (in fact was surprised to hear there *was* any), you get a kind of 'tunnel vision', seeing folk music only.

Folk music was actively practised by only a small and select minority in Milton Keynes. But its influence as both pleasant melodic music to listen to and the evocation of the kind of romantic 'world we have lost' so dear to English urban dwellers was felt in a range of contexts: through the creative use of folk music in perhaps unexpected settings like the Stantonbury musical plays on local historical themes or – even more widely – through the remarkable popularity of folk-based dance bands for annual barn dances at every kind of local social gathering from PTAs or sports clubs to ladies' keep-fit or fund-raising events. For the active folk performers, however, few though they were, the world of folk music was something which gave a deep meaning and value to their view of themselves and their experience: something that they 'spend more time thinking about than their work'; they 'live for folk'.

7

The world of musical theatre

There was a strong operatic and pantomime tradition in Milton Keynes, stemming from the older towns on to which the city was grafted. The Bletchley and Fenny Stratford Amateur Operatic Society was already putting on Gilbert and Sullivan operas before the First World War, a tradition which continued for many years (Wright et al. 1979, Pacey n.d.), while Newport Pagnell had a Gilbert and Sullivan Society at the turn of the century. Local schools too had long put on musical plays. Among them were the long-remembered Bletchley Road School productions of *The Rajah of Rajahpore* and *The Bandolero* between the wars, the latter to audiences of all the local celebrities and raising the then record sum of £128 (Wright et al. 1979).

This tradition was still very much alive in the 1980s, partly overlapping with classical music, but separate both organisationally and to some extent in personnel. It included a wide range of musical categories – light opera and operetta, musical plays and comedies, 'musicals', pantomimes and some music hall singing – all sharing the property of being presented through dramatic enactment on stage, often accompanied by the theatrical appurtenances of costume, make-up, lighting, and carefully produced dramatic 'spectacle'. The activities of those engaged in this well-established form of musical expression were not just separate one-off efforts but related together and organised within its own world of musical theatre. Within Milton Keynes this found expression in a flourishing amateur operatic society which had been putting on regular performances for a generation or more, as well as two active Gilbert and Sullivan societies, and musical plays and pantomimes were a constant feature of school and community group activities, above all at Christmas.

The continuing strength and attraction of the local operatic tradition can be illustrated from the Bletchley (later Milton Keynes) Amateur Operatic Society. This was started in 1952 by a local Bletchley businessman who got a few of his local and church friends together, saying how much he loved the music of *Lilac Time* and couldn't they have a go at it? He succeeded in his persuasions, and *Lilac Time* was soon followed by *The Maid of the Mountains* and *Quaker Girl*.

From then on the society snowballed, drawing in not only local business-men in Bletchley but enthusiastic participants from all backgrounds: teachers, bricklayers, electricians, secretaries, self-employed plumbers, housewives and professionals of various kinds; and it had close links to local churches. The list of patrons numbered many local notables, both those from the traditional land-owning families and, increasingly, public figures from local government or – like Dorian Williams – of national fame, and there was always financial and moral support from the local business community with whom the 'Amateur Operatic' had consistently beneficial links. The founder, Ray Holdom, was musical director for many years, and besides his musical leadership also used his business contacts in television maintenance to interest yet more potential members in Bletchley and, from the mid or late 1970s, in Milton Keynes as a whole. By the 1970s and early 1980s, the Milton Keynes Amateur Operatic Society was thus one of the most successful local societies with a very active membership of around 100, backed up by many part-time supporters and regularly enthusiastic audiences.

The centre of its activities was still, as from the beginning, its large-scale annual production in Bletchley. Over the years, these had included (among others) *Lilac Time, The Count of Luxembourg, My Fair Lady, Orpheus in the Underworld, Blossom Time, The Sound of Music, White Horse Inn, Waltz without End, Rose Marie, The Student Prince, Free as Air, The Gypsy Baron, South Pacific, Pink Champagne, Carousel, Half a Sixpence, Summer Song, The Pajama Game,* and *The Merry Widow,* some more than once. These annual productions were grand affairs with a run of five, six or seven performances, complete with London-hired costumes, full-scale stage man-agement, lighting and scene shifting, as well as lavish programmes contain-ing photographs of the main performers and officers, synopsis of the plot, and decorative, often witty, advertisements by local businessmen connected with the society. The cast usually included about 20 principals, a chorus of around 30, a troupe of dancers from one of the local dancing schools, and an orchestra of about 20 local instrumentalists. In addition, of course, as the programme seldom omitted to point out, 'there have to be two off-stage workers for every one on stage' (often spouses and friends of the per-formers), not to speak of three or four rehearsal pianists and both producer and musical director. These productions were acclaimed events in the locality, usually packed out on the later evenings and for many the occasion of an annual family outing. The society also often put on less elaborate 'variety concerts' or musical evenings of 'songs from the shows', while their week-long Christmas pantomimes were light-hearted affairs, extremely popular with local audiences. Their versions of *Aladdin, Dick Whittington, The Sleeping Beauty, Mother Goose* and many others were often booked solid well before the holiday, most of them written by Ken Branchette, a local test driver technician who had been a member of the society for twenty-five years.

These amateur operatic events received lavish coverage in the local press, no doubt partly because of their well-connected networks. The local papers often devoted nearly a page of review to the main annual productions, complete with photographs and a full cast list down to the names of every one of the chorus, dancers, orchestral players, scenery painters and builders, and lighting and stage assistants. Such accounts were presented with an air of analytic detachment but overall were extremely laudatory, in practice constituting one expected element in the shared celebration. The whole cast and their admirers could bask in such comments as 'And what a chorus the society now has!', 'The singing of all these principals, both in solo and in combination was a strong feature ... there was also considerable strength in the supporting parts', 'The speciality dancing ... was splendidly done', 'And once again the set designing genius and stage manager was Ken Branchette'.

Every year had its high points, but for the Amateur Operatic Society one of the largest occasions was their 'Silver Jubilee Year' of 1977, when they celebrated twenty-five years of active existence. A special 'jubilee committee' was set up including local businessmen who persuaded many local bodies to sponsor them. They put on a year's programme of *Babes in the Wood* in February, Schubert's *Lilac Time* in May, a variety show in the autumn and a Grand Finale in Bletchley Leisure Centre in October, with all proceeds going to a local hospital charity: 'it is felt that after the Society's 25 successful years in the area the adoption of the principal charity would be a most fitting way of saying "thank you" to the community as a whole for their loyal support during this period'. The year's events brought great satisfaction to the committee and organisers who recalled how twenty-five years before, the society had started off with many young members: 'many are still members and still looking young' and, still with a large number of young members and a supporting list of fifty or so patrons, were already 'looking forward to their Golden Jubilee in 2003'.

The Silver Jubilee was a specially grand event, but every year involved intensive effort and rehearsal by scores of participants. Preparations and rehearsals went on almost all year for the major annual productions, in a recognised cycle that started off with the enrolment and AGM evening in the autumn, then the start of the weekly or twice-weekly practices. As the time of the main public performances in April or May approached the pace of rehearsing increased. Even during the main part of the year 'it took over my life', as one member put it – attending regular rehearsals two nights a week

Figure 14 Scene from the Milton Keynes Amateur Operatic Society's pantomime *Babes in the Wood*, a sell-out at Stantonbury Theatre in January 1983

for acting, one for singing and yet another for dancing; near the end this turned into every night of the week and weekends too.

As with some other long-established clubs, the Milton Keynes Amateur Operatic Society was by the late 1970s and early 1980s a closely knit social group many of whose members knew each other well, in some cases also linked by kinship, love or marriage. A whole series of social activities as well as their joint musical production drew them together. In the summer and autumn of 1976, for example, during the 'resting season' between rehearsals, social occasions included a visit to Foscote Manor (the home of the society's President, Dorian Williams), provision of stalls at both the Bletchley and Newport Pagnell Carnivals (August), a car ramble (August) and a visit to a local Gilbert and Sullivan Society's *Pirates of Penzance* in September. As a long-established and economically stable society, the Amateur Operatic Society was undoubtedly one of the most flourishing local societies, drawing on a wide range of members, well connected with the local business and landed community and raising extensive funds for local causes.

There was more to this than just a financially effective business organisa-tion, though, since for most active participants it was the music that was paramount. Under the guidance of a series of energetic and gifted musical directors, local soloists flourished and even the less skilled chorus and small-part singers expanded, steeped in music for hours on end, attending constant rehearsals, studying their parts in every odd moment they could snatch from work or family – small wonder that one concluded 'I ate, slept and dreamt music.' Some members had before had relatively little systematic musical experience, and for them such experience could be a revelation – as for the local plumber unable to read notated music who talked and talked of the joy of singing in operas and pantomimes and his discovery of the beauties of listening to music. For their regular audiences too, the public performances were not only grand occasions of theatrical display, marked by colour, movement, dance and dramatic enactment as well as musical expression, but also an opportunity to hear well-known tunes and arrangements which even after the end of that year's performance could remain in the memory to evoke that special experience and lay the foundation for looking forward to the next year's production.

The Amateur Operatic may have been the oldest and best connected of the operatic/dramatic musical societies, but it was not the only one. In the Milton Keynes area, as so widely in Britain, the Gilbert and Sullivan tradition also flourished. The Wolverton and District Gilbert and Sullivan Society was founded in 1974 and was still presenting its grand annual productions of, for example, *The Mikado, Patience, The Yeomen of the Guard* and *The Pirates of Penzance* some ten years later under its musical director, the well-known local personality Arnold Jones, who had followed his foreman father into the Wolverton Railway Works early in the century. A similar cycle of rehearsals and productions was also followed by the Bletchley-based Milton Keynes Gilbert and Sullivan Society, an offshoot from the Amateur Operatic Society in 1972. Once again there was a strong link with local churches, and in some cases a tradition of giving smaller-scale concerts during the year for charity.

The drama societies also often had a musical side, like the long-established Bletchco Players, the New City Players, the Longueville Little Theatre Company, the Woughton Theatre Workshop, and various drama groups based on the Stantonbury Campus which had developed a striking series of musical plays based on local history. They produced musical plays and pantomimes from time to time, or co-operated with the operatic groups' productions by encouraging their own members to participate.

Pantomimes also played an important part in the musical and theatrical year. Most local dramatic societies put one on during the Christmas season, and for some, like the Bletchco Players, the Milton Keynes Amateur Operatic Society, and New City Players, it had become an annual obligation. Other groups who did not aspire to regular musical or theatrical productions also put on pantomimes at Christmas – Women's Institute branches, for example, church or village groups, and schools. These were especially popular when, as often, they were specially written or adapted to include local and topical references, and built on a long local tradition of amateur Christmas pantomimes directed to 'family entertainment'. Here again, however unpretentiously the pantomime was produced, a huge amount of work was always involved, not only in the many rehearsals but also in the co-ordination between large numbers of people exhibiting several art forms – dancing, speaking, acting, singing, playing.

One of the striking characteristics of the world of musical theatre was the amount of co-operation between the individuals and groups involved. There were joint occasions, for example, like the charity concert in December 1979 by the Milton Keynes Amateur Operatic Society and the Milton Keynes Gilbert and Sullivan Society. Singers and players from one society would also come along to help in productions by others: Amateur Operatic Society performances, for instance, included actors from the Bletchco Players and singers from the Gilbert and Sullivan Societies. Many of the same soloists appeared in the performances of several different groups during the yearly cycle, even though each society had a core of its 'own' leading singers who reappeared year after year, to the delight of the regular audiences.

Because of the complex of arts involved there was also contact with musical groups outside the theatrical world. This was partly due to overlapping membership, for many operatic singers also belonged to church choirs, and players in the accompanying orchestras often played in one or another of the local orchestral or instrumental groups. This could set up conflicts of loyalty, of course, when a musician had concurrent obligations which could not be met simultaneously, a situation that could and did lead to friction; alternatively it could be avoided by careful planning, as with the Wolverton and District Gilbert and Sullivan Society, which had extra rehearsals in the summer because the Wolverton Light Orchestra, which shared the same conductor and (in some cases) members, took a rest then. Other contacts were at a more formal level, as when the Newport Pagnell Singers joined the Stantonbury Drama Group in a production of *The Pirates of Penzance*. The local dancing schools too regularly co-operated in musical plays and pantomimes, adding a sparkle to the presentation that was much appreciated by local audiences (themselves swelled, of course, by parents and other relations of the dancers).

Besides the societies specifically formed to produce performances of musical theatre, this art form was also popular as one among a number of possible activities by groups such as churches, schools or community social clubs. The example of pantomimes at Christmas has already been mentioned, but the same pattern was also noticeable for many other kinds of musical. Many schools – especially those with younger pupils – liked to have a musical play on a nativity theme as their Christmas production, while both primary and secondary schools sometimes put on musicals as their main annual production. This sometimes led to complications because of copyright difficulties for well-known musicals, so many schools turned to writing their own. Such occasions necessitated a huge amount of effort and enthusiasm by children and staff alike and – though scarcely attaining the professionalism and scale of the Amateur Operatic Society's productions – still in their own way demanded the same range of theatrical skills on and off the stage. Church social groups too produced musical plays, sometimes composed and written by their own members, and these too could involve the members in many months of work and the need to draw on the varied resources of a wide number of people – not just chorus and actors, but also people to provide the costumes, props, backcloth and stage management generally.

Despite the heavy demands on time and expertise in this particular form of musical expression it still attracted considerable numbers both in societies organised specifically for the purpose and in other groups for whom this form was appealing in itself and popular with their potential audiences. Clearly the 'finish' of the various productions throughout the city varied considerably, but they all worked recognisably within the same musical theatrical framework.

The ideal model drew on the expert and lavish productions which were known from visits to professional shows (or to some extent from seeing broadcast or filmed versions), and this informed both the productions of the leading societies and, perhaps through their performances in turn, the smaller-scale events in the schools and other groups. But though this model helped to form the aspirations and expectations of local participants, the local amateur performances were not just imperfect copies of professional productions but made up a world in their own right which both transmitted and, in a sense, constituted the world of operatic and theatrical music for its admirers and executants in Milton Keynes and, no doubt, for many others through parallel institutions elsewhere in Britain.

8

Jazz

The world of jazz was more fragmented than those discussed so far, in its musical styles, social groupings, training, and the model drawn on by participants. Jazz was regarded as distinctive, but at the same time as shading on one side into rock or folk, on the other into brass band or classical music. Within 'jazz' too there were several differing traditions each with its own devotees, making up networks of individuals and groups rather than the more explicitly articulated worlds of, say, brass band or folk music. But, as will become clear in this chapter, jazz was certainly played and appreciated in Milton Keynes. To the outsider it was less visible than classical, operatic and brass band music on the one hand or the plentiful rock bands on the other, but for enthusiast 'in the know' there were many opportunities for both playing and hearing jazz.[1]

Take first the various playing groups. In the early 1980s there were about a dozen jazz bands in or around the Milton Keynes area. Some were local only in the sense of having one member living in the locality and making regular appearances there, but for many most of their members were locally based. A few were short lived, but some had been going for years (often with some change of personnel or developing from an earlier group) and in many cases put on regular performances with a healthy local following. Three of the bands playing in Milton Keynes in the early 1980s – the Original Grand Union Syncopators, the Fenny Stompers and the T-Bone Boogie Band – can illustrate some of the accepted patterns as well as differences in the local jazz scene.

The first two had much in common. They shared the same basic jazz format of six players: clarinet or saxophone, trumpet or cornet, and trombone (the 'front line' where the solo spots were concentrated) with a rhythm section of banjo, percussion and (string) bass, some players doubling on occasion as vocalists. Both bands put on regular performances both locally and (less often) further afield to enthusiastic audiences.

In other ways they differed considerably. The Original Grand Union Syncopators started up in Bletchley in 1975, reputedly the first real jazz band in Milton Keynes. From the start they were favoured by the new city planners, with whom the band leader (himself a senior management officer in local government) seemed to have consistent good relations. In contrast to other small bands they were encouraged to appear alongside the classical groups on large-scale occasions like the February Festival or the televised city centre Sunday Service in December 1981, and to represent Milton Keynes in cultural exchanges with its twin town of Bernkastel. Despite this official interest, the band very definitely regarded itself as an independent group, making a point of taking its name not from anything redolent of the 'new city' but from the historic Grand Union canal.

Their main performances were in local pubs and clubs, where they had built up a core of 50 or 60 regular followers. By the early 1980s they were putting on around 60 gigs a year, mainly of 'trad jazz' music, and reckoned they had a repertoire of around 200 tunes. They had occasional rehearsals in the winter (about once a month), but for the rest of the year were busy enough with performances not to need additional practice, appearing frequently in the Bull in Stony Stratford, the Swan in Woburn Sands, or the King's Arms in Newport Pagnell. Their most favoured engagements – as for most jazz bands – were 'residencies', as when they appeared regularly on alternate Sunday evenings at the White Hart in 1980 and fortnightly at the jazz evenings at the Cock in North Crawley, as well as regular appearances at (among others) the Woughton Centre and the Great Linford Arts Centre in Milton Keynes itself and WAP in Wavendon. They also travelled further afield to perform at jazz clubs at Watford or Nottingham as well as playing for private occasions like weddings or, from time to time, free for causes like Christian Aid or local charity organisations.

They took themselves seriously as musicians and as propagators of trad jazz, but had no intention of turning professional or regarding their playing as anything but a hobby, and so were content just to earn enough from fees to cover expenses like transport, amplification, advertising and telephone. The current members were in full-time paid employment: art lecturer, local government officer, teacher, musical instrument repairer, artificial limb maker and graphic artist. They could thus afford to engage in their passion for jazz in both the Original Grand Union Syncopators and the other bands they from time to time played or guested in, without having to worry unduly about finance. They did encounter the familiar difficulties of competing commitments, and the frustration of never quite being able to get a really flourishing jazz club going. Despite the problems, the band had stayed together as a named group for ten years or so, though, typically for a jazz band, there had been occasional changes both in instrumental composition and in personnel as people moved to other areas intending to resurrect jazz there too in the same way as the Original Grand Union Syncopators had done for Milton Keynes.

Figure 15 The Fenny Stompers in 1987: popular **traditional** jazz band playing since 1978, based on a constant nucleus of two brothers, Dennis and Brian Vick: publicity photograph in their band uniform

The Fenny Stompers had the same enthusiasm for traditional jazz but in other respects were very different. In contrast to the higher education or art diplomas of most of the Original Grand Union Syncopators all but one of the Fenny Stompers had finished full-time education at 15 or 16 and, by now in their thirties or forties, were involved in such work as warehouseman, self-employed plumber, school lab technician and carpenter; there was one teacher. Unlike the Original Grand Union Syncopators, some of whom had had some formal musical training, they were mostly self-taught as instrumentalists. They were formed in May 1978 under the title of Red River Stompers, soon changed to Fenny Stompers after Fenny Stratford, where their leader Dennis Vick lived. Despite some changes of personnel, especially among the drummers, the band with its nucleus of two brothers quickly took off, not least because of its leader's effective exploitation of free publicity in local newspapers. Within a few years their smart uniform of pink and white or red shirts with black trousers became well known to jazz audiences around the area and beyond.

By the early 1980s they were in demand for gigs two or three times a week. They performed not only at local pubs and clubs like the Bull Hotel in Fenny Stratford, the Bletchley Conservative and Naval Clubs or the Craufurd Arms in Wolverton, but also for paid performances at, for example, the Riverboat Shuffle for the Wimbledon Squash and Badminton Club, the

Horwood House fête arranged by British Telecom, or the British Stock Car Racing Supporters' Dinner Dance in Solihull, as well as working men's clubs around the area. They also played for fund-raising events, charitable occasions for senior citizens, and a Women's Institute Christmas party for the disabled. They also managed to arrange some regular bookings like the monthly Sunday lunchtime spot at the Swan Hotel in Fenny Stratford during 1979, and regular appearances at Ye Olde Swan, Woughton-on-the-Green, or the Coffee Pot at Yardley Gobion.

Like other bands, they too failed to get a permanent jazz club going within Milton Keynes to match the long-continuing jazz evenings at the Cock in North Crawley to which many enthusiasts went, and their various local attempts (like the Swan sessions in Fenny Stratford) were short-lived. But their playing regularly drew audiences of 70–100 people, and their total of around 140 performances a year by 1982 showed the appeal of jazz in the area despite its relatively fragmented organisation. They were said to be less adventurous musically than the Original Grand Union Syncopators and with a smaller repertoire, but their particular version of Dixieland New Orleans jazz for people 'to sing along to and have a good time' was popular with local audiences from a whole range of social backgrounds and organisations.

The T-Bone Boogie Band was different yet again. As they themselves publicised it, they went in for 'rhythm and blues with an element of self ridicule', for 'blues and mad jazz' and, as one of their admirers expressed it, 'boogie, ragtime, bop and riddum 'n' blooze'. They presented themselves as a zany 'fun band', but their act followed many traditional jazz and blues sequences, with beautiful traditional playing interspersed with their own wilder enactments of blues. They spoke of these as 'improvised out of nowhere, on the spur of the moment', but they were in practice based on long hours of jamming together as a group.

The nucleus of the band was the headmaster of a local school for handicapped children, Trevor Jeavons, an expert on the boogie piano, and Tracey Walters, a local youth worker who played the harmonica as well as producing extravagant vocals and wild clowning around for the audience. In all by 1982 it consisted of six players, including a schoolboy and a social worker. The somewhat unexpected but extremely popular combination of instruments was acoustic piano, saxophone, lead and bass guitars (sometimes replaced by string bass), harmonica, drums and vocals. The group had grown gradually from a series of informal jamming sessions by Trevor Jeavons and Tracey Walters in the foyer of the Woughton Centre at Sunday lunchtimes under the informal title of the Jam Band which used to draw in a large and enthusiastic audience. By September 1981 they had taken on the name of T-Bone Boogie Band to indicate both their rhythm-and-blues character (with a passing reference to T-Bone Walker as well as the T for

Figure 16 Trevor Jeavons and Tracey Walters in action: the two leading members of the T-Bone Boogie Band, the popular 'community mad jazz and blues band'

their lead vocalist Tracey) and Trevor Jeavons' boogie piano with its Dixieland overtones. They started getting widespread invitations to gigs, but – all busy people – preferred to keep these to about one a week, appearing regularly at their home base of the Woughton Centre as well as for a scattering of local social occasions and a few pub and outdoor performances.

They saw themselves as 'a community band', playing 'to give other people enjoyment ... and for our own enjoyment as well', a hobby rather than professional enterprise. When they were approached by a recording company and offered money to go professional, they turned it down. They did agree to do a recording live at Woughton with a local amateur recording engineer (which immediately sold out to local fans), but then decided to disband for a time, saying their performances were getting too serious and they wanted a rest. The upshot was the first of several 'Final Renditions' and 'Final Thrash Goodbye Concerts' – but both then and later, they were soon back again for a 'triumphant return' with only minor changes; their playing was too enjoyable and too well appreciated locally to keep away from for long.

Their entertainment aim was obvious in their performances. The lead singer's extravagant antics, the excited and active audience, the explicit air of enjoyment and their unconventional clothes were all part of the occasion. 'We like to entertain people', as Trevor Jeavons explained it, 'which is why we dress rather outrageously sometimes. People like it.' They themselves encouraged this extravagant image further by the ironically drawn self-portraits in their advertisements, designed to bring out the 'madness' so much appreciated by their fans. On their favourite home ground, the foyer in the Woughton Centre, their audiences regularly included people of all ages 'from babies to OAPs', which was just how they wanted it, and it was usual wherever they played for the venue to be filled to capacity. Some groups followed them from gig to gig, replying energetically to their jokes (musical, verbal and gestural), and T-Bone Boogie playing always stirred up the audience, not so much to actual dancing or singing along but to an active engagement with the performance. The band's own enjoyment was also clear as they played, with an air of mutual interaction, appreciation and, in a sense, pleased surprise as they presented their pieces from jokey songs like 'Little fishy' or 'My baby's gone down the plug hole' to a more traditional slow ballad.

The presentation of the T-Bone Boogie Band's music was designed to bring out their 'crazy' image, eliciting active audience participation and a 'fun' atmosphere. The emphasis on enjoyment should not obscure the enduring *musical* centre of their performances, however. The cassette that they recorded 'Live at Woughton' in 1982 was treated seriously in the 'Album of the Week' column in one of the local newspapers – which seldom took a local example – on the grounds that the band had 'proved that "fun music" can also be good music' in their 'remarkably professional sounding debut offering'. There was certainly far more to their playing than the visual clowning, not least the lyrics, music and piano playing of Trevor Jeavons himself, and the band's practised improvising in the traditional blues style. In some eyes the T-Bone Boogie Band's light-hearted exhibitionism made them less orthodox than the Original Grand Union Syncopators, Fenny Stompers, Momentum or the Mahogany Hall Jazzmen; but, whatever their idiosyncratic presentation, they were still part of the local jazz and blues offerings, one of the few local jazz groups performing at the local Great Linford Jazz Festival in July 1982, and immensely admired by some local jazz enthusiasts for their musical as well as 'fun' interest. Together with the other jazz bands in the area – all in practice varied in terms of instruments, personnel, background and detailed musical tastes – the T-Bone Boogie Band formed part of the contemporary realisation at the local level of the traditional jazz and blues storehouse of musical themes and idioms in a form no less 'real' than the more 'serious' offerings of other bands.

These three bands were not the only jazz groups functioning in Milton

Keynes, and the picture must be completed by briefly mentioning some of the others. These included the five-piece Momentum, putting on about twenty performances a year, mainly early fifties bebop, on a combination of flugelhorn/trumpet, reeds/saxophone, bass, keyboards and drums; the Mahogany Hall Jazzmen playing Dixieland early jazz and ragtime regularly once a fortnight or so in local pubs; and the long-lasting Wayfarers Jazz Band performing 'mainstream' and Dixieland jazz in pubs, wine bars, social clubs, colleges and fêtes in both the Milton Keynes and the Luton–Dunstable area – not quite a 'local' jazz band, though one very active member lived locally. Among the other local or near-local jazz bands (several of them overlapping in personnel with those already mentioned) were the Alan Fraser Band, the twosome blues and early jazz Bootleg Band, the Concorde Jazz Band, the Holt Jazz Quintet, the zany 1920s New Titanic Band with its stage pyrotechnics, the very fluid Stuart Green Band, the Colin James Trio, Oxide Brass and the John Dankworth Quartet (this last based on WAP and giving occasional performances there); there were also the short-lived Delta New Orleans Jazz, the New City Jazz Band, the Pat Archer Jazz Trio and (for a few struggling months) the MK Big Band.

All these bands put on public performances, sometimes singly, sometimes on a regular basis at particular pubs and clubs in the area. In addition there were probably several other groups who met more for the pleasure of jamming together or playing on private occasions than for taking on public engagements. The Saints group of six 11-year olds on clarinet, flute, trumpet, percussion and piano, for example, played jazz or pop together and performed in school assemblies and the end-of-term concert, while the highly educated all-female Slack Elastic Band played 'big band' and popular jazz of the thirties on trumpet, saxophone and string bass as a rehearsal rather than performing band, and the newer Jack and the Lads with trumpet, saxophone, guitar, bass guitar and drums were initially performing just for enjoyment on the Open University campus. There were doubtless other groups playing privately – an opportunity more open to them than to the larger and louder brass bands, operatic groups or amplified rock bands.

The administration of jazz bands differed from classical, operatic and brass band groups in that they seldom adopted the formal voluntary organisation framework. The numbers were smaller, for one thing: with a couple of exceptions like the short-lived MK Big Band, there were usually five or six players so that jazz groups were run on personal, not bureaucratic lines, geared to individual achievement rather than the hierarchical musical direction characteristic of larger groups. This also fitted their open-ended form, for though there were certain common groupings of instruments, the actual instrumental composition of jazz groups was more variable than in most other musical worlds.

This fluidity was also evident in the music-making itself. Jazz musicians were tied neither to written forms nor to exact memorisation, but rather engaged in a form of composition-in-performance following accepted stylistic and thematic patterns. This, of course, is a well-known characteristic of jazz more generally – not that anyone has ever managed to define 'jazz' too precisely – so it was no surprise to find it at the local level in the views and behaviour of those classifying themselves as jazz players. Local musicians often commented on the freedom they felt in jazz as compared to either classical music or rock. One commented that with rock 'it's all happened already' (i.e., already developed in prior rehearsals), whereas in jazz the performance itself was creative; another player explained his enthusiasm for jazz through the fact that 'it allows a lot of expression for the individual'. Similarly a local jazz drummer talked about how in classical playing, unlike jazz, he had had 'no real chance to create in a number, no choice about what to do' and so ultimately preferred playing jazz to classical music.

This aspect was also very apparent in the performance of local jazz players. Far more than other musicians they would break into smiles of recognition or admiration as one after another player took up the solo spot, and looked at each other in pleasure after the end of a number, as if having experienced something newly created as well as familiar. As one local jazz player put it, 'we improvise, with the tunes used as vehicles, so everything the group does is original'. Local jazz musicians often belonged to *several* jazz bands, moving easily between different groups. A musician who played both jazz and rock explained this in the following terms: with a rock band you are dependent on joint practising since the whole performance is very tight, whereas with jazz, providing you have learnt the basic conventions, 'I can play traditional jazz with a line-up I've not met before.' Jazz groups were thus less likely to have regular rehearsals than the other small bands: when they did play together it was often based on their general jazz skills rather than specific rehearsals of particular pieces. This open nature in performance also explained the high proportion of jazz 'residencies' by which the same band was booked to appear at the same venue once every fortnight or so. Audiences were likely to get tired of the same music time after time (a problem for rock and country and western bands), but were not bored by the more fluid jazz performances: 'numbers are practically made up on the spot'.

When jazz enthusiasts spoke of local jazz they often described it in terms of the venues where one could regularly hear jazz bands performing. Jazz was less prominent locally than other kinds of music and apparently did not have the historical roots found among local brass bands, operatic groups or choirs. But by the early 1980s there was a series of jazz clubs and pubs in and around Milton Keynes which could be visited in rotation by an enthusiast over any given week, chief among them being the Cock and the Bull Hotels in Stony Stratford, the Bull (Newport Pagnell), the Galleon (Wolverton), the Holt Hotel in Aspley Guise, and the Cock Inn in North Crawley. Other venues included the Swan at Fenny Stratford, the Coffee Pot at Yardley Gobion, Levi's bar at Woughton House Hotel, the Bedford Arms, Ridgmount, the Magpie Hotel, Woburn, the foyer bar at the Woughton Centre, the Swan in Woburn Sands, the regular 'Jazz at the Stables' evenings at WAP, Muzaks at the New Inn, and, for a few weeks in mid 1981, the Eight Belles in Bletchley. Some pubs organised weekly or fortnightly 'jazz clubs': for example the Bull in Newport Pagnell at one point ran a jazz club every Wednesday alternating the Mahogany Hall Jazzmen and the Alan Fraser Band, while the Holt Hotel Jazz Club functioned every Thursday. Other pubs put on either occasional jazz groups or, more often, arranged weekly, fortnightly or monthly jazz performances on a regular basis.

Some of these arrangements lasted longer than others, but at any one time there was live jazz being played in the area at least once or twice in the week, often more. For example June 1982 saw the following: the Original Grand Union Syncopators on alternate Thursday nights at the Woughton House Hotel, with the Cock Inn in North Crawley continuing its fortnightly jazz nights (already going for five years) on the other Thursdays; Momentum on alternate Fridays at the Cock Hotel, Stony Stratford; the Fenny Stompers on the last Saturday of every month at the Coffee Pot, Yardley Gobion; Tuesday jazz evenings at the Woughton Centre, alternating between the Alan Fraser Band and the Original Grand Union Syncopators; and the Mahogany Hall Jazzmen on the first and third Wednesday of every month at the Bull in Newport Pagnell. Most of these performances were in local pubs, and thus in a sense financed through market mechanisms and private enterprise. Unlike classical music and to some extent brass bands, jazz groups and performances, with the possible exception of the Original Grand Union Syncopators, had relatively little patronage from public bodies.

The regular jazz evenings in local pubs and clubs were the most visible performances. But bands were also asked to perform at private occasions like parties or weddings, or to entertain at local clubs (above all the working men's clubs), at special evenings for, say, the Angling Club, Bletchley Town Cricket Club, a local Conservative Club or Women's Institute, or at fêtes out of doors. Groups also played free for such causes as a local scouts jamboree appeal, Christian Aid, the Jimmy Savile Stoke Mandeville Appeal and Woburn Sands Brownies. Enthusiasts, of course, were also listening to broadcasts (including jazz on local radio stations, some not far away) and the occasional professional appearances in the area, like the successful concerts organised at WAP or the ambitious but sparsely attended Jazz Festival at the local Linford Arts Centre in mid 1982. In addition, music with a jazz flavour could be heard at other local events, notably at the Bletchley Middle School Festivals, when the specially composed pieces sometimes included jazz, and in events otherwise mainly devoted to folk, brass band or classical music modes. The main jazz world, however, insofar as it existed as something separate in Milton Keynes, was primarily represented by the players in the established jazz groups and their followers in the area.

Who were these local jazz players in Milton Keynes? Practically all fell towards the amateur end of the 'amateur/professional' continuum in the sense both of relying on other means than jazz for their income and in their view of their musical activity as basically enjoyment rather than job.[2] The question is an interesting one, however, because of the conflicting general views about this. For some, jazz is 'the people's music' (Finkelstein 1975), whereas others suggest that it is now an intellectual rather than truly popular form (see Collier 1978, pp. 3–4; Lloyd 1974). This ambiguity actually fitted quite well with the heterogeneous membership of local groups. On the one hand there were many highly educated jazz players, including teachers, administrators and community workers, and several who had developed their jazz enthusiasm at art school. But as demonstrated by the Fenny Stompers among others, there were also players who had left school early, were in skilled or semi-skilled manual work rather than professional jobs, or were unemployed; some were still at school. The one clear pattern was that they were overwhelmingly male (apart from the one explicitly female band) and predominantly in their thirties or forties. There were a few younger players like the primary school group, but essentially jazz playing seemed not to be a teens or twenties pursuit.

This lack of any single set of social characteristics also came out in the different channels through which local players were recruited into jazz. Some began through classical music at school, with the characteristic classical emphasis on reading music and executing it with little variation. Players coming through this route were usually confident about their instrumental skills and musical understanding but less happy performing in a context where – as in jazz – close reliance on *written* music was not appropriate; indeed such players were sometimes criticised by co-players for their lack of flexibility. Rather more players had taught themselves, sometimes via an interest in rock music. This often included some hints or informal help from friends or colleagues, but seldom any formal teaching (as that is understood in the classical music world), and meant learning jazz skills through listening to and copying recordings and, above all, playing within a group – a basic aspect of the jazz experience, whatever the original channel. Others again had a mixture of backgrounds, like the player who confessed he could 'read the dots' but had essentially 'learnt on the job'. Musically as well as socially, jazz musicians in Milton Keynes came from varied backgrounds.

The same complexity applied to audiences, for an interest in jazz did not appear to be the special preserve of any one section in Milton Keynes.

Certainly it was not confined to a single age group and included women as well as men. 'From babies to OAPs' was the T-Bone Boogie Band's boast, and this was probably the picture for other bands too, perhaps with particular emphasis on middle-aged groups. There was also the complication that some jazz clubs attracted audiences enthusiastic about one camp of jazz and unwilling to listen to others ('trad' as against 'modern' jazz in particular). Some bands, like the Original Grand Union Syncopators, Momentum or the T-Bone Boogie Band, built up their own fan groups who followed them from gig to gig and made up a large proportion of the audience when they appeared as the resident band. As with other kinds of performance, of course, such groups were probably attracted not only by the particular type of music offered but also by the company and social occasion, the dancing or talking in a pleasant atmosphere, or because of some link with the players. As one band member put it, you couldn't expect all the audience necessarily to be 'mad on jazz'; for another – as he explained not unappreciatively – his wife quite liked jazz, but really went along 'to chat with the other musicians' wives, laugh at us, and have a good chin-wag'.

Jazz in Milton Keynes, then, was more a fluid and impermanent series of bands and venues than an integrated and self-conscious musical world. There were not strong historical precursors in the area, and the local players never managed to set up a permanent venue where they could be sure of regularly hearing jazz by local and regional players over a matter of years. In addition, apart from the (general purpose) Musicians' Union, to which few local players belonged, there was no national association to which local groups could affiliate (unlike the classical, folk, operatic and brass band worlds) – or, if there was, it was apparently of little interest to Milton Keynes players. In all, there seemed to be a less distinctive view of what 'jazz' was and should be than with some of the other forms of music in Milton Keynes, and the experiences of jazz players and enthusiasts were defined more by the actual activities and interactions of local bands that labelled themselves as 'jazz' than by any clearly articulated ideal model.

Despite this, there *were* shared perceptions and experiences – unformulated though these were – of what it was to be a jazz player and to play jazz. This was shown most vividly in the way jazz players, far more strikingly than rock musicians, went in for membership of more than one jazz group and moved readily between bands; it was easy to ask guests to come and jam, from named stars from outside or ex-members who happened to be around to a ten-year-old boogie-woogie pianist from the audience. For though both the form of music-making and the constitution of the groups were in a sense fluid, there were definite shared expectations about the jazz style of playing, the traditional formulae, and the modes of improvising within recognised conventions: 'all jazz lovers know the tunes already', as one player expressed it. Players in other groups were recognised as fellow experts – more, or less, accomplished – in the same general tradition of music-making, and bands engaged in friendly rivalry with each other, going to each other's performances 'to smell out the opposition' or – on occasion – to look for a new player themselves. Similarly they were prepared to help out other bands, filling in at short notice if they were in difficulties.

Even though for practically all the players discussed here jazz was only a part-time leisure pursuit and not widely acclaimed throughout the city, both the musical activity itself, and the shared skills, pride and conventions that constituted jazz playing seemed to be a continuing element in their own identity and their perceptions of others. Once involved, 'as a musician, you need to play ... something you've got to do'; for, as another player put it, 'it's a blood thing, it's in your veins'.

9

The country and western world

Among certain sections of the Milton Keynes population the music labelled 'country and western' was extremely popular, and country and western events attracted a large and regular following. There were two established bands with regional – even national – reputations as well as local engagements; other more fluid bands; a flourishing country and western club with a healthy bank balance, known in the region as well as the immediate locality; several pubs putting on country and western evenings; 'Wild West' groups whose shows added variety and glamour to country and western musical performances; and a pool of regular attenders, based on family rather than just individual loyalty.

As with folk music I will start with the club organisation, before going on to explain the background and wider ramifications. In this case there was just one leading club, so a description of one of its events can provide a good introduction to the country and western world.

The Milton Keynes Divided Country and Western Club had been going strong since the mid 1970s, when it was founded by a small group of local enthusiasts in Bletchley. It held fortnightly Sunday meetings in a hall borrowed from the local football club next to the large sports fields on the edge of Bletchley. It was not easy to find for the newcomer – off the bus routes, across a narrow hump-back bridge over the canal, and past the playing fields – but, once known, the path was familiar to its many regular attenders who came on foot, bus, cycle, or (most frequently) in a shared car or taxi.

On this particular occasion – typical of many – the visiting band was due to start around 8.00 p.m. with the doors opening at 7.00. By 7.45 the hall was already well filled with 80 or so people (it rose to about 120 later on). Music was coming from records on the stage at one end, where the band members were setting up their instruments. The bar was at the opposite end and a table set up by the entrance for committee members 'on the door' to take entrance money, greet old and new members with a flourish and sell club mementoes. In contrast to rock and jazz events, the audience sitting round the tables was family based, with roughly equal numbers of men and women, several children, and people of every age from the twenties upwards, including middle-aged and elderly people; only the late teenagers were absent. It was a 'family night out' with most people in groups rather than singly, a policy encouraged by the club's organisers.

The club's name – the Divided Country and Western Club – indicated certain options. One of these was in dress: 'divided' between those who chose to come dressed 'just as you like' and those who preferred 'western dress'. Either was acceptable, and around half had opted for one or another version of 'western' gear. Some had only a token cowboy-style hat or scarf, but many of the men had elaborate costumes – a leather-look waistcoat, large leather belt with a holster and replica revolver on one side and bullets on the other, coloured neckcloth, jeans, badges (a star marked 'Sheriff Texas' for example), leather boots, a decorated cowboy hat, and sometimes a long coat which could be pushed back with a swagger to reach the belt and holster. Some women too were wearing hats or jeans, or in some cases leather jerkins or guns. The men in particular showed off their finery, strutting around in their long coats with hands on holsters. One strikingly smart group were dressed in matching black neckcloths and decorations: they were the local 'Wild Bunch', western enthusiasts who took a prominent part in local country and western events.

The band was introduced soon after 8 p.m. by the compère, the club secretary. It was an all-male group who had been to the club before and were known to many members; coming from Aylesbury, about half an hour's drive away, they were regarded as nearly local. They were given a big build-up and personal welcome by the compère, while the secretary welcomed individual visitors from other clubs to interest and smiles from his listeners – an established custom in country and western clubs, in keeping with their general atmosphere of friendliness and personal warmth.

The band then started up with electric guitars, pedal steel guitar, drums and vocals, with the main singer very much in the lead. The audience were free to talk, drink and walk round during the band's playing and later on to dance – a sociable evening out. But there were also some restraints on audience behaviour, and the setting was recognised as at least partly a musical one; children were discouraged from running round noisily during the performance and the close of each song was clearly marked. The band's playing was not just unheard background, either: the music was familiar to the audience – part of its appeal – and there was a lot of beating time and occasionally some quiet joining in with the catchy and rhythmic songs; the applause after each item was almost invariably highly enthusiastic. As the evening went on, more and more people got up to dance, adding to and developing the music through their rhythmic movements in the dance – one of the age-old modes of musical expression and appreciation. The atmosphere was relaxed and unselfconscious, and most people whatever their age, sex or build looked remarkably carefree as they danced to the band – the middle-aged woman in her tight jeans, jersey and big leather belt over her well-rounded bulges, the visiting technician and grandfather with his broken smoke-stained teeth, gleaming gun and cowboy gear, the young wife out for an evening with her husband, drawn in by his interest in country and western music and now sharing his enthusiasm – and scores of others.

About half-way through the evening there was the expected interval of fifteen to twenty minutes. This was both to give the band a break and to fit in announcements and other forms of entertainment.

Central to the interval was the 'shoot out' so typical of country and western events. Two men competed at a time. They took up their stand facing each other in the middle of the floor, their hands hovering over their holsters while the umpire counted out random numbers; when he reached the agreed figure each man seized his gun and after a great flash and bang, the quickest on the draw was declared the winner. The contest took about ten minutes and was regarded by the musicians and a few others as a noisy interruption, but for most it added the colour and glamour which was an accepted part of their country and western tradition.

This was followed by the regular fund-raising raffle. The entrance fee for the evening was regarded as relatively low at £1.25, but a substantial additional amount was expected from the attenders' contribution to the raffle, with the committee members taking the lead in lavish buying, often returning any prizes to the pool. The interval ended with some more personal club matters. One member stood up to make a short speech thanking friends for their letters, phone calls, and wreaths in her recent bereavement and finally, amid laughter, the club secretary was presented with a colossal birthday card.

As the evening went on, many people were on the floor dancing to the music, others chatting in groups, teasing, telling funny stories, all in an atmosphere of playfulness and light-hearted fun. The band – and the evening – were due to end at 11.00 p.m., and by 10.45 the audience were thinning out, calling cordial farewells as they left. Another of the fortnightly evenings of the Milton Keynes Divided Country and Western Club was drawing to its end, and the 120 members of the audience, the eight committee members and the six musicians went off in their various directions.

The tradition of country and western music which lay behind this event and the club which organised it was an accepted one in the locality. As in the folk music world, it was supported by a network of clubs throughout the country, publicised through national and regional publications, and visited readily by devotees from other areas, sometimes travelling in a jointly hired coach. Established country and western bands moved through this network, as well as being in demand from other more general sports and social clubs like the British Legion and working men's clubs, and if successful were advertised and reviewed in the national music press. The broadcast media too – including local radio – regularly had country and western spots, the timing and details all naturally known to enthusiasts. Country and western recordings were plentiful and in big demand, possibly second only to rock, a fact well appreciated by the local record shop run by a (self-styled) 'country and western music fanatic'. Country and western festivals and competitions were also established institutions, and the annual gathering at Wembley drew thousands (including many from Milton Keynes). At the national level country and western music had become big business in Britain, a commercial entertainment area in which a great deal of money changed hands – a contrast to some other musical worlds, in particular to the more intimate and less lavish folk clubs.

At the local level the social organisation of country and western music kept it distinct from other musical worlds. The Milton Keynes Divided Country and Western Club was the major focus, and its regular fortnightly meetings and big yearly events like the annual dance formed a consistent thread in many enthusiasts' lives. But there were also other specifically country and western events, advertised and recognised as such. There were country and western evenings for charity (like the one described in chapter 12), keenly anticipated by those on the network, and the occasional large-scale concert. Country and western evenings were also laid on by local pubs – not as frequent as the regular jazz, folk or rock entertainments but clearly differentiated as country and western nonetheless; some pub discos were also specifically advertised as country and western. The success of the Milton Keynes Divided Country and Western Club, however, pre-empted the development of other local clubs. Some pubs tried it: first the White Hart, then Levi's Bar put on a fortnightly 'Blue Yodel Country Music Club' combining records with live bands and attracting a nucleus of forty to fifty enthusiasts; but the income was not enough to meet expenses (generally heavier for country and western than for folk or rock bands), and their attempt did not last long. The social clubs too sometimes had country and western entertainment, often with bands from outside Milton Keynes. In this way, even when attending only local events local audiences shared the experience of taking part in the wider country and western world.

The same awareness of both a national and local framework was also evident in the locally based country and western bands. These were not professional in the sense of being made up solely of players whose primary income was from the band, but the two leading bands – Cuttin' Loose and Country Thinking – both had some members whose main occupation was music; the other players held full-time jobs elsewhere but were prepared to

93

miss or rearrange their work for the band. For these two ambitious bands their performance venues were regional, indeed near-national, rather than confined to the immediate locality.

Country Thinking – to take that group as one illustration – first began in Kent, but when some of its members moved to Milton Keynes in the late 1970s it re-formed locally under the influence of its leader. It was currently a five piece band (having started off smaller); the players were all male and of various ages from the twenties upwards. Between them they played electric lead and rhythm guitars, bass guitar, keyboards, percussion, pedal steel guitar and synthesiser. The lead singer took a prominent part, to support singing from one or two of the others, including much-admired high harmony vocals. Two of the five had jobs (coach worker with British Rail and piano tuner/builder respectively), but they still managed to perform widely throughout the country, mainly in country and western clubs but also for private occasions and, from time to time, at United States Air Force bases. These were organised by their energetic manager, who was also the secretary of the Milton Keynes Divided Country and Western Club and effectively exploited his network of connections throughout the country. They could command high fees, but since all expenses had to be met directly from these fees, in the long run made relatively little from their performances; travelling costs were among their heaviest expenses – not only petrol but insurance and a van (they had gone through three in two years) – and telephone: the kind of expenses which bands playing only locally did not incur.

By the early 1980s Country Thinking had built up a repertoire which stretched to many hours, but they still practised about once a week in a local village hall, especially if they were learning new material or settling in a new member. Typically of country and western bands, their songs were mostly familiar ones played in their own arrangements – mainly 'songs that tell a story' – but their leader also composed some original songs for them. One of them, 'Marrianne', had quite a success in 1982–3 and was played on regional radio stations, and they were currently marketing the cassette they recorded in a local studio with both that and older pieces like 'Old flames', 'Rainbow' and 'Just one time'. They had to work hard for their success, but this in no way damped their enthusiasm for their music and the subtleties of its performance – about which they and their manager could talk for hours – or for the particular combination of 'pleasure and leisure' that they had achieved, utilising their talents to entertain both themselves and others on the country club circuit.

There were also a few other country and western bands like Country Jems and Mississippi Showboat (which later became the Terry Anne Duo, then Terry Anne and the Country Dudes). These tended to be more amateur and short-lived than the two leading 'semi-pro' bands, but they too tried to

Figure 17 Country and western musical events: poster for a local show, and publicity in the form of a car sticker for the popular Milton Keynes Divided Country and Western Club

get engagements on the club circuit rather than just in Milton Keynes. They preferred the specialist country and western clubs but also appeared in country and western spots in political, sports and working men's clubs. The resulting networks of personal relationships throughout the country reinforced the awareness of a wider country and western world in which local performers took part.

The characterisation of this world as a rich and meaningful one in its own right was also supported by its participants' consciousness of harnessing a distinctive *musical* tradition of their own. The music that came to be classed as 'country and western' shared some of the same roots as 'folk' music, developed probably from a combination of the ballads and country music of white settlers in the American south-east with south-western rural music, and given further impetus and formulation by commercial recording and radio broadcasts.[1] By the 1980s, however, 'folk' and 'country and western' were perceived as very different. When I asked how, the answer was usually 'You just *feel* it' or 'hear it': even when the songs were about the same basic topics – marriage, divorce, life, death – and in similar melodic and strophic form the 'feel' was different. Some put it more explicitly: 'there's something missing in folk music: there's not that little extra zing that you get in country music', or explained that even though some tunes were in common the *presentation* was not the same. A few country and western enthusiasts tolerated what they called 'folky' music and its shared characteristic, as they saw it, of being music 'close to the people'; but mostly the music was experienced as distinctive: 'either you like country music or you like folk music – the two are worlds apart'.

The presentation was indeed very important. This included the settings in which country and western music was generally performed and the expected nature and behaviour of the audience. The actual instruments partly overlapped with those of folk bands, but were also different because of the stress on electric instruments and steel guitars as against the often acoustic folk. Thus the standard country and western instrumentation was electric lead, rhythm and bass guitars, vocals, drums/percussion, and in some cases pedal steel guitar, keyboards or synthesisers, with an emphasis on rhythm that was sometimes more akin to rock than folk presentation.

The background organisation was also important. Learning and playing followed the self-taught mode, with performance from memory and ear rather than written music. New items were learnt from recordings or radio, sometimes with the help of chord charts, one common method being to sit and listen to a cassette, perhaps writing out the words then gradually working out the instrumental arrangement. Many of the songs were of American origin and were little changed, for one of the characteristics of country and western performances was that the tunes were familiar, but the actual arrangements often individual to the band itself, with the occasional composition of new songs. But in sharp contrast to the rock world, where the band's own 'original material' was a constant theme, the main emphasis was on well-known music, presented in the band's own version. Musicians said they liked to take an old favourite and 'put a country accompaniment to it'.

One reason why there was little pressure to verbalise the boundary between folk and country and western music was that there was little direct encounter between the exponents of the two traditions. Country and western musicians and admirers operated within their own world. They had their recognised bands which played 'the circuit' of country music clubs, got reviewed in country and western publications (from the national *Country Music Round-up* to smaller regional newssheets like *Southern Country*, distributed through the local clubs), played on country and western slots in local radio stations and mixed with known country and western fans at specialist clubs and festivals. Folk clubs were emphatically not part of their circuit.

The description so far also indicates the divisions between the country and western and rock worlds – the music with which it overlapped at the other side from 'folk'. 'Country rock' was a category recognised by some, but by and large most Milton Keynes country and western music enthusiasts experienced their world as distinct from rock in the same kinds of ways as from folk: that is, in part musically but – even more important – socially. There were perceived differences in musical content and presentation, particularly the emphasis on familiar themes in the country and western songs – 'country stories' and 'western' themes were regarded as the appropriate and traditional topics – and on the relative 'quietness' of country music: 'people dance nice and quietly to country and western music', not like 'that rock music'. The social definition was important too: country and western clubs and bands were labelled as such and attended regularly, contrasting with the more haphazard nature of rock venues and rock records. It was often assumed that teenagers were likely to be attracted to rock for a time, but that the general *family* commitment to and experience of country and western music would continue.

The known historical overtones as well as current experience thus provided a shared background which helped to shape participants' awareness of partaking in a world with its own distinctive musical tradition. Country and western music was felt to be the kind of music which had developed from, and expressed the feelings of, 'ordinary people', treating everyone on a level with no false snobbery or show. 'Ordinary people' were featured in the music with its emphasis on 'stories with a tune'. The loves and trials depicted in the songs were those of common humanity – or at any rate rang a sympathetic chord with those who frequented country and western performances. At the same time the music also had its romantic side: the vision of the simple country life, the evocation of the great frontier days, the railroads, the cowboys and all the glamour of 'the West'. The known development of the country and western recording industry in America, especially in Nashville, was also part of the shared consciousness, together with some emphasis on the *British* contributions. 'Newmarket is *our* Nashville', one said, or 'we take an American tune and turn it into *our* version'. Given the mixed influences that have led into what is now defined as country and western music – blues, jazz, 'pop', ballads, black rural dance music, gospel – it was striking how clearly the country and western tradition was experienced as distinctive. As it was summed up by one enthusiast: 'you either take to country music or you detest it 100 per cent'.

What kind of people participated in this music? The answer to this too brings home the separate identity of the country and western world, for – at least in Milton Keynes – its membership was distinctive. In other musical worlds there was considerable overlap at the edges: classical musicians in touch with brass bands or jazz, folk club attenders recognising the existence of both classical and rock genres. But practically all such musicians equally professed ignorance of the country and western scene. Occasionally they voiced distaste but more often reacted blankly, expressing surprise if told of the local club and bands. Despite overlaps in some of the music itself, the paths of those in the country and western world seldom crossed those in the folk, classical, brass band or jazz worlds.

The regular audience at the Milton Keynes Divided Country and Western Club consisted largely of skilled manual workers and their families. There was a preponderance of train drivers (not surprising in the railway town of Bletchley), but also – to give a sample list – long-distance lorry drivers, bus drivers, workers in the gas, electricity and water industries, builders, forklift drivers, factory line worker, clerk, butcher, security officer, shop assistant, and unemployed.

It was the same in the bands. Their players were mostly in jobs such as lorry driver, milkman, dustman, builder, motor fitter, factory worker, coachbuilder or turner in the local British Rail works, and blind piano tuner at the local piano factory; others were unemployed, sometimes supplementing their band income by informal work on the side (as a motor mechanic, for example). Among local country and western performers the age of completing formal education was consistently low, in striking contrast to the high educational qualifications in the folk music world, and literacy could not be taken for granted. There were certainly exceptions, including some key figures active in the local organisation of country and western performances; the audience at the local club included the occasional member in junior or even senior management, and, especially among the 'Wild Bunch' and other costumed 'western' performers, a few highly educated professionals. But by and large the country and western world, unlike all the others discussed so far, was largely a working-class one – at least in terms of the occupations of the majority of its members. Interestingly this was the only musical world in Milton Keynes (not excluding the brass band and the rock worlds) that it seemed appropriate to characterise in class terms at all.

This did not mean that the concept of 'working class' or 'working-class culture' was particularly in people's minds. Certainly there was the 'ordinary' people image, and the bands prided themselves on 'being close to the people', 'knowing what the *people* (i.e. their audiences) want', but no explicitly 'class' ideology was evident. If one defines class in terms of occupation and perhaps educational or housing background then it is correct to speak of the local country and western world as primarily a 'working-class' one; but that was not how the participants themselves seemed to envisage it.

There was no overt shortage of money – within the country and western setting, that is, whatever the situation outside. Within the club people bought raffle tickets lavishly on top of the entrance fees and their drinks. Those with western costumes sometimes managed ingenious economies, but even so a full costume, complete with guns, was not cheap. The outfits of the 'Wild Bunch' and their emulators cost hundreds of pounds each, while the women went in for glamorous western costumes on gala occasions like the annual club dance. There was also much emphasis on raising money for charity, often by 'giving shows' ('western' shoot-outs or mini-dramas) or by performing free for a good cause. Country and western bands were more expensive than most to hire, and the whole entertainment business of which they formed part was one in which much money changed hands. All in all it was not surprising that starting from near nothing seven years before, the turnover in the Milton Keynes Divided Country and Western Club was in the region of £6,000 to £7,000 p.a. by 1982.

Among the co-members of the country and western world there was a great sense of comradeship and co-operation. The atmosphere at the clubs was conspicuously friendly and informal, with people always prepared to get into conversation with visitors and a general use of Christian names all round. For some, country and western commitments took up much of their non-working time. One engineering worker, for example, described how travelling for work gave him an opportunity to visit country and western clubs throughout the region. He would get home at 1.30 a.m., be up at 6.00 for work the next morning, be back at 4 p.m. for a wash and rest for a 'couple of hours', then off to a club again. His record was fourteen nights in a row at different country and western clubs, at all of which he met friends.

Many stories were told of the camaraderie of fellow enthusiasts up and down the country, linked through their music. One local band broke down twenty miles from their gig and far from home; when they finally arrived, the local club organisers not only changed the order of play for them but fed them, unloaded their equipment and booked them into an hotel at local expense. The local garage proprietor – a country and western fan – mended their van's gearbox, another lent them his car, and the local club members invited them in turns for meals. As the band leader ended up, 'we spent £85 on Interflora on the way home to thank them'. Again, one young local player lost all his money away at one of the big country music festivals, and, as his friends put it, 'being a bachelor he was carrying a good few shekels – £100'. When none of it turned up, 'the hat went round' for him. Another local band told how they too had broken down miles from home – the constant fear of any working band – stranding not only themselves but all their heavy equipment. They were rescued by the lead singer of a competing Milton Keynes band, who hired a van and towed them the whole way home: 'That's the country and western world for you – there are no friends like country music friends.'

This kind of support was not just in crises, but extended to routine behaviour. Fellow enthusiasts helped each other out and exchanged their skills in providing material for western outfits, helping to make the dresses for a country and western occasion or the new costumes for band performers, engraving badges for a friend, starting up a recalcitrant car, doing the artwork to advertise a performance, using personal contacts to get equipment cheap or to persuade a local group to put on a show for a particular charity, lending or exchanging records, getting a band's van mended through friends 'in the trade' – and a whole range of similar informal exchanges: 'you can call on help any time'. It was this kind of network as well as shared interest in a particular form of music that differentiated and maintained the country and western music world. So too did the less tangible acts of friendship and support – the formal and informal recognition of the central life events of co-members (the marking of both a bereavement and a birthday at the club evening was typical); the widespread enthusiasm for the colourful trappings of the country and western music world; and joint travelling in shared cars or taxis to local events and in coach expeditions to festivals like the annual Wembley event. The general sense of involvement was further intensified by the *family* rather than individual basis of much of the country and western allegiance, running across just about all ages (more like brass bands, therefore, than most rock settings) as well as by the sociableness characteristic of country and western music events: 'Country music is a great leveller', I was told, 'a great binder, where age, grade and area don't matter.'

Not all country and western music admirers, of course, were as closely linked as the leading members or organisers of the influential local club, or as performers in the local country and western bands. But a network of this sort was at the heart of the local country and western music world, with other enthusiasts more, or less, closely associated with it and to at least some extent entering into these relationships.

The country and western world was thus a distinctive one. But this did not mean it was monolithic, and there were different relationships and shades of opinion within it. In addition to some people being more committed than others, there were also different kinds of country and western music among which individuals had their own preferences. Some enthusiasts were extremely discriminating among the differing styles of, say, western swing, cajun, or rock-a-billy. (In some places 'bluegrass' is also a recognised and popular variant of country and western music, but this did not seem to be so with most Milton Keynes fans.[2]) One local pub tried out an all-graduate Oxford-based band, playing – as the compère put it – 'a fiddling kind of country music', with the idea that since they lived only an hour's drive away they might become the regular fortnightly band for the pub's country and western evening. But their particular style did not go down with the local audience – too quiet and 'folksy'. Audience numbers fell away and the band was discontinued.

One further division was between those who particularly emphasised 'western' elements (cowboy-style costumes and shooting) as against those who preferred to concentrate on the music, speaking often just of 'country music'. The two wings co-existed, even the music enthusiasts accepting that cowboy glamour was useful in attracting audiences and giving the band a brief break. Sometimes the western entertainment provided in this interval was even more elaborate, performances which appealed to both participants and audience, but were usually not allowed to encroach too far into the evening – at least in Milton Keynes. The organisers and, even more, the musicians complained that media coverage always highlighted western themes and costumes at the expense of the *music*, for them the main focus. Despite such complaints, however, the 'western' elements were tolerated – even encouraged – so long as they operated within unwritten but clearly understood constraints: shooting must take place only during the time set aside for it and certainly not during the music, and musicians had a right to be annoyed if, as happened occasionally, a gun went off while they were playing. In general the two different wings co-existed on mutually beneficial terms, with the basically musical framework of the evening providing an occasion for the western enthusiasts to engage in western drama and dress within the agreed conventions, and the added colour of the western element enhancing the overall atmosphere of the evening's entertainment even for those who came primarily for the music and dancing. This co-existence was also summed up in the name of the Milton Keynes Divided Country and Western Club – at first sight suggesting dissension but in practice symbolising fruitful co-operation and an ultimate sharing of interests between these wings of the country and western world.

The practice of country and western music in Milton Keynes, then, had certain characteristics which set it apart from other musical worlds not just in its musical context but also in personnel and social organisation, focussed very much round one leading club in the area. In contrast to the large number of active amateur bands playing rock or even, to a lesser extent, folk music, country and western players were mainly concentrated in a few bands, themselves of near-professional status, and the participation of the large number of local country and western fans (claimed as around a thousand by one of the local club organisers) tended to be more as audience, supporters and club members than performers. The relative roles of active musicians and supporting audiences were, therefore, different from those in the other local worlds. But (as further discussed in chapter 12), the audience's part too was one form of active and educated participation in local musical practice and certainly their role was an essential one, reinforced further by the personal network and family involvement characteristic of the country and western world.

10

Rock and pop

Milton Keynes was swarming with rock and pop bands. They were performing in the pubs and clubs, practising in garages, youth clubs, church halls and school classrooms, advertising for new members in the local papers and lugging their instruments around by car or on foot. There were probably around 100 groups, each with their own colourful names and brand of music. This chapter focusses on the activities of these local and largely amateur performers. It is not, in other words, intended as a contribution to the large – if very variable – literature on 'rock' and 'pop' music in general[1] (though some of this work will be referred to later as both influencing and, to some extent, misrepresenting local practice), nor is it concerned with nationally famous bands, or the recording industry, or musicological analysis. Rather it tries to fill what has been something of a gap in this more generalised literature by reporting on the practice of the grass-roots amateur musicians playing in local venues in one specific locality.[2]

A problem that needs to be tackled straightaway is that of what is being covered in this chapter. What exactly is meant by 'rock' and 'pop'? There were certainly large numbers of bands in Milton Keynes in the broad area popularly known as rock/pop; but precisely what kinds of music were involved, how to classify or sub-divide them, and where the lines should be drawn (and by whom) was all extremely elusive.

This was partly because of well-known changes and confusions over terminology. Despite confident labels in both the popular musical press and academic analyses, popular music classifications are far from agreed. Derek Jewell expressed this well:

The terminology of popular music is a maze. Meanings change; no authorities on usage exist; little wonder that newspapers, magazines, TV and radio employ the language of modern music so loosely. 'Rock 'n' roll' for some means the fairly crude music used for dancing or as general leisure background produced in the immediate wake of Elvis Presley; others use it to signify the very broad spectrum of youth

music, some simple, some very sophisticated, covering the whole of the 1960s and
1970s...

I can see the terminology which I employed down the years changing, as
definitions were revised and new words were invented. 'Pop' (even 'beat') was once
used to describe The Beatles. Then, as their music and that of others grew more
complex, more serious, more loaded with social, political, drug and mystical
references, 'rock' tended to be set in contra-distinction to 'pop' by the young pundits
who found their platform in journals like *Melody Maker, Rolling Stone* and *New
Musical Express*. No one has ever satisfactorily *defined* 'rock', any more than 'jazz'
has been defined satisfactorily – you suggest its properties, rather than pin it down
firmly – but the word carried overtones of toughness, protests, politics, seriousness
and sometimes of sophisticated and skilful musicianship compared with the frothy,
easy-listening and more childish connotations of 'pop'.

Towards the end of the 1960s and thereafter, rock and pop were used as separate
terms by some commentators and interchangeably by others ... Punk rock and disco
arrived in the later 1970s further to confuse the scene.

All this only begins to suggest the changes of popular fashion and the continual
flux of its vocabulary. (Jewell 1980, pp. 13–14)

The differing terms reflected not only changes in musical styles but also
differences among practising musicians themselves. From the outside 'rock'
and 'pop' may look more or less synonymous terms, but some musicians
made a point of differentiating them. 'Pop' was sometimes used by players as
a way of rejecting what they considered the wilder extremes of, say, heavy
metal or punk (which they called 'rock'); for others, 'pop' meant the Top
Ten (or Top Forty) records, which they regarded as distinct from other
popular styles like folk, country and western, soul, jazz, rock or reggae. But
these differentiations were not always observed, and some who themselves
preferred to distinguish 'pop' from other music were still prepared to accept
the term to describe their own tastes to outsiders.

The *general* terms 'rock' and 'pop' were in fact little used by local
musicians. The unqualified words 'rock' or 'pop' seldom or never appeared
in local bands' self-descriptions, for they preferred narrower and more
specific terms: 'punk', 'heavy metal', 'soft rock', 'light rock', 'new wave',
'M.O.R.' (Middle of the Road), 'late 60s early 70s feel, beat music', 'funky
soul', 'ska, blue beat and reggae', 'progressive rock', 'acid pop', 'power pop',
'high energy rock', 'high energy progressive folk rock (not heavy)', 'futurist',
'rock/pop', 'new wave/pop', 'blues rockers', or 'Golden Oldies, Classic
Oldies, 1960s, Beatles and Motown' – to quote just a few. Creating an image
for their own music sometimes led to quite complex descriptions in their
publicity material. The Kingsize Keen Band, for example, played 'Rock and
Roll and blues influenced music' or 'blues, soul and rock', Ha! Ha! Guru's
music was 'difficult to pigeon-hole. Melodic – verging on *avant garde* at
times, trying to bridge bland and abrasive music; a logical extension of
punk', while Dancing Counterparts played 'English punk/alternative dance.

The band admit to being greatly influenced by the punk explosion but prefer to describe their sounds as new wave with a late 60s psychedelic feel to it.' These bands all fell broadly within the 'rock' and 'pop' area, but it became clear both that the boundaries were not clear cut and that wider generalisations were of little interest to the practitioners. There seemed to be neither agreement nor concern among local bands and their admirers about such abstract questions as whether reggae or punk were forms of rock, how soul or ska fitted in, or whether rock 'n' roll was 'really' rock. What interested them was the particular form of music they themselves engaged in and *its* style.

Bands did of course differ among themselves. There were, for example, contrasts between heavy metal, rock 'n' roll, punk, and reggae – all commonly found categories in both the popular music press and academic works (e.g. Frith 1978, Vulliamy and Lee 1980, 1982, Middleton and Muncie 1981). However, the widely asssumed national associations of musical with social categories did not always fit the Milton Keynes situation. Thus the classification of a performance as, say, 'punk' depended as much on the image developed by a *particular* local band as on nationally detectable differences in musical style, general behaviour or class background. Similarly certain local pubs gained reputations for specific music – 'heavy rock' for example – drawing a clientele that defined themselves not only by musical allegiance but also by other local ties too, as with the Starting Gate motor bikers. Several local players had built up informal fan groups who followed *their* band without much interest in the wider typologies. These allegiances were reinforced by the stress on locally generated music, for as described in chapter 13 practically all these bands played a high proportion of their own compositions. What mattered was their own style rather than general labels, and though players sometimes like to relate themselves to nationally accepted images their typical interest was to get on with creating and performing their *own* music.

This came out clearly in a discussion at the Compass Club, a local youth club well known for its rock music. The members insisted that labels like 'punk', 'skinhead' and 'futurist' came from 'the media' rather than their own music or behaviour. 'OK, a lot of our clothes are taken from what's called new romantics – but we take the bits we like from it'; or again, 'People see someone walking down the street with different clothes on and they decide they're a futurist or something. I've been called everything – punk, Mohican, skinhead, futurist. I'm none of those ... I'm just me.' The musicians stressed that their *music* was central, and that only posers stuck to the media-created labels: 'They see something in the *Sun* and rush out to buy the right clothes. One week they're a skinhead, next they're a futurist. They think because they're into the clothes, they're into the music. I'm into the music. I don't care about the clothes.' Such statements no doubt under-estimated the

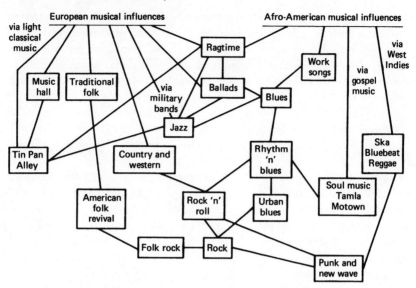

Figure 18 The interaction of European and Afro-American musical influences.

extent to which local musicians were affected by the media, but they were still making a valid point about how they themselves perceived their activities – as part of local bands with the autonomy to do their own thing without being determined by national labels.

Given both the local heterogeneity and the ambiguity of key terms, any general statement about the exact nature of this music is necessarily open to challenge. Indeed, the musical characteristics of rock and the processes by which Afro-American-originated music has developed in this country and elsewhere are still matters of controversy. However, a rough indication of the general area treated here can be taken from Vulliamy and Lee's outline (figure 18) and their suggested working summary of the term:

Rock covers a vast area of music from the more technically adventurous groups, whose music is to be found predominantly or even exclusively on LP records, to the more commercially orientated post-1964 derivations of earlier rock 'n' roll. It also covers the wide range of musical approaches thrown up by punk and the new wave. (Vulliamy and Lee 1982, p. 10)

Not all writers would accept this precise wording, and the varying links between the various forms in the Anglo-American/European chain are relative and overlapping rather than absolute, with rock sometimes given a narrower sense than here. Rock 'n' roll, soul, reggae and punk, for example, are sometimes taken as distinct forms, sometimes (as in this chapter) included under the broad general heading of 'rock'/'pop'. Both jazz and country and western music are commonly distinguished from rock and pop (as in Vulliamy and Lee's definition), and this distinction is broadly followed in this book.

One of the most striking features of the Milton Keynes local scene was the very large number of bands playing rock and pop in this wide sense of the terms, far exceeding those in the categories discussed earlier (jazz, folk, and country and western). Over about four years in the early 1980s I identified around 170 named rock or pop bands in Milton Keynes – and that only included those I heard of, certainly not all. Some were successive phases rather than co-existent groups, for another characteristic of these local bands was their transience, with 'new' bands constantly emerging from a reshuffling of existing players under different names. But even given this fluidity, I estimated that at any one time there were about 100 rock and pop bands practising in the locality. The following are some of the bands playing in 1980–4.[3]

Apollo	Flying Ducks
Basically Brian	Friends
Bitza	Home Brew
Corpse Corps	Illth
The Crew	The Inspectors
Dancing Counterparts	Javelen
Exit Stance	Kev's Numb Nuts
Ha! Ha! Guru	Legend
Herd of Fish	Malfunkshun
Ice	New Scientists
Imperial Sunset	Old Wave Band
Kingsize Keen Band	The Phazers
Lights Out	Plasam
Martial Law	The Ranking Dred
Malachi	Rephrase 594
The Memories	The Russians
The Offbeat	Scorpio
Rare Miranda	Seven Below
Renegade	Shakedowns
Rock Off	Skint
SNG	Spud and the Fabs
St Louis	State of Art
Scream and the Fits	Still Romantics
Seditious Impulse	Streets Ahead
Solstice	Suspects of Improvisation
Static Blue	System
Synonymous	Teaz
The Tempest	Ticketz
Typical Shit	Tokyo Rose
Under the Carpet	The Transistors

Musical worlds in Milton Keynes

Unit Six
The Void
Women's Band (no name yet)
All Stars
The Army
Art Nouveau
Backing Track
Band Aid [local band, 1981]
Black and White
Bottom of the Bill Band
Calico
Commercial Break
Dry Gin and Spangles
Dukes of Hazzard
Eddie Stanton Band
Entire Population of China
Ethnik Minority
Fab
Fictitious
Napalm Tan
The End
The Runaways
Split Decision
Two Incredible Mean Feet
Steve Dean Band
Freebird
No Komment
Jeff Gammon Band
Scratch
Mithras
Saracen
Escalators
Figures of Speech
Fools Errand
The Houndogs
M & T Rock Duo
Mick Cochran's Rock Duo/Trio
Niki Rhys Set
Norman Church and the Invasion
Lord Saracen
The Resistance
The Slack Elastic Band
Close Rivals
Fighter
Trail of Tears
Zenn Pleasure

Trevor's Jam Band
Twice As Nice
Urban Cows
Young Parisiennes
Fuck Authority
Blue Meanies
PH Sounds
Close Rivals
Buzz
Cosmic Force
Fore Play
Lights Out
Fighter
NA Pop 2000
Part One
The Moles
Safety Valve
Martyn and the Suggestions
Eddie Robbins Band
Suburbs
Kastaz
Swings and Roundabouts
Tleilaxu
Ugly Prince Eddie
Under Pressure Rock Band
Wide Open
Yamir and the Bohemians
The Fix
Osmosis
Final Solution
Cheyenne
Tulsa
Spirit of St Louis
Automatic Reaction
Neutrons
Synthetic Heroes
Synthetic Overdose
V12
Insight Straight
Unfinished Business
Immortal Resistance
Skewers
The Shakedowns
Rhesus
The G Men
The Black Tiger

108

Ha!	Equal Status
Street Graffiti	X-Invaders
Chantz	Out of Reach
Ultrablue	Flavour
One Up One	Foreign Legion
Subtle Entity	Black Water
The Face	Murda Squad
Made in Italy	The Streets
Hogargh's World	Zenana
Kay Terry Band	Friend or Foe
Click Click	Shanghai Rhythm
Night Watch	Scarlett Llama

Each band took pride in its own distinctive music, but in other respects usually shared certain formal features. Briefly, the typical group had four members, almost always male, playing lead guitar, rhythm guitar, bass (guitar) and percussion, with at least one player also singing; keyboard and synthesisers were used in some bands, and occasionally other instruments; electric instruments and amplification were preferred wherever possible. There were a few duos and trios and the occasional band with five, six or even – in a reggae band – seven players, but this was unusual. The players were regularly self-taught rather than classically trained. They normally practised at least once a week and either put on public performances or aspired to do so, most commonly in pubs and youth clubs. They also often made recordings for their own use or for 'demos' (sometimes for sale), the music usually consisting of their own compositions. A few groups had stayed together for years, but band break-ups followed by the members recombining in new groups were common.

These bands were amateur rather than professional in the sense that most players had other employment besides playing in the band; few belonged to the Musicians' Union. Most were not really organised for money-making; they did not have separate managers and seldom if ever used agents to arrange bookings. From the amount of time, trouble and (in many cases) money the players invested in their music, and from their own comments, it was clear that they got great social and personal satisfaction from their band membership – 'making people listen to what you say' and 'finding a way to express ourselves' – rather than regarding it primarily as a profitable enterprise.

Besides these general features there were also some notable differences. The players' ages, educational backgrounds and occupations were more varied than most of the generalisations about modern rock music and youth culture might suggest. Further, even the recurrent features concealed some interesting diversities. A thumb-nail sketch of six contrasting bands can illustrate some of these differing processes.

First, there were the young, relatively inexperienced and recently formed bands. There were many such groups, usually formed by boys at the same school, sometimes with one girl. They began by practising on the school premises and were dependent on parental support for finance or transport, but still regarded themselves as an independent group with its own name. That even this type could vary was shown by (among others) the two local bands The Tempest and Rare Miranda.

The Tempest had four teenage members, playing the standard self-taught combination of guitars, bass and drum. The players were male, but two girls helped with packing up, hoping they might end up as singers. The band had been going for nine months and had so far given only one public performance (supporting the T-Bone Boogie Band at a charity gig), but were hoping for more in the future; they had their first full booking lined up at a Hallowe'en dance at one of the local leisure centres. In the mean time they were composing further material and practising once a week at an ecumenical centre near their school; the guitar and bass players often started new material with a separate half-hour work-through, and then taught the others. They were also planning to make a cassette for their own use. In the absence of any fees from performances, they paid for equipment and its maintenance themselves, but parents helped out with transport. The band had no one leader but made collective decisions based on discussion after their weekly practices. Their fantasy for the future was to become 'famous and wealthy', but they were also realistically aware of the advantages of playing even in an unknown band, meeting people and finding personal expression: 'I can let myself go on stage, which I can't do playing in the park, so I think I'm quite privileged to do it.'

Rather different was Rare Miranda, two boys and a girl studying for A levels at a comprehensive school, together with one less closely attached player who had already left school. The three core members (guitars and vocals) attracted other friends to join them for particular occasions, both as vocalists and on the less usual instruments of viola and flute; the fourth member, temporarily away, played the bongos, which he had learnt in South Africa. The members had classical as well as rock experience: one had played the trumpet at a local music centre, another had had private guitar lessons, and a third had learnt the classical guitar for two years though she was self-taught as a singer and saw her particular contribution as the songwriting which she had been trying out for some years. The band was a year old, starting from lunchtime and afternoon practices at school but then moving to a convenient garage. Earlier there had been another member, but she had left, her place taken by the bongo player.

Rare Miranda defined their music as 'contemporary folk', but their associations were as much if not more in the world of rock. They were prepared to experiment with instruments and develop their music on the relatively cheap equipment they could afford. They had not yet got an extensive repertoire: around ten songs (a half-hour set). These included a couple of songs by others, but most had been composed by them, led by Sam, their female vocalist and song-writer: 'Meridian', 'Inside these walls', 'Peace pledge', 'Woman'. Once a song was ready they put it on cassette, and a couple of their songs ('Moon goddess' and 'I made these walls') had been used by the established local rock band Static Blue.

Rare Miranda had so far put on about six public performances, mostly unpaid, their audiences usually including twenty or so sixth-formers from their school. They had also played at a 'Glad to be Alive Day' at one of the leisure centres and in the backroom of a local pub. Unlike some, they said that their main ambition was not money or fame: they claimed that one of their principles was not to engage in commercial recording but to play free for good causes, and they saw the band's main rationale as voicing their political convictions, especially 'peace and feminism'. They aimed at lyrics 'important to the lives of people, to make people hear what young people think about certain issues ... We hope we can inspire people to fight for change and stand up for things they believe in ... music is one way of doing that'. Whether they would stay together as a band when they left school was uncertain, but for the moment they had built up an outlet and a following for their own views and at the same time had experienced great musical and personal satisfaction.

A second but no less typical category was of players who had left school and were beginning to perform in local pubs or youth clubs for a small fee. Here again there were many personal differences, and the number of performances ranged from, say, 10 to 20 a year, perhaps with the occasional appearance further afield. But such bands generally regarded themselves as reasonably well established though still near the start of, they hoped, an upward career.

Again, two examples can illustrate this. The first – Scream and the Fits – was another young band: four 18–19-year-olds (all male) in the usual vocals, guitar, bass and drums combination, this time describing their music as 'punk'. All had left school at 15 or 16, with a mixture of CSE and O level passes. They had not yet managed to get permanent jobs, but one was currently working with a local groundsman. The main difference from the earlier groups was this band's longer life (nearly three years) and the greater repertoire and web of bookings they had consequently built up. They had around 15 numbers ready for performance, including 'There is no truth', 'Broken hero', 'Fits', and 'Sex, drugs and chaos'. All but one were original to them, built up on an original idea by one guitarist with the others adding words and the rest of the tune. In the previous 12 months they had played at about 18 gigs, mainly in pubs and youth clubs but also for private occasions for friends, and had drawn audiences of up to 100–150, mainly 14–20-year-olds. They reckoned to get a small fee (though sometimes just beer) from the pubs and a cut of the door takings at youth clubs. For this they were practising two to three times a week at a local youth club, supplemented by extra practices in one member's garden shed. They had also acquired equipment worth around £500, produced their own T-shirts as publicity, and made three recordings at a local studio (Mikro). One of these, along with numbers by other bands, was released on the local 'Concrete Cow Label'.

The Scream and the Fits players were self-taught. The group had got going when two of them met in the changing room at their local comprehensive school and decided to found a band; at that stage they couldn't yet play but decided to start seriously. Finding a drummer proved – as often – the biggest problem: first they had one from school who only lasted three weeks, then a series of other hopefuls (among them a player's girlfriend), with the band contributing £25 each to buy a drum set. Their current drummer had been with them eight months, and had started to teach himself just a couple of months before that.

Their name fitted their 'punk' youth image, but they actually felt very sensitive about this, believing they were criticised just because they were young and played punk music. They much objected to criticism by 'those who can't play or can't be bothered', but accepted that there *was* sometimes trouble at their gigs, particularly when – as they put it – 'different youth cults were mixed and drunk'. Indeed the Craufurd Arms, one of the leading local rock pubs, refused to let punk bands play there, even for the local rock contest heats in autumn 1982. The first heat was eventually held at a local youth club and Scream and the Fits came third after a disastrous start in which, they said, everything went wrong, the sound was so bad they couldn't hear themselves, and the space too limited to allow their usual leaping around. They were conscious of their aggressive reputation and boasted they would never duck out of a fight, but at the same time became upset when they felt that their *music* was not taken seriously – something to which they'd been devoting themselves for three years. They also tried to counter their rebel image by posing for one of the local newpapers outside the peace pagoda 'to show that we're not a violent punk group, and don't go around smashing places up' (*Milton Keynes Express*, 24 June 1982). In their view popular labels in the media and community misrepresented their motivation and musical achievements.

What did they themselves get out of it? Band expenses ate up their resources for little or no return, and in addition they felt misunderstood and unappreciated. Nevertheless, they stuck at practising two or three times a week at the youth club where they'd been meeting for years, and producing their own compositions. One of their aims was, one day, to earn enough money to live on, but in the mean time they reckoned that playing together as a band 'gives you something to do in the week ... something to think about if you're a bit pissed off'. Despite misrepresentation by other people, it meant – to put it in their own understated terms – 'some achievement'.

Very different in social background but equally enthusiastic about their music were members of The Void, a three-piece all-male group (guitar, bass, drums and vocals) playing 'new wave/pop'. It had been founded eighteen months before by three ex-members of the Urban Cows re-forming under a new title chosen as 'short, snappy – and pessimistic'. They already had long contact with each other through school or work, and two had been friends since childhood. This was an older band (in their early twenties) and more highly educated than those described so far: one had a degree, the other two A levels and, in one case, City and Guilds qualifications, and all were in permanent jobs (banking, computer-aided design and multilingual data networking). Unlike the younger punk band, their music was more hobby than major commitment. But they still practised every week, and had a repertoire of twenty-two songs, most by the lead guitarist (the drummer providing lyrics), one or two by the bass player, and the rest in collaboration. Over the previous year they had put on a dozen performances in pubs and youth clubs, and, unlike Scream and the Fits, also played in halls and colleges further afield, mainly to audiences in their early twenties. They earned little from their appearances – they explained that they were usually 'desperate for a gig so would play for practically nothing' – but did get small fees (and beer) from local pubs. These were put towards expenses, but were nowhere near enough to cover equipment or transport, so the band were subsidised from their jobs: 'it's a charity', as they put it. Nevertheless, they were well enough off from other sources to afford the necessary costs, and for the band to possess its own PA and to hire transport.

The players had had varied musical experience. The drummer had learnt for a time in a military band, followed by self-learning, while the lead guitarist/vocalist had been playing on a self-taught basis for seven years and could also play bass and a range of recorders. The bass player/vocalist had played since he was 15 and before that had learnt the classical guitar, as well as taking violin, piano and singing lessons at school; he came from a musical family with piano and organ skills, while his mother had sung semi-professionally in a choir and around various clubs.

They were now wanting to reach wider audiences. Some of their songs, they felt, deserved publishing, and they also wanted to do more recording. So far they had produced one cassette with the local community radio (CRMK) and broadcast on Chiltern Radio, and had recently recorded 1,000 copies of a single of two songs ('Into the void' and 'I want you') at Wellingborough under their own label 'Hole in Space Records' – a title continuing their 'Void' theme by, as they put it, 'Trying to fill a hole in the music industry'. They were distributing this by mail order and advertising in the national music press, as well as pressing record shops in the Northampton and Milton Keynes areas to stock it, and selling at local gigs. If they broke even they intended to record another single. Meantime they were trying to develop their bookings by a publicity drive, distributing photographs (see Figure 19 (a)) projecting a 'new city' rather than a 'pub' image. They had persuaded a friend to act as informal manager, and were considering using an agent. They were particularly hoping to get on to the university and college circuit, as they did not see themselves as 'a pub band'. In general, their ambition was not so much to make money as to get a good name throughout the country: 'artistic and public acclaim'. The band was one way of getting through to people and influencing them, as well as having a lot of fun, and 'sharing some ability' and 'freedom of expression'.

The bands discussed so far were active and committed but not as yet with any large reputation. But there was also the third category: bands who though not of national stature had established a secure position in pub and club circuits, outside as well as within Milton Keynes, played in upwards of 50 or 100 performances a year and, while still towards the amateur rather than professional end of the scale, brought in substantial fees. Such bands in Milton Keynes in 1982/3 included, among others, Ice, Static Blue, Unit 6 (all giving 50–60 public performances a year), Synonymous (80–100), Bitza (110), and Solstice (100–150), with repertoires running to sets of at least one and a half hours and anything from 50 or 60 to several hundred songs.

Solstice were one of the best-known local bands, playing what they defined as 'high energy progressive folk rock (not heavy)'. They had taken their name because they saw themselves as hippies 'interested in Stonehenge', a theme kept up in their songs ('Sunrise', 'Pathways', 'Morning light', 'The journey' and 'Peace for a new age'). Despite these somewhat folksy overtones, they had roots 'in rock rather than folk' (as one local paper put it), and had built up a reputation in local pubs, youth clubs and colleges, as well as playing to audiences in some of the larger national centres and completing a tour of Scotland.

Solstice had four core players, with guitar, bass, drums, vocals and – less usually – violin. They had mostly been friends already when the band was founded, but there had been some changes over their two-and-a-half-year life (especially in their drummers) and they were currently looking for a new girl singer. The core members were men between 22 and 29, two of whom worked as engineers and one as a part-time violin teacher supplemented by busking, while the fourth was unemployed. They had varied musical backgrounds. The guitarist had started with a few private lessons some ten years before but was otherwise self-taught and currently teaching himself the flute; the drummer had been playing for eight years and had had some lessons from the well-known band Genesis; the bass guitarist had taught himself for about six years; and the violinist had had private lessons

Figure 19 Some local bands: a few of the hundred or more rock and pop bands of Milton Keynes: different music, different public images
(a) The Void: 'new wave post-punk pop'. Publicity photograph near the city centre
(b) Martial Law, after winning the local Archer Music Rock Competition in 1982, with their 'late 60's early 70's feel beat music'

Figure 19 (*cont.*)
(c) Seditious Impulse: controversial punk band
(d) Static Blue: a teenage rock band, with two members still at school (including –
unusually – a girl on the bass guitar), an upholsterer and an apprentice BR fitter

throughout childhood (he came from a classically inclined family, with clarinettist father and two musical sisters), but had taught himself keyboards, vocals and mandolin.

Despite their shortish life, Solstice had become extremely successful as a performing band. They had put on 100–150 performances in the previous 12 months, and though they still played locally were gradually drawing out of smaller venues to play at colleges, large pubs and clubs, as well as nationally recognised halls like the Venue and the Marquee in London or the Wheatsheaf in Dunstable, with audiences of several hundred at a time. By 1982 they could command good fees even for local gigs, where they usually played to sell-out audiences, not only 16–25-year-olds (the main nucleus) but also middle-aged and older people. Their performances were attracting interest outside the region, and early in 1983 they appeared on the cover of the national music paper *Sounds* and had had feelers from record companies. By mid 1983, local enthusiasts were seeing Solstice as 'Milton Keynes' own budding superstars'.

The Solstice participants put a great deal of effort into their band work. They composed their own material and practised two to three times a week at a local youth club and/or recording studio which on top of their regular gigs meant almost every night of the week devoted to music – a heavy commitment, especially for the two in full-time employment. They had recorded two cassettes locally – 'First light' and 'Pathways' – which they were successfully selling at gigs for £1 each, finding this outlet sufficient for the 500 and 600 copies they had made of each. They were also concerned about their publicity, arranging for band insignia like T-shirts and beginning to use an agent. So far their manager had been a friend, but now that negotiations with record companies were on the cards he needed experienced help. They took their hoped-for success *and* their own music seriously and had taken the precaution of depositing tapes of their compositions in the bank vault in copyright envelopes.

The band had found, however, that as their aspirations increased they still had financial problems. Their substantial fees were quickly eaten up by expenses for a PA, lighting, instruments, transport costs, and such extras as buying drinks for the unpaid 'roadies' who carried their extremely heavy and bulky equipment. The players had paid out for a PA and a 3-ton truck for touring, with the result that they were £1,500 in debt. This was a common pattern, for once a rock band started wanting its own PA, van, and other equipment (thousands – even tens of thousands – of pounds), plus the people to deal with it all, expenses mounted hugely and even large fees made little impression. The ever-increasing financial commitments of ambitious rock bands contrasted with folk, classical or brass band groups, where – though expenses were not negligible – there were not the same technological pressures to constantly escalating costs.

The current aims of Solstice members included commercial success: they wanted above all to get a record contract and to tour and play to large audiences. But such ambitions were not the only reason for the great commitment in time, money and personal involvement that they put in. They also felt the band provided an opportunity to communicate their own vision: 'you can put over your ideas – if you are subtle you can get over a message really well'. They liked to put on performances in keeping with their own ideology and had been glad to play free on such occasions as 'Good to be Alive Day' or the Greenham Common Peace Festival, and to support causes like CND or Amnesty International; they were also hoping to play at Glastonbury and Stonehenge. Playing in Solstice was not just a matter of money or managers but also of personal reward: the chance 'to do something you love doing ... I can play music. It's the only thing I'm good at.'

Synonymous were another successful local band. They resembled Solstice in their number of performances (80–100 a year), but in other ways were a contrast. They were older, with one member in his late twenties, one in his forties, and the two others in their thirties, all in reasonably well-paid jobs (a building estimator, sales engineer, electronics technician, and field sales manager); all but one had post-O level education, including two with higher education, of whom one had a degree. The all-male line-up had the standard instrumentation but were unusual in playing little of their own material, though they had added a few joke items like their 'bingo song' – new words to 'Football crazy'. In their eight-year life they had built up a repertoire of about 200 songs, enough for a three- to four-hour set, and were practising once a week at the home of one or other of the players. The members had long instrumental experience, partly through the band itself (for except for one guitarist, all had been with Synonymous from the start, and even he had been there four years), but also from experience in other bands, as each had been playing for 15–20 years or more. As so often most were self-taught, supplemented by a small amount of private guitar tuition and some school drum lessons; all three vocalists had also sung in school or church choirs as children.

Synonymous reckoned to be an entertainment 'family' band, playing anything 'from George Formby to rock 'n' roll; we try to reach everyone and tailor our material for kids in working men's clubs and also do stuff for grannies'. This approach fitted their performance contexts, for they opted for family-based clubs or dinner dances rather than the often youngish audiences of pubs. To suit their entertainment image they had a uniform of black trousers and waistcoats with bright contrasting shirts, and used coloured and fading lights to add to the effect: 'we try to put on a show rather than just get up and play'.

For these performances they received substantial fees, so that after putting some in the band kitty they could split the rest equally between the four. They had expenses like petrol, strings and equipment, but since each had their own transport and travelled separately they avoided the heavy cost of a band van or lorry. They collectively owned the PA, lights and leads (worth about £5,000 in all) and kept them insured. The band had a business approach to their earnings and organisation, with different members being in charge of electrics, agency, stage act and finance respectively so as to spread the work, and had paid tax for the previous three years. They found it worth joining the Musicians' Union, both for help with insurance and legal advice and because it was obligatory in certain venues.

Unlike Solstice they did not have the ambition to become nationally famous. Their only recordings were three or four demonstration tapes over the years and even these were really just for their own enjoyment. They produced some promotional literature (mainly business cards and photographs) and had been successful in local talent contests when they got through the regional heats in the Northampton Association of Working Men's Clubs and were recorded for BBC radio. But, perhaps because they were primarily performers rather than composers or (equally likely) because they were older and already securely employed, they were not trying to 'make it' in the professional world but were content with the substantial success they had already achieved. They were aware of the 'fun' the band gave them, 'the compliments at the end' and the 'ego trip' from performing, and said frankly that 'we're never likely to be famous or rich – but you feel you've achieved something'. They were real enthusiasts about their music-making: even the eldest (in his forties) admitted 'I still find it fun!' and, as another member put it, 'music is a life-time hobby – twenty-four hours a day'.

These brief accounts of six local bands playing in the rock/pop tradition illustrate both the similarities and the variety to be found in such bands. These can be further elaborated by some comments on the overall patterns and background.

The predominance of male players was striking: out of 125 players in the 1982–3 survey only 8 were women. In the bands in which women *were* included, however, they mostly took part on equal instrumental terms with the men rather than merely being the front singer – the 'sex symbol' role so castigated by feminist critics. In some of the bands from the local (mixed sex) comprehensive schools girls were certainly sometimes singers, but others insisted on playing guitars or percussion. Women also sometimes took a key role in the composition of the band's original material, notably Anita Tedder of The Crew and Sam Hill in Rare Miranda. A new all-female band had also been formed from the nucleus of the Crew which as a policy took only women. In addition, of course, the audiences included many women. Men were therefore strikingly in the majority among instrumentalists, but the rock world was not a totally male preserve and the few women who *were* members sometimes took equal, even leading, roles.

Another common pattern was the aim of live public performance – 'gigs', 'bookings', 'an act' or whatever the preferred term. Practically all bands aspired to this. Even the apparent exceptions implicitly accepted the value of public performances. The young Imperial Sunset typically explained that they had not yet 'got a set together' and did not want to go on stage 'till everything is perfect', while Malachi felt they must not perform before they were good enough 'because of the scepticism people have of reggae'. A few others had performed in the past but were not doing so for the moment because of temporary problems like having just recruited a new member and wanting to rehearse further first.

Despite this general emphasis on live performances, the number actually put on varied greatly from band to band. Of the 33 local bands questioned a quarter had put on no public performances at all in the previous year, nearly half had done 6 or fewer, nearly a quarter between 9 and 35 (mostly at the lower end of that range) and just under a fifth 50 – 150 a year. The ultimate aim might be the same, but for the basic functioning of the bands there was a vast difference between a group putting on two or three gigs a week throughout the year and one only doing one or two in the whole 12 months.

The venues also differed. By far the most common were pubs and youth clubs in or near Milton Keynes. Night clubs and colleges were favoured by some bands; also working men's clubs, other social clubs, and open air performances. Private occasions like weddings or parties provided another opportunity for band performance (often unpaid) – not perhaps the normal image of a rock band's activities, but one performance setting for at least a third of the bands. The audience numbers varied with venues. The big London clubs or, as with one band, American air bases could have audiences well into the hundreds and about half the bands said they had had audiences of 150 or more. Equally common, though, and for some bands the norm, were the smaller numbers typical of local pubs and youth clubs (usually 40–100), while 100–150 was characteristic of local social clubs. The differences in audiences were not just in numbers, for the familiar local audience with its core of personal supporters contrasted with the inevitably more impersonal atmosphere of larger, more distant venues to which the most successful local bands sometimes travelled.

Bands liked to get paid, but the amount varied greatly. Bands at local pubs got around £25, sometimes plus beer, and at youth clubs half the door takings. The social clubs, including political and working men's clubs, paid rather more (perhaps £75–£100, rarely up to £150) but were correspondingly more selective in who they invited, while the infrequent fees of over £150 were only from dinner dances and American air bases. Just about all the bands had also done free gigs. This was often just for the pleasure of having an audience, valuable for bands finding it hard to get paid bookings, or to enter a local competition like Pat Archer's Rock Contest in 1982; but bands also played free out of friendship and for a range of charitable causes – the National Abortion Campaign, the local CND festival at the Peace Pagoda, the Falkland Islands Fund, or local hospitals or handicapped children. It was clear from the number of unpaid appearances and from the common admission that fees did not cover costs that there was more to putting on performances than the payment.

These various patterns relating to gender, performances, venues and fees were not unexpected, but they did turn out to be more complex than appeared at first and gave more opportunity for experiment and variation than some of the more general comments on rock bands might suggest. In some other respects there was even more variety, some of it somewhat surprising in view of many widely held expectations about rock bands. Because some of these assumptions are so influential, indeed sometimes unquestioned, it is worth diverting to discuss them briefly.

Some arise from the succession of scholarly writings on and around the subject of popular music in general and rock and pop in particular. The influential mass culture theorists, for example, such as Adorno – strengthened from a somewhat different viewpoint by Leavis and his followers – saw popular music as essentially ruled by the market-place, soporific and non-artistic, delivered by non-creative and commercialised performers to passive and brain-washed mass audiences.[4] This is still one common view by outsiders of rock music – but, as will be clear from the account here, one that, apart from any other queries, it is not easy to recognise in the active amateur composers and performers in the Milton Keynes local bands. Later views have modified without totally dismissing these 'mass society' theories. Some Marxist writers have depicted popular music as almost totally dominated by a capitalist power elite. 'Pop music is produced within capitalist modes of production' is one such statement (Jones 1972, p. 130), while Charles Parker urges that 'pop is a master tool of social control by a ruling class' in which 'the illusion of rock-protest has been carefully sustained by a sort of shadow-boxing between the rulers and the ruled, authority and the young' (1975, p. 139). Others have stressed the active 'cultural struggle' they see going on in the sphere of rock and pop music, with the working class struggling to assert their own radical claims against the capitalist order (for instance Laing 1985), while the very influential 'subcultural theorists' speak of a 'working-class youth culture' or 'counterculture' expressed largely through rock music – in this view rock is seen as one form of working-class youth protest.[5]

One problem about such analyses has been their very generalised and polemical tone – only recently being replaced by cooler and more empirically based studies (such as Frith 1981b, 1983, Hustwitt 1986) – and their concentration on the *mass* media of television and the recording industry, which propagate the work of professional and nationally known bands. As such, even if valid in other respects, they cannot necessarily be expected to apply to the amateur grass-roots local performers and their face-to-face audiences – the subject of this volume. Nevertheless this succession of academic views – no doubt both reflecting and moulding some of the conventional wisdom of their times – has had its influence on common assumptions about the nature of rock music and its exponents, an influence also with its effect on the musicians and their audiences themselves. Thus there seemed to be a common series of images in Milton Keynes, encountered among people both inside and outside the rock world in general, that (variously) envisaged rock/pop as the protest music of the oppressed, as youth music (particularly amongst working-class youth), as the preserve of under-privileged, uneducated and unemployed working-class drop-outs, and (this last mainly by outsiders) as the kind of music (or non-music) which was essentially passive and derivative from the mass media, with no individual creativity – views clearly connected to the various academic analyses just quoted. Such views do not, of course, hang together into a coherent whole, and many of the musicians themselves were clear that certain aspects did not apply to their own practice. Nevertheless local participants and observers were still to some extent affected by this series of assumptions and were prepared from time to time to make effective use of such images in their own publicity.

How true were any or all of these varied assumptions about the nature of rock/pop music and its exponents?

One common – and not too contentious – view of rock is to regard it as part of 'youth culture(s)' or at any rate as 'the music of youth' (Frith 1978, p. 19, Grossman 1976, pp. 141–2). How true was this of the rock world in Milton Keynes in the early 1980s?

The evidence from the rock bands themselves certainly lends some support to this, but it was far from the whole truth. There was certainly great enthusiasm for particular bands among many young people, but 'youth culture' was not monolithic. Young people were not just differentiated by being 'young' but also sub-divided by age, interests, musical preferences, family background, locality and a whole range of other factors. It was true that teenagers were widely influenced by the popular music culture propagated in broadcasts, newspapers, recordings and local chain shops such as Virgin. But seen in terms of the active local participants, the picture looked much more diversified. A large proportion of band members were between 16 and 21, as were many of their audiences, but – as will have appeared from the earlier examples – these were individuals and groups with many *different* interests, musical tastes and backgrounds, not necessarily with a great deal of sympathy for, or interest in, each other's ideas or way of life or necessarily too concerned with each other's ages. Furthermore, other young people locally were keen on other pursuits, both other forms of music (classical, brass bands, operatic) and such activities as drama, sports or photography. Judged in relation to young people's active commitments in Milton Keynes the privileged position sometimes assumed for rock music as constituting either 'youth culture' in general or a series of differentiated youth 'sub-cultures' or 'counter-cultures' looks more like a wishful creation of the commercial recording outlets or the academic theorists than an exact description of actual grass-roots practice.

Age did, of course, sometimes play a part. In the teenage bands, age *was* of particular concern, so that young players advertising for co-band members commonly specified a particular age as one requirement: 'Drummer wanted for 16-year old M.O.R. band' or 'Drummer wishes to join or form a band with other enthusiastic players 17 to 19 years only.' Loyalty by school peers also often entered in: as for Rare Miranda, so for many others, school supporters numbered among a band's most steady followers. But this teenage interest in their contemporaries is not of course confined to music, and was of less relevance, even in rock bands, as they got older.

Playing and listening to live rock music, furthermore, was *not* the preserve only of the young. They were in the majority, certainly. Among the 125 band members surveyed in local rock bands about half were between 16 and 21; there were a few still younger players, and a further one-fifth in their early twenties. But – and here some commentators might be surprised – over a quarter were older: 16 in their late twenties, 16 in their thirties and 2 in their forties. Members of these older bands – Martial Law, for example – were often aware of the 'youth' image of rock music, ironically describing themselves as 'aging rockers' or objecting to the misconception of rock as 'just a teenage thing ... look at us, we're not exactly chickens'. In Milton Keynes, at least, enthusiasm for playing in rock music bands was certainly not confined to teenagers (or even teenagers/early twenties).

The emphasis on youth was more noticeable among the audiences. Many young bands directed themselves to teenagers (say, 14–18), this being the audience with whom they already had contacts and the most likely to be attracted into the youth clubs where they often played. Those who put on pub performances tried to construct a repertoire to appeal to young people between, say, 14 and 25; about half of the bands interviewed defined their audiences as mainly within that age range. Nearly as many, though, saw their audiences as including over-25s or mixed ages, while several bands, particularly those performing in working men's clubs, specifically mentioned middle-aged and older people, 'grannies as well as kids', '9–90 – from kids to parents'. Youth predominated, for even mixed audiences also included young people, but family audiences were nothing unusual and it would be misleading to conclude – despite the widespread image – that rock bands played exclusively to either teenagers or young people under 25. As far as the local rock players and their audiences went, therefore, generalised equations between rock music and 'youth' need some serious qualification; *not* all young people took an active part in playing or listening to live rock, nor were all rock players and audiences young.

Another popular view of rock music – and one also held by a number of local people – is the one that associates it particularly with uneducated and/ or unemployed youngsters. This stereotype too is worth investigating.

Were local rock players mainly unemployed? Or, alternatively, working outside the formal economy? On the basis of the 1982/3 interviews with thirty-three bands, supplemented by other local observation, the answer to both questions was no. Most local players did not rely on the band as their main source of livelihood, if for no other reason than that three-quarters found that fees did not cover their expenses. Of band members who gave details nearly two-thirds were in jobs, mostly full-time, under a third said that the band was their only employment, and the remainder were at school or college. Formal jobs clearly did not stop people taking an enthusiastic part in live rock music, and in Milton Keynes at any rate rock players were not mainly unemployed.

It was interesting, furthermore, to note the variety of occupations. Just to mention some of these: train driver, clerk, senior O. & M. officer, sales engineer, tutor on Youth Opportunities scheme, part-time violin teacher, barman, dental equipment engineer, part-time PE instructor, carpenter, forklift driver, car park supervisor, farm worker (on father's farm), shop workers, apprentice plasterer, telephone engineer, factory worker, hair-dresser, trainee telecommunications officer, upholsterer, graphic designer, warehouseman, buyer, trainee manager, and several schoolteachers. Even a summary list raises questions about the common stereotype of rock musicians as predominantly unqualified or non-conformist individuals on the edges of society.

For educational background the picture was again mixed. Of those band members who gave details, about two-thirds had ended full-time education at the minimum age, a pattern fitting one stereotype of rock musicians. However, the other third *had* stayed longer, several going on to higher education. Another way of looking at this was their educational achievements. Thirteen out of 125 were still at school or college, and of the rest half or more held some formal educational qualification:[6] thus many local rock players did indeed have little further educational experience, but once again the overall finding did not fit the stereotype of rock musicians as wholly or typically at the lower end of the population in educational terms; indeed, the fact that about half held CSEs or (more often) above meant that overall they were educationally not that different from the average population – certainly not markedly lower. There was no evidence, furthermore, that those with higher education had found this a disincentive for rock playing: indeed, they included some of the most influential local rock musicians such as Anita Tedder, Pete Lockwood or Ian Leech.

Another influential assumption is that rock bands express the protest of rebellious youth, more specifically of working-class youth. How far was this so of Milton Keynes rock players – or, at any rate, of those who *were* young (for, as we have seen, quite a proportion were scarcely classifiable as 'youth')?

The quick answer is scarcely surprising: bands varied. Some were certainly seen as 'a problem' by outsiders, and they and/or their audiences did sometimes get involved in fights. These bands did not always view themselves as 'protest bands', however, even if their particular form of behaviour, dress or followers were seen this way. Scream and the Fits, for example, were classified by local pubs and newpapers as 'punk' and 'skinhead' trouble-makers; but for *them* the music and fun of playing seemed to matter more than any political or anti-authority stance. Similarly, motor bike riders with their noisy machines and faceless get-up and the pub where they congregated to hear their favoured heavy rock seemed to outsiders like a threat from non-disciplined hooligans. Yet it looked rather different from their viewpoint as well as that of their local publican, their own followers and 'the motor bikers' mum'. Nor were they all in their teens or early twenties (in fact they ranged from twenties to late thirties). And their actions in organising a rock concert to buy a computer-aided device for a local handicapped child, then going to the school to present it, hardly fit with the general image of 'heavy rock addicts'. To interpret their activities in terms of 'youth revolt' or 'working-class protest' just because of their outward appearance or favoured genre of music would be very over-simplified.

In contrast, a small number of bands did label *themselves* as in some way opposed to authority, building on the common 'protest' image. Band names often indicated an implicit or explicit rejection of certain values that other influential people held to be important. Exit Stance was one clear example. The name needs some explanation. Originally several of the players – all in their mid to late teens – had played together as Ethnik Minority, a band catering for 'punk purists', and when two members left the remainder formed a new band called Fuck Authority. They gave some successful performances but ran into trouble when their 17-year old leader went to the main shopping centre on a Saturday in a black leather jacket with the band name in three-inch-high white letters on the back; the police were called and he was arrested. At the local Magistrates' Court the initial charge of behaviour likely to lead to a breach of the peace was withdrawn, but he was bound over and had to agree to remove the slogan and change the band name. The new name, Exit Stance, alluded to the loss of their old 'stance', but also in their eyes had some positive connotations (when said quickly it sounded like 'Existence'). This protest stance came out in their behaviour and personal appearance too and was also how they defined themselves. Their aim was 'to get over a message, anarchy and peace. We're a protest band against the system, social injustices ... We don't do it to please people, if they don't like it, tough. If we did what people like it would be crap ... We have never compromised: it will work because we want it to work ... We're pacifist drunkards who don't sniff glue. We believe in love and anarchy. We're a very individual band; we have different personal beliefs. We believe in life, not death ...' This 'protest' was of a very individual kind, therefore, based on specific ideals rather than a general or class-conscious rejection of the prevailing social order.

Reacting against parental control and ideals and stressing the opportunities for self-achievement was perhaps another aspect, but it would be hasty to take this as a central element in Exit Stance. For these youthful players were in fact *following* in their parents' musical footsteps rather than rejecting them. Like others too, they were not as alienated in their everyday lives as might appear from their overt philosophy. Of the four Exit Stance players, the 17-year old leader lived at home with his father, a special-school headmaster and himself a well-known local musician; another supported himself from part-time jobs; a third worked in the post office; while the drummer – himself the son of a jazz-drummer – worked as a carpenter. The idea of protest expressed in their original name was one aspect of their views, but so too was the secondary theme in their new name – 'Existence' – epitomised in their idealistic views of 'love and peace – life, not death', and in their insistence that 'we must live our own lives and control our own destiny', with the band as a medium 'to work things out for yourself'.

Other local bands too tried to project a rebellious image. Each had their own particular philosophy and problems, though. One example was the heavy metal band SNG (short for 'Sodom and Gomorrah', which grew out of Renegade, so named 'because we were!'). Their aims were not really political protest but to make money and be listened to: 'to make music that people appreciate'. Even their title was more a musical than political gesture: 'Renegade' because 'we refused to play cover versions' (i.e. they wouldn't perform others' compositions, only their own). Seditious Impulse was another local band regarded as 'punk', made up of four players in their late teens supported by a strong contingent of 50–70 'skinheads' who followed them about. They were banned from several local pubs and youth clubs, and had also been blamed – whether correctly or not – for a racist graffiti campaign in Bletchley and Wolverton. They explained their name as referring to 'sedition – arms against the state', but said their aims were mainly 'lots of birds ... a good laugh, a good piss-up, seeing lots of places and ... getting big – really rich'. The aggressive image they liked to project comes through well in their posed photograph (figure 19(c)). In other contexts, though, they were conformist. All had left school with at least some exam successes and were currently in jobs (machinist, painter, warehouseman/barman, BR vehicle builder, at least two with City and Guilds qualifications). Compared to some of their contemporaries they could be considered relatively privileged: but they still wanted the band as a context for letting off steam. Typical Shit is a final example of an apparently anti-authority band. This was a teenage and fairly inexperienced band playing 'punk' music (as they described it). Their name had come from the bass player's comment: sitting outside the shops he saw that people were giving him disgusted looks, so thought 'Typical shit'. Their special interest was in the opportunity to 'get a message across to people' outside commercial labels, especially their philosophy of 'making a stand against the way things are and the way people live. We're all pacifists ... we're all vegetarian, into animals' rights ... it's good fun – a good thing.'

These various bands were indeed questioning certain values and social arrangements – though perhaps in a less radical form than appeared on the surface – but most bands did not seem to see protest as in any sense their main purpose, even though they were keen to express their own personal views through their music. Again and again they stressed the comradeship of playing together in a band, the great feel of being on stage, 'giving people pleasure and excitement', self-expression, an outlet for their energy and expertise, making people think about their views and their music, getting some public recognition and, for some but not all, one day becoming professional musicians. When they did criticise the current situation, the criticism was directed against specific points and values rather than generalised protest.

The common image identifying rock music with protest – more especially with 'youth' and/or 'working-class' protest – was thus not generally borne out by this study. It may have been true of rock bands in other places or times (though I suggest that this always needs testing against the detailed evidence on the ground), but certainly among Milton Keynes bands most groups had other more important preoccupations and even the minority that did not often also had other interests and involvements. To select out just this (very varied) 'protest' element as somehow the most significant characteristic even of those bands, let alone of rock bands generally, downplays their many other interesting features in an ultimately reductionist and misleading way.

It should be clear by now that rock bands varied greatly both in outlook and in the type and organisation of their music, and that – perhaps unexpectedly – their members came from many different ages and backgrounds. Given this, is it reasonable to speak of a 'rock world'?

The answer has to be both yes and no. Rock music did present a particularly variegated scene. There were not the overall national organisations or formally linked associations to be found in, say, the classical, brass band, operatic, or even (to a degree) the folk or country and western worlds. The structure was more of individual forays into various sectors of the market-place than any hierarchical or overarching system, and bands were characteristically autonomous, separated by their own particular characteristics in regard to age, type of music, outlook and social networks. They were not necessarily in touch with other bands – particularly those in different age ranges, performance circuits or types of music – and when they did hear each other's performances sometimes regarded them with suspicion. Furthermore, most rock players played in one group at any time – a contrast to classical and jazz players – and thus were not immediately drawn into a wider musical world beyond their own band. On the other hand, the fluidity of rock bands meant that most players had belonged to several groups successively (or would do so in the future), some over a period of 20 or 25 years.

The relative lack of knowledge about other players in the local area was more marked than in the more hierarchically organised musical worlds, but was not different in kind. Even in the relatively tightly organised classical world by no means all musicians were personally acquainted, even though some leading personalities were widely known. Not so very different in the rock world: within particular forms at least (punk, say) the musicians knew each other, and certain individuals and bands were widely known. Jeff Donert, for example, the middle-aged chief car-park attendant in Central Milton Keynes – a life-long musician, leader of the Kingsize Keen Band, and local musical entrepreneur – was constantly mentioned, often with somewhat hostile envy as well as admiration, and the names of Dancing Counterparts (a long-established 'punk/alternative dance' band of players in their twenties) and 'Ferret' (the vocalist in Seditious Impulse) were also always cropping up.

Another shared characteristic was the set of conventions about playing and learning. The perceptions of both audiences and players were to a measure trained in rock performance idioms, further extended and revalidated by the coverage in the mass media, so that they could recognise with some appreciation the playing of other bands and the finer points of style. As one guitarist put it, to outsiders rock playing is 'quite a noise', but insiders can realise what is happening, which things are difficult to do, and what lies behind a particular performance. As far as learning went it was possible to take up an instrument, teach oneself, and join a rock band almost at once. One-fifth of the players in local bands had been teaching themselves for a year or less, a situation facilitated by the standard range of instruments: once players had mastered a few basic chords on the guitar or riffs on the drum, supplemented by self-learnt vocal skills, combining into a band became feasible. The contrast with the classical learning mode with its lengthy graded approach and wide range of instruments was a very marked one. The pattern was once again a complex and relative one, however. Self-learning was clearly the dominant mode, reinforced by the mutual help arising from the experience of band playing, but there was also a substantial minority of players (about one-third) who had learnt – or initially learnt – from more formal lessons at school, at work, or from private teachers, relations, colleagues or friends; a few had attended the local drum school run by Marshalls music shop through the seventies, and one had gone to music college.

The same complexity applied to the instruments. The standard combination was guitars (rhythm and lead), bass guitar, and drums, together with vocals,[7] but there were also occasional variations like violin, saxophone, harmonica, congas and bongos, sometimes supplemented by friends on other instruments (viola and flutes with Rare Miranda, for example). This range, furthermore, did not encompass the full musical expertise of band members, for several could play other instruments as well, including piano, brass, violin, cello, banjo, mouth organ, harmonica and mandolin: a spread of instruments which might be seen as fitting as readily into the folk or classical as the rock music worlds.

Perhaps the most prominent single characteristic of the preoccupations of rock players in Milton Keynes – apart from their variety – was their interest in expressing their own views and personality through music-making: a stress on individuality and artistic creation which accords ill with the mass theorists' delineation of popular music. This sense of individual achievement and creativity was particularly marked in rock bands. One need only recall the widespread emphasis on *self*-teaching for learning their instruments; the small-scale and independent form of rock groups, necessarily self-reliant and outside the formal organisation pattern typical of many other musical (and non-musical) groupings; the well-founded expectation that even a young musician just starting could play effectively with friends and perform in public; the parallel expectation that someone who had been playing for 20 or 25 years could still – without form-filling or permissions – find two or three like-minded people with whom to play for enjoyment to himself and others. There were certainly constraints for a band wanting expensive equipment, and finding venues for public performance needed negotiation; but to balance this, their independence of large-scale organisation or numbers meant that bands could be set up on the initiative of just two or three individuals. Most of all, the constant emphasis on composing their own original material (see chapter 13) gave players a clearly recognised channel in which to express their own musical and verbal insights in a recognised form – 'to do or die with our *own* music', as it was typically put by Static Blue (figure 19 (d)). Rock players were no doubt not the only local musicians to relish the opportunity for in some sense 'creating one's own world' in opposition to over-arching bureaucracy or 'mass society'. But perhaps there were indeed senses in which for rock players – and above all for the younger players – the currently understood conventions made up a special world in which they found a unique opportunity for personal expression and creativity.

The situation of rock players was thus a complex and heterogeneous one and one where individuals were participating in many different settings. Contrary to the views of some of the earlier academic theorists there is no *one* single profile of 'the rock musician' or of the role and background of rock/pop music. But there *were* enough characteristic features of live rock music in Milton Keynes to speak of the players – and at a further remove their audiences – as to a degree forming part of a wider rock world than just the individualised bands which they supported. The very autonomy and independence of the bands was itself an accepted feature of this world, together with their often ephemeral nature leading to changing combinations and re-combinations of the local players. So too was the concept and practice of being a rock band member: despite all other differences in background and musical style, there were accepted social and musical roles which individuals could take up and could recognise in others. It meant something predictable in terms of playing, practising and performing when someone said 'let's form a band' or inserted one of the many small ads for potential co-players in local newspapers. The accepted 'circuits' of local youth clubs and pubs, and (for the more successful) of social clubs and more distant venues, were common knowledge, even if in practice only experienced from time to time by any given band, as were the recognised conventions of instrumentation, performance and audience behaviour – within a range, anyway – and the great emphasis on original material. Acceptance of variation and experiment made this rock world a differentiated one; but that in itself, like the competition or conflict between differing bands each with their own followings, can be seen as yet another accepted characteristic of rock playing, one which to a degree distinguished it from other musical worlds in Milton Keynes.

In conclusion, it must be clear from the examples – few among many – that local rock players were extremely varied in their beliefs and backgrounds, and like any other groups had their quarrels and problems as well as successes.[8] Nevertheless, a sense of personal pride and achievement was one striking feature that seemed to run through all these bands. It was in such bands that their members felt they could really make some individual mark both now at the local level and, perhaps, more widely in the future. In contrast to the hierarchies and insecurities of school, work or the social services, playing in a band provided a medium where players could express their own personal aesthetic vision and through their music achieve a sense of controlling their own values, destiny and self-identity.

3

Contrasts and comparisons

The musical worlds of Milton Keynes have so far been presented as if autonomous and separate systems providing an essential, if often unnoticed, framework for local music-making. But they can also be seen in relation to each other. Some comparisons have already been implied, but this part adopts a directly comparative approach. This brings into sharper relief both the striking contrasts between the differing worlds and – in some other respects – their underlying similarities. The complex way in which the worlds both interpenetrate each other and have wider links outside the locality leads on to a reconsideration of the concept of 'musical world' as a route to understanding the practice of local music.

11

Learning music

It will be clear already that the many contrasts between the musical worlds of Milton Keynes were not haphazard differences but fell into a series of more or less consistent patterns. These related to such things as how people learnt and performed their music, the relation between 'originality' and 'performance', or the concept of what essentially constitutes a musical work.

This chapter (the first of three comparative discussions) considers the contrasting local conventions in the different musical worlds about how people should acquire their musical skills. These varying processes of teaching and learning have been touched on earlier, but this chapter brings them together in a more systematic comparison.

The most evident contrast is between the classical mode of professional and formalised teaching by recognised specialists on the one hand, and the self-taught or apprentice-type process of the more 'popular' music traditions on the other. Each of these is in turn linked to a wider set of conventions relating to social organisation and expectations as well as musical content.

The first mode is more familiar in the standard writing on music learning. It consists of a set of conventions drawn on in the official ideology of much school teaching, themselves in turn supported by the High Culture ideals of the classical music world. Here 'music' means the recognised theory and practice of Western classical music, made up of an accepted musical corpus and recognised instrumental skills which can (and should) be formally taught. Specialist instructors are responsible for this: school music teachers, peripatetic instrumental instructors employed by the local education authorities, or private teachers. Ideally their pupils move progressively through the graded examinations in both theory and practical instrumental playing conducted by national examining bodies such as the Associated Board of the Royal Schools of Music, Trinity College of Music or the London College of Music. It is thus always possible to specify a learner's stage of attainment precisely, and requirements like 'Grade III', 'Grade IV' etc. (still commonly expressed in Roman numerals) are recognised currency in the classical music world. These grades are also recognised by the nationally administered school examinations and in university entrance. What is involved is progressive admission through recognised grades, guarded by specialist teachers and examiners, to the highly regarded world of the classical music tradition.

This ideal model fitted well what was actually happening in Milton Keynes in the early 1980s. Thousands of children were learning classical instruments. This was often in a school context (where around 3,000 children were receiving instrumental tuition in 1982) or through the individual tuition provided to the county music scholars and others by forty or so full- or part-time instrumental teachers attached to the two LEA music centres. In addition, private music teaching flourished, especially for the piano (an instrument less catered for in school) but also for other classical instruments: strings, woodwind, brass, classical guitar, and voice. Both music centres kept lists of available instructors and were constantly being contacted by parents seeking teachers for their children. It was hard to estimate the total number of private teachers. Most or all of the centres' own teachers also taught privately, around forty additional teachers' names were on their lists in mid 1982, and many others with varying qualifications were teaching and contacting pupils through local grapevines or newspaper advertisements. Even so there was often said to be a shortage of instrumental teachers given the numbers of children (or parents) wanting their services, and piano teachers were particularly in demand. Not all pupils worked for recognised examinations, but many did, and many hundreds of practical examinations for the national examining boards were carried out each year in the Milton Keynes area.

The standard style of teaching and learning within this system was based on written (notated) music and its accompanying written signs, including the Italian musical terms. 'Learning music' and 'learning an instrument' meant learning to read music written in this form, some understanding of the theory that underlay it, and performing music composed by others. Formal instruction in instrumental skills was conducted within this taken-for-granted framework of acquiring measurable musical literacy.

The typical pattern was for a child to have a half-hour instrumental lesson once a week, usually on a one-to-one basis with an individual teacher. In each lesson, the teacher normally took the pupil through the various elements expected in this form of music learning. Since national examinations played so large a part, these elements often followed the demands of their syllabuses: scales; a limited number of pieces or studies; sight-reading; aural tests; and (either in the same or additional sessions) classical music theory. The weekly lesson was complemented by regular practice by the pupil on his or her own. Ideally (and at least sometimes in practice) this was around half an hour a day – less for younger children at the lower grades, more for the higher levels. In addition many of these children also played in groups, particularly in the Saturday morning activities organised by the local music centres or in the many voluntary school groups. In both private practising and most group playing, there was heavy reliance on written forms, and one of the responsibilities of teachers, parents and ensemble organisers was to obtain the necessary sheet music.

The investment of time and money in this system of learning was therefore a large one. The instruction fee was only one element, though, and, depending on the teacher's qualifications, this could amount to quite a sum over the years. In addition a huge amount of time was demanded from both child and parent. Some private teachers came to pupils' homes, but often children had to travel (and be transported) to their lessons. They also had to attend recognised centres for exams, where a predictable feature was the presence of proud (and extremely nervous) parents in the waiting room. Parents also had to obtain and pay for the instrument and printed music, and sometimes pay the examination fees. The most demanding commitment was providing support for practising. Some parents actually sat over their children as they went through the obligatory scales and pieces, while with others it was 'merely' ensuring the necessary facilities were available. This was actually no small matter since it meant providing the instrument, a suitable heated room, and practice time free from other obligations, as well as minimising other distractions in the same room – easier said than done since a piano was so often in the family living room. This was hard enough with one child practising one instrument; imagine the problems where several children in a family learnt (not at all uncommon), perhaps more than one instrument each, each needing its due practice! The demands on the child were heavy too, all the more so in that the end result was not always so very apparent (unlike in the various competing attractions), so that parental pressure or approval was often essential.

Many parents, especially mothers, became extremely committed to their children's music learning, partly of necessity – if they were going to encourage it at all they *had* to expend time, money and interest – partly because of the examination system. A child's progress could be clearly demonstrated in the sequence through numbered grades once or even twice a year, and parents became closely involved in the consequent dramas and pressures, very aware of their children's successes in nationally sanctioned gradings whose results were often published in the local newspapers. A common feature of everyday contacts between such parents was of one or both negotiating the conversation so as to bring in a comment about their own children's most recent exam success.

In this learning system, children ideally moved through the grades year by year, gradually working up to Grade VIII, the 'final' of the pre-diploma grades. The most successful sometimes then went on to further specialist training, often a full-time course outside Milton Keynes studying for a diploma or other specialist qualification as a basis for later work as professional teacher or performer. Many children dropped out earlier (though even then often with the satisfaction of having reached a specific grade); others persevered but gradually found that school examinations combined with the demands of the higher music grades was too much. The pyramid therefore narrowed sharply with increasing age and grade. Nevertheless many children did continue and managed to combine school studies with a high level of commitment to music (it had to be high, given the amount of time involved).

There was thus a regular cycle of development. At the early ages and stages large numbers of children were learning individually and playing in the many school groups and junior orchestras. Later there were fewer, but with many still contributing to school and local groups like the North Bucks Youth Orchestra (figure 8) or the Stantonbury Proteus Orchestra. A few teenagers who were musically advanced or played some sought-after instrument played in high-status amateur groups like the Sherwood Sinfonia or the scratch orchestras for local operatic performances or musical plays. They then largely disappeared from the local scene as they went off for further training (not necessarily in music), but some years later might surface as players or teachers in some local community, whether in Milton Keynes or elsewhere.

There was therefore a recognised and publicly validated 'career' in classical music learning. This was represented in Milton Keynes by the thousands of pupils and their specialist teachers, the series of nationally recognised and ranked examinations in local centres three times a year, and the agreed syllabuses and demands recognised by local teachers and pupils, all set within the conventions of Western classical music.

To those involved in that particular system, it is self-evidently *the* form of music learning. And yet there is another very different process, much less discussed. This is the mode of self-taught 'on the job' learning, which functions without any necessary reliance on written music or acquaintance with the classical music canons. Its most striking manifestation is among the many young musicians who, with little or no formal tuition, teach themselves to perform on guitar, percussion or vocals, playing with their peers in one or another of the many small bands that flourish throughout the country. This general process presents a striking contrast to the classical model and, despite outsiders' derogatory assessments, can be recognised as another system in its own right.

A high proportion of the musicians in local bands had learnt their skill in this way: through their own efforts and experience rather than being instructed formally by specialist teachers. In the 1982/3 survey of around 200 players in local Milton Keynes bands playing rock, jazz, folk, and country and western music by far the majority (particularly in rock) classed themselves as either totally self-taught or (less often) as mainly self-taught supplemented or initiated by some private lessons. Players could begin at any age, but one common pattern was for a teenager (usually a boy) to develop the ambition to play the guitar or drums, often inspired by a shared enthusiasm for some current popular number or player or by a friend or relation who played himself. Once he knew a few basic chords or rhythms it became feasible to contribute actively to group music-making and, usually without benefit of written music, to develop further skills in a group context which held not only all the satisfaction of joint musical experience, but also – very often – of peer group involvement in a valued and self-enhancing activity with rewards seen as self-chosen rather than set by external examinations or outside recognition.

To members of the classical world this mode looked overwhelmingly easy, undisciplined and 'low level' – not really a systematic way of learning at all. However, the picture was far from being as simple as the quick sketch above would suggest, and needs to be seen in relation to the amount put into this learning system by its adherents as well as to the nature of the music in which it was most frequently practised.

Some of those embarking on this kind of learning considered that it *was* an easy option or – just as in the classical mode – did not persevere with it vary far. For others, however, the self-learning process meant immense commitment and discrimination.

One leading local rock musician in her late twenties, for example, first got a guitar (acoustic) when she was 14 after hearing the Beatles. At first she did not know how to play, so just made up tunes – starting off on the track which led her to composing. She did have some school training in classical music, but this 'seemed quite separate from my own music', and the guitar was 'my own thing' which could be experimented on free from 'rules'. She was clear that teaching herself was a demanding task: 'I practised very very hard: it wasn't that I took it easy.' She used to work for hours at a time: 'I *really* wanted to do it.' Later she tried out an electric guitar under a fellow musician's influence and again had to work to master the technique. Apart from a couple of lessons when she was 18 she was totally self-taught on the guitar, learning both through her own experimentation and through singing and playing in a series of local rock groups.

There was also the local rock and jazz player (guitar, keyboard and vocals) who bought his first guitar for 18 shillings in London when he was 15, inspired by Lonnie Donegan, Buddy Holly and the Beatles. He had built up his skill over the years, partly through listening to records of his favourite singers and players – the same song 'perhaps 15 times a day'. It was a long hard struggle, but in this way he was able to lay the groundwork which he was still experimenting with and improving on through his frequent performances in local bands and as a soloist round the pubs and clubs. He envied those who had learnt 'the easy way' (of which his only personal experience was a few piano lessons at the age of nine), and wanted his own children to have formal lessons in the classical mode.

Another example was a versatile jazz/rock drummer who described his early enthusiasm on first hearing his school's 'Big Band': intensely exciting compared to the conventional school orchestra with its 'scratchy violins and squeaky clarinets'. He persuaded his father to buy him a second-hand drum kit for £5. At first he could not play at all, but avidly watched the drummers in the school group – and any others he could find – and tried it out at home at every opportunity, even with his mother's knitting needles. Since solitary drum playing was not very social, he also used to play pop records in a shed in the garden, and that too taught him a great deal. He described the huge difficulty of learning to work each hand and each foot independently, and at one point gave up in despair for six months. But he could not bear to leave it, so after a time resurrected the kit and his determination, and gradually began to develop the necessary skills. He let this be known at school, continued to listen and learn from yet more records, and finally was taken on in the school band. He hadn't looked back since, and by the 1980s was in great local demand for both jazz and rock bands.

In these cases – and the many others like them – the mode of learning was perceived by the musicians as a rigorous and lengthy one which made many demands on their time, energy and musical skill. It would be difficult to conclude on any objective grounds that this was an 'easier' or 'lower' form of learning (though that kind of judgement was a natural one for outsiders). Rather it was one distinct mode in its own right with its own standards and conventions, judged not by externally recognised criteria like examination marks but by the subjective evaluations and aspirations of the musicians themselves along with the shared judgements of those they regarded as their peers or models.

One interesting point about this learning mode was the frequent use of recorded versions on disc, cassette or tape, especially in the early stages. This was one option in instrumental learning which was not open – or at least not easily accessible – to musicians in the past. It is not surprising that it has given the opportunity for a revolution in music-learning processes; this is particularly so in the more recently recognised forms of music, whereas (as so often) the 'classical' and traditional form has tended to stick with its already-established institutions.

It is also relevant to note the nature of the music itself. The literate basis of classical music, with the player essentially a mouthpiece for the written compositions of others, was less relevant in other musical worlds, with their emphasis on *performance*. Learning the necessary skills in jazz, rock, and in some contexts folk and country and western music, did not demand written musical theory or notation but the acquisition of performance skills which could be effectively learnt by ear and on the job. Copying others' performances and developing in a group along with co-players were appropriate methods, different from, but not necessarily simpler than, receiving formal instruction from a specialist individual teacher as in the classical hierarchy.

For performance-oriented music, then, written learning and transmission were not central. Several leading local performers did in fact have some facility in reading music, but many did not. But even for those who could 'read the dots' this was usually not an important part of their musical skills. Some quite explicitly talked of the *constraints* of written music as against their own more 'creative' mode and criticised music-readers for their 'dependence' on written forms in both performance and repertoire. As the rock guitarist quoted earlier explained it, she found that not having to keep to written forms or to the rules of classical theory gave her the freedom to try out different tunings or experiment with unusual chords and modulations just as she liked, even ones that were 'wrong' in classical terms. Again, a folk musician commented on the richness and depth involved in playing by ear in contrast to the classical musicians, who 'are taught to play like typists who can type from one page to another without it going through their heads at all'.

The outlook and experience characteristic of these performance-oriented musical worlds also came out in the way members of the small popular bands set about learning a new number. In classical music the natural way was first to get 'the music' (by which, of course, was meant printed or written copies in standard notated form). In other forms of music this *was* sometimes one route, but it was more common to learn from a variety of non-written sources: hearing the piece from record, radio, or a live performance; obtaining a cassette for systematic listening and imitating; knowing the themes already but elaborating in performance; or learning by ear from one member of the group who might himself have got it from a recording or alternatively created all or parts of it himself, to be worked up by the group. Sometimes there was some initial use of chord charts as a basis for further development, often discarded later, or written or printed lyric sheets. With few exceptions, reliance on notated music was uncommon among local rock, jazz, folk and country music bands. In the 1982/3 band survey none of the local country and western groups used notated music at all, just over half of the jazz and folk groups did sometimes use written music to learn new items (most also using cassettes, tapes or records), but the rest never did, while among the 33 rock bands, only one did so. The lack of emphasis on reading music in this learning mode was thus supported by current practice in most local bands: full participation was possible without learning this skill. This practice was further reinforced by the fact that many of the rock bands played a high proportion of original material composed by themselves, material which was developed and learnt by ear and through joint playing rather than in written-out form (see chapter 13).

Within each of these contrasting learning worlds the conventions and the practical links between music and its organisation were well understood – indeed taken as natural – by the participants; and if each had a jaundiced view of the practices of the other this did not give rise to any particular problems so long as they operated in separate spheres. The contrasts were indeed quite striking. On the one hand there was the hierarchical and highly literate classical music training, with its externally validated system of grades and progress, entered upon primarily by children and strongly supported by parents, schools and the local network of paid teachers, with the aim of socialising children into the traditions of classical music theory and compositions through instruction in instrumental skills via written forms. Against this was the other mode: embarked on as a self-chosen mission primarily by adults and teenagers; not necessarily approved or encouraged by parents or schoolteachers; lacking external official validation, central bureaucratic organisation or any 'career' through progressive grades; resting on individual aspiration and achievement in a group music-making and 'oral' context rather than a hierarchically organised examination system; leading to skills of performance and variation by ear rather than the execution of already-written-out works; and finding expression in performance-oriented rather than written forms.

The difference between these two modes was a fundamental one. But though this is the central contrast I want to bring out in this chapter, there are some qualifications to be added before concluding. The two worlds of learning were not totally divergent, for there were overlaps in music, individuals and instruments.

First, it is worth remembering that the practice of self-teaching and learning on the job did not appear for the first time with the emergence of rock music, or, earlier, of jazz. Rather, it could be argued that it is the current extensive reliance on specialists to formally instruct and examine children in music that is in some respects new, hallowed though it often is by appeal to our musical traditions. Learning with minimal professional help and developing skills in the context of practice and performance had, for example, long been one of the routes by which church organists exercised their extremely influential role in both nineteenth-century and contemporary church music. A similar pattern was still evident in the parallel skill of piano playing. A number of the local pianists in great demand for accompanying (an essential function in many musical activities) followed a tradition that went back to the last century in that they had seldom or never had formal lessons or taken exams. This self-teaching sometimes led to some skill in reading music, but playing by ear was still often significant. Informal learning also had a long tradition in brass bands, and it was still common for brass players to have acquired their skill on a self-taught basis or through informal teaching in a family or band context. Local bands often had their own youth training sections one evening a week when experienced band members (often without any *formal* music qualifications) helped 'the youngsters coming on', and regarded playing in the band as itself part of their learning. This form of informal learning thus had continuities with the past and was still influential even outside the 'new' Afro-American forms of music.

Individual musicians, too, could and did participate in *both* these apparently opposed forms of training. Some began in classical music then moved to rock, jazz or folk, sometimes as a consequence explicitly rejecting their classical experience, sometimes making use of it while aware of the contrasts involved; a move in the other direction was less frequent, but sometimes happened. But for those involved in both kinds of learning simultaneously there could be conflicts. Children growing up in a context where learning by ear was highly regarded encountered problems when their classical teachers objected to their introducing variations into the music as written out. Some local musicians had learnt with apparent success in both modes, however, and, especially in jazz and folk music, provided a point of contact between the two, often supplementing earlier formal instruction on a typically classical instrument by self-learning on some instrument more suited to their newer interests.

There was also more overlap in instruments than might be expected. The preponderance of guitars, vocals and percussion in most small bands as against the mix of strings, keyboard, woodwind and brass in classical music sometimes gave rise to the argument that the 'easy' instruments of 'popular music' could be learnt by quick self-taught methods in contrast to the protracted and specialist process necessary for, say, the classical violin.

But it is doubtful if the *instruments* can really explain the different learning modes. It is true that with some instruments players could acquire basic skills for joint playing relatively rapidly (a few rudimentary chords on a guitar, for example, or riffs on a drum), whereas with others the *initial* stages took a long time. Similarly it is often claimed that it is quicker to train a brass band than a string orchestra. But several instruments in fact crossed the 'divide': the classical violin was the same *instrument* as the folk fiddle but with very different conventions for learning and playing; similarly with orchestral timpani as against rock or jazz percussion, or classical in contrast to popular guitar playing. Organs, pianos and electronic keyboard instruments could be played and learnt in various ways, and the same applied to the many other instruments which appeared in both 'classical' and 'popular' contexts, like brass, clarinets, flutes, and the voice. It seemed to be social convention and vested interest rather than technical instrumental requirements that led to the specific learning and performance modes attached to particular instruments – in the same way that it used to be 'common knowledge' that brass instruments were physically impossible for girls to blow. In Milton Keynes at least, there seemed few if any instruments which in themselves were impossible to learn to play with some confidence by informal self-learning processes. For example, a local 20-year old gave a 'one-girl show' for charity and raised £63 by performing on a selection of the twenty-three instruments she could play – all, with the sole exception of the bagpipes, self-taught.

The main point of this chapter has been to draw out the contrasts between two basically different systems of music learning, but, in addition to the qualifications just discussed, it may also be illuminating to end with a comment on resemblances between the two modes. In spite of the broad contrast which connects *performance* primarily with certain types of 'popular' music and transmission of *written* compositions with classical, it must also be remembered that classical music too is a performed art form and realised as such at the local level. Classical learning can include training in and through performance, an aspect explicitly encouraged by some local music organisers and teachers. Self-learning also occurs in practice as budding music pupils in the classical mode gain experience by taking part in local concerts, and the process of learning informally within a group or from friends and relatives also applies in some classical music learning, especially in choirs, operatic performances and local church music. Even some of the apparently 'specialist' music lessons at the local level are in practice conducted through family and friendship links and not always by teachers as highly qualified in professional terms as they and their pupils like to believe. These more informal aspects are often overshadowed not only by the very real importance of formal and specialist instruction, but also by the ideology of classical learning as expressed in the ideal model of classical music, which (as was suggested in chapter 4) does not necessarily provide a full account of local practice.

Both sides, therefore, ultimately share an interest in music as a performance art despite their differing emphases. The two systems of learning do indeed present many contrasts (ones typically unappreciated by those outside their conventions), but they also, finally, have in common the intensive demands that learning by *either* mode places upon the systematic commitment and application of those who acquire and practise the skills that underpin the continuance of local music.

12

Performances and their conditions

Local music is not just a matter of musical *works* encapsulated in musicians' memories or in written scores, as so many accounts of music have assumed, but, more centrally, of the active practice of local people: above all their performance of music. This has so far been taken as given, but some more detailed consideration is also needed both of the varied performance conventions of the differing musical worlds and their implications, and of the general significance of performance in music – a relatively neglected topic despite the increasing interest in performance in other contexts.[1]

Musical performances must obviously be organised in some way if they are to exist at all. This organisation takes place through the co-ordinated efforts of a whole series of participants working within specific cultural conventions. Leaving aside recorded music (generally outside the scope of this study), live performances generally fall somewhere along a continuum between informal playing on the one hand and, on the other, the formalised public occasion. Richard Bauman has usefully written of 'artistic *action*' – the doing itself – and 'artistic *event* – the performance situation, involving performer, art form, audience, and setting' (Bauman 1977, p. 4, also pp. 27ff). This chapter concentrates on the second of these categories: the artistic events of local 'concerts', 'gigs', 'bookings' and so on.

These performances are scheduled staged events which involve groups of people – including visual, kinaesthetic and interactional as well as the 'purely' auditory elements. Such performances must therefore be approached in context, with attention to the actual social conventions sustaining them, and not to the musical 'text' alone.

The idea of special performance events plays a central part in most local musical groups and activities. People do also find satisfaction in playing for themselves, listening, practising or just 'jamming together' in a context not defined as real 'performing' – and this activity too is one part of local music. Nevertheless it is generally taken for granted that 'performance' is a pre-eminent, even obligatory, part of music-making.

These 'performances' have a series of characteristics. There has to be some audience wider than the performers themselves. The performance has to be set apart in socially recognised ways. And it has to be worked up to through a set of prior activities. The audience or the preparations may be small or large, but these conditions are all normally present in one way or another for the musically realised enactment to constitute a performance.

This basic complex of conditions (audience, setting apart, and prior preparation) ran through all the music worlds in Milton Keynes, and musical performances on these lines were an accepted part of the local social activity. Schools regularly organised concerts and musical plays to enthusiastic audiences of hundreds of parents, relatives and friends after weeks or months of rehearsals. Local brass bands put on constant performances throughout the year at festivals and concerts. Hundreds of children through the city followed up their practising by playing or singing in school or church or music centre performances. Folk singers performed both in scheduled 'guest' appearances and in the less formal context of a local 'singers' night'. Rock bands met regularly to work up their repertoire for bookings in local pubs and clubs. In all these contexts – and many many more – the act of performance represented the high point and validation of a whole series of both musical and back-up activities by performers and supporters before and after the event, something which, apart from its utilitarian purpose, also gave a special symbolic value to these specially framed moments in time.

But if the general conditions for a 'performance' were widespread, the detailed form it was expected to take varied considerably. This might seem too obvious to mention were it not that the conventions held appropriate in one musical world were so often assumed to be the 'natural' and only ones, too familiar to need notice or explanation; others' conventions, by contrast, could look too strange to really constitute 'musical' enactment at all. Yet the performance conventions of each world were equally valid in principle and equally worthy of study. It is therefore worth providing a sketch of these contrasting conventions, even though to those within each musical tradition they will seem self-evident indeed.

These differences are very noticeable if one attends a succession of performances from *different* musical worlds – a contrast to the usual practice of staying within one's own familiar world(s), where one can follow tacitly agreed conventions without being even aware of their existence. Here, then, are brief accounts of three performance events, each representative of one musical tradition.[2]

First, a performance by a heavy metal band. This was in a local pub then well known for its music, especially for its regular weekly or fortnightly live rock performances. The event had been publicised both by an advertisement in the local newspaper and by word of mouth through the informal network of regular attenders; there were also hand-written posters on the pub windows. Admission was carefully controlled by the landlord, always concerned about the possibility of disturbance to neighbours which might lead to complaints and the loss of his entertainment licence, so people had to pass through a guard at the door as well as pay a small entrance fee. Inside, about forty people were sitting at tables and drinking in the semi-dark, a few standing at the bar along one side, while records were being played loudly from the wide low stage in the far corner. The audience, roughly equally male and female, were gathered in groups of two, three or four. They were mainly in their twenties with no one form of dress or hairstyle: trousers and jackets, not just jeans and jerseys, for the men, and skirts or dresses as well as jeans for the girls.

Time did not seem to be of particular moment, but the expectation was that the band would start up around 9.30 or 10.00. Presently the four players began appearing on the stage, fiddling with their instruments and PA while the potential audience – by now about 60 – carried on with their drinking, moving round and talking in loud voices in the intervals of the records. Finally the compère announced the band's title and origin (not their individual names): 'Give them a hand'. Everyone clapped in a restrained rather than wildly enthusiastic way, and the band made a tempestuous start: very loud, bright lights flashing, vigorous and eye-catching movements by the performers, especially the lead-singer, who was spectacular in his bright red tracksuit. Because of his vocal rather than instrumental focus he was able to leap about, head-shake violently, and sometimes move among the tables, encouraging others to join in his head movements. These visual and kinaesthetic features and their acclamation by the audience were clearly all part of the performance.

So too, of course, was the loud and rhythmic music performed by the standard all-male combination of electric guitars, bass guitar, drums and vocals. It was divided into separate items, each followed by somewhat desultory audience clapping. The performers marked the end of each piece more by its musical climax together with a briefly held pose than by any formal acknowledgment outside the playing proper, and immediately began retuning and checking their instruments again. At first they went straight on to the next piece after adjusting their instruments, but as the evening went on the leader made brief announcements about the name and, when it had been composed by others, the origin of the next item; there was no written programme.

Meantime the audience continued their relaxed drinking and smoking at their tables, sometimes turning their chairs to see the band better, or moving round to replenish their drinks in the gloom; the main lights were focussed on the band, though circulating coloured lights lit the rest of the room spasmodically. While the band were actually playing there was little talking – not so much through a convention of silent listening or undivided attention as through the sheer volume of highly amplified sound. Those present were to an extent joining in the band movement and rhythm, however, not by actually getting up to dance but by foot-tapping, rhythmic movements to the beat and in a few cases intermittent nodding along with the leader's violent head movements. There was thus some active audience participation and, despite the set-apart stage, relatively little separation between performers and audience.

Very different in both audience and performer behaviour was a concert I went to a few days later. This was a classical recital by a singer and pianist (both female) laid on by a small local music society in the unpretentious hall at one of the LEA music centres. This concert too had been advertised before hand, but in a different form from the pub one: a small note in the local newspaper supported by large printed posters in local libraries, shops, halls and churches. Once again there was someone on the door, both to check tickets (already held by most people) and – an essential part – give out the printed programme. In this concert this was a cyclostyled sheet and, as usual, listed the items to be played, giving title, composer, and brief notes for the pieces, and the names and personal background of the performers.

As audience members came in, they sometimes had a word or two with friends, but mostly went straight to the chairs set out in stiff rows facing towards that section of the room set apart for the performers, marked by a music stand and the grand piano. The audience were mixed in age, with a slight preponderance of middle-aged and elderly but also with some two-generation families, several groups of friends, and a few single members. Once again dress varied, the men in trousers and jackets with the occasional formal suit, the women in skirts or dresses: there was a general air that the adults at least had dressed up a bit, though certainly not so far as full evening clothes. It was hot, and people took off their coats and settled down ready to start.

The concert had been advertised for 7.45 p.m. By then, the audience – around sixty in all – were in their rows, chatting in quiet tones or sitting in silence looking through their programmes. They looked well settled by 7.40, but – even with everything ready – the formal proceedings could not commence until the advertised time. When 7.45 arrived the society's chairman went to the front to welcome the audience and call in and introduce by name the two soloists, who till then had waited unseen in a side room. They made a formal entrance, both wearing full-length evening dresses and carrying their music, and bowed ceremonially to lively clapping from the audience. The singer carefully put her printed music on the stand in the centre while the pianist sat at the piano with hers. There was an expectant hush as the audience consulted their programmes and waited for the first item.

Each piece or group of pieces was introduced briefly by one or other of the performers – not strictly necessary given the written programmes (and often not done in formal concerts) but accepted as a pleasant personal touch. The piece was then listened to in total and intent silence: not even low murmurs or whispering, with the very occasional – and carefully concealed – exception. How far everyone was as fully immersed in the intense inner experience ideally predicated for this form of musical participation was another question – but it was at least clear, first, that this conventional behaviour was familiar to the audience, and second that the socially enforced expectation *was* precisely that air of hushed concentration and awe, followed by a brief instant of silence and awakening, then a burst of applause after each item. The audience also took care to observe the classical convention that breaks between 'movements' in a single piece were not points for applause: the audience must still sit in silence (though they could shift slightly or cough), indicating that they knew the intricacies of correct behaviour. The performers acknowledged the audience's applause at the end of each item by formal bows, standing side by side and bending in unison.

As was usual in such concerts, the evening was split into two by an interval of around twenty minutes, preceded by the performers' ceremonial exit. The second half followed the same format: clapping from audience and bows by performers, and the resumption of the same hushed expectancy from the audience, back in their seats again after the informal moving round, talking and coffee during the interval. The proceedings were brought to a formal close with the completion first of the final item on the typed programme (followed by the normal convention of particularly intense applause from the audience, ceremonial bows, and exits then re-entrances by the performers), then an additional item (unscripted but expected) as an encore, marked by the same conventions of applause, bows, and procession out and in again, and, last of all (and not typical of all classical concerts), a brief comment of thanks to both audience and soloists by the society's chairman.

Despite the absence of a raised stage, the separation between audience and performers was clearer than in the pub, partly through the accepted formality of this concert form, partly because of the physical layout of the hall, and partly too because of the audience's apparent inactivity compared to the performers. They applauded, it is true, and at the end followed the accepted convention of clapping until the performers agreed to the 'encore' item. But otherwise they took a quiet role in comparison to most other performance traditions – no marked bodily movement to the rhythm (if there was the occasional gently tapping foot this was frowned down by others), no joining in with the songs, no calls of encouragement or appreciation during the performance. The separation of the performers was also marked by their distinctive costume and by their written music, which gave authority to their distinct specialist role.

There were some similarities between the two events. Each was announced in advance through both public media and personal networks; each was held at a specified and planned place and (within limits) time; each involved an audience, together with some separation between performers and audience; each had the specific items in the performances marked out by some kind of prior announcement and by applause at the end (most vehement by the classical audience, balancing their less active participation during the playing itself); and each involved groups, talk, and refreshments as well as the purely musical content.

Beyond these broad resemblances, however, the conventions which moulded the behaviour of players and listeners, the setting, and the performer/audience interaction were very different. Most noticeable was the relaxed mode for listening to the rock band, with people sitting informally at tables scattered through the room or moving around, drinking, smoking and eating even *during* the playing, in contrast to the tense silence during the classical performance, with the audience in straight rows of chairs, scarcely allowing themselves to move a limb or turn a head, no smoking, and refreshments and free conversation confined strictly to the interval; even in the spaces between items they only engaged in subdued talk. But there were also other differences: the typed programmes, printed tickets and posters, and reliance on written music by the performers in the classical mode, as against the much less 'literate' conventions of the pub band: no printed tickets or programmes for the audience, no written music for the band. Other differences were less radical, though still worth noting. The younger age of the rock audience, their more varied dress, the greater flexibility of timing, and the great volume of music contrasted with the older and more 'conventionally' dressed classical audience, the precisely timed start of the music, and the non-amplified sound interspersed with brief instants of silence, all in keeping with the hushed atmosphere taken for granted as the 'natural' reception for classical music. Finally – and related probably to all the other differences – there was the lack of physical audience participation in the classical performance as against the more direct part taken by the rock audience (not as great, admittedly, as in some performance traditions, but striking compared to classical expectations). Both *were* performances, but the contrasting conventions were clear, summed up in the different terms used of the two events – the music society 'concert' and the pub 'gig'.

Different yet again was a performance at a country and western evening in aid of a local school for handicapped children, held in the school hall. This followed the same broad lines already described in chapter 9, but yet another performance will be commented on briefly here in order to amplify this analysis and comparison of performance conventions. The band was Cuttin' Loose, a leading local group who usually played outside Milton Keynes, but had agreed to appear here 'for charity'. The setting was partly similar to the pub event. People sat at tables smoking and drinking, or moved around the hall and across to the nearby rooms to get food and drink. Near the door helpers were selling or checking tickets, while in one corner was the built-up stage with instruments laid out ready, but at first only records playing. Unlike the rock performance, however, the ages were very mixed – children, teenagers, early twenties and right up to the middle-aged and a few elderly, including several families, mostly seeming to know each other well. Dress varied, but there was quite a sprinkling of 'western' costumes and of dressy clothes – in all, clearly a festive occasion for which most people took pleasure in dressing up.

The timing was again flexible, with a general expectation that at some point – not too late – the band would appear; some were already there among the audience, chatting with their friends. By about 8.30 p.m. they gradually appeared on the stage adjusting their instruments, and finally the MC called the audience to attention and introduced the group by name as 'one of the best bands on the circuit'.

The leader started straight off on the guitar, then took up the song, joined shortly by the rest of the four-man band. As the evening went on, most songs were introduced by the leader, usually just giving the title with a brief comment on its style. The songs were clapped enthusiastically while the performers (especially the leader) gave a quick nod of acknowledgment or a brief 'Thank you very much' muttered into the microphone. Most were clearly familiar, chosen by the band from their extensive repertoire and greeted with pleasure by the audience. During the playing people were actively listening or looking at the stage rather than talking or moving round – but in a relaxed way as if it didn't matter if they *did* move or speak: a striking contrast to the intense concentration of the classical event. Many tapped their feet or part-hummed the tune.

About half-way through the evening there was a break. This was more for the band to have a short rest than (as with the classical interval) a change in the audience's format or activities, for the interval was also filled by entertainment – a short drama and 'shoot out' put on by the local Wild West group, emphasising the festival (rather than 'concert') atmosphere. This was further added to by the general atmosphere of a shared culture, among people who knew each other personally or were conscious of belonging to the same 'country and western' world with a noticeable camaraderie even between individuals otherwise unknown to each other.

By mid-evening there were about 100 there, and people got up to dance in front of the hall, first just two or three couples, then nearly half the audience. The strong rhythm of the music was enhanced by the repetitive and near-hypnotic swaying of all the dancers in unison to the beat. The music thus also found expression in dancing, as if in this context musical performance and its appreciation were not just something for the ears but also expressed by the body and enacted jointly with others through rhythm, gesture and bodily movement.

Here was yet another form of performance with its own conventions. Some details were of less significance – the particular ages, the fund-raising element (equally to be found in all the musical worlds), or the specific band or hall. The general conventions, however, are worth noting. They resembled the rock pub performance much more than the classical concert, with the audience's format (no straight rows), the atmosphere of social club rather than formal recital, the absence of written music or programme, and the desultory behaviour of the band (as it would seem to a classical devotee) in their entrances and exits or their acknowledgment of applause. The 'concert' mode of intent listening was also absent. But there were also differences from the rock event, chiefly in the nature of the active audience participation. The country tunes were already known, so the audience could hum along in a way difficult with original rock numbers. Most of all, there was the whole-hearted participation through *dancing*: an accepted mode for the appreciation, indeed the full realisation, of this form of music. And yet despite this full audience participation, in one sense there was still a marked separation in actual performance between audience (dancing, sitting, listening) and band (playing, singing, costumed, accepted as the specialists).

These three cases are presented merely as examples of some contrasts and comparisons between the local performance events in different musical worlds to bring out the conventional and differing nature of these expected patterns. They are not exclusive models, far less ideal types. For one thing, these examples did not exhaust the variations even in Milton Keynes. There were also, for example, the folk club performance conventions: again usually in a pub with informal seating and drink and food on tap throughout, but with a touch more 'concert' atmosphere because of the struggled-for ideal that people should be relatively quiet and still during a song; at the same time folk performances encouraged direct audience participation through their 'singalong' tradition, above all in the chorus songs. Or again, there was the pantomime tradition: partly like the classical event with fixed seats and audience/performers separation, but with a more relaxed atmosphere since the audience could talk and move around in their seats during the performance; and in certain phases direct audience participation was specifically encouraged. There was the church setting too when those who from one viewpoint constituted the audience (the congregation) themselves became full performers at certain points. These – and yet other cases again – represent only some of the varying conventions in local musical events.

The overlap between the performance conventions of the different musical worlds and the variations *within* them form another reason why the examples above cannot be taken as discrete models. They were reasonably

representative of performance conventions within the three worlds illustrated, but not every performance within these worlds was *exactly* on those
lines. There were variations according to how 'professional' the performers
were, their local connections, their personalities and aspirations, the scale of
the event, or how well members of the audience already knew each other. A
rock performance in a hall rather than a pub sometimes grew nearer to the
'concert' form, with rows of seats or a more formalised start, but still
differed in the expected audience behaviour; while some classical performances (to children, for example) were organised to encourage much more
active audience interaction.

It would be going too far, therefore, to try to establish a definitive
typology of performance models. The point that does emerge, however, is
the existence of differing conventions, well understood in the actual
situation by both players and listeners and tending to be more or less shared
within each musical world. These were often not part of people's explicit
consciousness, but when the expected conventions were *not* followed (by
children, for example), this was firmly conveyed to the offenders by other
audience members. Cases of conflict as well as the smoothly running
occasions illustrated the socially formed rather than 'natural' state of these
conventions, and the way they depended on learned assumptions (by
audience as well as performers) without which successful performances
could not take place.[3]

These performance conventions were also related to the varying assumptions about what was meant by 'music'. Many would assume that the
natural performance model is the 'classical concert', with the conclusion
that other types of performance are not really 'music' proper but 'merely
entertainment' or 'background'. But if classical performance expectations,
just as much as rock or country and western ones, are dependent on learned
conventions about appropriate behaviour, then it becomes clear that there
are several different but equally valid systems for musical enactment. In
particular, it is worth noting the performance modes which demand
audience interaction or direct audience participation in the performance,
whether through vocal, rhythmic, or, as in dancing, direct bodily participation. To one brought up in the classical world where music is often seen in
textual rather than performance terms, this form may seem unnatural or
peripheral. But this performance model has in fact a long tradition behind it;
it may be *different* from the usual contemporary classical performance, but
is not for that reason to be defined away as not 'real music'. Similarly the
temple-like atmosphere of classical concerts seemed artificial or pretentious
to rock enthusiasts, because of its emphasis on written communication and
its constraints on audience movement, but once again this was *to the
participants* the fully appropriate behaviour. Performance conventions are
thus not absolute conditions but, being contingent upon particular cultural

prescriptions, have to be empirically observed and studied – rather than just assumed – in their own right.

It is worth recalling the three elements that, it was suggested, are normally conditions for the definition of musical expression as 'performance': (1) the participation of a wider audience than the performers themselves; (2) the event being set apart and 'framed' in some way and (3) some prior preparation for the performance. Each of these conditions had its accepted forms in the various musical worlds, several of them apparent in the earlier examples. However, some comments on each can lead into further discussion about variations in performance forms.

First, conventions relating to the audience. Much of the previous discussion centred on this aspect, particularly the expected audience behaviour in particular musical traditions and the amount and nature of audience participation. To some readers this may seem perverse, for surely the behaviour of *performers* rather than audience constitutes 'performance'? In one sense the performers were of course central, but a 'performance' can also be seen as a whole, as an event involving all its participants. Audience expectations and behaviour were an essential part of this. This was most obvious when the audience directly participated in the music, but was also true where silent reception was the paradigm: without *that* particular form of audience participation the performance could not be regarded as successful.

Audiences for musical performances were varied – in age, sex, socio-economic background, and outlook – and it would be glib to generalise too readily about their composition. However, one general point that did emerge was that the audiences for most amateur musical events comprised people attending in virtue of some connection with the performers, with other audience members, or with the organisation running the event. That is, among the usual run of live performances throughout the year, there were few if any where the audience was a truly 'mass' or 'impersonal' one. Indeed many local audiences were made up mainly or wholly of the performers' friends, relatives and supporters (a few bands even had their own fan groups who followed them from performance to performance), and the experience of the audience was naturally coloured by these personal relationships as well as by the more general conventions already discussed. Thus there was simultaneously the idea that a performance – to be a proper 'performance' – had to be in some sense 'public' and the fact that much of the audience was actually recruited on a personal basis.

It was not just the audience that framed a 'performance' as a special event set apart from routine 'playing' or 'practising'. Some of these other framing conventions have already been touched on. They usually included at least some of the following. First, the time and place had to be announced in advance so 'publicity' was a regular prerequisite for setting up performances – even when it was widely accepted that word of mouth and personal pressure was what actually brought in the audience. Second, the venue – hall, church, pub or wherever – was usually marked by a special format or decoration for the occasion: either different from its everyday state, if only by special lighting or flowers, or indicating by its layout its special 'event' function. Third, there was often a distinctive costume or accoutrements for the performers, marking out the special nature of the occasion. Most choirs and all brass bands had performance uniforms, for example, dress was of the essence in theatrical musical events, school children were instructed on what to wear for concerts, and many of the small popular bands had special uniforms for their gigs; the audience often dressed up too. Fourth, the timing was often an indication of the set-apart nature of the event. Most musical performances were in the evenings or at weekends, fitting the accepted classification of these times as set aside from the rest of the day or week for 'leisure' or for 'cultural activity'. Fifth, the event was often marked by some quasi-ceremonial exchange between organisers (and/or audience) and the performers – the public exchange of speeches (a vote of thanks, for example, from the chairman at the end of a concert, acknowledged by the performers), or the making of a gift or payment to the musicians in return for their performance; often serving a symbolic as much as a financial function. Finally, as will have emerged from the earlier descriptions, there were the accepted rituals (differing in different music worlds) for starting and ending, entrances and exits, announcements, presentation, acknowledgment and applause. Not *all* of these elements were necessarily found in any given event, but some or most had to be present for a musical activity to be marked out as 'special' – a performance event.

This is also where the idea of rehearsing comes in – often a necessary complement to that of 'performing'. For most musical groups this was an essential preliminary to, and condition for, the final performance. Practices were sometimes an end in themselves, but the most frequent rationale was that they were directed to ultimate 'public' performance. For most regular groups the yearly cycle of weekly practices was punctuated by the intense moments of performance: the concert, gig, booking, or recording session.

Among musical groups in Milton Keynes it was quite striking how many hours were spent at practices. Choirs regularly rehearsed one evening a week with additional rehearsals coming up to a concert; brass bands twice a week or more; operatic clubs, besides the once or twice-weekly rehearsals through most of the year, had almost daily rehearsals before their main production. Most small bands too, organised on less bureaucratic lines and often regarded by their detractors as indisciplined, devoted many hours to regular practising together. There was also individual practising, particularly in the classical music world but also by self-teaching instrumentalists.

In all these cases there was a relation between the practices and performance, but its exact nature and the sharpness of the distinction between the two varied. Sometimes the 'performance' was a highly special and long-prepared-for event, the culmination of an organised rehearsal series, like many choir concerts or operatic performances. Sometimes the distinction was less clear, as with an individual player (a child learning perhaps) asked to 'perform' for a parent, a teacher, a visitor to the home (a not uncommon context), or an examiner. Some highly experienced bands and choirs found it difficult or unnecessary to have regular face to face rehearsals, and instead relied on preparatory communication to sketch out the programme, in one case interchanging cassettes through the post, followed by a quick run-through before or during the event. In other cases, such as a scratch group for a particular occasion (an orchestra accompanying an operatic performance, for example), one or two joint rehearsals from written music might be all that were held. The variations also related to the form of music. Rock and classical performances depended on prior preparation of a relatively fixed text whereas jazz performance rested on experience of the necessary skills and co-ordination; but even jazz bands often had rehearsals before a booking, or at least a discussion and a run-through just before the performance.

Amidst all these variations, the underlying pattern remained: an expectation that the performance event would be preceded by some musical as well as organisational preparation and that the performance was not just part of a seamless process of musical activity but a culmination of it.

The performance events discussed so far were thus the points at which activities reached their ideal fulfilment in a shared ritual widely recognised in local culture – the peak and rationale for the many hours of musical practice engaged in by local players. But performance events of this kind, however prominent, were not the only context in which local musicians experienced the satisfaction of music-making. To close this chapter some brief attention must also be paid to these other contexts: music-making without an audience, and performance for recording.

Preparation for later performance was often the explicit aim of musical practice, but, as will be obvious to anyone who has regularly taken part in music, practices could also be enjoyable themselves. As well as the experience of collective working towards a jointly valued aim and the attraction of 'a night out', there was the straight musical appeal of singing or playing together. This was attractive to individuals on their own too – learning new musical pieces and developing their skill as well as 'just playing for the pleasure of it'. For ensembles there was the additional satisfaction of participating in the musical blend and interaction that could not be achieved by one musician alone.

Such activity was also a kind of performing, especially in a large group – performing for each other or for their conductor. This applied more to some stages in regular practices than others: the group (or its leader or director) sometimes decided to go through a whole piece or section in a sustained way rather than the bitty mode typical of the rest of the session, and this difference might be marked by standing up to sing (the performance stance) rather than sitting in the rehearsal mode, or by the players carrying on to the end despite errors. Viewed in this light the difference between 'performing' and 'practising' was only a relative one – even though for most groups a 'performance' in the fullest sense was always the public event deliberately worked up to through a series of prior practices.

This only *relative* distinction between 'performing' and 'practising' provided the background to cases where music, a 'performed art' after all, was enjoyed by people who did not give public performances, but who yet in some sense regarded themselves as performing (rather than just practising at) their music. This applied to many local musicians, especially those who played the various keyboard instruments now available in their own homes. It was also true – if more rarely – of some music-making groups. Several small instrumental groups in the classical tradition met to play in each other's homes with no plans for public performance, while even among the small popular bands, though by far the majority wanted to give public performances, a few declared that they were not interested in taking bookings, and were content just to meet to play together. There was something about *musical* enactment, more so than in the performance arts of dance or drama, that meant it could be realised as at least a kind of performing even without all the accompaniments of a full event. Because, furthermore, the accepted conditions for a performance event were both multiple and relative, the line between 'mere playing' and full 'performance' could be a shifting one. Thus quite a small change in just one element – an outbreak of clapping at a final rehearsal, for instance, or the unexpected presence of outsiders – could tip the participants into reclarifying what before seemed a mere routine run-through into something verging on a 'performance' after all.

There was also the new form of 'performance' to which the small bands (in particular) were turning: recording their music on disc or cassette. With the proliferation of small but well-equipped local studios, not to speak of the ubiquitous access to cassette recorders, this had now become a possible medium for musical enactment for even the most local or unpretentious groups, and for a few bands seemed to be as important as 'live bookings', with comparable overtones of musical enactment and self-realisation.

Performing for recording was different from that for live events, but there were some interesting parallels. A session in one of the local studios was looked forward to as a high occasion in the band's musical activities, practised for with particular intensity. As well as the general preparations beforehand and the prior arrangements about payment and timing, the occasion was set apart from the usual run of everyday music-making. The physical format of the studios played a part, increasingly well known to bands and others as places specifically designed for this particular kind of performance. An audience in the usual sense was of course lacking and, as one experienced performer explained, you have to do something special in recording to make up for the absence of audience interaction and the glamour of live performance; but even here there were some parallels. The recording was not made in a vacuum, for there was constant critical exchange with other band members, with the recording experts (who in small local studios were fellow musicians and colleagues, sometimes already friends), and with the friends or supporters whom the band had encouraged to come along. After every stage of the recording – split up among separate players, tracks and sections as it often was – there was likely to be comment and discussion, not infrequently of a congratulatory kind: different from the applause following a performance at a more 'public' event, but with some similarity nonetheless. It is worth remembering too that such recordings were not usually circulated in large-scale impersonal form or through the mass media, but were played or given to friends, sold to fans and well-wishers on a personal network, or peddled to already enthused audiences at live performances.

Recordings, then, *were* different from live performances, but had enough in common to make it no strange step for local groups to regard recording events as one among the several engagements in their cycle of performances. Practically all the local small bands had made recordings of some kind, sometimes just home recordings for their own use or for informal demonstration tapes, but also surprisingly often in more permanent and technically sophisticated form. For some the importance of a recording session was comparable to live performance, for a few even more 'creative' because of its special challenge. But however it was precisely defined, the spread of small local studios and their use by local bands was certainly a most significant extension of what had been – till recently – the familiar round of live performances in the locality.

These extensions in the practice of performances must be noted, but for all that 'live performance events' remained the highlight of the practising and active music-making cycle of most music groups – the fullest and most appropriate realisation of music-making. This was implied even by those who, as it was sometimes put, enjoyed 'just' jamming together, or 'only' played for their own enjoyment. The ritual of public performance – 'concerts', 'recitals', 'bookings', 'gigs', 'engagements', or whatever the chosen term – was the epitome of musical enactment.[4]

That this was not just an empty ideal was shown by the amount of time and effort put into organising performances and the number of performance events that took place. It was near impossible to find out exactly how many

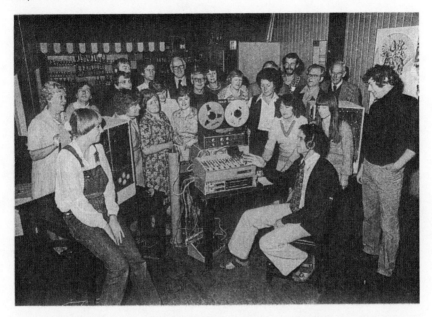

Figure 20 Mike Skeet of the local Whitetower studio records the Stratford Singers: nowa-days recording is one form of 'performance' made possible by the proliferation of small local studios

performance events took place within a given space of time within the Milton Keynes area, for they were often publicised among a limited circle of intimates, but hundreds were referred to each year in the advertisements, notices and 'What's on' notes in local newspapers.[5] To these must be added regular church services; musical societies; additional weekly or fortnightly entertainment at local pubs or social clubs; private occasions like weddings, dances, and PTA and other voluntary associations' annual socials; termly concerts at local music centres; and many many others, most known only to the participants. There were also certain seasonal high points when perfor-mances clustered in even larger numbers, among them the end of the educational year in late June/early July when many schools held perfor-mances, and, even more, round Christmas when just about every choir, school, and church had musical celebrations, when brass bands performed almost daily, clubs held socials, and local dramatic and operatic societies put on their shows. Musical rituals were thus not rare events, for throughout the year – and especially at such high points – they constantly punctuated the musical and social life of Milton Keynes.

From the viewpoint of the musical groups, too, the performance events they created both structured and crowned their musical activities. The main patterns have already been indicated, but the significance and amount of this for the groups themselves also needs stressing. A few groups did not go in for public performances, but most did and the number was quite extensive. Among the fifty small local bands interviewed, only a handful were currently taking no bookings, and about a quarter regularly put on performances once or twice a week on average (some as many as 150 times a year); this included bands from the different musical worlds of folk, jazz, country and western and the various forms of rock. It will be clear too from the earlier discussion that most classical and operatic groups had a yearly cycle of performances prepared through a succession of rehearsals, usually with at least one major production during the year and one or more lesser ones. Many, such as the Canzonetta Singers, put on far more, and church choirs regularly performed each week. Brass bands too had a busy programme of engagements, not just at the high point of Christmas when they might be out playing as many as 15 or 20 times but also throughout the year. Putting on a performance was *not* just something provided by outside professionals visiting the area or a rare event for local groups, but an accepted and practised part of local musical life.

The performance event was also regarded as an essential part of most local groups' activity. Just meeting to practise had an appeal, but the standard explanation was that it was preparation for a performance. The performance event, by contrast, was not regarded as needing explanation. Admittedly groups were pleased with applause or a fee, but these were pleasant additions: the central musical enactment, the performance, was its own justification. The shared subjective experience of performing was also part of the expectations of group music-making – an aspect left out in many sociological and musicological works, but of great significance to the performers themselves, clear to anyone either observing or participating in such performances. This was not true just of 'popular' music like jazz or rock either, for in classical music too – for all its stress on writing and theory – the practice of working up to a performance was central to the behaviour and self-image of the local musicians. This element also came out in explicit comments by performers – being 'high' during or after a performance, 'making music that people appreciate', 'a great way of expressing yourself', 'artistic expression'.[6] Unless questioned about it, however, people did not feel the need to explain why they should attach so much importance to working up to and taking part in the performance ritual itself – it was self-evidently justified.

Perhaps, then, a fourth should be added to the conditions for something to be a 'performance', at least in the sense of the 'performance events' focussed on here. Three conditions have already been discussed: mechanisms to frame the occasion as somehow apart, prior preparation by organisers, and the crucial presence of an audience, not just as passive recipients but as active and experienced participants themselves playing an essential role in constituting the occasion as a musical event. To these can now be added a fourth point – that the event was classified as, in some sense and under some locally understood concept, a performance event. In Milton Keynes such terms included 'gig', 'booking', 'recital', 'concert', 'engagement', and perhaps 'recording session'. In all these cases, people took it for granted that participation in these rituals was a fitting end in itself, a fundamental and unquestioned value – one central dimension of the enactment and evaluation of music as art that is totally missed by the only too common concentration on the purely textual aspects of music.

13

Composition, creativity and performance

It is commonly believed, especially within the classical music world, that all composers worthy of that name are either dead or (if alive) men of genius far removed from ordinary life. Even for cynics (or social scientists) who might question the absolute superiority of the accepted canon of 'great composers', it is still easy to assume that the composition of music is something specialised and esoteric, unlikely to be encountered among grass-roots musicians. It therefore came as a surprise to me to discover that musical composition was a quite common activity at the local level. This chapter is about some of the differing systems by which this took place.

The first is the well-known classical mode of prior written composition by an individual. This mode is assumed to be *the* natural form of 'composition' in most serious writing about music. It also fits conventional wisdom, not least because of the long association in western high art (both literary and musical) between *writing* and authorship. Whether this can any longer be taken as a necessary association has now become open to question even for literary works (see e.g. Chadwick 1932–40, Lord 1960, Finnegan 1977), and as this chapter will illustrate it is also not true of all musical composition. Nevertheless the classical model was a powerful and widely held one, in local as in national music, and it is thus reasonable to start with it.

In its extreme form, this high-art model assumes a canon of accepted composers, notably the 'greats' like Bach, Mozart, Beethoven or Chopin but also others, lesser known or more recent, who have become relatively accepted. Classical music consists of works by these individual composers in the sense that later musicians follow their written scripts with relatively little change. There is therefore a separation between composition and performance, a separation both in time (sometimes of many centuries) and in personnel: composers are the originators, performers merely the executants.

This was one common form in which local music was practised. Local choirs, orchestras, ensembles and individual musicians worked from written texts – known, revealingly, as their 'music' – which gave them the necessary directions for performing works by earlier composers. Among their obligations was to obtain this 'music', which they could then read and translate into performance. The annual cycles of the many classical groups and individuals, with their performances of Handel's *Messiah*, Brahms or Mozart symphonies, Bach suites and fugues, Beethoven quartets, madrigals by Orlando Gibbons, sonatas by Scarlatti or Schubert, religious music by Byrd, Vivaldi, Bruckner, or Albinoni, choral or orchestral works by Elgar or Vaughan Williams, and innumerable others, all followed this classical model of composition followed by, and separated from, performance. The most frequent performances were of works handed down in writing over generations or centuries, but there was also a sprinkling of twentieth-century works which were becoming assimilated into the same canon.

This model of written composition followed by later performance was most prominent in the classical music world. But it was also to be found, if in slightly different format, among the brass bands, where a band's store of printed music was one of its investments. Local operatic performances too often included music by such composers as Chopin, Schubert, Offenbach, Johann Strauss, and, of course (Gilbert and) Sullivan, all encapsulated in written scores. Much church and school music also fell within the same general model, performances from musical texts which had been laid down by others. It was on these works by earlier writers, then, that local practitioners drew for their material, a resource without which the activities of the many classical musicians and audiences could not have taken place.

But this simple, if widely accepted, model did not fully comprehend the actual practices of local musicians, even those in the classical world. For one thing, their actual performing involved much more than the blind reproduction of earlier scripts (a point to be returned to later). For another, musical composition in written form was not just the preserve of the dead and gone, but was still engaged in by many local musicians. This perhaps unexpected fact needs some elaboration.

Written composition at the local level took various forms. One intersected with the professional and national music world. This was by musicians commuting from local addresses to the London music colleges, for example, or the well-known John Dankworth, who, though based at Wavendon in the Milton Keynes area, functioned nationally and internationally rather than primarily through local musical networks. There were also a few cases where local groups, sometimes with the backing of the Borough of Milton Keynes, commissioned works by contemporary composers for a first performance in Milton Keynes, the professional Milton Keynes Chamber Orchestra being the leading exponents. In addition to such instances, however, written composition was also taking place in a more local and amateur context, usually designed in the first place for performance by local musicians of the kind discussed in this volume.

Contrasts and comparisons

There was more of this than might at first be imagined. The music teachers and advanced classical students in particular wrote their own works, sometimes getting little further than producing a manuscript, sometimes having them performed locally. Several musicians associated with local choirs or orchestras produced compositions for them, usually distributed in photocopied manuscript scores. The brass teacher Malcolm Crane, for example, wrote 'Festival fanfare' and 'Overture to a concert' for his youth wind groups, as well as the short 'One summer's evening' for his choir; John Dankworth, then the Hon. President of the North Bucks Music Centre, composed 'One horse shay' for the combined choirs and youth orchestras of the two local music centres; the well-known local teacher Harold Nutt produced a series of works for local school festivals; and there were many other similar examples. Such composition was extremely time-consuming (one composer complained that his work took over a year to compose, then lasted just 14 minutes in performance!). The separate parts also had to be written out by hand, legibly enough for the performers to read clearly and quickly: a huge task. Nevertheless several individuals did compose in this form, if often on a small scale to fit the practicalities of local performance. Others just wrote for their own satisfaction, a category sometimes tapped by the Composers Class in the annual Festival of Arts.

There was also a strong tradition of composing hymns and carols for local groups. One leading instance was the well-known Bletchley musician Mrs Trude Bedford, the organist and for many years choir director at the Spurgeon Baptist Church. Her choir was famous for its tradition of more than twenty years of putting on a carol evening each Christmas for which each year she composed a new four-part carol; some years the whole programme was of her own compositions. Her church had its own printed collection of 20 of her hymn tunes and others had been published in national collections but her main focus continued to be the local church choir, and, as she put it, what her own choir liked did not necessarily appeal to the publishing world. In 1981 one of the set choral works at the local Festival of Arts was her anthem 'The Miracle of Spring' and choirs had to apply to the organizers for photocopies of her beautifully written-out manuscript (figure 21).

Mrs Bedford was perhaps unique in the quantity and popularity of her output but the tradition of composition for religious occasions was still very much alive in the early 1980s. Several of the local clergy had written hymns for their services, while the minister at one Church of England/Baptist ecumenical church had composed three communion services, the Gloria being particularly popular with his congregation. The priest of a local catholic church had composed a series of metrical psalms and the local Salvation Army played recently composed songs by its members. The Trinity Church in the Woughton Ecumenical Parish printed its own *Trinity*

162

Figure 21 From Mrs Trude Bedford's manuscript of 'The Miracle of Spring', set piece for choirs at the local Festival of Arts, and one of the many hymns and carols she has composed

Songbook in 1984, a collection of 32 original songs and hymns with words, music and attractive cover by members of the local congregation. New carols were particularly widespread. A local carol competition sponsored by Volkswagen drew 19 entries in 1980, the winner being the Alex Campbell Middle School with 'Jesus in Jerusalem' (see figure 22). Among many other examples were the small school band of piano, xylophone, recorders and voices at Fulbrook Middle School who composed their own 'Follow the star to Jesus', while at a more sophisticated level (in classical terms) there was the carol for choir, piano, flutes and glockenspiels by Laurence Gillam, a senior pupil at one of the Bletchley comprehensive schools. This was performed at school concerts and in local Methodist churches by friends and fellow pupils, with the composer conducting from the piano.

Concerts at the local music centres and by music departments in the secondary schools also provided opportunities for performing new works, and over the years there was a regular scattering of works by local composers, including students. Local school music festivals were even more important. The yearly Middle School Music Festivals in Bletchley which brought together pupils from a dozen local schools and attracted audiences of hundreds of parents and friends regularly included choral and instrumental performances written by local musicians: a jazzy piece for two violins

Figure 22 Singing a new song: composition and performance. Prize-giving ceremony for a local carol-writing competition won by the Alex,Campbell Middle School

and double bass, for example, or 'Three country dances' for recorders. They also included large-scale works composed by local teachers which took up a large proportion of the concert, each performed by an orchestra of eighty or so middle-school children and a two hundred strong massed choir.

Musical plays were another common context for original composition. Here the extent of innovation was sometimes unclear, for when it was stated that, say, a school had written the musical they were staging, this could mean mainly new words to old tunes, supplemented by spoken dialogue; and even specially written music might well mean rearrangement or variation rather than totally new material. Nevertheless, the amount of composition in *some* sense was extensive, in at least some cases including music. School after school produced their own musicals every year, and even those who would have preferred a published version sometimes gave this up because of copyright costs and instead wrote their own. And local operatic societies and drama clubs regularly produced pantomimes which they had written.

The Stantonbury drama group with their specially written documentary plays on local historical themes were well-known instances of local composition. *Days of Pride*, for example, was a musical play based on local sources about Wolverton and New Bradwell between 1913 and 1918 which depended on the co-operation of many local musicians, both classical and folk. Much of the music was by the local musician Rod Hall, a primary teacher with classical training but a particular interest in traditional folk forms (and the creator of the posters shown in figure 13). The drama thus included such vocal and instrumental pieces as 'Song of the regiments', 'Brass band song', 'Song of the Stallard brothers', 'Do you remember England?', 'Rest and relief song', 'Hawtin's anabasis', 'Back home again', 'Suet pud gag' and 'Days of pride', all with music composed by Rod Hall, together with three 'traditional items arranged by Rod Hall' ('Washing day', 'Morris on' and 'Shepherd's hey (Armistice)'). Other music in the play was also by local songwriters: 'Song of the recruits', 'Dad's song', 'Violet's song', 'Khaki train song' by 'J.' Cunningham, and 'In memoriam', 'The parapet song', 'The valley of the shadow' and 'Who are the heroes, who are the cowards?' by Paul Clark and (jointly with 'J.') 'Bob a bloody day'. A list like this may seem bare to all but the enthusiastic audience at the play itself or listeners to the cassette made for local sale, but this one case indicates something of the extent of local composition for public performance.

The examples just mentioned are only some that I came across during my research; there were doubtless many others. The forms varied and perhaps included some which a purist might not consider 'truly original' in the highest sense – though of course the line between 'arranging' and 'original composition' is a shaky one, even for the 'great' composers. But even without the possibly marginal cases, it is clear that local compositions like those in Milton Keynes were far from irrelevant – as many might start by assuming – to the processes of composition in this country. Mrs Bedford's hymns, Rod Hall's songs, local church compositions, or the new cantatas for school concerts and music festivals were not written in the leading music schools or nationally known through publication or professional performance, but they were still concrete examples of the imaginative creation of original musical works in one long-recognised mode of composition: the writing down of new musical texts by an individual prior to, and separate from, its actual performance.

But this was not the only form of local musical composition. New musical items can also be developed during performance itself. This process has by now been well established for literary composition. It used to be assumed that the only way literature could be created was either in writing or – for non-literates – by word-for-word memorisation. However, research on oral literature has drawn attention to another form: composition-*in*-performance. Here the composer relies on a body of formulaic phrases, traditional themes, and well-known story patterns and poetic devices which enable him to compose on the spot – in a sense improvising, but from a familiar storehouse of material from which he can draw at will to fill up a line, complete a stage in the story or, as he feels appropriate for the particular audience he is addressing, lengthen or shorten or embroider or vary his exposition. There is no single correct text composed beforehand, for each exposition is a unique and authentic performance. The prevalence of this 'oral-formulaic' process in non-literate contexts has perhaps sometimes been exaggerated, but composition-in-performance is now accepted as one widespread mode of artistic composition (see, for example, Lord 1960, Finnegan 1977, chap. 3, Foley 1985).

The parallel with musical composition will be clear. Indeed some of the earlier writers about oral poetic performance started from an analogy with musical improvisation (as in Chadwick, vol. 3, 1940, pp. 181–2), while in more recent studies jazz has been taken to illustrate how what are in a sense 'new' works are created on familiar themes in performance (Middleton 1972, pp. 51ff, Ware 1976; cf. Baker 1969).

This composition-in-performance form could certainly be found in Milton Keynes. In the jazz bands, the basic themes and structures were well known to performers (and, at a less conscious level, to listeners), but the actual way they were realised on any one occasion was not laid down in advance. The players seldom used written music, and when they did it was as an *aide-mémoire* rather than a prescriptive score. The reactions of the players during and after playing also indicated their sense of creativity in that unique performance.

Local jazz players were quite explicit about his. Asked how far they performed 'original material', one band's players replied that 'everything the group does is original because we improvise and change standards'. Another band expressed it differently, saying they played little of their own material though their actual performance was 'very fluid – the numbers are practically made up on the spot', while the T-Bone Boogie Band reckoned that many of their numbers were 'improvised out of nowhere – we could go on all night'.

The emphasis on composition-in-performance fitted well with the jazz bands' working patterns, which contrasted to some extent with other small bands. All groups liked regular bookings at the same place – but jazz bands were the most successful precisely because their performances sounded new week after week. Indeed the mixture of creativity and familiarity was clearly of immense appeal to devotees, so that though there were relatively few jazz bands, those there were attracted enthusiastic followers prepared to go from place to place to hear their favourite group. For the same reason, it was easier for jazz than rock players to move between different groups, for they did not have to reproduce specific group-developed pieces, but performed on the basis of shared skills and of a store of tunes, musical structures and chord sequences. This too explained why jazz groups practised less regularly than other bands; for once the players had acquired the basic skills and got used to playing together, they could perform with relatively little rehearsal and allow visitors to join temporarily as 'guests'.

Jazz players valued this opportunity for individual expression, and contrasted the flexibility of jazz in performance with the constraints of both rock and classical music. At the same time, jazz composition was collective as well as individual – 'a team effort' – and, unlike both classical composition and the solo performance of individual artists, depended on the co-operation and shared expectations of a group. This composition-in-performance system, which meant textual variation and originality in *each* performance, was thus distinct from the other composition modes discussed in this chapter. It was neither better nor worse – merely different and appropriate to the practice of jazz musicians and their audiences.

There is also a third type of composition much used by contemporary musicians: the rock mode of collective prior composition. This is another distinctive and important form. It was also a remarkably prevalent one locally, for most of the many rock bands in Milton Keynes composed their own music.[1]

This was not prior composition in writing, for local rock bands did not work from written music.[2] Nor was it composition-in-performance on the jazz model, for despite the outward air of improvisation the items were worked out *beforehand* by the players. The actual process of composition was thus distinctive and yet settled enough to be familiar to rock musicians and their audiences. It could be labelled the 'prior-composition-through-practice mode'. Each term in this phrase needs some explanation, however, for this form may not be familiar to all readers, and it has relatively seldom been discussed in works on modern music (some recent exceptions are Bennett 1980 (on a rather different aspect), White 1983, Becker 1982, pp. 10–11).

This system of 'prior composition' is different from that of the classical model not just in being non-written but also because a piece is not by just one individual or fully worked out before being given to the players. Rather, it is developed through a series of practices by a whole group who then themselves perform it as their own joint composition. One member of the group usually starts it off by 'coming up with an original idea' – a snatch of tune, riff, theme, set of rhythms or chords, or (less often) a verbal phrase or verse. This is played or sung to the group and gradually worked up into a complete piece.

This process was very evident at a series of rehearsals I attended by the rock band Basically Brian. The keyboard player had brought along one of his songs which he played to the others, and provided skeleton chord charts. They played it through roughly then stopped to discuss how to change and develop it – should the intro be repeated twice? How could the chorus, verse and break be combined best? What should be the chord sequences just there? How about trying them this way (partial demonstration by one player) or those that way? How about trying this bit again with different percussion combinations? Was it all 'too E-minor-ish'? Then came another play-through, with the drummer trying out new developments, breaking off to discuss yet again and readjusting the electrical equipment. The rhythm guitarist was encouraged to 'do something special if he felt inspired', with the others giving him a cushion to take off from. Later they went on to other pieces with similar stops and starts: was it too 'jolly', needing 'sharpening up'? Would the bass be more effective playing a simple leisurely downwards scale rather than cluttering it with chords? Would the words sound better changed round? Was B minor or D minor more effective on the keyboard? Should the drummer play less forcefully just there or was it brilliant the way it was? Similar try-outs and discussions went on with all the pieces, for hours in all over a series of weekly rehearsals, resulting finally in a public performance at a local booking. The two main composers mostly took the leading roles in the discussion, but it was not a case of individuals directing a group but of creative participation by all four players, working out the piece collectively for joint performance.

This was not an isolated case, for almost all the bands stressed the collective and protracted process of developing their own material, at the same time often attributing responsibility for particular elements to named individual players. The basic pattern, together with its variations, can be illustrated from comments by the players on how they themselves perceived this: 'We develop the tune from the bass line – go over it together and improve it'; 'Brent usually gets the original idea and plays it to the band – they add ideas on'; 'At practices we always have ideas – we work on them together'; 'Gary and Tony write lyrics. The drummer's style is completely different, so what he contributes is also original composition'; 'Collectively. Wally usually gets an original idea [on the guitar] and others add words and the rest of the tune'; 'Improvise together – written by feel'; 'Sam composes a song, takes it to the band; they work on it together; when it's good enough they put it on a cassette'; 'At first from one member of the band, then the band fits lyrics round the idea'; 'Anita usually gets original idea – everyone adds ideas and modifies the song – collectively composed and learnt'. There were differences of detail, depending perhaps on the individuals and group dynamics of each band, but the recurrent theme was the collective develop-ment of ideas first generated by one or more of the players through actual playing rather than silent planning. The lyrics were sometimes written down at some stage, but it was more common to work them out in conjunction with the instrumental development, by ear and action rather than by eye.

This form of composition fitted in with various other characteristics of the rock world. The oral and active group learning mode, rather than the written forms typical of individual classical learning, meant that rock players were in any case used to working out their own contribution jointly with other players and independent of written texts. The regular practising typical of local rock bands also made sense, for since their performances consisted of their own material this had to be worked on beforehand (not improvised at the time); indeed rock bands who said they were not ready for public gigs were referring not so much to instrumental competence as to not yet having worked up enough original material in their practices. Developments in musical technology too had led to new opportunities for musical composition and performance. In the end, though, there may be no all-embracing *explanation* for this form other than to say that it had become accepted as the appropriate one for the type of music and of musical organisation that most rock bands in Milton Keynes (and doubtless elsewhere) were following in the early 1980s.

The exactness of repetition from practice into performance was not complete, for, as will be discussed later, *every* performance, whatever the composition mode, must involve some leeway for individual creativity. What was clear, though, was that rock players conventionally had much less freedom than jazz players to improvise in the notes and rhythms themselves – the musical 'text' by some definitions. Rock groups thus had to stay together to be successful, for if one member left it was difficult to perform publicly until a new player either had learnt the group's numbers or joined in creating new ones. Particular rock bands varied in their scope for individual variation in performance, not least according to the specific type of music they favoured. In general terms, though, the constraints on innovation in performance were stricter than might be expected from the common assumption that in non-written or popular performance there is *always* textual variation.[3]

Adherents of the other musical worlds – and of 'high culture' generally – commonly picture rock music as essentially derivative, passively taken over from the mass media, or else as disorganised and anarchic. The implicit contrast here is the classical model, with its stress on individual inspiration, long-considered composition, and written theory, against which rock music is seen as crude, collective, and not 'really' considered or original. It was clear in the local research, however, that to those personally involved, a band's own compositions *were* new and original, a contrast to the wearisome series of note after note characteristic of classical music. Certainly, rock music often made use of familiar and up to a point predictable musical structures, rhythms and chord sequences, and this very familiarity was part of its attraction; but exactly the same could surely be said of classical composition or jazz performance, where the beauty equally lies in the combination of the new and unpredicted with the familiar and expected. It would be strange too to dismiss as 'non-original' the many songs by local musicians *just* because they happened not to have been produced in writing or within the context of orchestral instrumentation or classical concert conventions. For the performance-orientated work of rock musicians the criteria of originality were necessarily different from classical music. Rather than the variation or manipulation of the formal structure of the piece, typical in classical composition, the development instead was closely tied to performance: 'in rock, the elaboration comes from inflections, notably of rhythm and of the manner of approaching and articulating notes, and from the importance placed on the highly personal timbres used by individual singers and instrumentalists' (Vulliamy and Lee 1982, p. 4). A band's originality arose from their development of such inflections first in joint practice and then in performance of their 'own material'.

The composers themselves, both bands and individuals, certainly regarded what they were doing as original. The bands' names, the song titles, the instrumental arrangements, the words of the vocals – all were part of the band's creativity and personal expression. The productions of some groups, certainly, were considered more effective than others. Local assessments varied too, and the music or players favoured by some were not necessarily popular with all. But it was abundantly clear that for the devotees and exponents of this form of music-making – the first-hand practitioners – composition and performance of the band's own numbers was rightly labelled as their own original work, indeed far more creative and personal to them than the well-worn tunes of jazz performance or handed-down works from the classics.

Most of these compositions were in the form of songs, and a quick list of some of their titles can give some indication of the many different subjects on which their creators wished to comment: 'The point of no return' or 'Total amnesia' (The Memories), 'Black boy, white boy' (Martial Law), 'There is no truth', 'Sex, drugs and chaos!' and 'Broken hero' (Scream and the Fits), 'Algiers 1957' and 'Alternatives to Majesty' (Ha! Ha! Guru), 'So much hate' and 'Get out and run' (Ice), 'The robot' and 'Thought of distortion' (Imperial Sunset), 'Struggle for me' (Lights Out), 'Armageddon', 'Try talking to me' and 'Infants of infinity' (Dancing Counterparts), 'Reflections' and 'Parodies' (Synonymous), 'Into the void', 'Searching for the word' and 'No bus on Sundays' (The Void). The performance as a whole was of course a musical rather than just a literary one, and sometimes the words were very sparse. As a local rock composer explained, if you have an important message in the lyrics then 'you don't need a great tune or accompaniment', while a complex instrumental piece can have simple lyrics – sometimes 'just nonsense really'. The words did not stand alone, for it was the way they were realised in actual performances that manifested even their formal qualities (rhyme and rhythm for instance), let alone their intended impact and meaning.[4] But even leaving out the music, the variety of the lyrics makes it difficult to dismiss them as merely the passive copying of ready-made matter. To the players and audiences they were creative ways of expressing their personal experience and insights in words and music.

Some further titles of songs and (in a few cases) instrumentals by local bands are listed below. These titles represent only *some* of the pieces composed by *some* of the rock bands working in Milton Keynes; and if one remembers the musical arranging and developing through practice after practice that had to go into each of these, it is evident that the amount of composition by local rock bands must have been immense. In contrast to the relatively isolated cases of classical composition – important as these were to those directly involved – the creation of original material by the recognised prior-composition-through-practice mode was a regular procedure by practically all the many local rock bands.

Some titles of original pieces composed and performed by rock groups
(mostly songs, a few instrumentals)

'Untold truth'
'Vengeance'
'Queen & country'
'Call the law'
'So this is Britain'
(Legion)

'Tone'
(Apollo)

'Pressure on our lives'
'I'm no frog'
'Strange cigarette'
'Secrets of your heart'
'Rock & roll dreamer'
(Basically Brian)

'I'm leaving you for another'
'I can give you everything'
'Wake up'
'Why? why? why?'
'Miles away'
(Bitza)

'Rectangle'
'Moody side of me'
(Corpse Corps)

'Josie'
'Fuck the Gazette'
(The Crew)

'They built the bomb'
'Just another hymn'
'Political violence'

'I have no gun, but I can spit'
'They kill dogs'
(Exit Stance)

'Whatever happened to Baby Jane?'
'Room in this choir'
'Algiers 1957'·
'Alternatives to Majesty'

'Cigarette Jim'
'Never more'
(Ha! Ha! Guru)

'It's all right'
(Herd of fish)

'Lady you're a fool'
'So much hate'
'All night long'
'Midnight stroll'
'Ice has melted'
'Get out and run'
(Ice)

'The robot'
'I saw'
'Mirror'
'Thoughts of distortion'
(Imperial Sunset)

'Nobody's there'
'Struggle for me'
'For always'
'Cinderella'

Contrasts and comparisons

'Natural born hooker'
'For you'
(Lights Out)

'United people'
(Malachi)

'Treading on thin ice'
'Diary'
'Black boy, white boy'
'Why do ya?'
'You – you are'
'Thoughts of you'
(Martial Law)

'The point of no return'
'Only you know (how it feels)'
'Warning signs'
'No go zone'
'Total amnesia'
(The Memories)

'Union Jack'
'Winning combination'
'Media murder'
'Electric avenue'
'Not what you thought'
'The in thing'
'Time for tomorrow'
(The Offbeat)

'Meridian'
'Inside these walls'
'Peace pledge'
'Woman'
'Moon Goddess'
(Rare Miranda)

'Trip to nowhere'
'Changes in my life'
'On the rocks'
'I want to make love to you'
'City Lights'
'Is that true?'
(Members of Rock Off)

'Tears of a city'
'63° below reason'
'Scarlett ribbons'

'Shoot'
'Rock & roll hero'
'Misguided fool'
(SNG)

'Let her go'
'Protest song'
'Do I?'
'You always lie alone'
'First love'
'What price a life'
(St Louis)

'The task'
'There is no truth'
'Killer'
'Broken hero'
'Sex, drugs & chaos'
'Fits'
(Scream and the Fits)

'In the past'
'Concert halls'
'Sick joke'
'Curb crawler'
'Space animals'
(Seditious Impulse)

'Sunrise'
'White lady'
'Morning light'
'The journey'
'Peace for a new age'
'Pathways'
(Solstice)

'Silverbird'
'Caverns'
'The vixen'
'Rowena'
'Joe's cafe'
'Scarecrow'
(Static Blue)

'Reflections'
'The bingo song'
'Parodies'
(Synonymous)

'Close your eyes'
'The game'
(The Tempest)

'Chicken run'
(Typical shit)

'Under the carpet'
'Kevin & Karen'
'Back in 69'
'Jenny'
'Walking in the park'
(Under the Carpet)

'Into the void'
'I want you'
'Searching for the word'
'Why do you keep on staring?'
'Living in stereo'
'No bus on Sundays'
(The Void)

'Look to the stars'
'Josie'
'Songs like these'
'Times remembered'
'Love you in the dark'
'Automatic clock radio'
(Members of Women's Band)

'Prime directive'
'Word love'
'Sleep'
'Horse & carriage'
'Armageddon'
'Try talking to me'
'Natural instincts'
'Infants of infinity'
'Pap'
(Dancing counterparts)

This, then, was the third main system of local composition. In contrast to the widely recognised classical or (by now) jazz modes, the rock form has been virtually ignored in discussions of musical composition. And yet this form of composition is widely practised – composition which takes place in a gradual and, in a sense, collective manner through active and prior practice, resulting not in a written text but in a joint *performance*. It needs to be recognised as one authentic system in its own right, rather than somehow inferior to, or an unsuccessful copy of, classical or jazz compositional models.

The central point, then, is the far-reaching differentiation between three equally authentic systems for composition. These differences link in with the other differing conventions between the musical worlds in terms of performance, transmission, training, and attitudes to copyright and to the nature of music. Against that background, however, there were also overlaps, for in practice elements from two or more modes sometimes combined in particular cases. The rest of this chapter comments briefly on some of these complications.

First, the significance of performance. While the concept of composition-in-performance was of course peculiarly applicable to jazz, something of this process was also evident everywhere. Music is a *performed* art – at least, this is the view assumed in this work – so its realisation therefore essentially depends on its performance by active individuals in actual situations. There was always some opportunity for performers to mould the music, though this varied according to the specific genre and its mode of composition. The greatest scope for performer input was in jazz, affecting the basic notation, length and instrumentation, but to a degree it was found in other traditions too. Rock music, despite its constraints, allowed *some* change by musicians in performance. As one rock musician said, 'I never play it the same twice', meaning not that the fundamental structure of the piece changed but that there could be differences in timbre, in decoration, in dynamics, techniques, intensity – points which might seem superficialities and yet greatly affected the final performance as actually experienced by both musicians and audience. And because in rock the music was essentially defined as the *performed piece* rather than the written script, even small variations of this kind could be crucial in the final product. Despite its real differences from the jazz mode, then, rock music too included some element of composition-in-performance. This also extended to the visual components of the performance – costume, lighting, dancing, the physical movements of the performers – and the reactions and participation of the audience (further elaborated in chapter 12). In both rock and jazz the emphasis on the music-as-performed made these aspects (which the classical musician might consider extraneous to the *music*) essential parts of the work in its full sense. In this sense too, then, part of the composition of a piece of music in both the jazz and the rock traditions came through the performance.

Classical music seems the odd one out, for the 'music' was pictured as formulated in the notated score, existing independently of its various contingent performances, in some sense 'out of time'. This ideology was a powerful one and affected both the perceptions and the actions of those within this world. And yet people's behaviour did not altogether fit with this ideal. After all in the classical tradition too, above all in its earlier forms, there *was* a certain freedom, even obligation, to adapt, interpret, or even change in some respects. Classical music too can be viewed as a performed art and in that context it is clear that the elements necessary for performance could *not* all be laid down in the conventional notated format. It is true that the basic notes and rhythms *were* (mostly) indicated in the written scores, together with some (incomplete) indications of dynamics or tempo, but they always demanded interpretation and supplementation according to the current powerful – if unstated – performance traditions (see, for instance, Schutz 1951, Ohmiya 1986, Darbellay 1986). And there were other elements too which either could not be represented in writing at all or were conventionally recognised as unwritten: the relative prominence of various parts and instruments, the timbre, the enunciation of the words, the intensity, and a host of similar points. Such aspects were well known to performers though infrequently put in words (the vocabulary in this area is, perhaps significantly, little developed within classical musicology). For performers a whole series of small decisions had to be made about (for example) the detailed exposition of the text, the numbers and blend of performers, whether words should be sung in the original or in translation, whether repetitions, even whole movements, should be omitted. This process, recognised or not, could have a large cumulative effect on the shape and impact of the work as actually performed. Here again there was arguably an element of composition in or leading up to performance. It was more circumscribed than for jazz or rock, but insofar as a musical work receives its full realisation in actual performance rather than in abstract non-performed script, this aspect unavoidably entered into the actual performances of classical compositions in local musical practice.

This runs counter to much received wisdom about composition in classical music, but will be familiar in *practice* to anyone who has taken part in classical rehearsals and performances. Certainly among the local classical music groups – choirs, orchestras, small ensembles – this aspect was a regular part of rehearsing and performing. It has often been pointed out that for jazz or rock written notation is inadequate for representing many characteristics essential to the performed work (see, for example, Middleton 1972, pp. 51ff., Vulliamy and Lee 1982, pp. 3 ff); the same basic point was also true of classical music, for though the written musical score might be taken as a major defining component of the piece (unlike rock or jazz) it did not and could not provide a complete delineation of it as performed, and much still had to be worked out by its performers. Paradoxically, then, understanding the contrasting modes of composition in their differing relations to performance brings out similarities which might not otherwise be obvious, above all the greater significance of creativity in actual performance, *even* in the classical mode, than our traditional respect for the charter of the score and the unchangeability of the written word normally allows us to recognise.

There were also a number of other ways in which musicians sometimes drew on elements from several composition modes for particular purposes. In jazz, for example, not all players relied on composition-in-performance in every piece. Some bands used written music to play standards by, say, Fats Waller, Gershwin, Duke Ellington or Count Basie, sticking more, or less, closely to the texts according to the nature of the band or performance. Others used written forms to recall *certain* elements of the music, like basic chording, tune, or words. Similarly rock musicians occasionally used music sheets for the compositions of others, or rehearsed with chord charts or lyrics written out by hand by one of the composer-performers, expecting to dispense with them in public performance. They might also take in a written list of the main numbers to be played, perhaps with some minimal direction (see figure 23). So rock and jazz players did not necessarily avoid written forms totally: they were just not the basis of their usual procedure and were used for only limited purposes.

There were also varying combinations in the classical world too. Classical performance typically depended on reading from written music, but there were exceptions and some performers played or sang by ear what others read from notated forms. This was especially so in operatic performances, for though these regularly consisted of works for which printed parts were available, some singers did not read music at all, or only did so with difficulty. There was the secretary, for instance, who at first learnt her parts by ear but gradually taught herself to sight-read, or the self-employed plumber who memorised his many roles by ear; he intended to stay that way too, and made the most of the oddities of printed music: 'What are all these little tadpoles swimming about?' The singers could not use their written parts in public performance, so that memorising was accepted as a necessity at some stage anyhow. Learning by ear was not uncommon in the many choral performances in schools (though adult choirs were more likely to cling to their printed copies). Playing or singing without music was also stressed by many who were perfectly prepared to read from written music in other contexts. This was especially so among folk musicians, often skilled in classical music but preferring to avoid what they saw as the rigidity of written parts. In fact 'folk music' as practised locally was an interesting blend of elements from the different composition modes. Sometimes there was heavy reliance on writing (some musicians going to great trouble to hunt out manuscript sources from folk archives); sometimes a group of players or singers worked out a performance from a remembered theme or dance tune to their own arrangements; and sometimes a soloist composed a song beforehand (perhaps written down, perhaps not), which then went on to circulate in an unwritten form through performances or recordings among singers other than the composer himself or herself. In some cases, a blend of all these modes could be found in a single piece.

The 'rock model' too had its varieties and overlaps. The commonest mode was certainly for a piece to be performed by those who had jointly contributed to its composition; but this was not invariably the case. A few rock bands performed numbers by others, learning them from listening to recordings, from song sheets (sometimes with chord charts), from the memory of one of the players, or in a very few cases from notated music. The different backgrounds were not necessarily distinguishable in performance (though bands often mentioned when they were playing someone else's composition) and still depended on joint practising and development, the difference being that the scope for innovation extended to fewer elements. Reproduction of pieces by others did not just apply to compositions by nationally famous composers. Several bands played pieces generated by just one of their members, originally composed at a time when they were playing in a different band. This was quite common when a new band included experienced rock players with their own material who wanted to

---

BASICALLY BRIAN.

HALLOWEEN DANCE October 31st 1981

Running Order

1. Careless Love (trad.)
   Scott first solo.

2. How High The Moon (?)
   Scott first solo.

3. Scott's Waltz (Forest)
   George solo first eight bars; no theme; John Close
   first solo; theme stated at end.

4. And I Love Her (Lennon-McCartney)
   intro leading to theme; John Close phaser pedal on
   theme; Scott first solo; repeat intro at end.

5. Norwegian Wood (Lennon-McCartney)
   2 choruses leading into jam in A major/minor;
   restatement of theme at end.

6. A La Mole Towards C Sharp (Close)
   Scott first solo; John Close solo leads into
   George solo followed by general collapse.

7. Home Brew Phase Two (Corfield)
   John Carter/ George start quietly on A. John Close
   phaser pedal on theme, then first solo.

8. Waiting for a Bee (Close)
   General melee; George takes all breaks. Finish on
   cry of "Change!"
9. Basically Brian (Close)
   John Carter/ George start on C;theme, then Scott
   solo, John Close solo then repeat theme with last
   line repeated several times till "Last Time!".
   Big ham ending.

Personnel;   Scott Forest (sax)
              John Close (piano)
              George Corfield (bass)
              John Carter (drums)

Figure 23 Running order for a local gig: Basically Brian

move quickly into public performance without waiting to develop every-thing from scratch. Another practice was to take over a piece by another local band. Thus Static Blue had as part of their repertoire two songs 'written by friends' in Rare Miranda: 'Moon goddess' and 'Inside these walls'. Because of the rock music tradition of relatively faithful reproduc-tion, once the pieces had been taken into their repertoire, the processes of practising and performing were not ultimately so different from the repeated reproduction of their own compositions.

Another area of overlap was in individual versus group contribution. On the face of it, there was a clear contrast between the classical form of *individual* originality (introspective and distanced from performance), the jazz form of individual creativity developed in interaction with others in live performance and, finally, rock composition, collective decision-making in the process of actual playing. This was true, but needs some qualification. In the local context composing on classical lines was quite often directed to performance by known players or singers and in consequence sometimes involved modification in the light of the performers' capacities and of how it sounded when actually tried out. In jazz, even given the general outlines of composition-in-performance, the structure and details of a performance – and thus of scope for individual creation – were more, or less, flexible according to the music, occasion, piece, and the band's general policy and make-up. Composition in rock music too could rest more on individual and long-considered composition than the contrast between rock and classical models might seem to suggest, for though the regular pattern was for a band to work on a preliminary idea, how that original idea was first generated and how fully worked out it was by the composer varied considerably. Sometimes a piece was already well on when it was first brought to the band, so that the individual process by which the composer had worked on it beforehand was not so very different from classical composition. In other cases, the initial idea was more rudimentary – just a snatch of words or a drum riff, say – so that the contribution by the other players was relatively greater, right up to the extreme case where, as the members of Typical Shit put it, 'We make a noise till we like it, then do it again till we do it right.' Even there, however, individual creativity was still of the essence in that each member of a small band had to put in his or her own contribution, and the composition as it was finally worked out ultimately rested on the input of individuals working together.

It would be over-simple, then, to regard the three main modes of composition-performance as always mutually exclusive. One and the same musician or group could use more than one, and even for those who mainly worked within just one world, elements of the others might from time to time come into their actual music-making. One advantage of distinguishing these three main modes, then, is that it brings into sharper focus not only their differences but also the ways in which they overlap and mutually enrich each other.

The other benefit in recognising these three contrasting models is that it clarifies the different ways in which local musicians in fact create their own original music. When only one mode of composition is held in mind – often the widely revered classical model – it is tempting to speak, as some have done, of the 'passivity' of the population or the lack of originality of the youth. But once one understands the validity of these *differing* systems for creating original music, each autonomous in its own terms, it becomes clear that there is indeed a remarkable amount of musical creativity at the grass roots. In all forms of music, but perhaps most strikingly of all in the prior-composition-through-practice of rock groups, the local musicians are quite consciously and deliberately among the modern-day musical composers.

14

Plural worlds

Local music, it will now be clear, is not just unrelated individual events, but structured in a series of differing musical worlds. These worlds, further, are themselves both divided and united by a number of systematic, if sometimes unappreciated, conventions for organising the learning, performance and creation of music.

So far I have described these local music-making practices in terms of contrasting 'musical worlds'. This chapter, however, opens up the question of whether these worlds between them cover all aspects of the local practice of music, and if not, what has been left out. This in turn leads to some reconsideration of the costs and benefits of this central idea of 'musical worlds' in preparation for the discussion in the second half of the book.

Among the merits of adopting Howard Becker's seminal concept of differing art 'worlds' is that it points us to the sustained and systematic notion of what otherwise might look haphazard and individual. Equally important, it gets us away from the idea that there is just *one* way in which music can and should be enacted – an implicit assumption that has bedevilled much writing on music and art. It turns out that even in one quite small town there are indeed many different forms. These are not random variations, furthermore, but established systems that are taken for granted within their own particular social settings. What is right and natural in one world is not necessarily so in another, and it is when criteria appropriate for one are applied to another that misunderstandings appear.

This part has therefore explored how these differences are exhibited in a range of interrelated conventions: the forms of practising, performance and audience behaviour, and their relation to composition and originality; the modes of recruitment and learning; venues, conditions and audiences; the relative significance of written and unwritten forms; and the expectations that individuals hold for themselves and others about what counts as 'music'. What is beautiful or absorbing within one world seems uncreative in another: just a boring series of 'so many notes strung together' or 'dreadful' or 'mindless' (to quote some local comments about *others'* musical worlds), or maybe just 'noise', even a 'nuisance' leading to lawsuits. Conflicts take place between teachers and pupils over the 'right' way to play – how much improvisation around written notation is acceptable, for example – or between audience and performers about, say, the volume or instrumentation. Certainly there are also some underlying similarities, but overall the main impression from this first look at local music is of the *diversity* of different musical worlds, each with its own organised standards and participants.

This plurality of equally authentic local musics is thus one major conclusion of this book. But by this stage it may be becoming apparent that such a summary of the practice of local music also needs some qualification. For though it is illuminating to present musical activities as mutually exclusive worlds, this metaphor cannot be taken literally.

For one thing, despite the real contrasts, these 'worlds' are not totally self-contained. In Milton Keynes people tended to operate mainly within just one, if for no other reason than limitation of time, but there was a scattering of individuals who belonged to more. Brass band players often played for operatic performances, in classical or jazz concerts, or even – though less often – in rock bands. Some musicians began from learning in the classical mode, then switched to rock, jazz or folk, while a few became interested in classical or operatic music after earlier involvement with rock. A few regularly played in a variety of musical styles and became involved in the social activities and groupings that went with these without necessarily finding this stressful or feeling the 'pull between two worlds' that has become a cliché in other contexts. Some worlds were more open to overlapping membership than others: classical, operatic and brass flowed easily into each other, unlike, say, rock and classical (though there were a few surprises). In some areas of music, interactions in style or membership provided for new musical development, as with folk/rock, jazz styles within classical models, or the meeting of jazz and rock. Operatic performances drew on a wide range of musical styles and performers, especially in the musical dramas based on local history, and there was particularly lively interchange between jazz, folk and classical music under the influence of the Wavendon Allmusic Plan, set up by John Dankworth and Cleo Laine. Musicians in these contexts were often particularly aware of the contrasting expectations in different traditions and of some of the consequent problems – getting appreciative and knowledgeable audiences, for example. But at the same time these less usual combinations were forms through which individuals and groups could in a sense create their own musical worlds through the innovative blending of several traditions.

The musical worlds thus to some extent interpenetrated one another. Their boundaries were shiftable – and were shifted – by their participants even if for the most part and for most musicians they were taken as given. The musical worlds were thus in practice more relative, changing and subject to their participants' individual pressures than the earlier exposition might have implied.

The presentation so far might also seem to imply that only a limited number of musical worlds operated in Milton Keynes, so that an account of classical, operatic, jazz, brass, folk, country and western, and rock and pop music necessarily covered all the significant forms of musical activity. This would be unjustified. Certainly these were all relatively large and visible traditions in terms both of the numbers of their local participants and (in many cases) the scale of their organisation, often linking into wider national institutions. But there were also local musical activities which did not possess all these features. The music in the old people's clubs,[1] for instance, did not fit neatly into those discussed already but was still important to those concerned – singing old favourites round the piano or joining in with visiting artists who specialised in this kind of musical evening. Scattered and small-scale as these performances were, they still shared many of the characteristics of the musical activities already discussed, in their emotive links with a whole host of musical and other associations, and their symbolic value for the participants. Perhaps it is only subjective evaluation not to include all this as one musical world? Or again, take music that sometimes cropped up in local events without exactly fitting into any of the earlier 'worlds': the performances of 'Old Time Music Hall' or variety concerts (very popular from time to time in a whole range of contexts), musical evenings at local Women's Institutes, where 'Jerusalem' was still regularly sung, pub pianists playing a range of light music, or church bell ringing – once again, perhaps not 'worlds' in the earlier sense but no doubt often of deep meaning for those involved.

Other local activities outside the worlds discussed so far were more structured. The dance schools made up another kind of world or worlds (ones not unrelated to music). So did the local radio station, with its fluctuating fortunes in the early 1980s, supported by a group of local volunteers, many of whom were extremely knowledgeable about popular music of various kinds and in touch with the local performing groups as well as recorded music. Again, some local associations organised their activities along similar lines to those in some of the musical worlds already presented. The local branch of the Royal Scottish Country Dancing Society, for example, or the Milton Keynes and District Pipe Band co-operated with various other musical organisations in Milton Keynes without falling fully into any of the worlds described earlier – another instance of the unsettled and relative boundaries of such 'worlds'. The Milton Keynes Organ Society was another vigorous group. It met regularly once a month to hear guest organists and possessed two organs of its own: for its participants a focus of continuing satisfaction, but relatively unknown to non-participants. Here and in similar cases it might seem stretching the term to speak of 'worlds', and yet in view of the participants' own perceptions and their links with some wider traditions, there might seem to be an almost infinite multiplicity of differing worlds of music: some well established and highly visible locally, like those selected for discussion earlier, others smaller (in their local representation anyway) but perhaps of equal value for their members.

This leads to the further important point that it would be misleading to envisage musical worlds and musical activities as fully contained within Milton Keynes itself. But of course no town in Britain is *only* local, isolated from the wider region, country, or civilisation of which it forms part. It will already be clear, for example, that brass bands, classical music groups and folk clubs were also linked to institutions outside Milton Keynes. So too were aspects of the 'amateur'/'professional' interaction, while the ideologies and conventions associated with the various musical worlds were clearly more than purely local manifestations.

These wider interactions came out in different ways in the different musical worlds. For classical, brass band, operatic and to some extent folk music there were national organisations which facilitated communication, general support, shared events and (in some cases) financial redistribution among the various local groups within a formal bureaucratic framework.[2] Relationships with the national organisations in these forms of music were often an accepted part of local societies, though perhaps not always as central to local activity – or as friction-free – as the top–down view from the national headquarters often assumed. In the more 'popular' musical worlds, formally organised extra-local associations were less conspicuous. The Musicians' Union, despite their drive for members, did not have much influence, and if there were other national groupings they had relatively little *local* significance. Not a few bands did have national ambitions, however (even if not always realistically), unlike most local classical amateurs. National or regional publications were also important, like the *New Musical Express, Country Music Round Up* and *Melody Maker*, all on regular sale in local stationers, as well as those with a limited circulation to subscribers only or distributed through local clubs, like the regional folk or country and western magazines. Such publications were followed not just by readers interested in national events and leading bands but also for information relevant for local fans and performers such as announcements of local events, advertisements, regional round-ups, and reviews of recent performances.

Competitions or festivals were another way in which local groups or individuals participated in a wider musical context outside the local world. Some of the glamorous competitions like the BBC's 'Young Musician of the Year' competition in the classical music tradition or the more broadly based

National Festival of Music for Youth as well as other more regionally based ones all began with heats involving local players and organisers, while in the brass band world there were the national contests conducted through regional heats, as well as regional competitions including one in Milton Keynes itself. Other competitions too had local links. There was the informal opinion poll on the best country and western music clubs in the region, for example (the local one came out highly), a local choir's successful visit to the Eisteddfod, the Hamilton Taverns 'Pub Entertainer of 1981' contest with heats in the local pubs, or the *Melody Maker* 'Rock 80' national contest, won by a local band. Occasions, such as these – remembered and noted when local groups were involved – could have a big impact on the self-confidence and sense of identity of local performers and their followers.

The same applied to local concerts by visiting professionals and national music events reported in the press or broadcast on radio or television. Such performances could set the standards and fashions for local players. Together with the constant output through both recordings and broadcasts, these obviously affected people's assumptions about their own and others' music and the development of local and semi-local counterparts to some of the more publicised national performances or recordings. The national framework thus affected local groups and players, but once again the influence was not just one way and there was also a sense in which the large national and commercial interests were themselves dependent upon the grass-roots musical tradition.[3]

Musical activities outside the area were also important for those who travelled outside Milton Keynes or came to the area for the first time, given the existence of accepted musical models more or less shared throughout the country. Thus folk music enthusiasts could feel 'at home' in their familiar world *wherever* they went into a folk club, and many carried a folk club directory for that precise purpose whenever they travelled. Again, brass or jazz players often felt they knew the ropes well enough to 'go along for a blow' when they went to a new area, while newcomers could insert advertisements in local papers for co-players in some specified form of music in the knowledge that if and when they met together they would have some shared understanding. Similarly a suitably experienced visitor from another area (or even country) could be asked to conduct a local choir for one evening without raising too many problems of differing expectations, just as new recruits who had sung in choirs before slipped easily into the accepted rehearsal and performance routines. Local musical groups and activities, for all their loyalty and in a sense uniqueness, were also in one way merely local manifestations of more widely existing patterns throughout the country.

These wider links, then, were important aspects of local musical practice. Musical worlds, in other words, were bound into complex relationships with a series of institutions and patterns outside the city. In addition, the existence of wider groupings and ideas *outside* as well as inside Milton Keynes meant that even a small active group of musicians – making little impact within the city – might be a local offshoot of an organised and self-conscious world to which local participants related but which was mainly manifested outside Milton Keynes. Regarded in this way, the local organ or pipe band societies mentioned earlier could indeed be regarded as representatives of wider musical worlds for all that their local adherents were relatively few: yet another possible addition to the local worlds.

There were also other instances (not mentioned so far) where music was practised in both a local and a wider setting. One of the most prominent was the world of Irish music. Here there *was* something of a substantial local grouping, and there were said to be around 9,000 Irish people in Milton Keynes in the early 1980s.⁴ Some spoke of them as a 'community', but they were really linked by shared but intermittent cultural or religious interests rather than permanent local or political allegiances. Several of the Catholic churches had substantial Irish congregations, sometimes manifested in celebrations like the St Patrick's Day Mass organised by the Milton Keynes Irish Society at Our Lady of Lourdes in 1981, with the local Erin Singers leading the hymns. There were also two locally based Irish societies which formed the setting for some of the structured musical activities in the area. One – the Green Grass Social Club described in chapter 17 – put on regular Irish music every week, while the Milton Keynes Irish Society was founded in 1980 to 'foster and promote all aspects of Irish culture in the Milton Keynes area' in a non-political and non-sectarian context, concentrating on 'Irish traditional music and song, dancing and drama', with special emphasis on the music. By mid 1981 the society had built up a steady membership of about 200 and was running several events a year – concerts by visiting bands, 'musical evenings', ceilidhs and dances, with the usual mix including at least some audience participation in the music. Their all-female choir, the Erin Singers, met once a week and performed at Irish occasions, specialising in Irish music. In all these activities, the definition of 'Irishness' was almost always in terms of music (or music-with-dance), and it was this rather than any distinctive local community or shared political stance that linked an otherwise disparate population. Music experienced as 'Irish' led not only to enjoyment and conviviality but also to a shared image of the people involved as participants in a wider and valued tradition.

The same point could be made for other cultural groupings in Milton Keynes, many less organised than the Irish, but to a degree maintaining contact with some outside cultural and musical world: the Bletchley Edelweiss Club, with its evenings for Austrian, Swiss and German music, the Milton Keynes Welsh Society, or the Hindu Youth Organisation of Milton Keynes that celebrated the Diwali festival in December 1982 with artists

Figure 24 Dragon Dance to celebrate the Chinese New Year, performed outside the Peartree Bridge Centre

from Milton Keynes, Luton and London. The strong Italian community too had several associations as well as regular services by a visiting Italian priest at one of the local Catholic churches, singing Italian hymns. There were also groupings that were sometimes referred to as local communities: 'ethnic' groups by some definitions. There were 32 Vietnamese families in Milton Keynes by early 1984, for example, more closely linked than the scattered and in practice very English 'Irish' community, and in consequence with ties not so limited to just *musical* interests. Music played a part in their shared cultural values, for the group included an acclaimed musician in Vietnamese circles and met from time to time for musically decorated festivities like the Chinese New Year celebrations with dragon and drum beat (see figure 24). Other relatively recently arrived groups of Asian origin were particularly drawn together by their religious ties: the small Buddhist group associated with the Peace Pagoda, or the rather larger Sikh community, each with its own musical traditions. The largest was the Muslim population, amounting to perhaps 2,000 in all, centred particularly in Stony Stratford and the Bangladeshi community round the mosque in Duncombe Street in Bletchley.

It would be exaggerated to portray all these as necessarily constituting either self-conscious 'ethnic communities' or 'musical worlds' on any but an occasional or situational basis. But they cannot be entirely omitted, since

Figure 25 The Milton Keynes Pipe and Drum Band marching to the annual Remembrance Ceremony in Bletchley

these events did provide links into some wider musical and cultural worlds, even if manifested only from time to time by people in Milton Keynes. Music among these groupings had nothing of the widespread visibility in Milton Keynes generally that was characteristic of, say, rock music or the brass band world. Nevertheless to those concerned their musical traditions were equally real, in some cases perhaps the more valued amidst what in some respects was otherwise an alien culture. Certainly the quality of the experience or the intensity of participation cannot be assumed to be less just because there were fewer participants than in, say, Western classical music, or because they were less reported in the local newspapers.

Were these too 'musical worlds' like those in earlier chapters? Most scarcely seem comparable in view of the small numbers (of both individuals and activities) involved, and the relatively minor role sometimes often played by music compared to other ties. And yet their participants might retort that the same could be said for the 'classical music world' which, though not everyone takes an active part in it, is so often just *assumed* as an unquestioned part of our culture; the same for the active folk musicians – small in absolute numbers despite their effective public relations. And if a relationship to national or international art traditions outside the city gives a group some claim to be regarded as partaking in a wider musical world, many of these cases certainly qualified. Indeed it could be argued that when we come to the Asian musics in Milton Keynes we have returned once more, after our long excursus among popular musics, to the world of high art. For each of these Eastern musics linked with and represented a long and self-conscious tradition of musical learning as established and sophisticated as the Western classical world with which this presentation of Milton Keynes musics started.

This leads back once more to the problematics of the term 'world' for describing local musical activities. Certainly the concept has the essential role of reminding us that different musics can be treated as equally valid forms, not to be judged by the criteria of others. Rock is not failed classical music, nor is the behaviour of country and western audiences 'wrong' because it is different from listening to organ playing in church. The concept of 'world' too alerts us to the way the system can outlast the rise and fall of particular groups or individuals, and that music is not just a question of pure art *works* produced in a social vacuum but of collective activity by people working in co-operation and sharing certain artistic conventions – points so well exemplified in Becker's work (e.g. 1974 and 1982).

But this image can have misleading implications as well as useful insights. Becker did not intend his 'art worlds' as concrete and bounded realities: indeed he stresses that they do *not* have clear boundaries around them, that they vary in their independence, and that people can be members of more than one such 'world' (especially 1982, pp. 34ff). But since the term 'world' somehow suggests something rather concrete and coherent, with some sort of absolute and perhaps large-scale existence, it is worth stressing that the term itself does not automatically prove a clear-cut and unambiguous reality and that there are several *different* senses in which musical practices can be seen as forming 'musical worlds'. In some cases it is a large number of people spending a great deal of time on music in a highly visible way with clearly established conventions and ideology (brass bands, for example); in others relatively infrequent meetings by a small group of people (say, the Milton Keynes Organ Society) but very keen for all that and linking with wider interests outside the locality; and in yet others, like the Vietnamese musicians, represented by only a tiny handful of local participants and yet fitting into a venerable tradition in international perspective. Thus some worlds are manifested by people actually living and interacting on the ground at a local level, others by largely symbolic ties linking them into more widely recognised conventions seldom realised in practice in the local setting. Structured musical activities always mean some joint organisation and shared symbols, but in a given locality or situation not all 'worlds' are equally concretised.

Similarly, the suggestion of autonomy about the term 'world' has to be approached carefully. It is a helpful starting point to disabuse us of ethnocentric evaluations, but it will be clear from the examples already given that musical worlds in Milton Keynes overlapped or interpenetrated each other in complex ways. Furthermore they also depended on non-musical elements 'outside' as well as 'inside' these worlds – not just the national associations but also the various patrons and networks to be treated later. The concept of 'world' too gives the impression, however much this is denied, of an all-including framework dominating the lives of those within it. This notion had some truth, but most participants had many other links or interests and it is worth remembering again that (unlike the professional jazz players studied by Becker (1951)) most of the musicians in this study were more amateurs than professionals. In every case the local participants entered into many other worlds besides the musical ones focussed on here.

The concept of 'world' does not have to imply coherence, either, but because it is a common connotation of the word it is worth commenting again that none of the musical worlds discussed was *totally* consistent in either musical style or people's social expectations. Many were far from harmonious, and the rather static impression given by the term 'world' was often belied by the changes in personnel and conventions over time.

A 'world' somehow sounds large too. In terms of numbers of people and/or historical depth, some certainly were. But, as in some examples earlier in this chapter, some groupings and activities were large in neither sense – and yet to the participants shared many of the other features of what have been counted as musical worlds elsewhere, so that it is hard to deny them the same term. But then one reaches the position that even the smallest groups or sets of shared activities (even one person perhaps?) form a kind of 'world' – a not unreasonable conclusion, no doubt, but not quite the collective shared social action that was one of the attractions of the concept of 'world' in the first place.

A further difficulty is the way the term can shift between referring primarily to the *people* involved in certain musical activities and a particular musical *style* (often accompanied by its own conventions about, for example, performance, composition or expertise). It is tempting to move between the two and conclude that what is a world in one respect necessarily is in the other. That it often tends to be so is one of the interesting findings about musical 'worlds'. But one cannot just assume this, and many of the misleading generalisations in studies of music have come from confusing the two. It is unjustified, for instance, to conclude that because certain music can be labelled 'rock' or 'jazz' *all* those who play it are the same kinds of people or necessarily know each other (the basis, for example, for the misconceptions about rock as a working-class 'counter-culture' discussed in chapter 10). This is a confusion to which I am aware that my use of the concept of 'musical world' in this part could lead,[5] so let me re-emphasise that the activities presented under this head, though certainly with enough coherence in musical convention and social interaction to make it reasonable to label them as 'worlds', were in practice without definitive boundaries, the fruit not just of accepted tradition but also of changing and individually selected action.

Even used with care, therefore, the term 'world' becomes difficult to apply without the implications of coherence, concreteness, stability, comprehensiveness and autonomy that tend to cluster round it. The flexibility and relativity of local musical systems – the very characteristics so well illuminated initially by the concept of 'world' – eventually get obscured if the term is pressed too hard. Parts 4 and 5 thus mainly move away from the terminology of 'musical worlds', and the somewhat static view that this perhaps implies, to concentrate on some of the processes by which people in a sense 'trod out their musical pathways'. This complementary metaphor highlights not only the personal element in people's musical activities but also the active and time-consuming *work* needed to maintain and recreate even the established conventions of the 'worlds' discussed in this part, let alone the innovations.

The final point is to stress again that in the limited sense in which the metaphor of 'musical world' is meaningful, there is a *plurality* of such worlds in local music-making. In principle perhaps there are an infinite number, and arguably more than just the 'main' ones elaborated in Parts 2 and 3. To a degree, these worlds do indeed represent separable and clearly structured musical conventions and personnel, which we need to understand to appreciate the often hidden system behind local musical practices. But they are at the same time relative, shifting and situational, dependent on individual action and creation as well as on externally established convention.

4

The organisation and work of local music

This part moves away from the description and comparisons of distinctive musical worlds to some more general questions. Case studies from the grass-roots amateur groupings of Milton Keynes musicians are still used for illustration, but the concentration is now on the social contexts and problems that to some degree or another run through local musical practice whatever the particular musical world. These illuminate such questions – not so far treated – as the general ways local musical activities are organised, the contribution of institutions like the church or the state, the support and patronage system, and how it is that local music continues year after year after year.

15

Music in the home and school

Cutting across the musical worlds discussed earlier are the settings in which music is regularly performed and organised, some common to most or all of these worlds, some associated particularly with just a few. Some will be obvious from the discussion so far – the halls in which concerts or rehearsals take place, the recognised music and leisure centres, or (to be discussed in chapter 20) the music shops – but others demand more explicit consideration. The home, school and church, as well as the local pubs and social clubs, serve as more than just the physical *places* for music-making, for they also provide a complex of expected roles and opportunities for music. Music does not just happen 'naturally' in any society, but has to have its recognised time and place, its organisation of personnel, resources, and physical locations. It is thus worth drawing attention to some of the institutions which invisibly underpin musical practice in our society in the 1980s, the contemporary counterpart to other similar – but in detail different – arrangements in other cultures or at other historical periods.

It is part of conventional wisdom to recall the supposed golden age of 'Victorian music-making' with its instrumental ensembles and family sing-songs round the piano, contrasting this with a modern family life which leaves no room for active music-making, with its 'canned' music via the mass media and the breakdown of family-centred leisure. Judging by the findings on Milton Keynes in the 1980s, there have indeed been relevant changes in the social and the physical structure of domestic life, but as far as music is concerned the generalised and negative form in which this is often put gives a misleading picture. The reality was more complex and more interesting.

The first point is that homes *varied* not only in composition (for it is worth remembering that not all were made up of the assumed 'norm' of two parents with dependent children) but also, more central to our subject, in their musical involvement. In some homes there was little or no active participation in music, and the conventional model above may partially apply. In others, active music-making was an accepted part of family life, often a crucially important if hidden background for the more public musical activities described in this book.

The more musically active homes are discussed later, but first some comment on the 'unmusical' ones. Whatever the detailed changes it would seem that active processes of the greatest relevance to the continuity and maintenance of music were still taking place within local homes.

This applied above all to the initial socialisation that all children receive as part of their general acquisition of the culture in which they grow up. In music this must include both an appreciation of what sounds are classified as 'music' (something learned, not absolute) and some understanding of the kinds of melodies, harmonies, rhythms or performances expected and familiar within one or more of the accepted musical worlds. Hearing sounds *as music*, or as particular kinds of music, does not just 'happen', so there has to be some mechanism through which children learn these skills. While it is true that nowadays this may involve electronic media and pre-recorded music rather than learning songs 'at the mother's knee', the process is still primarily initiated within the home. Small and not so small children consistently hear music from television, radio or tapes/cassettes/discs, and learn to classify and to respond to it as in some sense musical – a process of the utmost importance for our continuing and changing musical culture.

It may be argued that this is often just music as 'background' and that this cannot therefore be 'real' musical education. But that is to apply just one model of music, for (as described in chapter 12) there are other accepted modes of audience reception than that of the intense and *outwardly* 'passive' classical model. In some homes, children did learn that classical convention; in others, they learnt other skills instead (or as well), not necessarily on the conscious level but still deeply engrained in their musical experience, through coming to appreciate particular patterns of movement, verbal response or critical assessment which laid the foundation for later listening or performing. Without this, a whole range of popular music would lack the musically aware public on which it draws. In other words, musical education in Milton Keynes (as elsewhere) was not just a matter of formal teaching or of learning the accepted classical skills, but also extended to socialisation into many different musics and learned responses to those musics. For all these aspects, the home, despite so many changes in detailed patterns, was still one major centre.

This informal musical education to some extent continued through all age groups. One of the differences, however, from earlier home-based music was the greater choice of musical styles, for though some speak of all mass-distributed music as equally 'pap', young people at least were often highly discriminating within different forms of music. Technological devices, furthermore, have led to opportunities for *individual* (rather than family) selection, and local teenagers spent hours listening to playing after playing of their favourite recordings: quite apart from the opportunity this gave for instrumental self-teaching (of which more later), this intensive listening could result in great expertise on their chosen forms of music. Changes in living arrangements during this century have some relevance here. Many more homes now have heat and light throughout the house, with more opportunity for both privacy and the pursuit of individual interests, so young people who rejected their parents' musical styles did not necessarily have to go outside to find alternatives, but could withdraw to another room and have access to different forms through recorded music. Thus though the specific opportunities, the technology and the detailed musical styles were different from those of the past the home still remained one major setting for informal musical learning and experience.

In some homes more active music-making took place. Such households were doubtless in the minority, but for those involved their home experience was of great significance, connected too with the hereditary trend in music which surely relates to the learned patterns of early socialisation and life-long habitude as much as to genetic predisposition. In 'musical' households this early socialisation went beyond implicit absorption. The knowledge of parental musical interest or performance provided early models for young children, reinforced further as they grew up. Active instruction was some-times an additional factor. One common pattern was for one or both parents to teach children nursery rhymes and songs in the early years, then to move on to help them with instruments, especially recorders – often started at home – or, for families within the brass band world, brass instruments. Parental support for the many other musical activities which some children developed as they grew up also played a crucial part. Their facilitating of instrumental practice at home, joining in playing or singing, and providing material resources all laid foundations for people's musical pathways later in life.

Homes were also the *location* for musical activities and their related resources. They provided the storage place and, in some cases, the finance for buying and maintaining some of the necessary physical equipment, from small items like sheet music and music stands (essential for some music) to the instruments themselves. Perhaps chief among them was the piano, once the symbolic instrument for family music and still, for all the current alternatives, an accepted item in a very large number of homes. Other instruments too were often around or easily acquired in the musical homes, and this presence of instruments was itself an encouragement for younger members to take one up, adding yet another strand to hereditary tendencies in music. Some households built up a store of sheet music over the generations: a further resource and sense of continuity for budding musicians within the family, above all in the classical tradition.

The musical activities that took place in the home varied. The most common were practising by children and young people related to their formal instrumental tuition, adult playing for pleasure, self-learning by teenagers in various popular music styles, and some (but perhaps not so much) group playing.

First, practising. The standard pattern for learning an instrument in the classical tradition was one weekly lesson, with (ideally) regular practices of half an hour or so on each intervening day. This is described in chapter 11, but here it can just be recalled that this procedure was followed by hundreds of local pupils each year, many working for the national graded examinations. Since this practising regularly took place at home it can be imagined how many hours of playing in this mode alone went on in local homes, mostly on pianos but also on violins, violas, cellos, flutes, clarinets, oboes, trumpets and guitars – to mention only the most popular. The mass media may indeed have been powerful in many households, but that should not blind us to the intensive participation in music by hundreds of youthful players in homes throughout the city.

Individual adult playing for enjoyment was another form of home musical activity. How common this was was difficult to discover, but it was certainly not unusual. Piano playing still appealed to many people, but one striking development over recent years has been the increasing popularity of electronic organs. These were often particularly attractive to adult beginners because of the facility of hearing oneself through earphones without disturbing other household members.

Self-teaching (discussed in chapter 11) is also worth mentioning in connection with home music-making. The combination of recent technological developments and domestic privacy made it feasible to learn not just from a formal teacher, another family member, or self-instruction manual, but from imitating recorded music. This was one accepted channel of musical learning. Much of the music most appreciated by teenagers could be learnt from 'playing along' with records better than from written formulations or classical-type tuition. There were difficulties for certain instruments, particularly percussion, where one person's 'music' was another's 'noise' or 'nuisance', so home was not always a problem-free base; garden sheds, cellars or separate garages were one possibility, but sometimes there was no alternative but to persist in annoying others or go elsewhere. For most other instruments, however, including the widely popular guitar, homes were the main locales – better than, say, school or youth club – where teenagers could count on hours of relatively private and undisturbed learning.

The home was also sometimes the setting for joint music-making in pairs or larger groups. Parents played piano accompaniment for their children's early instrumental efforts, siblings performed duets or trios, or pupils played with their music teachers. Adults visited each other's houses in turn to play in classical chamber groups or sing in small choirs (an option more open to small classical or folk groups than bands with amplified music). Rock players were extremely keen to practise together; if they were relative beginners and small in numbers (for both reasons unlikely to have much money) they could often not afford to hire a hall for practising and so made do at home, either playing without full amplification or risking complaints from neighbours; but they preferred elsewhere, and the youth clubs, schools and church halls that provided facilities were in great demand. As a consequence, playing in this type of group, in contrast both to small classical groups and individual playing, drew musicians away from rather than towards the home. The same was true of participation in larger groups like the orchestras, operatic societies, big choirs and brass bands, which all met outside private houses and to which people therefore had to go out.

Private homes therefore interact with other settings in providing facilities for local music. For some purposes, their use is limited. For others, however, they remain major locales and facilitators of local music-making partly through the family setting for primary musical socialisation – a process of more importance than is often recognised – and also more directly in those homes where music-making is actively pursued on an individual or group basis. I have no figures for such homes in Milton Keynes or elsewhere, and no doubt they formed a minority. Given the number of established and learning musicians in the area, however, and the basis in home activity likely to lie behind the more public performances, such homes clearly play an important, if unpublicised, role in local music.

The contribution of the schools was also basic to much local musical practice. Schools are in general important locales for the arts – particularly the musical arts – given that they are centres of regular and intensive social activity in a context conducive to musical learning and expression and also widely expected to be so. Schools play an essential part in children's socialisation and in laying the foundations for individuals' musical interests and expertise in later life, thus constituting one crucial mechanism for the transmission of musical culture from one generation to the next and for its differential distribution among the population. These general expectations about schools and music were supported by my research on Milton Keynes schools in the early 1980s.[1]

'Music' was taught in the schools as part of the curriculum, so some music was a compulsory part of most children's education up to about 13, when most dropped music as a school subject. This formal exposure to music was relatively small, but nonetheless provided a supplement to informal home socialisation, and sometimes fired a child's interest either in music generally or in particular types of music unfamiliar from home. Some pupils chose to continue music, studying for CSE or O level examinations in music, a very few going on to A levels. This was the main pool for potential entrants to higher education in music (both teacher training and the music schools); such students had usually also had additional teaching through the local LEA music centres or instrumental tuition from peripatetic or private music teachers. Each year a handful went on to specialist music training, often in due course returning to schools as music teachers. This formal musical education was mainly within the classical music tradition, increasingly so with the more advanced work.

Other elements were more informal. These are the ones I intend to focus on, partly because they are less often discussed, partly because for most children these were the processes through which they participated most fully and enthusiastically in musical pursuits. The remainder of this section will therefore discuss these less formalised – but nonetheless structured – activities, with their importance not only for musical socialisation but as a form of musical experience in its own right.

There was a remarkable amount of extra-curricular musical activity in local schools. Indeed almost every school had at least one voluntary musical ensemble – orchestras, choirs and other musical groups arranged as optional activities at lunchtimes or outside the time-tabled school day. In the 46 primary and secondary schools responding to my 1982 survey (catering for around 16,000 children in all) there were 72 recorder groups, 33 choirs, 19 orchestral and similar groups, 14 guitar groups, 5 wind bands, 3 jazz groups, 4 percussion groups and 2 string ensembles, together with one each of a barber shop group, brass band, rock shop, dance band, Gilbert and Sullivan group, and folk group – 158 in all. (These figures were from just over half the schools in the Milton Keynes division – excluding the special schools – so the total was probably considerably higher.) Some schools had a whole range of groups, notably the comprehensive schools with their larger numbers and more experienced pupils. At Leon Comprehensive School, for example, there were in 1982 two orchestras, a wind band, two recorder groups, a jazz group, a brass band of 12 players, a folk guitar group, a woodwind ensemble, a six-piece percussion ensemble, a rock shop, a dance band, a Gilbert and Sullivan group, a barber shop group, a timbrel band, and the 15-member Leon Singers, while the Radcliffe Comprehensive School had two orchestras, a junior and a senior choir, a recorder group, a folk club and a jazz group. Even the smaller primary schools sometimes had several groups: the 247 pupils at St Thomas Aquinas Combined School, for example, between them fielded four recorder groups, two guitar groups, and a 30-member choir accompanied by glockenspiels, xylophones and percussion.

Figures and lists do not convey much in themselves, but it must be stressed that each group depended directly on the active participation of its members, and this in turn meant continued commitment of time and co-operation by large numbers of people. Just about all groups met regularly to

Figure 26 A young performer at the annual Bletchley and District Middle Schools concert

Figure 27 (a) and (b) Performances at the annual Leon School music week

play together, some daily, more commonly once a week. The total was striking, for it meant that (even counting just over half the schools) 2,000 or more 'child hours' of musical practice were going on every week of term in Milton Keynes schools.[2] When other forms of voluntary instrumental playing and learning were included, around 10–15 per cent of the school population were directly participating in self-chosen extra-curricular musical activity – a minority, but a not inconsiderable one in the light of the continuing skilled effort needed to keep musical groups and learning in being.

Musical expression was not just an internal activity but was also used by schools to embellish their more public occasions, give pupils experience in performance, involve members of the local community and generally advertise their achievements. Almost all the schools held concerts of one kind or another as a regular part of their yearly cycle. This feature of the school year was well known to parents – or, at least, those with children involved in school music – as well as reported from time to time in the local press. In the 1982 survey, all but four of the 51 schools reporting (including the special schools) had had at least one public musical event in the previous year, and the vast majority two or more; two of the comprehensive schools had had seven or eight. The most common cycle was one event at Christmas (in 1982 there were 25 carol services/carol concerts, 3 Christmas pantomimes, and 2 Christmas entertainments), and a summer concert. There were also other musical occasions, often combined with drama or dancing, as in the very common musical plays, operas, and pantomimes. In addition there were Old Time Music Hall performances, harvest, autumn and Easter festivals, 'musical extravaganzas', a dramatic and musical 'Third world exhibition', a musical week, a soloist evening, and a wind quartet at the annual speech day.

Once again a list sounds stark, but remember that each single item – the Leon School's soloists' evening, the Lord Grey carol concert or the Rickley Middle School musical evening – marked a joint musical performance which for the participants was the highlight of many weeks', sometimes months', work and meant constant rehearsals and pressure in the days beforehand. Each single instance formed part of an organised pattern in these and other schools across the years. The work and co-ordination needed are also brought home by the numbers involved – almost always at least twenty and in many cases a hundred or more, sometimes with all the school's pupils taking part.

Concerts also linked school with the local community outside. Performances had to have audiences, and though a few were internal only, most were thrown open more widely, attended by relatives of the performers or friends of the school. When one considers the other possible attractions the audience numbers were remarkable, commonly around 100–150 or higher,

Music in the home and school

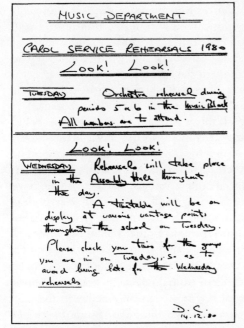

Figure 28 Organising a school carol service: even the simplest musical event places additional demands on teachers, pupils, photocopiers and dinner queues

201

and in cases where a show had more than one performance sometimes as many as 400–700, even 1,000. For the 134 different performances in local schools in 1982 the audiences totalled nearly 22,000 in all – and that left 40 schools uncounted. School musical events thus drew large and consistent audiences, sometimes limited only by the size of the school hall – more perhaps attended them than the much-vaunted school sports activities.

Audiences were prepared to pay too, for in about half of these events there was a collection or entry charge ranging from 10p to 75p. The proceeds mostly went towards expenses or to school funds or music departments, but other bodies also sometimes benefited: charities, church funds, a brass band, and occasionally the PTA.

Schools also took their music outside, for though school halls were the most common locale, performances were also put on elsewhere. Most schools took part in inter-school events like the Middle School Festivals, and there were also performances in local churches, community halls, and old people's clubs or homes, as well as in a local hospital; less usually, one comprehensive school choir travelled to Hampshire to sing. This in itself linked the school to a wider setting, a link further reinforced by the accepted custom that a proportion of concerts were 'for charity', for some cause outside the school.

The schools, then, were among the local centres that organised musical activity – locales where musical resources were owned and stored, musicians could gather and play together, musical skills could be transmitted, and public musical events prepared and performed. A considerable amount of local musical practice regularly and consistently, and without much public acclaim, thus took place in and through the schools.

This leads on to the question of *which* children participated. It is frequently assumed that music (like many other minority pursuits) is primarily a 'middle-class' preserve. If this was so in Milton Keynes we could expect the 10–15 per cent of children actively engaged in music in the schools to be predominantly selected according to class background. This would be difficult to test conclusively, but there certainly seemed to be no overwhelming evidence that either the social and economic factors which have (variously) been associated with the concept of class or subjective ideas about 'class' were of primary significance in determining which children took an active interest in music (perhaps unlike other school activities).

There was, for one thing, little evidence that schools in the less well-off areas were less musically active. Leon Comprehensive School, for example, was usually considered to draw children from a relatively 'poor' catchment area – but was incontestably one of the most musically active in the city. Other schools in reputedly tough areas (like the Lakes Estate) were not noticeably less musical, and the few private schools no more musically active than the state ones. The key factor, it seemed, was not the children's social and economic background but individual teacher(s) at particular schools at any given time. Leon, for example, had an outstandingly successful head of music and a strong supporting department in the early 1980s, as, at a primary and less specialist level, did the Lakes schools (to take just a couple of examples).

Judging from the 1982 survey, few music teachers themselves saw the differential participation of children in school music in 'class' terms at all. I had expected a number of responses to bring in 'class' quite explicitly in answer to an open-ended question almost inviting this answer,[3] but out of 51 responses only three used the term at all. One was unambiguous ('More middle-class snobs than working class – they've got the bread to buy instruments, and they value the status of it'); one suggested it was often but not invariably part of the background ('Most reliable children come from parents who are "keen middle class", although there are some surprises'); and the third denied its relevance ('No social class distinctions, but parental encouragement is most helpful'). Others stressed that the home background of children participating was very varied ('seems to make little difference'; 'varies'; those with individual lessons 'tend to be from "better off" homes, but other members of the school orchestra have very varied backgrounds'; 'parental background varies but generally very supportive'). Indeed the factor most commonly noted was not social or economic background at all but whether or not parents took a positive interest in their children's musical activities. Terms such as 'supportive', 'encouraging', 'interested', 'caring' or 'backing' came spontaneously in about a third of the responses; and one Combined teacher spoke of parental backing as 'crucial'. Some analysts might argue that 'supportive' necessarily implies 'middle class', but this seems quite an assumption to make, certainly not proven by any hard evidence in Milton Keynes. Certainly whatever the actual basis of differential participation, the vast majority of teachers who commented did not see it in class-related terms at all.

Gender was in fact more to the fore. In the younger age groups, musically active children at school were predominantly girls – an imbalance partially corrected later on, and also offset by the larger involvement of teenage boys in rock groups *outside* school. The main choir, orchestral and ensemble members were girls, and though boys *did* participate, it required greater effort on their part to do so given the prevailing image: 'cissy' for boys to be musical but 'natural' to be sporty. Some schools had more success than others in breaking down the stereotype, and those boys who did persevere were all the keener precisely because of the extra commitment needed (they were sometimes supported by classically minded parents). In general, though, apart perhaps from the instruments popularly viewed as 'for boys' (brass and percussion), there were far more obstacles to engaging in school music for boys than for girls.

Academic ability has sometimes been associated with music. Was this so in local schools? The results of the local survey were mixed. Musically inclined children, some said, were 'average to above in academic ability', 'usually fairly bright', 'more above average than not' etc., but this was usually linked to other factors as well, like 'caring parents'. Others denied any association ('mixed ability', 'academic achievement seems to make very little difference', 'participants come from all years and abilities', 'full comprehensive range'). Even more suggested that the overall picture was a complex one, as in 'Group starting any tuition are very mixed, but those who persevere are usually those with supportive parents'; *'Usually* the "brighter" child learns to play the recorder more quickly. The ability to co-ordinate is essential – although I have had one or two "bright" children who have found it very difficult to begin with', or 'A correlation between intelligence and musicality, but then one or two exceptions to the rule'.

Overall the interesting point was that no *one* factor was seen as determining musical involvement. Some characteristics certainly did often seem to play a part – gender (especially at the primary stage), parental attitude, academic ability (within limits), and possibly income (especially if payment for music lessons was needed). Another influential factor, under-standably not mentioned by the respondents, was the impact of individual teachers. But no *one* of these was all-powerful. There was thus no simple way of categorising the sizable minority of children who chose for one or another of a whole range of individual reasons and backgrounds to participate – or continue to participate or not to participate – in school musical activities.

This may seem a negative conclusion. But it can also be interpreted in a more positive light: although there certainly were constraints for individual children (especially the younger boys), there was some real choice involved and the opportunities to take part were not – as sometimes suggested – effectively closed to all except a select few.

Voluntary musical activities did not just include the children. The teachers who took responsibility for music in the schools (whether formally or personally) also played a key role. Interestingly, many of them lacked specialist musical qualifications in the classical music mode. There were some highly qualified teachers with specialist music qualifications (dip-lomas, teachers' certificates, degrees) and some musically active schools had highly qualified staff, but the teachers responsible for music in well over half of the schools apparently held no specialist music qualification whatsoever (or if they did so, did not consider this worth mentioning despite a specific question). It was not only schools with highly qualified music teachers, however, that maintained an active musical tradition of regularly practising musical groups and regular concerts: yet another instance of the long amateur tradition of music in England, where the contribution of those with first-hand experience and informally acquired skills has complemented and enhanced those few with specialist qualifications. The key factor in school music was as much the enthusiasm and energy of the teacher(s) as the amount of formal training.

In the kind of music fostered, the main emphasis was on the classical tradition. This has been a long interest of the schools and interacted effectively with the peripatetic teachers and local centres supported by the education authorities. But this was interpreted in a broad sense, and other traditions too had some representation. It is not easy to sum up musical styles succinctly, but the overall pattern was a mixture of 'classical' and 'light classical'/'easy listening' music (often of course at an elementary level in the first schools), together with the fund of popular songs and accompaniments well known from musical shows, pantomimes, and Gilbert and Sullivan operas, and some brass band and 'folk' music.

There were almost no explicit references in teachers' replies to music of the Afro-American tradition – jazz, blues, rock etc.; the only exceptions were three 'jazz groups', one 'dance band' and one 'rock shop' (i.e. 5 out of 158 examples) and in five schools references to a 'pop cantata', a 'jazz cantata', or 'pop type' music. This was a remarkable absence given the huge enthusiasm of so many teenagers and pre-teenagers for rock music in all its many forms. The lack of rock and pop may not have been as complete it appeared, however. It was unlikely that the fourteen 'guitar groups' and four 'percussion groups' did not play at least some Afro-American music. Inter-school musical occasions included at least some jazz and 'music with a beat', and teenage rock bands sometimes negotiated the use of school premises to practise (even though this was not really considered part of 'school activities'). It is significant that such music was hardly mentioned, whether because it was defined out by teachers as not something to notice or publicise – maybe not really quite 'music' – or because the general tradition of music teaching in school, together with constraints related to cost, noise and availability of amplified rock instruments, made it more difficult to incorporate directly. Either way it would be interesting to see whether this submerged form of music-making comes more to the surface in the future in local schools, possibly accompanied by increasing participation of boys in school music.

The schools are thus important centres for the execution and transmission of music, to some extent involving *all* their pupils in general musical socialisation, and in addition providing specific opportunities for those who, within certain constraints, choose to pursue music in a school context. The schools interact with other local contexts, and in particular the home, for forming and expressing musical experience. Some forms of music were not directly catered for in Milton Keynes schools – large brass groups, for example, or rock bands – but even here the schools played some part. Rock bands often arose from school friendships, and the larger musical groups in the town were fed by children coming from local schools, leading to a mutually reinforcing relationship between school and town musical activities.

It would be easy to over-stress the narrowly *functional* role of extra-curricular music in schools, important though this is in providing musical centres and learning opportunities for their localities. For school musical activity is also a manifestation of musical expression and performance in its own right. It is tempting to take the 'top–down' view and assume that children engaging in school music are 'merely learning', copying adults rather than taking part in the 'real' world – a model used for various other school activities. But in the case of music it can equally well be said that young people are truly participating in music in their musical groups and concerts and that their performances are as valid as those performed by adults. The school-based musical activities are not totally distinct from the general complex of local music-making, especially given the lack of a definitive divide between professional and amateur in local music generally. Many school musicians are also members of local groups outside, where (with the exception of some teenage rock bands) musical competence matters more than age. The schools are something more than just channels to lay the foundations for 'proper' musical participation in later life; they are *themselves* organised centres of music – a real part of local musical practice.

16

The churches and music

In the past the church was one major patron and facilitator of music – not just the church in general but the series of churches up and down the country, providing the locale and impetus for musical activity. Something of this role is still played by local churches in the 1980s. It is true that they are not the *sole* context for music and attract only certain sections of the population, but this can still mean a sizable number of people. Judging from the local evidence to be presented in this chapter, the churches are still major centres for the training and organisation of music-making, with effects spread widely into the community.[1]

There were around seventy churches or religious groups in Milton Keynes. The number was increasing with the growth of the new city, and some older parish churches which had been near-empty in the 1970s were filling up once again. At the time of the main survey for this study (1983), they included Church of England (12), Methodist (9), Roman Catholic (8) and Baptist (5) churches, together with about a dozen churches designated separately or in groups as 'Local Ecumenical Projects' sponsored by the Church of England and by Baptist, Methodist and United Reformed churches. There were also two United Reformed churches and about nineteen other churches or religious groups (among them the Christadelphians, the Christian Scientists, the Pentecostal Church, the Society of Friends (Quakers), the Seventh-day Adventists, the Spiritualist Church and the Salvation Army). In addition there was a synagogue, a mosque, a Buddhist community based on the Milton Keynes Peace Pagoda, and a Sikh group.

With the sole exception of the Quakers, the churches and religious groups all included music in their regular gatherings (even the Quakers held musical events from time to time outside their meetings for worship). This ranged from unaccompanied hymns in very small churches to congregational singing with piano or organ, or – the most common – choir and organ leading the congregation, sometimes with choral solos or intoned responses.

Churches and church halls were also used for musical or partly musical occasions – weddings and funerals, Sunday schools, meetings of church groups such as the Brownies, or church musical evenings.

A great deal of music was thus performed week by week as a taken-for-granted part of church life. This apparently 'natural' locale of music – too familiar to need comment – concealed the great amount of work, organisation and commitment needed to sustain the constant musical practice to be described in the following pages.

First, just about every religious group had either an organ or piano (sometimes both), the only exceptions being the Quakers, one Church of England group just starting up, and the non-Christian groups. The organ particularly was felt to play a central role in musical and religious life. For an English church-goer the organ sounds are steeped with long associations of worship and continuity, evoking the special sacred atmosphere and recalling too other more personal rituals associated with weddings, funerals, or baptisms. The organ provides a frame for the start and finish of the service and ushers people through the transition between 'ordinary' events outside church and the ritual enactment within it. It also forms a recurrent thread during the service, playing during the interludes between spoken or sung actions and, in its own inimitable way, accompanying congregational choir singing. It has obvious utilitarian functions too in providing a decent veil over the shuffling and whispers as people enter and leave or, even more directly, setting the note for hymns or chants, leading and controlling the collective singing (often an essential task in the absence of a conductor to co-ordinate large groups of people), and adding musical harmony and resonance to support the often unrehearsed singing of congregations. Perhaps most significant of all is the symbolic role of the organ, bringing together religious and musical experience.

This symbolic element is often below people's overt consciousness – assumed rather than explicitly enunciated – but people in Milton Keynes seemed well aware of the importance of organ playing. At least three-quarters of the Christian churches had organs, and in the few cases where there were no permanent installations, members of the congregation were prevailed on to lend portable ones. Even those without organs commented that, for example, 'the organ is associated in people's minds with the religious atmosphere', and 'there's something about playing an organ that's special'. Groups who had only recently acquired an organ or had difficulty in getting an organist were particularly aware of its importance: 'without an organ we struggle... organ music helps the meeting' (the Church of Jesus Christ of Latter-day Saints) and 'the most suitable type of instrument for this type of service' (Seventh-day Adventists, who had also tried a guitar and found it less appropriate). Churches went to great trouble and expense to buy, maintain or renovate their organs, and the burdensome 'organ fund' was a stock joke.

Some churches had pianos, not with the same continuity and richness but similarly framing and phasing the service, providing a musical thread, and accompanying singing. Churches with both piano and organ often selected according to the type of music: organ for traditional hymns, piano for the 'folk' or 'chorus' songs seen as more contemporary or appropriate for young people's services. Others, such as the Methodist church at Wolverton, used the organ for services, but piano for social occasions.

Pianos or organs were thus common to just about all the churches in Milton Keynes, used extensively in both services and related church activities. But – contrary to what one often unthinkingly assumes – they did not just come naturally, for their use as well as maintenance needed a great deal of organisation.

There was, to start with, the expense of buying and maintaining church instruments. Among Milton Keynes churches, around a third had acquired their organ within the previous ten years – one sign of their continuing popularity. This was not a trouble-free event, for it often involved both a contentious decision (was an organ the best way to use scarce resources?) and finding the necessary money, usually dependent on a lengthy process of fund-raising which *someone* had to organise and contribute to. One parish church, for example, had just raised £4,300 for an electronic organ after their old pipe organ became unusable, while others had gone in for major work on older organs. St Martin's in Fenny Stratford had their 1897 organ rebuilt and resited in 1982, paid for by selling a church-owned house as well as general fund-raising, while St Peter's and St Paul's in Newport Pagnell faced having to raise £50,000 or more in the next fifteen years to have their Victorian organ rebuilt for the second time. Other churches had reasonable organs already (including many Victorian or old cinema organs), but still had to arrange maintenance. At the very least there had to be regular tuning, and maintenance and repairs were a constant expense whether by a formal service contract or personal contacts through the congregation. In one church the organist paid her honorarium straight into the maintenance fund, and several churches were wondering how long they could afford an organ or considering changing their pipe organ for a new electronic one – not that new ones were free from maintenance problems either. All in all the continued provision of a playable organ was far from simple and depended on a series of decisions, arrangements and monetary resources from the congregation and their friends.

The actual playing also needed to be organised. The organ sounds duly floating out as one enters or leaves a church and at the appropriate points in a service or wedding or funeral are a familiar part of many people's experience – but churches had somehow to ensure that this *would* in fact happen. The most common system was for a principal organist (sometimes though not always paid a small honorarium) supported by at least one, more often two, three, or even five, assistants who helped out in the main organist's absence or in a pre-arranged rota. In some churches this was quite arduous since as well as several Sunday services plus others during the week, there were also weddings, funerals and other church events – sometimes three or more weddings every Saturday all through the summer. These organists were not full time. Some of them were unemployed, retired, or, like housewives, engaged in non-paid work (all people, in fact, who usually had many other responsibilities in addition to church services); but most organ players were in employment, and so had to fit their playing in with the demands of their jobs.

The churches attached great importance to these local musical experts and it was remarkable that so many people were in fact able and prepared to fulfil this essential role. It was not all plain sailing. Some organists played better than others, some had to negotiate the peculiarities of particular instruments or settings (over-loud perhaps in their original Victorian siting for today's smaller choirs), and some were still in the early stages of learning. Churches could not just take it for granted that if one organist left another would automatically come forward. At the time of our survey, for example, the church of Our Lady of Lourdes was advertising on the church board for a young person to sponsor since their current organist was going off to university. But, with all the problems, the arrangements mostly worked, and just about all the churches in Milton Keynes could count on music by a series of local musicians, mainly on the organ but also in some cases (with similar if less formalised arrangements) on the piano.

These many musicians came from a wide variety of backgrounds and occupations. The organists – almost equally male and female – included several teachers, housewives, schoolchildren and retired people, together with a farmer, organ builder, piano tuner, civil engineer, ticket officer in the underground, electrician, accountant, nursing assistant, photographer, salesman, manager of the local ironmonger's shop, solicitor, ex-lorry driver, painter at the Wolverton works, and retired opera singer. In some respects they had little in common, but they did share a commitment to a church and to music, combined with the ability and willingness to provide the musical services with which the life of the local church was bound up. Without these musicians the taken-for-granted accoutrements of religious worship and of the church's social activities could not function – nor, in turn, would one of the main centres of local music continue to function.

This went beyond just instrumental playing, for these musicians also fulfilled an important local role in co-ordinating and teaching musical skills. There was the lead their playing provided for congregational singing (not least in new hymns and music), but an even more far-reaching contribution was the responsibility they so frequently held for recruiting and training the choir and other incipient musicians. In the past local organists were among the main channels of musical education and mobility, encouraging local children to undertake formal musical education or self-training, perhaps to become organists or music teachers themselves. Several of the elderly music teachers and performers in Bletchley still remembered being helped as children by church organists early in the century, the essential basis for their later careers and interests. By the early 1980s, there were other channels, not least the schools and self-recruiting teenage bands, but something of the influence of the organists still remained. Many local musicians – from youthful rock players to established brass band members or folk-singers – spoke of early training in a local church choir as the start of later musical interest.

Church choirs were another still flourishing institution. More than half of the Christian churches in Milton Keynes had choirs in 1983, with several more either having had choirs in the recent past or – as was common in small churches just starting up – looking forward to one in the future. These choirs too directly contributed to local music, for it was also through their activities that the churches acted as local centres of musical practice: providing the locale and incentive for collective groupings of people – male and female, young and old, educated or not so educated – to meet, learn, practise and jointly perform the forms of music conceived as appropriate for church occasions. Having a choir of several singers, accompanied on the organ or piano, was thus an explicit part of most local services, and this in itself engaged many people in music. In 1983, the local church choirs mostly contained between 6 and 25 people, with just a couple below 5 and the two largest with 30; some were subdivided into junior and adult choirs, who sometimes practised and performed separately. Week after week after week, these choirs performed at services in the local churches or met to learn and practise their music, activities which have somehow remained invisible in most treatments of popular culture in this country.

Once again, the taken-for-granted role of the musicians who provided this choral music involved a fair amount of work and active organisation by a series of people, both directly participating and in the background: singers, organist, pianist, choirmaster/mistress, parents (of child singers), congregation generally, and vicar, minister or priest. Choirs did not just run themselves, however, or go without challenge, for while it was accepted custom for churches to have choirs, not all did, and making and implementing decisions on this was not always easy. Small new churches had to struggle to get a choir together at all, existing choirs sometimes fell in numbers or dissolved totally, and some ministers (supported presumably by at least some of their congregations) held that the 'elitist' nature of choirs was undesirable. One vicar was quite explicit: 'when I arrived at this church, people came just to hear the choir. So we banned it, and now all the congregation are involved.'

Even when a choir was accepted as routine, members still had to be recruited, kept, and trained – all processes which could not just be taken for granted. For a start, there was no one pool of potential members, and choirs were very varied in composition. Their age range was enormous: anything from small children to people in their eighties, sometimes together, sometimes divided into adult and junior choirs. In some churches, the choirs were less varied (in one mostly in their twenties and thirties, in another mainly middle-aged), but in general stratification by age was not a typical feature: those choirs who boasted that they included people from 6 to 70 or 14 to 84 were by no means unusual. The male–female balance also varied: a few had more men (indeed in St George's Wolverton, girls had only recently been allowed) and a handful of choirs were female only, but the more common pattern was for a slight preponderance of women (often 3:2). Amidst this heterogeneity there was thus no one clear pattern. Indeed, it is hard to see choir membership as anything but an essentially personal and unpredictable matter – we must remember, of course, that it was drawn from those who were in any case attracted to the church, interested in music or the social participation facilitated through music, and in many cases with a family connection with both church and music. Given this individual tendency, together with the necessarily competing commitments of those concerned, it is not surprising that the membership of church choirs fluctuated – rather, perhaps, that they continued to flourish as such a strong element in local religious and musical life.

Choirs also had to be organised, and to learn and practise their repertoire. There were various ways of arranging this, from the appointment of a formal director of music in a few churches to a more informal system by which choirs more or less ran themselves. One common pattern was for the principal church organist or, lacking that, pianist to act as choirmaster/ mistress; less often these roles were divided, or the choir was made the responsibility of the minister or of a special choir 'leader'. The choir's essential task was to master the music needed in church services so as to give a lead to the congregation and, in some cases, perform on their own. This meant knowing the established church repertoire of hymns (and sometimes anthems or responses) as well as from time to time learning new music. The standard way of achieving this was by holding regular choir practices at the church, normally lasting an hour to an hour and a half one evening a week. This requirement had been the downfall of several choirs, who found themselves unable to find a time to get together regularly, but many persisted with this by no means light obligation: one evening a week for which each member had to say 'I can't – it's choir practice.'

Practice sessions were not just for putting a gloss on performances but also – especially with the younger choirs – for learning the craft of choral singing which usually (not always) meant singing from notated music, in some cases four-part harmony. This was reinforced through the repeated performances in church, normally at least once every Sunday, for some more often; a few churches had as many as four services on a Sunday, three of these with choir. Some choirs also sang for weddings and other church occasions (occasionally for a small fee, though in general choir members were not paid), as well as in the special concerts and festivals which many churches put on from time to time. All in all, membership of church choirs not only gave local musicians an occasion to practise their art, but also provided the development of musical skills and interests.

The type of music in the church choirs varied more than I had expected. In most of the mainstream Christian churches, long-transmitted church music and the old favourite hymns were still going strong, much valued by congregations. Milton Keynes practice thus well bore out Temperley's conclusions in his treatment of English parish church music on the importance and continuity of hymnody: 'the same words and tunes, from all periods of the Church's history, including the middle ages, supplemented from post-Tridentine Catholic, Lutheran, Methodist, Nonconformist, and humanist sources, are sung in churches everywhere. The music ... is a strong emotional bond for those who remain in the Church, and even between them and those outside' (1979, p. 348). But in some churches there was also an interest in jazz or folk-based music, in rhythmic songs to appeal to young people, and in newly produced hymn books, many of them more ecumenically based than in the past: not of course to the taste of everyone. One Anglican church with a flourishing choir had 'styles ranging from Purcell to calypso folk stuff', while in some Catholic churches the succession of Sunday services geared to different congregations had varying music – some with 'all folk hymns', others 'traditional mass hymns' led by the choir, while the service by a visiting Italian priest had all Italian hymns. Most clergy also spoke of their desire to introduce *new* hymns and music, as well as of the resistance to this, and saw choirs as providing a useful lead for innovation. Indeed a number had produced their own compositions or arrangements for their choir, and then congregation, to sing at services.

Church choirs did not confine their music to routine church services, for most also performed on special church occasions in the religious year – Holy Week in Catholic churches laid particularly heavy demands on the choir – and sometimes also sang in concerts or musical evenings. The choir at the Methodist Freeman Memorial church performed a specially rehearsed cantata every Palm Sunday, while the Spurgeon Baptist church choir were famous for their 'Carols for Everybody' before Christmas, usually with at least one newly composed carol. In any one year, several local churches were likely to be holding 'festivals', and for these too the choir usually sang, sometimes supplemented by instrumentalists and singers from related churches. In addition, church choirs and other musicians from the congregation performed in more light-hearted social events. The Spurgeon Baptist choirmaster put on an evening's entertainment in 1983, for example, in aid of Christian work in Brazil, consisting of a Victorian evening with duets, solos, comic tunes, and a barber shop quartet. Some choirs were invited to other churches; the choir of St Francis de Sales in Wolverton was asked to sing in Bedford, and St Lawrence's choir regularly sang for the twice-monthly service at the Old Bradwell Methodist church. The church choirs were thus among the musical resources of the locality, not only in their own regular church services but also in the musical life of other churches and in their special-occasion musical performances.

Not all church singing was by choirs. Congregational singing was often important too, even in the Catholic churches, which in the past had set less store by collective singing; no local churches followed the cathedral model of music being the sole responsibility of a specialist choir, with little participation by others. As has been noted already, up to a third of the churches did not have choirs at any one time, and some ministers were doubtful about having a choir. The minister at one Anglican church with a strong musical tradition confessed that: 'I have sometimes had hesitations about the value of the choir – but on the whole I think it's good', while a priest and others commented on the problems of a group separate from the rest of the congregation. Others refused to have a choir at all or spoke of music as likely to become distracting, while the Jehovah's Witnesses were quite clear that 'We don't have choirs because we feel people should all have the opportunity to participate whether they've got a good voice or not' – sentiments which recall the still significant suspicion in several churches of too prominent a place for music (see Martin 1984).

The absence of a choir did not mean lack of music, for singing was important in just about all the churches, usually to instrumental accompaniment. Sometimes having no choir went along with extremely active congregational participation, especially in smaller churches. The local Seventh-day Adventist church was notable here. It was mainly West Indian, with a tradition of people getting up and doing things – perhaps preparing songs or instrumental items and then presenting them, or just coming along for a sing-song with someone going to the front to lead. Among the local Jehovah's Witnesses a limited number of scripture-based songs were sung and resung at meetings so that everyone knew them well and could join in – 'the participation is more important than the end product'. In other churches the existence of a choir seemed to have the effect of facilitating *greater* congregational involvement and strengthening the joint musical performance. As one priest put it, the choir 'encouraged the vocal participation of the people and lifted their hearts up to the Lord'.

Whatever the varying attitudes to choirs, congregational singing was a taken-for-granted part of church services, as if for most churches religious ritual could not really be envisaged without singing in some form or another. This implicit assumption was sometimes articulated explicitly, as in the claim (from a member of a parish church) that 'Music has always been seen as an essential element in Christian worship. Nearly everyone enjoys singing even if they can't sing very well ... it is still essential' or St Augustine's comment, quoted by one priest, that 'He who sings praises twice.' Such views were even more to the fore in some of the free churches where, as one Baptist put it, 'hymns take the place of liturgy ... it's really difficult to imagine our worship without music', or (from a URC member) 'hymns provide an opportunity to ... say something during the service, a musical response, affirmation of faith'. In the local Church of God, music was seen as the vehicle which could take people away from the problems of the world and 'concentrate our eyes on God: we're called the singing church!', and for the Jehovah's Witnesses singing was 'a very important part of worship and has always been since the beginning of man'.

In some churches instrumental groups had a parallel role to the choirs. Nearly two-thirds of the churches in 1983 had some organised instrumentalists, from the occasional accompaniment of a couple of guitars to organised and regularly performing groups of ten or more. Between them they included just about every common instrument. Recorders and guitars (both acoustic and electric) were the favourites, but there were also wind instruments (especially flutes and clarinets, but also oboe, bassoon, tin whistle), brass (trombone, tenor horn and trumpet), violins, cellos, accordions, drums and other percussion, as well as a range of less common instruments like xylophone, glockenspiel, melodica, tambourine, mandolin and maraca. This wide variety demonstrated the contingent nature of these groups, less routinised than choirs and arising more from the personal interests and abilities of particular church members at any given time than from the need to fill a regular slot. Many players were young and formed transient groupings which did not necessarily continue after their departure. But in some churches they were beginning to form an expected part of church life and to be creating their own niche, adding an element that was thought to appeal particularly to the younger people and was especially appropriate as an accompaninent to songs with a 'folk' or 'pop' flavour.

A few churches – like St Mary's, Bletchley – ran children's recorder groups with a regular teacher, but most instrumental groups were informal. Even so they sometimes provided an important input into the church's music. The minister of one ecumenical Church of England/Baptist church, for example, had written out arrangements for 50–100 hymns for flutes, guitars, recorders, drums and piano; though the full instrumental group in his church only played from time to time, they provided one valued element in the service: 'music communicates to you in a way words don't; if there were no music we would be saying less actually to people and to God'. Again, at St James in New Bradwell a music group functioned on an ad hoc basis according to who was available, sometimes accompanying regular services, sometimes putting on special performances. One Sunday service included two guitars, recorders, clarinet and brass instruments, while on another a local folk-singer from the congregation sang to accompaniment at the start of the service. Usually the group chose pieces they knew already or could learn in three or four short practices and accompanied the more rhythmic songs like 'When the saints come marching in'. The group at St Mary's, Wavendon again demonstrated the coincidental nature of many of these groups, for in 1983 there 'just happened to be a group of children who played music'. These were a number of 10–14 year-olds who had been playing together for a year and a half on the clarinet, tenor horn, violin, trombone and recorders. They could by then play all the standard hymns without problems and used to accompany the service every six weeks or so. Despite their competence, though, their efforts still involved work, for the organist had to write out all the parts and they had three practices before each service. The varied group of guitars, violins, mandolins, clarinets, recorders, flute, xylophone and glockenspiel at the All Saints Catholic church in Bletchley, on the other hand, used to practise just before the 11 a.m. mass, with only occasional additional rehearsals. In some other churches, instruments were used just for the odd occasions, or earlier groups had disbanded when particular individuals had moved away. Getting an instrumental group going involved time and organisation, even when capable players were around. The Spurgeon Baptist church for one was finding this in 1983, for even with its strong musical tradition and several string and brass players among the church members (the minister himself playing the trumpet), its hoped-for church orchestra somehow never quite got off the ground. In the Pentecostal church most people played by ear, so they just turned up with their instruments and played along with the hymns and choruses – a situation apparently needing little overt organisation; but even then the tradition of being able and ready to participate in this way still needed to be established by constant practice for it to be effective.

Different again and yet in some ways parallel were the non-Christian religions, which have as yet scarcely been mentioned. There different instruments were used, taking precedence over the traditional Christian mix of organ and singing. Each had its own particular forms: the Buddhists associated with the Peace Pagoda with drums, bell and Sanskrit or Pali chants, regarding music as 'an aid to meditation'; the Muslims with their mosque in Bletchley; the local Sikh community with traditional Indian instruments like drums, sitar and harmonium, supplemented by electronic organs, for whom music was 'fundamental and soothing' and well worth the practice they put in at home before performing. The Sikhs were having difficulty in passing on their skills (untaught in local schools), and though they ran their own Friday evening school there was no local music teacher and the previous practice of taking children to Southall for music lessons had lapsed. The numbers attached to these religions were small, but it is worth remembering that for those involved their own cultural and musical traditions were as valued and meaningful as the church music heritage for Christians and, furthermore, that the religious setting for music and musicians, while perhaps in some sense universal, does not always and everywhere take the particular 'hymn–prayer sandwich' form characteristic of Christian churches, with their emphasis on organ/piano, choir and congregational singing.

Returning to the Christian churches it is worth adding some further general comments on the varied contribution these made to the maintenance of local music. Their musical actions were, of course, to serve their own purposes: instrumentalists or choir could uplift the congregation with their music, provide a marker to set apart the rituals of service and sacred place, attach individuals yet more closely to the group, or quieten people down and get them in the right mood at the start of a service. The minister for a small ecumenical group in unaccustomed premises described how 'People chat in the community group: the only way they stop is when the music starts up. For our communion service, the whole atmosphere of worship is created by the music group.' At a different level was the deep symbolic association of music and religion, expressing itself in the experience of the participants, drawn together 'into one', as it was often put, through the combination of joint music-making and joint worship. Precisely because of this centrality to their own interests, the churches encouraged music, and this in turn had further consequences for music-making in general and for the continuity of music in the locality.

The churches therefore (rather like the schools) provided *locales* for music-making and, to an extent, its necessary material equipment. Large expensive items such as an organ, a piano, and sometimes percussion and other instruments were owned and maintained by the churches – no cheap or easy responsibility – and were stored there ready for use by the appropriate musicians. The churches were also places available for music-making, with their upkeep, maintenance and heating organised through church resources, providing a welcome to singers and instrumentalists who took a musical part in the regular services Sunday after Sunday. Churches were often chosen for local concerts not just by their own musical groups but also via more tenuous personal connections. Not only all the regular musically embellished services but also school carol services, local choir recitals, brass band concerts, organ recitals, chamber ensembles, voice and instrumental recitals, local music society concerts, large-scale oratorio performances – all these were regularly laid on and organised for local audiences through the ready availability and approval of local churches.

This went further than just the provision of premises, for it will be clear that the churches also provided a focus of *organisation*, an established framework and a network of committed people – all elements which facilitated and stimulated music-making. The need to provide musical services within the church meant the presence of organists, pianists and/or choirmasters, and of organised groups of musical participants in choirs, instrumental groups or congregational singers; and this in turn implied behind-the-scenes support. It was because of all this background organisation that the church and its social networks were able to join in the general arrangements for local music as well as in the 'central' church musical performances.

A further consequence was musical education within church contexts. Sometimes this was deliberately and separately arranged, as in the church-based summer camps run by one of the URC ministers and his helpers in which children spent a fortnight working at the musical and other preparations for a final production of, say, *Swinging Samson*, or *Joseph and his amazing technicolor dreamcoat*. Other processes were more informal and taken for granted. Church organists and pianists had sometimes had formal training on their instruments, but surprisingly many had little by way of formal qualifications and were self-taught 'on the job', often over very many years (the lady in one URC church who had played the organ in church for fifty years was not exceptional). They had been brought on by the need to provide a valued service for which they had some initial skills and commitment: one highly motivated form of learning. Most of the orchestral instrumentalists who played in church had probably had or were having some formal lessons (less so with guitarists and percussionists), but even for them the incentive to play in a group and 'in public' provided a valuable and additional learning resource.

This was even more obvious with the choirs. Churches occasionally followed formal training courses, like those laid down by the Royal School of Church Music. This was not the most usual learning mode, however, for just about all the churches had at the least some recognised conductor or leader with the responsibility for teaching not only a particular repertoire but, with it, basic musical skills – a function explicitly acknowledged by many musicians in later life as they reflected on their early experience in church choirs. Nor should one forget the congregations. They too were invisibly trained in the appreciation and execution of the church's music, a process perhaps now all the more necessary with less attention paid in the schools to teaching children the old hymns and carols. It is easy to agree with one minister's assessment that 'we have a musical tradition in the

Methodist Church and so [the congregation] pick up things quite well', but also easy to forget that for a tradition of that kind to remain active it had to be passed on and learnt by whole series of congregations, year after year after year; and that this, furthermore, even if most notable among Methodists, to some extent applied to all singing in local churches. Ministers and organists were well aware of the problems of introducing new hymns and songs, but even the *old* ones had to be learnt over the months and years. Through this lengthy process, too, all those participating in church services – not just the musical 'experts' – engaged in the experience of learning the musical arts of appreciation and performance in the context of the church: from recognising and appreciating the traditional organ repertoire or new 'folk-style' mass, to the skills of singing the old and the new religious songs.

This musical education through the churches is often overlooked, but in practice complemented school music teaching, though operating at a more informal and unnoticed level. For those directly involved, the churches' role in musical training was fundamental, the more so because it was often imbued with profound personal significance arising from family and group experiences over many years. This could add an extra dimension to the learning of music, well expressed by a choir member in one of the local churches:

As a member of the choir for thirty three years I think I can safely say it's a wonderful place to belong. I feel privileged to take my seat each week ... When you belong to a church choir there is always something to look forward to. Can you think of a better way to spend your life than singing praises to God. (*The Stantonbury L.E.P.'er*, no. 21, 2 October 1983)

Those directly participating in these musical performances and learning processes were of course only a minority; universal attendance at church services, if it ever existed, is a thing of the past. The numbers were not negligible, though. Religious statistics are notoriously elusive, but the estimate in 1984 by the Rural Dean of Milton Keynes that approximately 5 per cent of the local population attended church on a regular weekly basis (reported in the *Milton Keynes Mirror*, 9 February 1984) was certainly, judging by my own figures, not too high – if anything, it perhaps should be slightly greater. My own estimate would be that every week around 8,000–10,000 people (including children) took part in a religious service.[2] (If this does not at first sound large, it is worth remembering that if a consistent figure of this order turned out to, say, a football match each week in a town of the size of Milton Keynes, this would be considered a significant part of local popular culture.) On special occasions such as Easter and, above all, Christmas, attendance was higher, probably by thousands. It was sometimes necessary to arrive an hour early to get a seat at all for a midnight Christmas service, with 300, even 500, participants not unusual, some churches having to shut their doors against late-comers for lack of room.

These participants in church services and their music came from varied backgrounds. This sounds obvious but is worth stressing given the claims still sometimes made that Christianity today is a 'traditional' and 'middle-class phenomenon', with the implication that it is somehow sectional, marginal, or out-dated. The Milton Keynes churches drew on a variety of people, decided in part by the church's own location, in part by people's own preferences: churches that had several services on a Sunday often found that their successive congregations differed markedly in age, domestic situation or, sometimes, ethnic background. Some churches did predominantly attract limited groupings in terms of job or income, especially those located either in the less wealthy (and in some cases older) areas or in traditionally well-off localities – though this in turn was being affected by new building programmes. The spokesmen for some churches described their congregations in terms of social background: some spoke of 'mainly middle class', others mentioned 'working class/lower-middle class', 'more of an artisan flavour ... more lower-income groups', or 'dominated by the Wolverton works' (to quote some comments from the 1983 interviews). Many churches did not seem to see themselves in these terms at all, or explicitly mentioned the *mix* of social backgrounds they attracted. The Spurgeon Baptist church stressed its variety ('upper-working class – carpenters, fitters – through to professional people'), others commented on having 'a fair mixture', 'a pretty wide cross-section', 'a complete spread in this parish'. The populous Catholic churches were particularly mixed: St Thomas Aquinas' congregation included English, Irish and Italian people, and St Francis de Sales in Wolverton had Polish, Italian, West Indian, Irish and 'a fair proportion of old Wolvertonians'. Some of the smaller religious bodies drew on particular categories, and there was a high proportion of West Indians among the Seventh-day Adventists. In age too congregations were mixed, with different churches (and specific services) sometimes catering for different age groups; there was no overall pattern except perhaps for the relative shortfall of single people in their late teens and early twenties (a cohort likely to return later). Overall it would certainly be misleading to suggest that the participants in church music came from only certain social or ethnic sections, for the churches attracted people in a whole mix of jobs and non-jobs. Music through the local churches in Milton Keynes in the early 1980s was not just the preserve of the traditional 'English middle class'.

The churches thus form one set of centres for the many practising amateur musicians that constitute so characteristic an element in English culture. Organists, pianists, composers, arrangers, choirmasters, cantors, choirs, instrumentalists, and trained congregational singers – all are clustered round the local churches, and, through them, learn and practise their musical art. One must not exaggerate this, for of course the churches are only one among several contexts for the practice of music. Indeed one of the other characteristics of music in England is the way known musicians function – and are in demand – in many *different* contexts. This was evident in the Milton Keynes churches too, for most of the musicians active as organists, choirmasters or players also appeared in other musical roles and groups. The organist in one Methodist church conducted the local Gilbert and Sullivan Society, a Baptist choirmaster was the musical director for Amateur Operatic Society productions, instrumentalists played in local orchestras and brass bands, singers appeared at folk clubs, and members of church choirs also belonged to local choirs or operatic societies. In conjunction with these many other organisations, the churches help to maintain the network of amateur musicians in the locality – and in this network, they themselves constitute one of the continuing nodes of musical practice.

The value system that lies behind this is not an unambiguous one, for there are those who query as well as those who applaud the presence of music. In Milton Keynes, there were fears about music 'taking over' as an end in itself, of people coming to church thinking more of the musical execution than worship, or of the dangers of music as 'entertainment'. Nevertheless the dominant ideology was of a close link between music and religion, with music contributing to church worship or forming one aspect of religious experience – 'a spirit of one-ness – of one mind'. This link was not just something drawn out by the outside observer but was expressed in many explicit comments: 'an art form that has been part of our worship for so many centuries I can't imagine worship without a huge content of music'; 'music is the most important vehicle to get people "in tune"'; 'music is one expression of the glory of the creator'; 'music ... has a unity function, a meditative function: it enables people to express something that's deep in their hearts that words can't express; it adds to the celebrative aspect of something; it is at the very centre of worship ...' – these were only some of the many local comments across the whole range of denominations.

Given these deep-rooted values associating music and religion, it is hardly surprising that despite the many historical changes in the position of the Christian church over the centuries, the churches have continued to form major – if often 'invisible' – centres for the maintenance, transmission and encouragement of music. This comes out not just in formal pronouncements by the churches at a national level or support from national church movements and associations to the sometimes struggling local groups, but also, and in the last analysis most fundamentally, through the work and commitment of hundreds of thousands of individuals in the local churches up and down the country. In this process, the many musicians and their supporters in the local churches in Milton Keynes were, as elsewhere, playing their essential part.

17

Club and pub music

Music is also often performed and organised in pubs and social clubs. These musical contexts may be less familiar to some readers, so it is worth stressing once again that within any English town – certainly in Milton Keynes – there are many different locales for music. These further settings are illustrated in this chapter.

There were many kinds of social clubs in Milton Keynes: youth clubs, working men's clubs, firms' social clubs, and the general social and recreational clubs in specific neighbourhoods. These were not specialist music societies, but many included music among their services, and though at any one time there were always a few in financial difficulties, overall they provided another continuing setting for local musical activity, unnoticed though this often was by those not directly involved.[1]

The working men's clubs – to start with them – regularly provided live musical entertainment.[2] Of the seven in Milton Keynes almost all were founded near the start of the century and by the 1980s had memberships of 1,000 or more each. Amidst their various attractions of pool, darts, skittles, crib, snooker, dominoes, bingo, and a congenial place to drink, live music was usually on offer every Saturday night. These were family-based social occasions, often supplemented by a separate organist and sometimes the occasional 'variety' or 'cabaret' show. A characteristic pattern was that in the 1,500-member Wolverton Central Working Men's Club (founded 1907). It had a disco plus bingo on Friday evenings, a live band on Saturday evenings which usually attracted around 150–200 (including many families with children), and a live band together with bingo on Sundays which brought in about 100 mainly middle-aged people, mostly couples. An additional Saturday attraction was an organist playing downstairs in 'old time style', with many of the older members joining in the sing-songs.

This blend of musical forms was common in the working men's clubs, which aimed to appeal to all tastes 'from toddlers to pensioners'; discos were generally for the younger groups (a minority), organists and 'old time' sing-songs for the oldest, and the live bands in between; all the clubs tried to insist on broad-based music from their bands: 'in a club you have to entertain everyone'. The clubs did not usually go for nationally acclaimed artists, but they did attract bands from a wider area than just Milton Keynes and paid higher fees than the pubs. Not all members took a direct interest in the music, of course, but it was assumed as one regular part of the club. 'Live entertainment is very popular' was a constant theme, something thought necessary to keep a good atmosphere as well as increasing bar takings, offering the opportunity for members to have a pleasant musical background or participate more actively as they wished, and in addition provide a limited number of paid engagements for local bands.

Other clubs with their own premises followed a similar pattern. The Green Grass Social Club, for example, had been founded in 1978 by a group from one of the local working men's clubs who took over a near-derelict building on the edge of Bletchley and turned it into a centre for Irish music and mutual help, mainly intended for local working-class men of Irish background. The main attraction was the music ('90 per cent Irish'), by local or near-local performers from Milton Keynes, Buckingham and Northampton – often relatively cheap 'one-man bands', with larger groups every two or three weeks. This regular weekly music had consistent audiences of 90–100 a time, mainly men of 25 upwards: the club attracted the older age groups (including many over-60s) and thus did not find it appropriate to put on discos. At the weekends there was also impromptu jamming and Irish singing, though anti-British songs were banned because of the club's non-political position. The club saw itself as providing an important service for local Irish people: 'there is nothing else that caters for their music'.

The main 'political' and armed services clubs also provided music, like the 50-year old Conservative Club in Bletchley with its bands or solo performers every Saturday, and a similar variety of music to appeal to the families 'from a wide spectrum of society' which made up a large proportion of the 1,600 membership. The Milton Keynes Rugby Club had its own particular pattern. It staged live bands from outside the area on weekly social nights throughout the summer (the non-playing season), but most Saturday games were followed by sing-songs in the bar, especially if the local team had won.

There were also the neighbourhood 'social' or 'sports and social' clubs. Many had been founded during the new city development and had as yet relatively few members and resources. They too aspired to provide live music, if only on a fortnightly or monthly basis, and despite struggling finances were trying to engage at least a guitarist singer, organist, duo or occasional band, to encourage sing-songs or, on occasion, persuade members to come up with cockney, Scottish or Irish songs at the end of a disco. The much older Woburn Sands Sports and Social Club did manage a regular local organist for people to waltz to and Saturday night groups attracting 150–300 members, many of them middle-aged couples, with carefully-chosen music ('no pop stuff'), while every month or so someone would bring along records for a sing-song. Despite financial cutbacks, music was taken for granted: 'we have to have it to keep the club running'. Firms' clubs, on the other hand, were less interested. Many claimed there was 'no demand' for live music; often they did not have their own premises (beyond access to the works canteen) so that opportunities were in any case limited. There were some exceptions, like the sing-songs and local bands at the Bletchley Post Office Social Club, but in general firms' clubs took little part in organising local musical activity.

This leaves the youth clubs, of which there were around sixty. Given the common association between 'youth' and 'popular music', these might be expected to be a major setting for local music. But though recorded background music and discos were common, many youth clubs had no live musical performances of the kind put on by the working men's and similar social clubs. The physical constraints of the buildings and apparent lack of interest in live music among the early teens partly explained this, but equally important was the view of many leaders that live music was divisive; in discos, unlike a live band, a balance of different music could be struck. A further complication according to some was that the boys found a live performance threatening: *they* would have liked to have been in front doing it and were jealous of the players' skill and self-exhibition. Youth clubs varied (and some exceptions are noted below), but for the most part, surprisingly, they had little or no scheduled live music.

What they did provide, however, was practice room. It was common for two or three rock bands to be 'based' at a club in the sense of regularly practising there once or more a week. Such bands were sometimes asked to play more directly for their fellow members or, as with the three bands that rehearsed at the Stantonbury Youth Club, used to leave the door open so that people could listen. Since finding a regular practice venue was a real problem for rock bands the provision of a room – and an indirect audience – was an important service.

There were also other exceptions to the general lack of live music in youth clubs, and at any one time there was usually at least one which did put on regular gigs. A lot depended on individual enthusiasts, but these clubs were generally among the more lavishly endowed, drawing on a city-wide rather than neighbourhood membership. In some years the Compass Youth Club in Bletchley was *the* place to go for rock bands. It also attracted its own rehearsal bands, like the two skinhead groups who practised once a week in 1983 as well as an all-black reggae group putting on a performance for members every two to three weeks. At other times the Compass Club had financial problems or troubles arising from musically generated disagreements, and other clubs, particularly that at Peartree Bridge Centre, came to the fore.

Peartree Bridge was set up to 'promote the performing arts' with an enthusiastic group of organisers, themselves keen on music. It was popular with local musicians because a large donation from the internationally famous band Police after a performance in the Milton Keynes Bowl had enabled them to install recording equipment as well as a stage and lighting for large-scale gigs. By 1983 bands from well outside the area were ringing up and offering to play at their Saturday music nights, which, together with a series of local bands, were attracting audiences of 150, or up to 250 for the local favourites, Solstice. They too had had their problems with opposing camps and some younger members did not really want live music, but for the many live music enthusiasts, preparing for or participating in the Peartree Bridge gigs was one continuing attraction.

The Peartree Bridge rehearsal facilities also helped to start off new bands. This was more than just the *physical* facility, for the general enthusiasm for music in the club encouraged players' interests and ambition. Sometimes the club organisers took an active part. One club leader described how 'four bored punks' were at the club one day and started 'mucking around' with some guitars and other instruments there. They enjoyed themselves and in a short time had made up a song about rape – but after some discussion with the leader agreed it was not really a fit subject for glorification. 'Their next effort', he continued, 'went so: "Fuck fuck fuck shit shit fuck fuck fuck" ad nauseam. However, the next week they returned to the club having become very enthusiastic about having a group. They had written a song about the horrors of Hiroshima.' This start to what resulted in a series of enthusiastic bands under various names was one example of the role which local youth clubs could play by providing both a practice and support locale.

Peartree Bridge also facilitated local recordings, not just by their equipment but also, on one occasion, co-operating in a 'Make-it-Yourself' scheme financed by Inter Action in London; local teenagers set up their own committee to do market research and then organised a recording of local bands, hiring the Woughton Campus hall so that each band could play in public; a high-priced ticket gave a discount on the recording. The committee also arranged the distribution of the album, entitled *A warped sense of humour*, selling some hundreds through local outlets – a strong encouragement to the confidence and achievement of a series of local players, many of them still musically active some years later.

The interesting thing about the local youth clubs, then, was that despite some striking exceptions and their general provision of much-needed practice facilities, *active* musical performances were only put on by a small minority of members – almost always male – and for the small neighbourhood youth clubs live musical engagements were the exception. Active music-making or live performances were thus *not* a universal or obligatory part of local 'youth culture', but rather a matter of personal choice within specific youth clubs.

The same kind of selectivity, combined with sets of accepted musical pathways for those interested, was evident all through the social clubs. Some had little or no live music. Even in those that did – most notably the working men's clubs – not all members necessarily paid much attention to the *musical* offerings. For those who did, however, there were accustomed channels which they could and did follow; applauding and dancing to 'middle of the road' music by small groups and singing 'old time' songs to a visiting organist were the most common. As in other spheres of music, active participation was by a minority only, but overall this minority amounted to many hundreds of people every weekend involved in some way or another in live music, while for the local bands the clubs provided an alternative (and more lucrative) opening to the pubs. Social clubs are less often considered as settings for local musical activity than the apparently more formalised settings of specialised music clubs or even of schools and churches, but in Milton Keynes at any rate many were providing an unpretentious and structured setting which, however varied over the years, was still, cumulatively, the context for a great deal of locally based musical practice.

Finally, that other traditional English institution, the pub. Considering the widespread view of pubs as 'unique to England' (Jackson 1976, p. 5), English pubs are surprisingly little studied.[3] This is the more striking because of the way pubs have long been one focus of social life through their provision of many kinds of recreation (not just drinking): games and sports (both legal and illegal), plays, striptease, dancing, music hall, and a whole variety of singing and instrumental music. The pubs in Milton Keynes continued that tradition, for they were the scene of a great deal of organised entertainment.[4]

Their significance as settings for music was often invisible to those who did not frequent the pubs or moved mainly in the classical or operatic music worlds. But it was quite startling to find how much local music went on there. I think for example of the White Hart, a pub not five minutes' walk from my house, which I passed several times a day with no inkling that it was the venue for a 1,000-member music club. It put on either live music or regular disco nights four to five evenings a week and was a recognised centre for local and regional bands. Club members paid £1 for a year and had free (or reduced) entry to the music nights. Most bands were 'progressive' or 'heavy metal' (the landlord's favourites) and played in the 'entertainment lounge' – a large room with a shallow stage at one side (doubling as small dance floor), bar at the other, and chairs and tables for the audience. It easily held 200, and did in fact attract that many on the occasions when particularly popular bands were playing, though on a poor night there were only 30 or so, and people were attracted not just from the immediate locality but from all over Milton Keynes, sometimes beyond. The local newspapers took notice too, and spoke of the White Hart 'becoming THE place ... for young music fans'. This did not necessarily mean an impersonal mass audience, however, for at least a nucleus of the same people, mainly in their twenties and both male and female, came back and back and regarded White Hart music evenings (especially the Wednesday 'rock nights') as regular occasions and, for them, 'local'.

A sample list of advertised White Hart attractions over two weeks in October 1981 will illustrate the bill of fare:

Wednesday 7 October: Exciters and Ice [a local band]; Thursday 8th: Sounds of the '60s with DJ Michael Dee; Friday 9th: Disco with Tony Charles; Saturday 10th: Disco with DJ Flip; Sunday 11th: lunchtime Jam 12 till 2 – 'Come along, listen, or play'; Wednesday 14th: The Void [local band]; Thursday 15th: Country Night with Ann and Ray Brett and Cuttin' Loose [local band and performers]; Friday 16th: Hit group of late '60s 'Marmalade' (O-bla-Dee etc.) [non-local band]; Sunday 18th: lunchtime Jam 12 till 2 – 'listen or play'; Wednesday 21st: Safety Valve [local band].

In theory the pub made money from membership fees, entrance charges for non-members, and the increased custom for drinks, but the financial element was in practice ambiguous, at best bringing in a very small profit. The landlord had other motives besides economic ones; he was himself a rock enthusiast and, on occasion, performer and was keen to fill his pub with fellow fans and to keep up contacts with musicians in Milton Keynes and beyond. He was also eager to create a musical reputation for his pub and build up the particular clientele this was attracting. He followed the tradition common to many English pubs of putting on events 'for charity' and liked to raise money for the hostel for the mentally handicapped a couple of hundred yards away; the pub also hosted a charity concert in December 1981 for the community radio (then under threat of closing down), featuring 'top local rock bands' like Martin S and the Suggestions and Seven Below, and raising £125 through door takings and a raffle for which the landlord put up the prize.

Not all pubs were so centred round music or organised their musical events in quite the same way as the White Hart. But it is an instructive case, for it illustrates how some energetically pursued local music could be quite unnoticed by other sections of the population. For those who knew where to look pubs were centres of musical activity, manifested in small notices in local newspapers, handwritten posters on pub windows, and informed interest by individual performers, listeners, and bands.

At any given period, particular pubs took leading roles only to lose interest or be supplanted by others as landlords, managements, financial policy or local tastes changed. (By early 1983, for instance, the landlord of the White Hart had been replaced, and the pub had given up live music.) Some pubs retained a reputation for music over long periods. One example was the Craufurd Arms in Wolverton, running weekly gigs for local bands like Safety Valve, Abacus, Weekend, Flavour, Ice, The Moles and the New Titanic Band and attracting regular local audiences over several years.

Another well-known rock pub (in 1982) was the Starting Gate in Central Milton Keynes, with 'heavy rock' every Friday and Saturday. The regular audience were local motor bikers. They and their supporters, aged from 20 to their late thirties, were themselves informally organised by the 'Mum of the bikers', whose daughters were married to local bikers. Well-known bands were invited, some from the region rather than the immediate locality such as Marrillion (from Aylesbury), Energy or Apocalypse, others from Milton Keynes itself (Solstice or Ice). On big occasions the lounge was packed out with around 200 people, adding other musical enthusiasts to the regular nucleus of motor bikers. As with the White Hart, there was also an emphasis on music for charity. One example was in mid 1982, arising from the pub's earlier Christmas gift of toys to the local handicapped children's school which engaged the motor bikers' interest, so they asked what further they could do ('I think', said the headmaster, 'they wanted to get away from this image people have of greasers'). When told of the appeal for a special head-band-operated computer for a little paralysed girl, they organised a 12-hour rock festival at the Starting Gate and rode over as a group to present the £100 raised from 'their' pub.

The old coaching inn of the Bull in Stony Stratford was different in concentrating on folk music. Every Sunday lunchtime their Vaults bar saw a regular sing-song by local folk performers like Matt Armour with a roomful of 50–100 people joining in. The Bull also sometimes joined with the other coaching inn down the road, the Cock (the originals for the 'Cock and Bull' stories), in running The Cock and Bull Folk Festival with local folk bands and performers. From time to time too it acted as host for events with a musical flavour like the 'charity pigroast' with local Morris dancers, jazz band, and rock group, an 'organ spectacular', a special session for one of the local jazz bands, or a barn-dance with a local ceilidh band for the Falklands Fund ('dress patriotic').

These cases illustrate the kind of music that went on in some leading Milton Keynes pubs, well enough patronised for some local observers to conclude that 'pub gigs' were now more popular than 'concerts' (*Milton Keynes Express*, 5 November 1981). How typical, however, were these examples? To answer this, a survey of all Milton Keynes pubs was carried out in the winter of 1982/3 which made clear that despite much variation in format and frequency music was indeed a feature of many local pubs.[5] Well over half at any given time were putting on live musical performances on an occasional or regular basis with yet others running discos or having had music in the past; under one-third provided only background music or juke boxes; and a small minority provided no music at all. In addition 20–25 other pubs within a 15- or so mile radius of Milton Keynes regularly provided musical attractions.

Some pubs found it difficult to cater for live musical performance because of their small premises, whereas others considered it too expensive, the brewery was against it, or the landlord did not like music. Most, however, took it for granted that music was advantageous; it gives 'good contact with the community; people who come just for music will later come back to use the pub', according to one landlord, while others commented that music brings a 'good atmosphere which gives the place character'. It was widely believed that music brought in more clients and that – since 'pubs today can't sit on their backsides and wait for custom to come in' – it was up to the landlords to lay on something special. Many saw live music as the best attraction. The established pattern of pub music meant that bands regularly phoned up offering to play and there was already a potential audience of people who had expectations of hearing live music in a context where both sociability and (to the pubs' direct advantage) alcoholic drinking was the norm. As one landlord congratulated himself, his musical arrangements 'attract the right sort of people – musicians are good drinkers'.

Though live music was common, any one pub did not necessarily put on musical entertainment on a weekly, let alone daily basis, and only a few (like the White Hart at its peak) offered live music several nights a week. About a quarter of those providing live musical entertainment arranged only occasional music evenings, say three or four times a year on 'promotion nights' or special occasions like the Royal Wedding in 1981 or festival days in the yearly calendar like Hallowe'en, New Year's Eve, St Patrick's Night, or Christmas (the choices depending on the pub and its clientele); occasionally pubs provided meeting places for competition heats or for charity events like pig roasts. At the other extreme, about a quarter had live music once a week or more often. Another quarter or so had performers once a fortnight, once a month or – less often – three times a month with the rest made up by more or less regular sing-songs. Fridays and Saturdays were the most popular evenings, but others were sometimes chosen, precisely because 'there's not much on anywhere that night'; Mondays or Tuesdays were sometimes favoured for regular music because there was less competition (or perhaps because some special attraction was needed to bring people out there).

With a few exceptions, then, any one pub did not provide musical performances all that frequently. Nevertheless the sum total was extensive and on any given night there were likely to be several musical events in local pubs (above all on Fridays and Saturdays). Despite the competing attractions, the numbers attending each were far from negligible, from around a dozen to 200 plus, with audiences of 100 or more quite common.

Pub music was typically provided by groups. There were also some sing-songs in the bar (some planned, some spontaneous), and about a quarter of performances were by soloists: keyboard (acoustic or electric piano, or organ), a singer/guitarist (the most common) or (occasionally) a singer with synthesiser. But over half the pubs went for group performers (duos, trios, or full four- or five-piece bands), and since bands were favoured by the most active pubs, band performances were overall the most frequent, mostly drawn from Milton Keynes itself or from the area regarded as in a way still 'local' – (within about a 20-mile radius, i.e. easy driving distance). Pubs were therefore among the main performance opportunities for local bands: those just starting up; those already reasonably successful in a wider area but still wanting some local gigs; and those without serious ambitions to go further but glad to have an audience to give them the pleasure of performing and perhaps a minimal fee to set towards expenses. Ice, Scream and the Fits, Bitza, Oxide Brass, Momentum, Martial Law, Safety Valve, The Moles, the New Titanic Band, Flavour and the Fenny Stompers were just a few of the many bands playing in local pubs in 1982–3.

Various forms of music were played – a point worth making given the common assumption that pub music is exclusively loud rock played to unselective audiences in their late teens and early twenties. Rock was certainly common, but individual pubs built up reputations for particular kinds of music (or for particular types on different nights of the week) and attracted audiences accordingly.

Jazz was played in a number of pubs, often to regular fans. The Galleon in Wolverton put on modern jazz on Tuesday evenings with a hard-core jazz following, about one-third, according to the landlord, coming 'just for the music', many of them policemen (the Galleon was near the police station). Others had resident jazz performers (the Fenny Stompers at the Station Hotel in Woburn Sands, for example, or Oxide Brass monthly at the Cock in Stony Stratford) or like the Bull in Newport Pagnell ran regular jazz 'clubs' for older audiences: 'jazz keeps the youngsters out', as one landlord summed it up. In some pubs jazz attracted the largest numbers, consistently 70–100 a night, and at any one time seemed to be being promoted by ten or so pubs, especially those in the old coaching inns.

Country and western music was played in around eight pubs, but was both costlier than rock and more repetitive than jazz. Many pubs therefore preferred just the occasional country and western performer or tried for a time and then, as with the Red Lion at Fenny Stratford, gave it up because 'he sang the same songs every evening and got very dull'.

Pubs were also the main locales for the folk clubs, which met in their private bars or special function rooms; also on occasion – as in the Black Horse 'folk days' – in pub grounds. In the summer, Morris dancers too appeared, complete with accompanying music. Regular events in the early eighties were the Castle Morris dancers' two-day tour in traditional narrow boats round pubs on the Grand Union Canal and the May Day 'Day of Dance' when local Morris groups danced in turn at seven different pubs in and around the city.

Brass bands also occasionally appeared at pubs. This was usually in the summer when they could play outside, as with the Woburn Sands Band in the Wheatsheaf gardens in Aspley Guise, but there were also winter occasions like the Wolverton Town Brass Band's carol-playing at the Walnut Tree in front of the Mayor and Mayoress. Other pubs also put on carol concerts. The Eager Poet on a new housing estate near the city centre tried to arrange 'community things' for recently arrived local people in the form of music, among them two successful carol concerts: one with the Wolverton Town Brass Band, one with a small community choir when the place was 'packed out – you couldn't move; the landlord was tickled pink', all the more because 'they took round the beer mug' and collected a good sum for the favourite local charity, Willen Hospice.

Rock was very popular with the pubs. This was partly because of costs since local rock bands had relatively few outlets and were prepared to come for little or no pay. They were also likely to draw large numbers, so long as they were publicised in the right areas, for local rock audiences were selective in their tastes and pubs became known at a given period (and for particular days of the week) for putting on specific types of rock. Some pubs specialised in heavy metal, others in 'punk', 'rock 'n' roll', 'funk', 'folksy rock', 'chart music', or 'sixties stuff'. Each drew its own audience, which in turn both reinforced that form of music and helped to define it.

Pubs were thus important locales for music not only for their physical facilities but also as organised settings within which group and individual definitions were worked out, with music as a reference point. This took place in a more selective way than is conveyed by the common picture – held mainly by outsiders – that music in pubs is an impersonal or simple 'mass' phenomenon, perhaps patronised almost exclusively by 'the youth' or, as some put it, 'the rough elements'.

This heterogeneity also applied to audience composition. Ages were generally quite varied, but of course specific pubs or types of music could attract particular age groups. Just over half the landlords described their audience's ages as either very varied (for instance, 'youngsters to OAPs') or as 'middle aged', just under a quarter as 18 or 20 upwards, and the rest as mainly in their twenties. The age groups sometimes sorted themselves out by coming on different nights and to different events, a pattern landlords were well aware of when they selected their entertainment.

The tradition that more men than women frequent pubs still applied. This was more extreme in some cases than others, however, and nearly half of the live music events attracted roughly equal numbers of men and women.

Publicans wanted to encourage more women and saw music as one way of achieving this. Sometimes it did not work – one landlord was asked to put on live music so that the men could bring their wives for a night out: 'they didn't though!' – but in many cases people came as couples, sometimes dancing to the music together.

Pubs tried to build up a nucleus of regular attenders for their music nights. Sometimes this was formalised through 'club' membership (as at the White Hart); more often the 'regulars' just turned up to music evenings, with additional listeners brought in when a well-known band was billed to play. Pubs were sometimes packed out when a band was publicised as in some of the advertisements pictured in figure 30, but pub policy was often to avoid attracting too many 'outsiders' and despite the financial advantage of numbers preferred to have known audiences: mixed groups and unfamiliar faces were more likely to lead to trouble. Pub audiences at musical performances usually contained a core of people who knew each other or at least had the common (and uniting) experience of shared participation in specific forms of music, aware of the unwritten traditions of that particular pub and usually with the same conventions for listening to musical performance. This lent credence to publicans' claims that audiences for *live* music (unlike discos) were not a problem to control. This personal atmosphere within pubs was encouraged by most landlords, and it had become the fashion for them to publicise their facilities under their own personal names (a number of the local pubs were run by couples). Advertisements on the lines of 'Alan and Sandra welcome you to live music, every Friday evening' were characteristic.

There was often a link between performers and audience. Particular performers were invited in response to direct requests from the pub 'regulars' or with reference to their expected preferences. This was mostly through personal contact, for unlike social clubs few pubs used agencies or recruited many performers from outside the local area.

Performers themselves often took the initiative in approaching the pub, sometimes over the telephone, sometimes coming to see the publican or sounding him out over a drink. The landlord then usually checked their suitability by asking around, hearing them at some other local venue, or requesting a sample tape. Equally often, the performers came through personal contacts. When one pub's electric piano player left, for example, his brother arranged a trio for them; or again, the barmaid knew Rod Hall (a well-known local musician) and he contacted others, 'then we got rid of the ones we didn't like'; or, from another landlord, 'I enquire of friends who run pubs.' In a couple of cases the Musicians' Union approached pubs to employ their members, but even this was done on a personal basis by the MU's local organiser, himself known to be a keen band player and living in the area.

Club and pub music

Some pubs preferred 'resident' bands performing weekly, fortnightly or monthly over several months. The jazz and folk 'clubs' held at local pubs were a version of this, an arrangement which often suited performers, pubs, and audiences alike. Others did not appear on such a predictable basis, but might nevertheless be asked back frequently, as familiar guests. Sometimes the audience numbers were swollen further by the band bringing their own followers, as with the T-Bone Boogie Band or Momentum's performances at the Cock, where about 90 per cent of the weekly audience went just to hear them play. Some landlords had strong musical preferences and irrespective of their regulars' tastes persevered with their chosen type of music. The result was that the regulars gradually selected themselves into those who liked – or tolerated – that form of music. Sometimes the selection was made by a club; artists for the folk club at the Cock in Stony Stratford, for example, were arranged by the club organiser through his regional or national folk contacts. The jazz clubs were more localised, resident bands being local favourites like the Fenny Stompers, Momentum, or the Mahogany Hall Jazz Band. These personal tastes and contacts, building largely on local networks, moulded the choice of pub music and performers, and, as a consequence, most performers playing at local pubs had many friends or acquaintances among their audience.

The term 'audience' has been used so far. These were not audiences in the sense of listeners to a classical concert, for the atmosphere was a relaxed one, and people were drinking and moving around, talking as well as listening. The music, however, was important in setting the atmosphere and defining the situation; it was, after all, performed *music* that was in question rather than, say, juggling, visual display, political speeches, or striptease (to mention some possible alternatives). But that many people were also listening at least for a portion of the time seemed obvious both from observation and from comments by audience members and by the publicans (who had to keep a watchful eye on customers' preferences). The audience's reception depended very much on their assessment of the performers – sometimes lively applause after every song, with listeners taking a great interest in the music or asking for more, sometimes bored and not staying, sometimes *appearing* uninterested but in fact coming back in large numbers every music night: 'the performers think the audience are not listening – but they do. People ring to check the performer is on.'

One way people showed their involvement was singing along, especially in folk, Golden Oldies and country and western pub evenings or, particularly as the evening wore on, in dancing. The amount was unpredictable but was generally taken to be a mark of appreciation of the music: 'some nights there is little reaction; other nights they really enjoy it and get up and dance.'

Insofar as dancing was one form of musical participation it is also worth mentioning briefly the 'disco' evenings (sessions for dancing to popular records) – not strictly active music-making, but with some resemblances to it. Dancing can constitute not just audience participation but a kind of musical activity and realisation in itself; in addition the music in discos was not just impersonal canned music but presented by an individual who himself added a performance element, sometimes supplemented by visual display or spoken additions to the music played. Local disco outfits built up particular reputations and involved known *individuals* with their own equipment and personal contacts with the pub regulars – a contrast to the faceless technology suggested by the term 'disco'.

Discos were common, run by about one-third of the pubs interviewed in 1982–3; over half of those put on discos once a week or more which attracted large numbers (often over 100, sometimes 250 plus). They attracted rather younger attenders than live music and had less male preponderance. The music varied but was also sometimes carefully chosen to appeal to particular audiences, like the Bletchley Arms 'Golden Oldies' and 'Country and Western' discos. The apparatus and presentation were sometimes organised by an outside outfit hired by the landlord (at a cost of around £25–30), but as far as possible a presenter familiar to the customers was selected, sometimes himself 'one of the regulars' or someone recommended by the customers; at the Bradwell Monk the landlord did it himself. Personal links were thus again important but probably less so than for fully 'live' music, partly because of the larger disco audiences. Consequently landlords found disco evenings harder to control and some actively disliked them, preferring the personal atmosphere of live groups.

The financial arrangements for pub music were on the face of it simple. Live performers sometimes played free but were often paid around £25–50 for a group and £15–20 for soloists, sometimes supplemented by beer, other drinks or occasionally food (but nothing additional for expenses). Apart from the clubs meeting in pub premises there was usually no entrance charge for live events, but customers financed the occasion indirectly by attending in larger numbers and buying more drinks.

In practice the financial aspects were more complex. Publicans were often uncertain whether live music was really financially worth while, and though occasionally performances were seen as bringing in a profit the general picture was the vague one of 'just breaking even' or making just a small amount. Discos, by contrast, were clearly profitable, which is not surprising given the large numbers they pulled in. One pub moved from average takings of £1,700 to £4,000 per week after introducing discos, and as one publican put it 'discos three nights a week drives you bonkers – but those three nights pay the bills; the rest of the week you can have a nice local pub'. It might seem surprising therefore that so many pubs still went in for live music – except that financial profit was not the only factor. With few exceptions live music was seen as more attractive in itself than discos, less prone to trouble, and generally valued for its atmosphere: 'it adds a sort of air to the reputation of the place'. On the other hand, certain *types* of live music were sometimes frowned on; at one pub 'heavy rock' and at another 'punk rock' were in turn seen as 'bringing in the wrong crowd' and were discontinued. The overall aim was – as one landlord put it – that 'the music I have suits my particular pub'. Much therefore turned not so much on money as on the image, landlord and expected clientele of each pub, things which often changed over the years.

Musical events thus formed one common facet of pub activity, for the most part arranged to fit the varying interests and networks in the locality rather than on a mass entertainment basis. The pubs themselves were thus one structured and predictable locale for music, with their own contribution to the organisation of local music. They had a mutual relationship with local bands and other performers and provided musical entertainment for large numbers of people in conditions which were to them congenial and appropriate settings for musical performance and appreciation – an essential part, for many, of local musical life.

The local pubs and clubs and the groups who played there can be seen as the counterpart, at the local and amateur level, of the professionals who have 'made it' and play in public entertainment venues in the national context. But local pub and club playing is more than just a pale reflection of those well-known groups which to some scholars and admirers have seemed more 'real' because picked out by the limelight of the national mass media. Bands in the local pubs and social clubs have an essential role in feeding the national scene, both directly in the groups that come up through local circuits, and indirectly through the moulding of the audience perceptions and interests initiated or enhanced at the local level. These local venues, furthermore, and the musical performances that take place there, have their own reality too: not just the foundation for or reflection of commercially successful groups, but a locally expressed and tangible manifestation of music in its own right, one continuing – if seldom studied – expression of twentieth-century English culture.

18

Working at it: organisation and administration in music groups – the case of the Sherwood Choir

Music, like any other performed art, does not just float up naturally, but has to be *made* to happen. This should already be clear from the earlier discussion, but in this chapter is explored more directly and related to the problem of organisation underlying the musical practices described earlier. It is also illustrated in more detail through its application to one particular local group.

Local music is dependent on local action and on the cultural definitions that – wherever they may have been first generated – are accepted and perpetuated by the active participants. This may seem too obvious to need stating. But it in fact runs counter to the common view of music as somehow beyond social conventions, the preserve of innate musical talent. Contrary to this view, the practice of music is essentially dependent on its social organisation and on the actions and administration through which it is on any specific occasion actively realised. It is always taken for granted that *professional* music demands work and organisation, just as the administration of large-scale organisations is accepted as important for the maintenance of these institutions and of self-evident interest to researchers. But the informal and less 'visible' activities underlying local amateur music *also* involve administration, arguably as interesting as the structures of large bureaucracies or the dispensers of public money.

There are a series of common problems with which local musical groups have to find ways of coping, the larger and more formal organisations (the focus of this chapter) as well as the small bands (chapter 19). These are almost always the responsibility of local people working on a voluntary basis, using their own time and contacts to enable the musical activity they support to go ahead in the circumstances they consider appropriate.

One specific case, the Sherwood Choral Society, will be used to illustrate these general processes. This was a four-part choir founded in Bletchley in 1973, which by the 1980s was drawing members from throughout Milton Keynes and its surrounding area. Over the years the numbers varied between

30 and 70; members were mainly middle-aged to elderly, but there were a few schoolchildren and many of the members had church connections. As was common in choirs, women were in the majority. The choir followed the typical choral cycle of two main concerts a year, mostly drawn from the classical repertory by such composers as Handel, Brahms, Haydn, and Vivaldi, supplemented by the occasional performance of modern and more light-hearted works.

This all seems quite straightforward and usual, and for most of the time was indeed reasonably problem-free. But consider what was involved in keeping these arrangements going and making the choir's enjoyment of their singing possible at all: the subject of this chapter.

The choir had to be started in the first place. This may sound simple enough, but a host of hitches were possible and there had been optimistic groups and individuals who had *not* managed to get a choir off the ground. There were various requirements: a qualified and enthusiastic conductor; an accompanist; a place for regular rehearsals, with heating, piano and coffee-making facilities; people prepared to undertake secretarial, financial and social chores; and a large number of keen singers, preferably with experience, willing to commit themselves for an evening a week for the foreseeable future.

There was a conductor available: Malcolm Crane, who had recently been recruited to the LEA North Bucks Music Centre as a peripatetic brass teacher. He was keen to start up a choir and persuaded the Music Centre and its Director to back him.

Contacting and enlisting potential singers was another thing again. Would enough people be interested? and how to get in touch with them? This was partly done by local press advertisements, partly by contacting existing organisations and individuals likely to take an interest. The Music Centre was particularly important here. It was a focus for a whole circle in Bletchley and beyond: small groups used its hall for practising, people met to discuss and enjoy music, music teachers left their names with the secretary, people phoned up asking about local music or prospective teachers, and there was constant contact with the schools through the peripatetic teachers and the Centre's Saturday morning orchestras. The Centre also had its own mailing list, and the services of a part-time secretary and a duplicator. All these channels were activated to call people for an initial meeting at the Music Centre – not just formal letters but innumerable phone calls, private conversations, and a whole network of personal contacts.

Equally important were the known conventions of English choral singing. It could rightly be presumed that there was local interest and expertise to be tapped, backed by the long local choral tradition. But there *was* a gap in the local offerings, for there was currently no independent four-part choir in

Bletchley that could undertake the kind of major works Malcolm Crane was suggesting: Fauré's *Requiem* and Handel's *Messiah*.

At the inaugural meeting that resulted at the Music Centre on 10 January 1973, it was agreed to start a choir entitled the Sherwood Choral Society. Crucial decisions were also taken about general policy on performance, timing, accompanist and subscriptions. Leaving aside the details of this first meeting – which itself had to be carefully managed with consideration for both established interests and individual personalities – it is worth empha-sising that even then the initial development was by no means complete. More singers had to be drawn in, the pattern of rehearsing developed, and the new committee and office-holders work out their mutual responsibilities. Decisions had to be followed up about music, finance, the first concert, and the arrangements for tea- and coffee-making at rehearsals. There were known precedents from other choirs and clubs – and many new members came with this experience – so not everything had to be worked out from first principles, but such decisions did not just make themselves and depended on co-operation (sometimes conflict) between a number of people and on their ability to carry others with them.

The Sherwood Choir, as they were informally called, started rehearsals in the early months of 1973 with a paid-up membership of 45 (£2 a head), and gave their first concert in Buckingham Church in June 1973. The main choral work was Fauré's *Requiem*, and it was accompanied by the newly formed Sherwood Sinfonia orchestra, who provided the music for the other half of the concert – an appropriate collaboration given the personal links between choir and orchestra and their connection with the North Bucks Music Centre. But even after this successful début problems continued, demanding effort, decisions and tact. This was not because the choir was particularly trouble-prone – it was not – but because the successful maintenance of any such organisation demands constant work by the participants.

First, fluctuating membership was always a matter for concern. No one was quite sure why it went down from time to time over the years. Was it the music? Fauré's *Requiem* and the *Messiah* were favourites in the choral repertory, but numbers fell off for less familiar works. Was it competition from other choirs as the new city grew, some with the high prestige of being directed by professionally connected musicians? Was it conflicts within the choir (of which there was the usual quota) over personalities, musical policy, or organisational details? People disagreed, sometimes loudly, more often in sotto voce mutterings, about the choice of music (must we have so much Latin? or, alternatively, so many modern works?) or about soloists, the concert pattern, the accompanist, the conduct of rehearsals, the coffee/tea roster, and so on and so on – the familiar issues of most choral groups. Towards the end of the choir's first ten years the membership had more or less settled to around 35–45 (rather small for some) with a steady nucleus of long-term members, but even this varied and it was always a matter of anxiety how many would turn up to start a new season.

It was not surprising, then, that the conductor and officers were always urging members to bring along new singers. Most came through personal contacts but some were attracted by having heard the choir sing, read advertisements or reports in the press, or themselves initiated inquiries if they had recently moved into the area. Some joined only for a season or two but most stayed several years, learning the art of choral singing as they participated or drawing on and developing their existing choral experience (some had been singing for over 40 years and knew the standard repertoire from cover to cover). There was always some loss: schoolchildren grew up and went off, people moved away, demands from jobs or families changed, the current music did not appeal, friends suggested a different choir, transport arrangements broke down, illness or increasing age made evening outings a problem ... and a host of other reasons. In fact, when one considers people's different responsibilities and the problems of juggling time and commitments to guarantee a particular evening free each week, let alone arranging to get there, the wonder was not that people left but that so many continued to turn out to rehearsals and concerts season after season.

Mere numbers were not enough, for a balance of voices was also needed. Like others, the Sherwood Choir was usually shortest of tenors and basses (particularly the former). Not that these sections were necessarily always the weakest, for a few experienced men held their own against a preponderance of women; but when, say, there were only two or three tenors in all, any crisis that kept away even one could radically affect the balance in four-part (even more eight-part) singing. At other times there were worries about the sopranos: their numbers were fine, but did they need more young voices to improve the high notes? And would a rearrangement in seating help to balance some current deficiency? There was always some problem to contend with, and the need for both conductor and choir to co-operate in its solution.

The registered membership was one thing, but the actual turnout at rehearsals something yet again. Week after week the conductor had to look at empty chairs – sometimes only one or two, sometimes great expanses – and every now and then was provoked into launching into that well-known diatribe in all musical groups: castigating those who were there with the irresponsible absence of those who weren't. From the point of view of individual singers, there were a hundred and one reasons why they might be missing: illness; a conflicting engagement (Wednesday evenings might be a regular commitment but there were always one-off events like a family visit, church occasion or another concert); travelling away for work or family; extreme bad weather; transport break-downs; baby-sitting problems. The conductor and chairman spoke emotively of the need to regard choir practice as 'absolute *top priority*, everything else coming second' – and people would nod agreement enthusiastically or smugly, but in practice there were obstacles for somebody just about every week. Some consistently found it harder than others, particularly mothers of young children, London commuters, and the elderly (especially susceptible to illness and the fear of illness); some individuals had a particularly heavy round of evening commitments at certain times of the year, for example during the annual Festival of Arts, in which several members took leading roles. Despite all resolves, the weekly commitment was not easy to fulfil and a great deal of perseverance was needed to ensure that for most of the time most of the members did indeed turn up.

Just recruiting and retaining the choir members and getting them to rehearsal thus involved effort enough. But this was far from the end of the tasks needed to keep the choir going.

Some were dealt with by the officers, for like most choirs the Sherwood Choral Society had a formally organised structure with a constitution laying down the rules for the management of the society's affairs and its overall aims (common ones in choir constitutions): 'The Objects of the Society shall be to educate the public in the arts and sciences, and in particular the art and science of music, by the presentation of concerts and other activities.' There was a regular and predictable annual cycle for the payment of membership dues, auditing of accounts, Annual General Meeting, and election of officers (Chairman, Secretary and Treasurer) and of committee. There was seldom if ever any contest over these honorary posts, partly because of the outward consensus philosophy on which the choir was run (which didn't prevent disagreements behind the scenes), but perhaps mainly because of the work involved: the difficulty was more to talk people into taking on official responsibilities than a plenitude of candidates. The committee members and officers were primarily responsible for most of the necessary chores, but help was needed from other members and their acquaintances, help on which the success of the choir was ultimately dependent.

Some further examples will help to bring this home. Take just the routine running of rehearsals. Once people had been persuaded to attend that might seem to be that. But even leaving aside the *musical* matters much still remained to be done. The room, for example: the choir were fortunate in being able to use the North Bucks Music Centre Hall – not something which could have been taken for granted (indeed many other choirs had much greater difficulty and expense); but even here there were constraints, for the Centre closed during school holidays and any rehearsals outside the usual Wednesday evenings had to be negotiated with other users or accommodated elsewhere. The room had to be opened (and there were occasions when the arriving choir had to wait outside in the cold until someone came late with the key), and though the heating was supplied both this and the lights sometimes failed. During the day the hall was used for other purposes, so the stacked-up chairs had to be put out in the correct rows and numbers for the current choir sections. This was theoretically the men's job, complementing the women's responsibility for tea and coffee, but in practice most of the early arrivals took a hand and at the end everyone stacked up their own chairs. But every now and then there were queries about this division of labour to be settled.

A break of fifteen minutes or so was an essential part of each rehearsal, not only for a brief rest and drink, but for a chance to exchange gossip. This too had to be arranged.

A woman committee member always had the job of drawing up a rota for preparing the tea and coffee, collecting the payment, and washing up. The designated pair had to get there early, put out the cups and saucers ready on the tables at the end, then fill up the large electric urn. That done, they could join the rehearsal, keeping an ear for the urn boiling too wildly, and ready to go out for the final preparations a few moments before the interval. Then they were busy pouring out and refilling the jugs from the heavy scalding boiler at the same time as trying to look cool and hospitable as they handed out the cups. Afterwards came the washing up, putting away, cleaning up and – worst job of all – emptying out the still-steaming urn: it was seldom that they managed to get back to their seats without missing yet more singing. It was not the done thing to complain, but people heaved a sigh of relief when their turn was over and they could just sing for another few weeks. The committee member in charge had no let-up, however, checking every week that the duty pair were there, giving a hand herself if there were problems, cajoling people to commit themselves for later dates, taking the urn home and bringing it back again each week, providing two clean tea towels, buying the tea, coffee, sugar and milk and *always* being on time with them, and checking that all was in order afterwards with the takings delivered to the Treasurer. All trivia, it could be said. But they were trivia that were essential to the happy functioning of the choir, trivia that had to be organised by *someone*.

Other requirements were closer to the musical tasks. The Sherwood Choir were lucky in having the use of a tuned piano already in the hall, so the instrument itself seldom caused problems. But a skilled accompanist was also needed, to provide far more than just a piano background. He or she also had to play out the parts with each section, sound the initial notes, hammer out lines where singers were having trouble, and develop a sixth sense for where the conductor wanted to restart. The choir were generally fortunate in their series of accompanists who, barring the occasional controversy, got on well, turned up on time, and could sight-read as well as cope with differing musical styles. By the early 1980s, the choir could boast with some justice that their current accompanist – the middle-school teacher Ros Whatmore – was 'the best in Milton Keynes'.

The conductor himself took a central role. The detailed rehearsal techniques will not be pursued here except to comment that these too involved a series of decisions by the conductor, often implicitly negotiated with the choir, about how to interpret a work, attain certain effects, and help develop the choir's skills. Other points are worth noting, however. The conductor had to arrive in good time for each rehearsal (a practice seldom broken) and persuade choir members to be equally prompt (not so successful). There were also the concurrent but conflicting desires of choir members, on the one hand to get on with the rehearsal, on the other to exchange news with their neighbours or comment on the bit of music they had just been trying to sing – they'd partly come for a social night out, not *just* for the music. The result was some element of hidden struggle between conductor and choir, the conductor trying to keep people's full attention throughout the practising, the choir accepting this in principle but still wanting just to make their own personal remark to their neighbours. Mostly this was conducted with great good humour (with the occasional outburst), but it was yet another instance of how even the apparently unproblematic process of a rehearsal itself involved questions of control, decision making and organisation.

The choir sang from written music – typical of the classical musical world – and this was yet something else to be arranged. Some choirs asked members to purchase their own copies, but this was not generally true of the Sherwood Choir and would not have been easy for the choir's many short items; but the music had to be procured somehow before even one effective rehearsal could be held. It was the job of the 'librarian' committee member to search out sources of multiple copies, negotiate to borrow them, arrange for postage or delivery, distribute them at the start of rehearsals, keep track of who had what copy, and ensure they were all returned promptly after the concert – an arduous task. If printed music was not available or a piece was specially arranged or composed for the choir a manuscript copy had to be laboriously written out by hand and photocopied.

The routines of rehearsing thus demanded considerable effort and organisation. The same was true of the lengthy arrangements necessary for putting on concerts. For the two main concerts which the choir gave most years the date was settled up to a year in advance, essential to avoid a clash of dates with other performances. Forgetting to check on competing claims on the same potential audiences and players could be disastrous, as when one of the local Gilbert and Sullivan societies scheduled a performance for the same evening as a Sherwood Choir concert, both hoping to use scratch orchestras from the same small nucleus. The Sherwood Choir that time got in first but did not altogether win, for their accompanist had to go to the other society (for which she also played) to compensate for their lack of orchestra. The local arts association tried to keep a central music diary to avoid clashes, but this was not always consulted or fully up to date, so conflicts still occurred.

Booking the hall also had to take place early, usually a simple enough matter but still needing to be remembered. Most halls used for Sherwood Choir concerts (like the College of Further Education hall in Bletchley or the parish church) had other demands on them which sometimes made use impossible on the night the choir wanted, leading to real problems if the booking was left late. Other details also needed checking: was there a piano? an organ? were they playable? who would get the piano tuned? was the hall available for a final afternoon rehearsal? what about lighting? heating? a room for the soloists? and for the choir to gather in beforehand? facilities for making and serving refreshments in the interval? platforms for the choir or space for the orchestra? seating arrangements for the audience? and if the acoustics were dreadful was it possible to rearrange the hall? All this had to be discovered or, if known from previous use, rechecked.

There were also the outside performers. Most of the choir's big concerts involved soloists, necessary for many works in the choral repertory and yet another reason why concert dates had to be settled well in advance. The soloists themselves were of various kinds, depending on the choir finances, the musical work and scale of the concert. Local soloists were often used and given a token fee or presentation. They included local teachers who had specialised in music, a part-time choirmaster well known as a soloist in the area, a sixth-former hoping to take up music – there was no shortage of local talent. In the more light-hearted concerts, solo parts were sometimes taken by members of the choir itself, but for big occasions soloists were formally booked from outside, often young singers still early in their careers. It was one of the committee jobs to sift through their brochures, deciding on suitability and likely fee as well as on availability, assisted by any personal contacts. All this once again meant work – not just selecting soloist(s), but negotiating date and fee, finding alternatives if necessary, and sometimes getting a last-minute substitute.

Other additional performers might also be needed. The many choral works with orchestral accompaniment always presented a problem. Fortunately, as with many choirs, several members had contacts with local instrumentalists, sometimes themselves playing in orchestral groups; the peripatetic music staff and their contacts were a frequent resource, and many a time the choir were supported by a group led by the violinist head of the North Bucks Music Centre. Each time, however, this had to be negotiated, and since it was not a permanent group its composition changed depending on who was available, what senior pupils or music students were around, and what else was on that evening. It was basically on friendship lines, but a token amount was also usually paid to players and this too had to be decided – and however little it was per player it was still an expense for the choir, a constraint on how often they could choose music needing an orchestra. The expense was even greater when local players needed supplementing by outside and more expensive instrumentalists in works where one instrument took a prominent role, like the trumpet in *Messiah* or the harp in Fauré's *Requiem*.

Many concerts had piano or organ accompaniment alone – both easier and cheaper, for the regular accompanist could play and for some music this was the most suitable form in any case. It was not totally problem-free, for the instruments at the concert venue were variable indeed, especially the idiosyncratic organs which often caused problems for both players and choir, but it was a frequent arrangement, one felt especially appropriate for the concerts in local churches.

The choir sometimes performed jointly with others, often some local group to which one or more choir members themselves belonged. The conductor's brass expertise came in useful and the choir frequently joined with wind groups for which he played or conducted: the Boot Brass Ensemble (local brass players), Sarabande (early music on replica instruments by teachers from Hertfordshire, Bedfordshire, and Buckinghamshire, several with Milton Keynes connections), and the North Bucks Youth Wind Band. Decisions had to be made in advance and the music negotiated, but co-operation of this kind was straightforward to organise and of benefit to both sides.

There was yet more to be done at the time of the performance itself. Rehearsals were intensive leading up to a concert, sometimes supplemented by additional practices the week or so before (provided a place could be found and singers were able to come outside their usual schedule). For every main concert there was also a full rehearsal in the hall itself on the afternoon of the performance, one reason for scheduling most concerts on Saturday or Sunday, so performers could be free for the rehearsal as well as the concert.

A great deal had to be done at that final rehearsal. The choir's seating had to be ordered, usually easier said than done in an unfamiliar setting (so singers often had to accept unfamiliar seating – always an occasion for grumbles), and spaces had to be left for absentees, preceded by searching inquiry as to whether they were or were not coming on the night. The conductor's position had to be tested out – did he need a platform to be seen? And what about the location of instrumentalists, piano, soloists? There were standard conventions for all this, but they still had to be reviewed in the actual hall and its acoustics. Lighting had to be thought about, and the provision of music stands, the setting up and testing of microphones for any recording, and in some cases the audience seating.

Figure 29 The Sherwood Choir perform Brahms' *German Requiem* in Buckingham Parish Church jointly with the Market Harborough Choral Society and a local orchestra led by David Stevenson

Where more than one work was involved the performers had to know the order, so someone had to arrange to distribute typed copies of the programme to each singer, and the choir exhorted to get their music tidily in order (sometimes in special folders, also needing providing) and *not* to keep rustling it. All this was essential organisation before even thinking about the musical side. That, of course, formed the central focus of the final rehearsal and was long and intensive: adjusting volume, tempo or balance according to the acoustics and the combination with unfamiliar soloists or instrumentalists, sorting out differences in the scores held by the choir and those joining them (sometimes a real problem), checking choir–soloists joins, and going over again and yet again some familiar problem spot in the choir's performance. After two to three hours the choir went home exhausted, with only a couple of hours or less to eat and change before having to be back at the hall again.

For the conductor it was often longer still, for he often had to stay for yet further rehearsal with soloists or instrumentalists. He had also usually been implicated in other last-minute arrangements, from lugging around portable platforms to fetching music stands or, on a few dire occasions, phoning round all his musical friends to get a last-minute replacement for a soloist struck down by illness.

There were also other matters. The hall had to be open and ready for the audience, preparations made for refreshments in the interval, and the tickets and programmes ready; as the Secretary commented, 'Everyone takes it as just natural that Sue will provide the programmes every time, but it's a lot of work' – which, indeed it was, needing typing, the paper bought, and copies run off on the Music Centre mimeograph. For special occasions, too, flowers were prepared by particularly skilled choir members. Where the soloists were to have a presentation this also had to be in hand, usually bouquets for the women soloists, a frequent ceremony at the close of a classical concert. Visiting singers or instrumentalists also had to be looked after: usually arranged in advance, with choir members volunteering to take them home after the afternoon rehearsal to have tea and change before the evening, but occasionally there were embarrassing last-minute gaps – yet something else to get organised.

There was then a general rush to get ready for the concert. Some had to travel quite a way home after the afternoon rehearsal, others were preparing tea for their families or looking after soloists, and all were tired but at the same time expectant, looking forward to the evening. The singers had to dress in their 'concert uniform' – long black skirts, white blouses and purple neckbands for the women, and for the men dark suits and purple bow ties (something else needing organising). Soloists had to change too, usually long dresses for the women, formal evening wear for the men, in keeping with the ceremonial dress expected in a classical concert.

Somehow the performers managed to get back to the hall by the appointed time. Whatever their private scrambles, they were now all elaborately dressed ready for the big occasion. Visiting musicians were brought by their hosts of the afternoon – a point that might seem too obvious to mention, except that there could be hitches. There was the famous occasion on the grand Tenth Anniversary Concert when the choir's (usually highly efficient) Chairman entertained three of the soloists for tea, then drove off with only two, leaving the baritone soloist in the empty house with no idea of how to reach the hall. The mistake wasn't realised for some time and the concert began late – but the baritone still sang beautifully.

There were usually special arrangements for the performers at the hall. The soloists had to have their own room for any final preparations and for waiting when not on stage while the choir usually gathered in another, leaving their coats and making final adjustments to their appearance. For big concerts they filed into their places shortly before the beginning, marshalled by one of the committee after the conductor had appeared for a brief word. In less formal affairs they went straight to their places when they arrived having first left their coats in some place arranged beforehand (another job for some committee member).

The musical conduct of the concert and the conventions of the actual performance will be left on one side, except to recall the amount of *musical* organisation involved in the performance itself as well as in its preparation. It is also worth recalling again that the responsibility for the event did not just lie with the performers. As described in chapter 12, the audience too had a part to play not only by making the effort to get there at all but also by reacting during the performance: applauding, commenting, congratulating their friends during the interval and at the end, and providing by their mode of sitting and their behaving the element of ceremony that defined the occasion as a musical event.

The performance over, there were still things to do: the hall to be tidied up and any platforms or equipment put back, the music on loan to be collected and sent off, and the soloists thanked and paid. Visiting musicians might need overnight hospitality or a drink and snack before leaving. Mostly the choir were free to leave soon after, going off with friends or relatives they had invited to the concert – who, in performance of their audience duties, discussed and praised the performance. There was sometimes a regular Wednesday meeting following the concert, the choir agog to hear the conductor's reactions, but often they were free until the start of the next session some weeks later, when the rehearsal round would begin again.

The organising described so far was only part of what was needed to set up a concert. The point has already been made that one absolute essential for a public performance in the full sense was an *audience*. Once again this could not just be assumed and a great deal of time was conventionally spent on securing this. Everyone accepted that 'publicity' was essential: posters were printed and small ads placed in local newspapers or sent in good time to one of the free local events brochures, and singers who had contacts with local papers pressed them to preview the concert.

All this sounds straightforward, relying on the printed media to advertise the coming event. But in practice this was only the start, and the choir themselves had to organise effective communication. The posters had to be *displayed* to be successful, so after collection from the printers the bundle was brought to the next practice and every member given several to put up. Everyone had their chosen spots – the local libraries, music shops, music centres, local corner shops, people's own windows, their place of work, schools, churches, clubs – or wherever individuals could gain access or cajole permission, and be bothered to remember to do it. Announcements were also sometimes produced for other groups regarded as friendly (usually because of overlapping membership), a reciprocal arrangement beneficial to both sides. Dissemination thus essentially rested on the networks built up round each individual choir member and the work he or she put in to keep them effective.

'Publicity' was seen as an essential prelude to a concert, something which helped to define it as a 'proper' public performance. How far this in itself sold tickets or brought in the audience was less clear; indeed some doubted whether anyone ever came to a concert just from having seen a poster. Most probably depended on the informal efforts of the choir itself. The weeks leading up to a concert were always characterised by announcements that tickets were on the piano for members to take to sell, followed by heartfelt pleas from the conductor *please* to get rid of them: 'if each of you just take four we'll have at least a respectable audience'. Friends and relations of the performers always made up a large proportion of the audience, and without their willingness to come or the choir's work in persuading them the concerts would probably have been total flops. The occasion when only eight people turned up ('and four of *them* were brought by the bass soloist') was long notorious in the choir's mythology. Occasionally tickets were also sold through music shops, direct from the secretary, or, on the few occasions when the bigger centres were used, through their box offices, but the effective sales were through personal pressure. One additional reason for collaboration with the North Bucks Youth Wind Band was precisely that they drew in an additional network, including parents supporting their children's music (they often had to transport them anyway, so might as well stay to listen!). Probably everyone who finally came had something else he or she might have done instead; so getting the audience was far from automatic but depended upon a great deal of effort by a large number of people, listeners as well as performers.

Besides their two main concerts, the Sherwood Choir also gave some less formal performances by invitation – in nearby churches, for example, or for the local Masonic Christmas social (through a contact in the choir, naturally). These meant less organising from the choir's side: publicity was arranged by the hosts, the local arrangements were not the choir's concern, and since such events were often during the week and not grand occasions with specially engaged soloists, practices were not so fraught and the final afternoon rehearsal was sometimes omitted. Even these occasions meant *some* arranging, not least the initial contact which led to the invitation, but the choir always particularly enjoyed them because they could just sing without having to think about the chores, and as one member rightly said of one such performance, 'In these village churches you can *always* count on an audience.'

All these rehearsals and performances depended on the back-up work by the officers and committee. Much of it was basically like that in any other voluntary association, the correspondence and finance above all. It was the secretary's job not just to write up minutes after the AGM (not an arduous task), but also to take responsibility for official communications like applications for grants, negotiating with possible soloists, booking halls, arranging for piano tuning, and on occasion writing to individual members at times of personal celebration or crisis. The Secretary was the main official contact point between the choir and those outside, and his or her correspondence and telephone calls covered a wide range of topics and were a constant and time-consuming activity.

Finance was another thing which could not just look after itself. People were singing for love, not money, but even so there were costs. The Treasurer had to keep the books balanced, arrange the auditing and collect the yearly subscription which went some way to paying for halls, soloists, publicity, and music, but other sources were also needed. Part was sometimes met by grants from such bodies as the National Federation of Music Societies, the Borough of Milton Keynes, or the Milton Keynes Arts Association, but this usually demanded a vast effort of form-filling by Secretary or Treasurer – they sometimes wondered if it was all worth it. Other amounts had to come from the choir's own efforts: fund-raising activities like jumble sales, social evenings, selling Christmas cards or cassettes of a recent performance, raffles, collecting 'voluntary' donations at rehearsals, or a coffee morning laid on by one of the choir, a familiar local institution in which guests (often themselves members or friends of the choir) paid a high price for coffee and took a generous part in the bring-and-buy stall.

Many of the contacts which lay behind the continued existence of the Sherwood Choir were informal and personal, but official communication was also an element, and over the years the choir were amassing their own collection of written records. Shortly before their first ten years were up these already filled three hefty files and folders: the Secretary's correspondence with soloists, choir members, or institutions like the National Federation of Music Societies; records of concert arrangements, halls, and advertising; past posters and programmes; membership lists; financial statements; AGM minutes; brochures from would-be soloists; material from the National Federation of Music Societies and the Incorporated Society of Musicians; and miscellaneous correspondence and notes. In all, the bundle weighed over ten pounds – just part of the work of just one small choir!

The Sherwood Choir, then, provides just one example of the activities needed for the practice of local music. Nevertheless, it illustrates well some of the characteristic processes behind the continuing existence and effective functioning of a local organisation, however small and informal. Just because these procedures often took place through personal rather than marketed or formalised links did not mean an absence of organised effort. Many of the tasks were small matters in themselves but did have to be accomplished by some means for the choir to continue.

The organisation and work of local music

This aspect of local amateur music is too often forgotten in the vague assumption by both administrators and academics that it somehow just carries on of itself in a cost-free and voluntary manner. Indeed many of the classic problems of administration studied in larger-scale and more bureaucratic institutions could be found, if in a less formal context, in the workings of the Sherwood Choir: modes of decision making and decision implementation; strategies of leadership, control and consent; media of communication both within and outside the choir; routinised procedures for accomplishing certain ends; division and delegation of responsibilities; and the problems of acquiring and retaining the necessary resources of both personnel and materials within known but sometimes negotiable constraints. Once again it must be insisted that – small and relatively unformalised as the Sherwood Choir was – it depended ultimately on just the same kinds of effort and organisation that are well known in larger and more visible organisations.

Similar processes were found in other performing groups in Milton Keynes, for though the Sherwood Choir of course had peculiar features of its own, many of the same problems and procedures recurred whatever the musical tradition. All groups, in other words, had to attract members of the right kind and keep them together despite the other commitments that pulled them away. This applied equally to the classical choirs and orchestras, the operatic clubs, and the brass bands, the old-established as well as the newly founded (it was also found in the small popular bands playing folk, jazz, country and western, and rock music, though with the particular problems to be described in the next chapter). During the time of the research several groups tried to start up but never really got going (the New City Choral Society, the Bull and Butcher Singers' Club, the Blue Yodel Country Music Club, and the Milton Keynes Big Band) while yet others, like the Concrete Cow Folk Club or the New City Jazz Band, flourished for a while then lapsed, and in early 1985 the Sherwood Choir itself seemed on the brink of dissolution. And there were still more in the history of the constituent towns and villages that later became part of Milton Keynes, with the rise and fall through the years of many active musical groups. Such vicissitudes remind us that even the most flourishing groups' membership remained constantly problematic in the sense of depending on continued participation and the successful manipulation of whole series of commitments by large numbers of people. None of this could just be taken for granted.

The same was true for other aspects illustrated in the Sherwood Choir case study. All groups had to find ways of meeting to play together, negotiating suitable times and places – often not easy. A few fortunate groups such as the Woburn Sands Brass Band had their own accommodation. They had had a struggle to get it when they lost their previous site, and even then there was still work to be done to keep it in good order – as evidenced by prominently displayed notices like 'Music folders ought to be taken home for practice not scattered over the floor', 'Please use music files when floor is full!', and *'Please* put music into folders after rehearsal.' Keeping agreed times and places for rehearsals meant constant pressure, most obviously for those groups (the majority) who practised at least weekly. It is hard to see this kind of music-making as something carefree and easy in whichever musical 'world' the musicians participated.

Public performances too always needed careful organisation. The main processes were usually very similar to those exemplified by the Sherwood Choir – booking halls, soloists and co-artists, publicity, rehearsal, and the crucial problems of co-ordinating not just the performers but also an audience on the night. There were a number of other variations around the same general theme, the common factor always being that however the work was distributed it always had to be done by someone (usually unpaid), through an accepted set of organisational procedures. Some performances relied on the framework of schools, churches, or clubs where the performers as such often had little direct responsibility for the physical arrangements, or on external invitations, like several of the brass bands. Even then, such openings did not float up naturally or in a vacuum, for as one brass band secretary put it, 'nothing ever comes without some tenuous link with *some* member of the band'.

The local clubs catering for various forms of music have been mentioned several times. Examples were the North Bucks (later renamed Milton Keynes) Music Society (arranging recitals of mainly classical music), Muzaks (popular music from folk and jazz to rock and country and western in a local pub), the Milton Keynes Divided Country and Western Club, the occasional jazz club, and the various local folk clubs. These too demanded time and organising, often through a formal system of officers and committee, sometimes theoretically so but in practice by just a few people (as one of these put it, 'the best committee number is three, with two ill in bed'), sometimes just by a couple of individuals. But whatever the system, there had to be people to take responsibility for ordering whatever activities the club was promoting. The tasks varied but always included engaging performers for the club's programme, planning dates, booking or confirming halls, making the physical preparations, and – a feature of most club activities – ensuring that refreshments were available. Finance was usually a problem, balancing the costs of hall, postage, phone, publicity, hospitality and performers' fees with dues from members, selling tickets, and fund-raising through raffles or socials. In addition there was the job of keeping up a decent membership, not only for viable financing but for the existence of the club itself. This was similar to the performing groups' problems of keeping personnel, but with the difference that the members in this case were mostly audience rather than performers – simpler and demanding less intensive commitment but with fewer immediate rewards, certainly without the exhilaration of active musical performance. There might also need to be other social attractions in addition to the music, and these too had to be catered for by the organisers.

This may all sound very straightforward and familiar – and so in a sense it was. But the need for continued organisational effort to keep such clubs in being was demonstrated not just by the amount of time put in by those responsible, backed up by all the people they enlisted for this or that task – from displaying posters in their front window to using their office photo-copier to run off the annual financial statement – but also by the number of clubs which did *not* survive or were only being saved by a desperate struggle.

Local music – however 'voluntary' or 'amateur' – does not happen automatically. In Milton Keynes, as no doubt elsewhere, it essentially depended on the commitment of the many individuals who devoted so many hours to upholding these institutions, made possible by the existence of the well-known conventions and procedures which structured their individual actions, conventions which in turn depended on the continuing efforts of individuals. None of this was cost-free, even though few of these activities were directly paid for. Very many people laboured to keep open the local musical pathways being followed and re-created in local musical practice.

Exactly how much work actually went into this kind of activity in Milton Keynes in the early 1980s is really impossible to quantify, not least because even the participants were not always aware of the efforts being made by others besides themselves. As one brass band secretary remarked, most players had no idea how much background work went on on their behalf, whereas all *they* had to do was 'turn up and blow'; on the other hand the players knew about the musical and organisational effort that *they* put into that apparently simple act of turning up, again and again and yet again, musically prepared and with their instruments in order and at the right time and place. Such effort is often – like 'good housekeeping' – invisible and, again like housekeeping, seldom or never counted in official statistics. A few guesses can be attempted, such as the estimate one reviewer made of a performance of Brahms' *German Requiem* by the Milton Keynes Chamber Orchestra, the Milton Keynes Chorale and the Danesborough Chorus as having 'represented at least 2,000 man hours': an underestimate if anything.

Some idea of the scope can perhaps be glimpsed by recalling the effort that, it emerged earlier, was needed to keep just one fairly small choir going. Remember, then, that that choir was only one of many choirs in Milton Keynes and that there were also the other classical orchestral groups, large and small (see chapter 4); then all the other groups and clubs and societies outside classical music as such, not only the operatic societies, but the jazz groups, folk and ceilidh bands, folk clubs, country and western bands and clubs, the half-dozen brass bands with their heavy schedules, music (or partly music) clubs, and a hundred or more small rock or pop bands. Not all needed precisely the same tasks as the Sherwood Choir: some perhaps needed less work, some, like the operatic groups, definitely more, some had these tasks carried out mainly by the performers, others partly by outsiders, some were informal, others more bureaucratic – but all meant demands on time that were in principle not so different from those discussed earlier. Even if ultimately unquantifiable, it is fair to conclude that the amount of work and organisation that was invested in running local music in Milton Keynes in the early eighties must have been immense, probably far surpassing not only the expectations of scholars of such topics as urban development, culture, or public administration, but even the awareness of the participants themselves.

The conclusion should not be drawn from this that every group operated successfully and achieved all its objectives (even where these were agreed). This was certainly not so. Not all groups survived or stayed in the same channels as envisaged by their founders, and some had a constant struggle to keep going at all. Some closed down, and others were only kept going by subsidies from local enthusiasts. Some events were flops, and after such disasters the organisers regularly castigated the people of Milton Keynes for their 'apathy'. Some groups going for years found that with new circumstances their supporters were drifting away. Not every group, then, was happy, successful and harmonious, and local music was characterised by frustration as well as by achievement. But this is the very point to emphasise: music activities *only* survived with constant struggle. Not surprisingly some groups were more effective than others in attracting the necessary personnel, coping with the various constraints, and more or less meeting their participants' aspirations, but even the smallest of them – the precarious church choir of four members as much as the 90-strong Milton Keynes Chorale – ultimately depended on the ordered commitment of its participants: without that none could continue.

When one thinks of local music, then, the correct impression should not be either of the 'cultural desert' that some picture, or of a set of smartly operated and highly efficient groups, or yet of the natural co-operation of communally oriented or selfless individuals, but rather a variegated landscape made up of a whole series of differing kinds of groups and activities, some tightly organised, visible and populous, others more informal, some struggling or on their last legs, some starting up and perhaps benefiting from the dissolution of others, some established but still vulnerable, some in direct competition with other groups at some times but joining in co-operative ventures at others, some lasting over the years, and some appearing for just one or two events then lapsing. In the rich tapestry that makes up local music, what all these groups and activities have in common – whether large or small, 'successful' or not, harmonious or quarrelsome or mixed – is the need for a constant input of organised co-ordinated effort from those who at one level or another participate in them.

Many of the pictures we are given of cultural activity in this country rest on a top–down model (patronage coming from the state or the large commercial concerns) or on a model of culture, and more specifically music, as essentially and ideally the preserve of specialists or as primarily conducted through the mass media or large-scale professional concerts. Local music-making falls easily within none of these models. Nor does it fit the also common idea that amateur cultural activities are somehow natural, easy and carefree, costing nothing and outside the normal sphere of those who are interested in organisational processes. On the contrary, the organisational processes of effective work, decision making, communication, choice between alternative methods of achieving objectives, delegation of responsi-bilities, and, above all, co-operation in the attaining of more or less agreed ends can all be found in the processes of running local amateur music – indeed they must be found there if it is to continue. As the anthropologist Cato Wadel put it, there are a number of activities which 'are not termed work in common parlance [but] are nevertheless necessary for the mainten-ance of widely valued institutions' (Wadel 1979, p. 379). Such institutions certainly include the often hidden practice of local music exemplified in this volume.

19

Small working bands and their organisation

The last chapter illustrated the organisation behind local music in a relatively established formal society, but there are also the less formalised groups, above all the huge numbers of small bands. This multiplicity of groups, with their personal and often ephemeral membership, constantly breaking up and reforming, looks at first sight disorganised and anarchic. But behind this impression of formlessness can be found a measure of ordered predictability. Despite their informal make-up, the small bands too work according to predictable procedures which provide an organised structure to musical action in a parallel, if different, way from the more bureaucratic and larger bodies. Here too local music (or certain forms of it) is only possible through the organised efforts of a large number of committed individuals working together within a system of recognised conventions.

The many small bands of Milton Keynes – mainly consisting of three to six players – were at first sight very different from each other. They played a range of different musics, from rock, pop, or country and western to jazz or folk, and varied in experience, reputation and financial rewards. Most were on the amateur end of the spectrum, but some also included players who could arguably be regarded as 'professional' (or would so describe themselves). Some put on 100–150 gigs a year, others only a handful if that, with payments ranging from £10–20 (or nothing) to the occasional £200 or more. But there were also similarities in the way they got going, developed, arranged their affairs, put on performances and, in some cases, came to an end. Local bands had their conventional routines for coping with both the specific problems and the continuing pressures inherent in the maintenance of their forms of music.

The life-cycle of bands, whatever the form of music, had certain recurrent stages and characteristics. The most obvious was their short life. Over the years there were constant changes in the band names being talked about locally, a contrast to the relative permanence of organisations like orchestras, brass bands, operatic societies or choirs which, with their large numbers and abiding bureaucratic organisation, could outlast changing membership and policies in a way impossible with small and personal groups.

Bands usually got started in one of two ways. The first was for a group of young players, often schoolfriends, to set up together, teaching themselves the art of band playing and gradually building up skills and repertoire. As illustrated by the rock bands described in chapter 10, they then usually tried to put on public performances, first in local pubs or youth clubs, later in the better-paid social club circuit both locally and further afield. The second way was for relatively experienced players to come together, perhaps initially in just a one-off performance, and then decide on – or drift into – performing jointly. The ceilidh dance band Sunday Suits and Muddy Boots, for example, was made up of experienced folk musicians who first played together for one country dance; when it went well, they stayed together and in time found themselves in great demand for barn dances. Similarly, the Stewart Green Band began in 1981 with BBC employees who had just moved to the Open University putting on a performance at the local BBC club. Not just school or neighbourhood but any kind of contact could be built on, including work, advertisements for additional members, previous experience of playing together, or news through the musical grapevine. The national club networks in jazz, folk, and country and western were particularly useful and provided opportunities of playing with a number of different colleagues. In rock the lengthy joint development of a group working out their own repertoire was more common than the rapid consolidation of a new group of experienced musicians based on the already shared skills or familiar repertoire of the jazz, folk and country and western musicians. But both patterns of band formation were recognised as standard ways of starting up a group in every type of music.

Once formed, the next question was how the band was to keep going. Many forces pulled individuals away from the great commitment of time and energy that band membership depended on. But, as will be described later, there were also ties which increasingly bound them to the other players.

There were recurrent points in the life cycles of both individuals and bands where this joint membership – essential for the band's performance and existence – was particularly vulnerable to change. One was when members of a school-based band came to leave school. Provided they stayed in the neighbourhood they might struggle to continue, though practice venues became a problem, but many bands broke up when one or more of their members went off to further training or a job elsewhere. A large proportion of the sixth-form bands at any given period were unlikely to be in existence a couple of years later (though the ex-members might be playing in other bands elsewhere).

Another turning point was at marriage or parenthood. For some teenage bands, marriage was regarded as a symbol of moving to a new stage incompatible with band membership (even in cases where both parties were band members). This applied especially to female singers. One local soloist with a professional background spoke of how alarmed her band leader had been when she and another player married, and he made her conceal this from her audience by removing her rings for performances. Married women did perform in local bands – some very successfully, often jointly with their husbands and occasionally children – but in the youthful bands there was some pressure to withdraw when they married. A married man was more likely to continue, but now with additional obligations which made him less available for practising and performing: it was a standard joke that he was no longer his own master: 'his old missus is getting on to him something terrible'. Competing claims were even more intense for parents, and time after time the explanation for a band break-up was given as domestic commitments. When playing in a band so often involved most of the members' free time, sometimes including frequent late trips, it was not surprising that it was often difficult to keep up all obligations, especially if in addition (as with the majority of older players) they were also in full-time work.

Jobs also caused conflicts. Practices were often disrupted when a player had to undertake extra work in the evenings or travel away, or had to move because of his job. This was a hazard for all musical groups, but the small bands were particularly vulnerable both because of the intensity of their activities – even a couple of extra evenings at work could quickly eat into the three or four evenings previously spent on the band – and because of their size: the absence of just one member drastically affected the band's viability.

There were also internal pressures, and groups split up or lost members over disagreements on band policy. Bands often worked together happily in the early stages while the main emphasis was on building a repertoire and performing in a small way locally, but they then sometimes reached a turning point when they had to decide whether to continue on the same lines or try to become more commercially 'successful'. When bands had to question their ultimate aims members sometimes found they disagreed about priorities. Financial calculations could enter in too: commercial offers, attractive at first sight, might not pay off in the end, or might involve musical or personal sacrifices unacceptable to some or all of the band members.

One such case was The Crew, who in summer 1980 became the 'Milton Keynes success' in a national rock competition, first winning the regional final of the *Melody Maker* 'Battle of the Bands', then, after a tough final in

London when as a member of the band put it 'everything went wrong' from snapped guitar strings to broken drum sticks, coming through as the winners. They seemed set for a successful commercial future, not least because the prize, in addition to a cheque for £1,000, was a contract with a leading record company. Some of the players were doubtful, however, and not long afterwards the band split up, with the various members pursuing their own musical choices. Another example was the T-Bone Boogie Band, the local 'blues and mad jazz' band playing regularly to enthusiastic local audiences for charity, not money, led by the headmaster of a local special school. When they were made an offer to 'go professional' in early 1982 they turned it down, partly presumably because of their other local commitments, partly because 'we're a community band'. Possibly not all the members saw it the same way, for one left shortly after to join a London band, replaced by a local schoolboy who gradually played himself in with the band as they continued the tuneful and self-mocking performances so popular with local audiences. They gave a 'farewell' performance in 1983 (the first of several!) – soon to be back again in other equally amateur guises. Even 'success' could thus lead to disruption or refocussing.

Less drastic challenges too led to realignments or withdrawals. At some point in a band's development latent musical disagreements sometimes became explicit. The Hot Rubber Band, for example, was started off by two local enthusiasts for traditional jazz music. But the rock interest of members joining later became more dominant and one founder finally left as the band moved towards rock, with the remaining members re-forming as Basically Brian. In other cases, the band continued but individuals left. Ice, for example, was initially a heavy rock six-piece band, but as the interests of the majority shifted to more commercial rock the original vocalist and keyboard player left. The remaining players decided they sounded better without them so continued as a foursome.

There were thus recurrent crisis points when bands' continuity was typically brought into question. Not all occurred in every band, nor were they the only points at which band membership might dissolve. Indeed the membership of bands, with their lack of formalised authority, was constantly subject to external and internal pressures which made the continued existence of any given band precarious. Even a 'sudden rush of work' (i.e. of bookings) could conflict with other activities to which members were already committed, especially difficult for players with jobs: 'they are under pressure', as a member of Momentum put it; 'they come home for a couple of hours and go out again – living two lives'. It was especially complicated for bands of which some members were in full-time jobs and others not, for this had to be taken into account in planning bookings. Holidays too were a problem, so that bands with a large number of bookings through the year had to use stand-ins. Social commitments were another constraint. Two players commented bitterly that 'the other two weren't pulling their weight – their heart wasn't in it. They had girl friends etc.' and, as another put it, a major problem of working in a performing band was coping with disruptions to your personal life: 'it demands sacrifices by other members of your family: either you're not there when needed or you're tired from getting in at 3 a.m. It becomes very jading at times.' It was not therefore surprising that so many bands lapsed over time and few groups that had lasted over several years had managed this with no changes in personnel.

The constant effort of retaining the current band membership, maintaining agreement on musical and non-musical policy and keeping it working effectively and harmoniously together was not just a matter of coping with the major crises, but also of keeping up enthusiasm and co-operation over long periods. One problem was how band decision making should take place, a topic that deserves some treatment.

There was a clear contrast in decision processes between the informal make-up of the small local bands and the authority structure typical of larger musical groups. In the orchestras, brass bands or operatic societies, even if there was informal politicking behind the scenes, there was at least the continuity of *some* formal authority and decision-making machinery in the form of officers, committee and, often, a constitution laying down the aims, procedures and composition of the group. The small bands were different. Their basis was a personal one, their aims and current practices constantly open to negotiation and renegotiation, and any change of personnel (or even of the personal circumstances or outlook of just one player) was likely to have a crucial impact. Even more than other musical groups, a band rested on the individual personalities and personal relations of its members.

A few bands had managers, and this could ease the burden of decision making about bookings, finance, workload, transport etc. But even then, responsibility for the musical decisions was usually held by one or more players. As the manager of a successful local country and western band explained it, some involvement by other members of the band, however minimal, was also needed: 'although manager, I do heavily involve Alan [the leading musician] on the movements of the band – a sort of joint management although leaving the administrative/publicity side to me'.

Most local bands worked without managers, however, so decisions about organisational as about musical matters had somehow to be settled among their four or five members. The concept of band 'leader' was a familiar one and many bands were quite clear which one (or sometimes two) of their members this term referred to. But this was always an informal personal arrangement, not an official post, and one which could imperceptibly change over time without players always being aware of it. The role of 'leader' was also interpreted differently by different bands: for some, the main presenter and leader on stage; for others, the most respected musician, or often (especially in rock bands) their main composer. Some bands liked to divide up the leadership roles. In the Bootleg band, for example, 'John does the organisation and Judy is the front person on stage', while in another, one was the stage front man with 'all being leaders in different ways offstage', or, again, 'we try to keep it democratic to spread the load'. Other divisions too occurred: in the Kingsize Keen Band one person was the 'musical leader' and another the 'overall leader', while Ha! Ha! Guru described one as 'the leader idealistically' but another as having 'more musical control' and in Synonymous the division of functions went further still with one player responsible for finance, another for electrics and the other two for the agency and stage side respectively. Some bands made such divisions explicit, but in practice distribution of responsibility probably applied generally as players defined and redefined their positions and skills vis-à-vis others in the band according to their detailed circumstances and personal relations. The term 'leader', therefore, did not always imply overall direction but a somewhat unformulated role in one or more familiar situations: stage presentation, musical leadership or organising public performances.

Even when there was an accepted leader, the band's own development could lead to changes. One or two people had often taken the original initiative and for a time retained the leading role, but as the band began to perform more widely different people sometimes came to the fore; or a band was founded by mutual agreement but one player gradually emerged as dominant. Thus a member of the then new Rock Off explained that their band was 'pretty much a democratic thing' but that probably Kevin (as the most experienced musician) would 'end up one of the leaders'. Static Blue started off with the idea of not having any one leader but one member began to compose and organise so, as one player put it, 'things are changing'.

The bands' ideologies on this varied. Some, particularly jazz bands, did like to have a definite leader(s). Others emphasised their equality, especially the younger rock bands, who insisted that they were 'all equal', 'there's no leader', or 'we all make decisions as one'; a reggae band stressed that though they had a leader 'one rule of the band is that if there is anything to be said it must be discussed and voted on'. This democratic ethos was possibly more an ideal than actuality, but the players were making a real point: compared to the hierarchical and often impersonal structures associated with school, large-scale organisations and many types of jobs, leadership and decision making in small popular bands *was* diffused and democratic, with all members potentially taking a direct part. Co-operation at the personal level was essential for the band to continue, the more so given the particular music in most of these bands, which depended on the individual player's memory and skill rather than written-out scores. It was not surprising that even a recognised leader was likely to take serious account of his co-players' views; 'other members must have a say', explained one, 'and I try to compromise'.

Good personal relations among the members were thus crucial, but could be disrupted for a whole number of reasons, from professional or marital jealousies to suspicion of new recruits, a feeling that someone was not pulling his weight, or disagreements about how or where to play. Just about all the familiar human frictions could turn up in bands with the added edge given by the highly charged atmosphere of public performance and the dire effects that the disaffection of just one member could have. The occasional row could be smoothed, but constant problems were liable to lead to the departure of one or more, or the demise of the band as a whole.

Some types of bands tolerated changing membership better than others. The ceilidh dance bands often had stand-ins, useful for the frequent performances typical of such bands; their music was often based on familiar tunes, with the option of various combinations of instruments, so some fluidity in membership was feasible. The same applied to jazz, in which occasional changes did not affect a band's overall character provided guests shared the same jazz background. Rock bands, however – often smaller in number and generating their own material – were especially vulnerable to personnel changes and, though there were occasional stand-ins, were particularly dependent on the continued co-operation and activity of their own committed players.

What happened when players did leave depended on the personal relations and confidence of those remaining. Sometimes two or more players saw themselves as the core of the band, particularly if they in any sense included the leader, founder or main composer: the situation was then defined as the other (peripheral) players having 'left the band' with themselves (the nucleus) continuing the name and tradition. Sometimes they carried on on their own, in a smaller group. Ice went on as a four-piece when they lost two players, and when The Void's bass player left, the remaining three – who had known each other for years – decided to continue on their own. Other bands again had a lengthy history of changing personnel with just two or three musicians providing continuity. Bitza had a nucleus of three (including a husband and wife) with others coming and going, a 'whole series' of players passed through Philip the Toad (later renamed the Hemlock Cock and Bull band), the Fenny Stompers jazz band had two brothers as a constant core while attracting other musicians for longer or shorter periods through the jazz clubs, and the Wayfarers Jazz Band had kept going for over twenty years, still with two of the original members.

In other cases, disagreements led to a change of name even when some players went on playing together. In one rock band, for example, three members constantly disagreed with their bass player, so they re-formed under a new name as a way of 'kicking him out'. The various permutations could become quite complicated. The members of Ha! Ha! Guru recounted that their band was based on an earlier group (Yimir and the Bohemians) which used to contain five musicians. The bass guitarist decided to leave, much to the regret of two players who considered he was 'the only one worth hanging on to' since the others were 'diluting our ideals'. Their recourse was to 'kick out' the others and team up with the bass – but only by admitting the demise of the previous group and taking on a new name.

Sometimes the remaining members spoke of one of the players being 'fired' (terminology that probably did not match the dissident's interpretation). One player was 'sacked for unprofessionalism', another kicked out because he 'did not fit in with the band', another because he tried to get all the attention for himself or because he was 'totally hopeless – he didn't know how to drum when he joined the band and didn't progress'. Occasionally two members of a band spoke of 'firing' the other two – as in Spirit of St Louis – but it was a moot point who really inherited the name and the remaining two compromised by shortening it to St Louis.

Other bands continued as mainly stable entities but with a continuing problem over one musical slot, whether because that particular role was difficult to fill or because the existing group was so closely bound together that any newcomer, however accomplished, found it difficult to be accepted. The most troublesome role was vocalist, particularly female vocalists with predominantly male bands. One band had seven vocalists – 'each lasted less than a month and then got kicked out by the rest of the band'; others used various girl singers over longer periods but none became permanent. Finding a drummer was also often difficult: Scream and the Fits had had a whole series over the years, while in Unit Six, going since 1964, twenty-three people had passed through: 'drummers last six months, bass players a year', often leaving to take up better opportunities.

There were established ways of recruiting a new player. One strategy was to use the band's personal network – through school, neighbourhood, or work, members of the same family, or 'the musical grapevine', a commonly used phrase. Specialist music club networks were important for jazz and folk bands and pub or club contacts for rock groups, while for certain types of music there were key personalities regarded as particularly knowledgeable about the local scene. Sometimes there were already friends or relatives waiting their chance, and then the only problem was the sometimes embarrassing one of deciding whether they were acceptable to the other members. If there were no suitable recruits on this informal basis or if, as with some successful bands, they wished to draw from a wider field, they tried advertising: handwritten postcards in a local newsagents or music shop, an entry in a local newspaper (one for a time provided a free 'Noticeboard' for musicians on its leisure page), or, for the richer few, an advertisement in one of the national music papers. This was followed by auditions and/or the player joining in some band performances. If the recruit was acceptable, there was then often a phase of intensive rehearsing, especially for bands playing their own material, perhaps withdrawing a little from public performances until the new line-up had been developed.

Recruiting involved other than purely musical factors. Suitably qualified players might not want to play with a given band, might feel they were the wrong age (important in teenage bands), or not appreciate the band's musical material, policy, or likely venues; and experienced players of certain instruments (particularly saxophone and drums) were in short supply. Some bands tried to take on players in the early stages of learning, thus ensuring their musical skills and repertoire were compatible with those of the group.

The same general processes were also followed by bands who decided – less commonly – to expand their numbers or add a particular instrument. Sometimes this was in response to a friend or fellow-musician pressing to join. Country Thinking, for example, a four-piece country and western band, was approached by a local fan, a blind piano tuner, who both expressed admiration and suggested that one thing was missing from their sound: a pedal steel guitar. He offered to learn the instrument and they on their side agreed to take him if and when he became proficient. Amazingly, within four months he felt ready to practise with the band and soon became accepted as a regular member. Again The Offbeat played for a year as a three-piece, but when another friend's band broke up, they drew him in, largely with the idea of scrapping their earlier mainly reggae-influenced set to work on 'better songs'. In other cases enlarging the current line-up was an explicit decision, leading to the same process of looking for potential players.

In these forms of changing membership, a band might or might not achieve its aims, for any one of the recruiting stages – finding potential players, trying them out, assimilating them into the band – could be unsuccessful. But for many bands the process was a successful and familiar one, following the accepted procedures for maintaining or enlarging their membership.

So far, the emphasis has been on pressures undermining bands' continuing integration and strategies for dealing with these, the background to the short life-cycle of so many local bands and the way new bands constantly built on and replaced the earlier ones. The pressures were not all towards disintegration, however, and there were also recognised factors which held bands together.

First, and most important, bands had *names*. This may seem trivial but in fact was a potent symbol of unity and identity. The name was the focus of allegiance, an identification of both group and individual in conversing with outsiders and often a crisp epitomising of the group's shared philosophy. When they performed in public players were announced and applauded under their *band's* name and it was prominently displayed in their publicity, usually with no reference to the players' individual names.

Something of the variety of band names will have appeared in earlier chapters, a variety that itself queries the stereotype of popular bands as unthinking followers of the same packaged mass culture; indeed a whole study could probably be written on the imaginativeness and wit of local band names. Some focussed on key terms which to the knowledgeable indicated the type of music: 'stompers' or 'syncopators' in jazz band names, compounds of 'country' in country and western groups (like Country Thinking, Country Jems, Terry Anne and the Country Dudes), or 'folk' and rural-sounding terms in folk and ceilidh bands (Music Folk, Merlin's Isle), with a more varied series (sometimes including variants of 'rock', 'rockin'', 'beat') in the various rock and pop bands. Some bands by contrast tried to avoid pinning themselves down and purposely chose a name without musical connotations. Basically Brian was 'a nice anonymous name' (based on a joke from one of the Monty Python shows: why had a football team lost to their rivals? 'Basically, Brian, they scored more goals'). Similarly Ha! Ha! Guru was chosen as 'a name that wouldn't pigeon-hole our music: we wanted it nebulous'; this reflected the group's own view of their music which, however others might assess it, they themselves saw as innovative and personal, not fitting into the usual pigeon-holes.

Other names represented some shared philosophy in the band, a comment on the state of the world. Solstice, for example, fitted the band's 'hippie' image with its interest in Stonehenge, while The Void was liked because of its 'pessimistic' ring. Martial Law was so called as 'appropriate to today's situation', while another group considered that social problems like being on the dole were ignored by society – so called themselves Under the Carpet. The name Malachi was taken by a reggae band because their leader wanted a biblical name; for him Malachi, being the last book in the Old Testament, signified the end of an old way of life, just as joining the band meant getting out of the rut.

Often the names had a self-mocking twist. Bitza was 'a bit of this, a bit of that' (the band had one player from Scotland, one from America), while others were tongue in cheek: Bottom of the Bill Band, Hole in the Head Gang, Numb Nuts, Old Wave Band. Herd of Fish was chosen because the band had 'an obsession with fish' and wanted 'a really stupid name – a name people could laugh at'. Others may have been adopted to shock but often had ironic overtones as well, like Typical Shit, SNG (for Sodom and Gomorrah), Seditious Impulse, Lights Out (replacing Foreplay when the band 'got sick of that name') or Fuck Authority, later changed to Exit Stance. The humorously named NA Pop 2000 was chosen as a gesture against others' seriousness: 'other bands all have names that mean something deep or arty – we thought we'd be different' (later though, they or their followers decided it was 'really' a shortened form of 'North American Population of 200,000,000').

Other names were more neutral but recalled some personal or local connection. There were the Fenny Stompers, changed from the original Red River Stompers in honour of their leader's home in Fenny Stratford (once a separate village on the main coach route north and still regarded with some sentiment by long-term residents). The Concrete Cows was a mocking reference to the notorious sculptures of Milton Keynes, while the Original Grand Union Syncopators decided they did not want a 'new city' name and instead took a local historical feature, the Grand Union canal. The Hemlock Cock and Bull Band got its name from the older Hemlock (a 'folky sounding name') and added the two famous and still active coaching inns in Stony Stratford, the traditional sites for travellers' 'Cock and Bull stories'.

Yet other names were just liked for their pleasing ring or their literary or personal association. The Gaberlunzies barn dance band was from the lowland Scots word for beggarmen, while Rare Miranda was chosen because one of its members – an A level student – had just been reading two works about a character called Miranda. The sound of the name was sometimes as important as its meaning: Synonymous came from searching the dictionary when the band could not think of a name, just as another player happened on Pennyroyal in a medical dictionary and just 'liked the word'. Imperial Sunset was chosen after its lead guitarist went to the library and saw a book of that title on the shelves.

The name was the key focus in any promotional literature or insignia. Bands often produced publicity items to be sold or given away to fans and potential customers: photographs of the band projecting their own 'image' (like those in figures 15 and 19), often with their name inserted in large letters, 'business cards', T-shirts featuring their name or, for a successful band, a recorded cassette or disc, again with a cover or inset highlighting the band name. Some also had logos or graphic symbols associated with their names which they used on posters, tickets or music cases. Some bands went even further and developed their own uniform, sometimes closely associated with their name like Ice's white sparkling costumes.

When a group was first formed it had no real identity, but once it had a name took on a new quality. The very fact that the band had its own title gave its players a mark of unity and shared purpose for both themselves and outsiders. The life-cycle of bands was short and their organisation informal and precarious: but through the system of band names, each group marked out its well-recognised claim to its own unique identity and pride.

Band equipment was a further element drawing together the interests of individual members. In some bands, especially those of young or inexperienced players, this was just the members' individually owned instruments. Even then, however, the replacement of items like strings, plectrums, reeds or drumsticks made constant financial demands, sometimes partly met as 'band expenses' when any income was shared out. This also applied to the larger items which bands possessed or aspired to. Drum kits were particularly expensive, and though some drummers had their own, this was essential equipment to which the members might contribute, sometimes even buy on behalf of the band; fees were also sometimes used to add to an existing kit, an investment for the band as a whole. For ambitious bands there was also much other equipment which they could purchase outright, hire or buy on HP – various forms of amplification, a full PA system, lighting, or a van or truck. Such items were expensive and some bands amassed equipment worth several thousand pounds, sometimes paid for over many years. Again recording, which many bands liked to undertake for demonstration tapes or for sale, often involved a heavy pre-payment. The joint responsibility for such equipment and investment was thus another force which bound members to the band, or, at the least – for the joint financial investment also sometimes led to quarrels and disillusion – made it costly or complicated for individuals to leave.

Practising together was part of the accepted experience of just about all local bands, and this too played a part in band unity. For most bands this was not just an occasional meeting, but part of a regular weekly cycle. Over four-fifths of the bands surveyed in 1982–3 practised regularly at least once a week, the most common pattern being one weekly practice, with two or three a week a close second (especially among rock bands), and a handful even more often.

Bands commonly practised intensively in the early stages, often several times a week. Once they had started playing together with more confidence and built up some mastery of their material, they often had fewer practices, though still at least one a week. Later practising might diminish still further and, especially in jazz bands, amount to little more than a discussion just before performing. Ceilidh dance bands and some country and western bands also sometimes had just a quick run-through before the audience turned up if they had worked together for some years; they practised together sometimes too, but this was often concentrated rehearsing just before a recording or special performance rather than a regular weekly commitment.

Whichever pattern was followed, however, there was a large amount of social and musical interaction between band members through intensive practice and/or frequent performances. This was in itself already a considerable commitment. The sheer time involved was one element. So too was the organisation and co-ordination needed to mount the practices. A place had to be arranged, for one thing. This was sometimes a private house or garage belonging to one player (or their parents or relatives); no fees would then be involved, but it still needed negotiation with other members of the household and perhaps the neighbours (those who had to practise in private homes often only heard themselves fully amplified at public performances – or never). Others met in local youth clubs, function rooms at pubs, community centres or village halls. Sometimes this meant payment and in practically all cases arranging in advance. As well, the players and their gear had to be got there: humping heavy drum kits and PAs along corridors and stairs, often on top of several miles' drive – and some sort of transport was virtually essential – to the practice venue. All in all these regular practices placed many obligations on the members, an investment not to be lightly thrown away once the players had committed themselves to the band.

There was more to practising than just time and effort. Developing collaborative musical skills with the enthusiasm of a self-chosen occupation and voluntary selection of colleagues meant a commitment of self as well as time. It was in a context too which set it apart from the run of events in the rest of the week; perhaps this is always one aspect of what is meant by artistic activity, but in any case it was strikingly evident in the work of the bands discussed here. The musical content and its particular forms of composition and performance must also be remembered, for with many bands there was the additional creative act of forming the (unwritten) music itself. Even when the music was already familiar, the arrangement, the interaction of the parts and the dynamics of the performance had to be worked out by the players themselves. Sometimes even the basic material was totally new, or perceived as such, the players performing the band's own material, worked out by them and owing nothing to outsiders. That was most common in rock bands, but even in the other forms 'practising' and 'playing together' conveyed far more than a routine run through pre-formed material. The hours spent in such activity formed an act of creation and discovery in which all members of the band participated.

The mode of learning in small bands should be remembered too: often informal self-teaching and playing by ear, learning *with* others by playing in a group. Both individuals and bands developed as they hammered out the form and interaction of the various parts together, built up the sequences and blends within the band, and explored new skills because of the demands and responses of their co-members. As one experienced jazz drummer put it, speaking of the importance of learning in a group: 'it develops one's understanding of other musicians' ideas as well as enabling one to further one's own aims and proficiency musically'. At the very least, the practices provided an occasion for musical discovery in a group situation, and a band who had gradually developed together on such lines had common interests and understandings over and above the mere total of the (probably large) number of hours they had spent together.

The small size of the bands was another factor. Not only was each player a principal (the only player for his or her particular part), but the balance, interaction, even the musical content was worked out by individual players while rehearsing and/or performing with no overall director separate from themselves. In this sense band members played a more independent part in the creative process than was open to those in large conducted ensembles. The players worked in an atmosphere of autonomy and self-fulfilment of an arguably different quality from that in some other musical traditions. That this did not necessarily prevent dissension was obvious from the short life of many bands; indeed, the personal intensity of this mode of musical expression perhaps rendered such break-ups particularly emotive. Nevertheless the creative experience inherent in this musical co-operation was one element pulling the members together in a highly personal commitment to the band and its joint achievements.

This was further reinforced by the experience of putting on performances in public. This too meant time and organising. Band members had to approach the possible venues, phone up pub landlords, send copies of publicity material, provide demo tapes, discuss with potential organisers, build up their personal networks. As they all discovered, it was no good sitting round waiting for bookings – you had to go out and look for them. They also had to fix times, arrange terms, co-ordinate their movements, get themselves and their instruments there on time – no light task – and, perhaps even more of an effort, get them all back home again at the end of the evening.

The experience of participating in the performance itself was something else that drew players together both as members of a shared band world and in a commitment to their own group. Player after player commented on the sense of achievement in joint public performance: 'it's good to make good music'; 'you get a good feeling, a really big ego trip'; 'once anyone gets on stage I defy them to stop'; 'the satisfaction of hearing the audience shouting for more'. The intensity of such moments was no doubt highlighted by the lengthy preparations that conventionally led up to and framed such events, booking the place and date, advertising under the band's name, word-of-mouth publicity, pre-gig practising, travel, the arrival of the audience, and the preparation of the room, instruments and stage. Then followed the introduction of the band by their chosen name, the presentation, the applause, and yet more applause as the band went through their numbers. Even with a thin or inattentive audience, the trappings were enough to bring some sense of excitement, but on a 'good night' the band's own skill, the audience response and acclaim, their participation in the mood or the beat or the dancing, and the plaudits of the band's own following could bring something even more, a sense of exhilaration and self-fulfilment.

Working together in a group has sometimes been called one of the most profoundly human of experiences. How much more this must apply when the joint work constituted an act – that of artistic expression – widely

268

recognised as a deeply valued one and acclaimed by the band's close friends. This was enhanced by the glamour linked to the whole concept of 'public performance': something set apart as special, given something of the status of a ritual activity in contemporary English culture. This could not in itself keep players together, but was certainly experienced as one of the deep rewards of participating in a band and building on the jointly acquired skills of playing together which alone made the experience of public performance possible.

Players who had chosen instruments unsuitable for solo work particularly valued playing in a group. As one drummer explained, a band gives 'comradeship in music-making – the ability to use talent that could not be used individually'. The same applied to bass guitarists and (in this context) to keyboard players. Even players and singers who *could* perform solo found group support enabled them to perform in public in a way they would otherwise have found impossible. One keen but inexperienced guitarist explained that 'playing with other people raises the standard of your own playing. You play music you otherwise may not; it gives more possibilities of playing in public than if I were playing solo.' The same was true of some singers, even experienced ones, and for some kinds of music like the fast and loud playing needed at barn dances effective performance depended on group co-operation. Band membership was also valuable for those keen on composing. Rock was in one sense a group product, but a single individual often took the lead, and belonging to a band which could work up and perform their compositions in public was greatly valued. The main song-writer in the teenage band Rare Miranda, for example, had found real expression for the first time: 'before she was in a band she wrote songs, but they got nowhere'. As others put it, 'it's nice to take something you've written and play it to people', and 'the biggest kick of my life was both to play with others and to play *my* song'. For these composers, their band went further than just manual interaction and performance, for it was also the creative outlet for their own work.

The close co-operation that such activities demanded was both a mark and cause of a band's mutual interdependence. There were of course costs as well as benefits in mutual co-operation. In rock a member had to be solely loyal to his *own* band and not spread his interests, so that if a rock player did want to play with another band, this really meant leaving and thus probably breaking up his existing one; the terminology of 'stealing' players had a point to it. Other types of bands were more flexible and among jazz and folk players roughly half played in more than one band and some also performed as individuals; additional musical activity by one member was less likely to threaten the line-up. The musical benefits and costs of belonging to small bands thus varied depending on the particular style; but for the many players who continued to play such an active part in local band life it was clear that the advantages of group performance and of band membership far outweighed the problems.

There were also all the attractions of social interaction and identity which apply to small groups generally, musical or not. This was something of which many band members were well aware, stressing the 'fun' and 'enjoyment' of group work, elaborated in such comments as 'we do it as a social thing – most of our evenings out we play', 'there's a social side – we're all friends, we meet new people, break down barriers; you express yourself as a group rather than individuals', and 'camaraderie – perhaps the same thing as you'd find in a rugby side, good humour and mutual understanding'. For a group already working together, even the recurrent problems, of finance, transport, and organisation, could strengthen the mutual bonds as they jointly tackled and, for the bands that lasted, surmounted their difficulties.

Amidst the social and musical pressures within bands – some towards continuity and integration, others to change or dissolution – it was interesting to see the different ways these worked out in practice. Some of the pulls which on the face of it drew people together, such as mutual interdependence, the euphoria of joint performance, social interaction, also sometimes formed the focus of disagreements which weakened or eventually broke the ties. The intensity of small group interaction had its harsh as well as smooth side, with personality clashes the more bitter for being within the close group: 'you can get the best musicians in the world together – but if they won't work together it won't work'. Even when musicians had operated successfully for a time, it was sometimes hard to maintain interest. The long-established Unit Six had problems 'keeping it together – keeping people together and happy, making sure they don't get bored', and the same point was made by many bands: familiarity had its attractions but could also impel people to seek out new experiences, no longer challenged by the old. Even the satisfactions of joint musical performance could produce division rather than integration: joint euphoria could turn to competitiveness or 'bigheadedness' or, as one rock player put it, 'one person may get carried away a bit and think it's his own band'. And then there were all the frictions liable to assail any small group, succinctly summed up by one rock player as 'human nature'. He elaborated: 'all the nasty sides of human nature – jealousy etc. Being misunderstood or misinterpreted in communication within the band – disappointment – after months of work things go wrong'.

The general pattern of local band activity was thus characterised by the relatively short life-cycle of individual named bands while at the same time there were always a large number of active bands made up of players who were for the moment committed to their own bands, with their high involvement of time, energy, musical skill and personal loyalty. A few bands survived over many years, usually with some change in personnel, but most lasted two to three years or less, to be replaced by new bands or by recombinations of the same players under different names. How far this turnover was due to the increasing population of the 'new city' of Milton Keynes – for the area as a whole had more than doubled its numbers in ten years – was not altogether clear. This must have had some effect, expressed among other things in advertisements by newcomers wanting to form a band or by incomers arriving with their already-established groups. But the same basic processes were equally evident among the less changing population centred on Bletchley. Indeed the various patterns of band formation, of the turning points in a band's life-cycle, and of a balance of forces leading to both continuation and dissolution are probably widely found in small band activity.

Within Milton Keynes, at any rate, it was this complex of performing bands – staying together and breaking up, commitment and disagreement, the focus for frustration and competition as well as the experience of profound personal achievement and the exhilaration of artistic creation – that made up the accepted framework within which band players operated. Whatever their chosen form of music they could take pride in this world of small bands and recognise it as in one sense their own, shared with other band players both in the area and beyond. For each band member, no doubt his or her own experience was unique, and there was not necessarily explicit awareness of the general patterns. Yet so much of the experience had common features: being fired to learn an instrument or to sing; teaching oneself not only alone but in the context of group playing; joining a band or a series of bands, quite often helping to choose its name, create its repertoire, and build its reputation; attending regular practices to work up its offerings; organising the practice places and ways of getting there; agreeing with others over decisions and policy; somehow getting together the funds for instruments; listening to other bands 'to smell out the competition', make comparisons, and drop hints about their own availability; undergoing the hassles of organising gigs, and, for the bands with farther off bookings, the travelling to get themselves and their instruments there, with the initial tension and afterwards the joking and release during the journey home; the working up for public booking or recording studio, and the interaction with the audience, the problems or successes of gaining the desired response, the nerves and the satisfaction, and the experience of exhilaration that went with successful performance; finally the acclaim and (perhaps) the fee marking the successful act which, even when barely covering expenses through the year, was still a potent symbol of achievement.

This shared organisational background was supplemented by the joint perceptions band players often had of their activities. This included standard tales about audience response (or lack of response), terrible experiences with instruments breaking, going to a gig and finding another band double-booked there before you, the jokes, sex, and drinking (perhaps sometimes more put on than real), experiences in the recording studio, competition between bands with others 'stealing' players, coping with audiences or landlords wanting different music from your own and problem after problem with travel and transport. Repeated stories were told of driving home down the motorway 'high' after performing to find that between euphoria and exhaustion they were over the speed limit, or – an even more common picture – of the clapped-out transit van broken down by the side of the road laden with equipment and musicians. Such band mythology gave people an awareness of belonging to a wider band world, meaningful in its own right, a shared background to their own activities.

Experiences of this kind were expected and common ones among local band members. A player's work with his band was one continuing path amidst the other activities of his life, a continuity marked by the experience of personal and artistic achievement that so frequently seemed to go with band membership. 'Being able to satisfy the creative side that drives the thing along' was one way this was put. The context within which this thread was set, furthermore, was a valued one accepted by many others beside himself. For though at one level each experience was an individual one and the overall patterns not necessarily fully perceived by many players, the extent of shared conventions and expectations among the practices of the small local performing bands was considerable. This was sometimes locally expressed as the 'local music scene', with comments about how 'incestuous' it was. There was a sense in which, at least for the duration, each member had his 'home' in his own local band, a home that was in turn part of the wider pathways of the ever-changing but still continuing local bands.

The accepted routines and conventions among these small bands are no doubt less tightly formulated than the more explicit rules of groups like orchestras or brass bands. But they demand no less work and commitment, and, in their different way, make up a comparable – if less publicly recognised – system of structured procedures, experiences and expectations: the framework for the organisation of one significant set of local music activities.

20

Resources, rewards and support

For musicians to practise their art there has to be some system for the supply of the necessary equipment and for the material and non-material support that musical performance demands. Even at the local level music rests on a system of suppliers, of patronage and of costs and rewards for the various participants. And though local amateurs are essentially self-supporting, earning their livelihood from some other source than musical performance, there is, even so, an economic side to their music. There are costs for instruments, equipment, music, places to play, publicity, training and transport. Why and how are people prepared to meet these costs? And what are the rewards or the patrons which underlie local music? Certain aspects of the background organisation and values have already been explained (especially in chapters 18 and 19), and of course each musical world and set of local contexts (as explored in parts 2 and 4) has its own detailed support and distribution system. This chapter will not repeat these points but rather put earlier references in some perspective by using the Milton Keynes example to point to some of the more general processes of supply and patronage behind local music-making.

First the material resources. Even local music is big business where a great deal of money changes hands. By this I do not mean the mass music industry, though radio, television and outlets for mass-produced recording are also part of the local scene, or the system of national and international production and distribution which also lies behind local activities. Rather the focus here is on the local supply of goods and services that directly facilitate the musical activities of local practitioners.

Music shops play an important role. In Milton Keynes there were about eight of these, selling musical instruments and accessories, plus four or five record shops in addition to the big stores which included records among their merchandise. The number and identity of the music shops fluctuated over time and as some opened others closed; the expansion of the city shopping centre attracted new shops, and the opening of a branch of the large West End firm of Chappells in December 1980 was probably one factor in the closure of others, especially in the organ business. Between them these shops provided the broad range of supplies needed by local musicians: recorders for schools; sheet music and work books for classical players and examinees; string, wind, percussion and keyboard instruments; accessories such as reeds, strings, plectrums or music stands; and equipment for bands such as amplifiers, microphones, PAs or drum kits – goods costing from a few pence to hundreds or thousands of pounds. Some also hired out instruments, a valued service for those unable to buy outright, or undertook repairs. Some customers went further afield, searching out alternative suppliers in such places as Leighton Buzzard, Bedford (both widely used by Milton Keynes customers), Northampton or London; but for most routine musical needs the local music shops provided the essential source.

Most of these shops were more or less specialised. Not many carried a wide range of sheet music, for example, and the expensive electronic organ market was fully exploited by only a handful. Others such as Eastcote Music stressed the school, brass band and orchestral side, and others again the electrical rock business. Some shops were explicit about their sectional interests. Vanner and Sons in Stony Stratford directed their appeal to buyers of country and western records, claiming to have '1,000 titles in stock', while Archer Music made their interest in popular band equipment clear in their advertisements: 'All group gear – guitars, amps, keyboards, percussion, PA and all accessories', and Oak Music stocked 'all types of disco, lighting and group equipment. For sale, hire and repair'. Local musicians gravitated towards the shops most suitable for their needs and often became regular customers or friends of the staff.

The contribution of such shops to local musical life did not just lie in the supply of goods, however. Among other things, they provided one outlet for locally produced wares like pianos (from Kembles in Bletchley and Mayells in Stony Stratford) and, perhaps of more interest to local practising musicians, for locally recorded discs and cassettes. They also often functioned as teaching centres and the source of expert advice and communication for local musical enthusiasts.

The staff of most local music shops included people with long experience of music, often practising musicians themselves. This often meant considerable instrumental skill – one Bletchley music shop assistant could play twenty-three instruments and advise on even more – or some involvement with local music societies. Even more common were assistants with band-playing experience so that they could advise on the technical questions of amplifiers, PAs, mixers, and lighting systems. These shops had a constant stream of both customers and visitors looking at the equipment on offer and discussing it in highly specialist terms with one or other of the staff.

The local music shops were also effective communication centres. They displayed posters about local concerts or small ads for bands looking for new bookings or new members, and had handouts about local groups, locally produced 'fanzines' (a cross between a fan-club magazine and a newsletter about selected local groups) or tickets for local events. Even more important was their informal communication function. People came in not only to buy, bring instruments for repair or leave posters but also just to look and to chat with other enthusiasts. Current gossip and news about local musicians and events were effectively passed on through the informal network of the music shops.

Some shops took their role as centres of expertise even further and reckoned to provide other services too – at a price, naturally. Several offered lessons, an extra attraction for would-be instrument purchasers as well as (in some cases) part of the owner's own enthusiasm. The long-established Bletchley music shop Marshalls, for example, for years ran the Jim Marshall Drumming School over the shop. Between 1950 and 1980 it taught hundreds of pupils, among them budding national players as well as local band members. Other lessons concentrated on purchasers of electronic organs. Mr Music, for example, publicised its 'Play-time plan', under which for £5 a week the customer not only had an organ and 'de luxe padded stool' but was also promised a 'one hour lesson per week, a special easy play music course, mono–stereo practice headphones. WE WILL GUARANTEE you will play the first time you try'; while Chappells made great play of its prestigious 'Yamaha Music School', which opened shortly after the shop.

Running music lessons had obvious advantages for the shop in attracting potential customers for instruments they might not otherwise feel themselves competent to cope with, and also filled a gap in the teaching and learning of certain instruments. The traditional classical instruments were normally bought by players who had already had formal classical-type lessons or were planning them in the near future, but for other instruments there were fewer teaching opportunities; many practitioners were of course happy to teach themselves or learn while playing with others, but for those who wanted more formalised tuition the music shops offered one possible venue.

Music shops also assisted in local musical occasions. Two Bletchley music shops regularly put on displays of instruments at school musical evenings – good publicity for the shops, no doubt, but also much appreciated as an extra embellishment to the evening. Many of the music shops also organised or sponsored concerts. Minns Music, for instance, laid on several concerts-cum-displays in 1980 to promote Kimball organs after opening their new shop in Central Milton Keynes. They advertised prominently in the local newspaper: 'Kimball Organ Jamboree, featuring MICHAEL BRENT, playing the *new* exciting range of Kimball Organs at the JENNIE LEE THEATRE, BLETCHLEY on Tuesday April 5th, at 8 p.m. Admission by

The Pilgrims Bottle
Linford Local Centre

Come along and listen to

DENNIS playing the piano

every Friday evening

A full range of basket meals and snacks available

Tel. MILTON KEYNES 679616

KINGSIZE KEEN
AND HIS
ROCKIN' MACHINE

A FEW DATES STILL
AVAILABLE FOR THE
FESTIVE SEASON

See them—

The Crawford Arms
WOLVERTON
Every Thursday

**And this Saturday
8th November**

Also

Wed, 12th Nov.
The Walnut Tree
COFFEE HALL
BOOK NOW
MK 661570

**ROSE &
CROWN**

Silver Street
Newport Pagnell

A friendly
welcome
and
live music
on
Saturday
evening

Tel.
Milton Keynes
611686

Musical Instruments   S

BARGAIN : Organ, worth £525, want
sell, £200 (no offers). Telephone
Milton Keynes (0529). 29-KO-561

GUITAR, Les Paul copy. With case
£90. Telephone Leighton Buzzard
377983 (after £.00 p.m.). 29-KO-561

GUITAR (Gibson copy). £25 o.n.o
Telephone Milton Keynes 676975.
29-KO-561

PIANOS tuned, hired, repaired and
purchased. Reconditioned and new
instruments sold. Complete service.
Mayrell Pianos, 67 Wolverton Road,
Stony Stratford, Milton Keynes
562596 (showrooms/workshops): or
563096 (after hours/Sundays).
29-C-56GP

**COUNTRY
AND
WESTERN
MUSIC**
at
**THE BULL
AND BUTCHER**
Fenny Stratford

On Saturday evening
June 11

Music by
PHIL CHARLES

cm/23J

**Sunday, 25th Oct.
LUNCHTIME
SING-A-LONG**
with Dave Cox Sound

**MASTER INSTRUMENT
MAKER & REPAIRERS**

offer all repairs at trade prices

**BRASS, STRINGS
and WOODWIND**

SPECIAL OFFER FOR MARCH

B-FLAT CLARINET OVERHAULS: £25

Pick-up and delivery in M.K. arranged at £3 extra
We will be at CHAPPELLS THIS SATURDAY,
25th FEBRUARY, 10.30 a.m. to 2.30 p.m.
for on-the-spot repairs to woodwind and strings

Tel.: **MILTON KEYNES 568768** or call at:

EUROPEAN INSTRUMENT SERVICES
20 BURNERS LANE, KILN FARM, MILTON KEYNES

VICTORIA HOTEL
WOLVERTON
Saturday, August 16th
THE MICK COCHRAN TRIO
(Remember Elvis Night)
Free Admission
Saturday, August 30
England's answer to Jerry Lee Lewis
FREDDY FINGERS LEE plus MICK COCHRAN
Tickets £3. Limited number

*Streetwalker
Sounds*

Discos for all occasions
Specialist in Charity Functions

16 Broadwater, Tinkers Bridge,
Milton Keynes.
Telephone: M.K. (0908) 607151.
Harrow 4211664

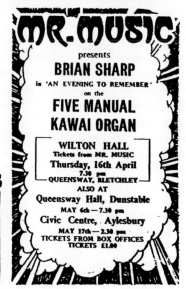

MR. MUSIC

presents

BRIAN SHARP

in 'AN EVENING TO REMEMBER'
on the

**FIVE MANUAL
KAWAI ORGAN**

WILTON HALL
Tickets from MR. MUSIC
Thursday, 16th April
7.30 pm
QUEENSWAY, BLETCHLEY

ALSO AT

Queensway Hall, Dunstable
MAY 6th — 7.30 pm

Civic Centre, Aylesbury
MAY 17th — 2.30 pm

TICKETS FROM BOX OFFICES
TICKETS £1.00

Criminal Rec rds

for JAZZ . . . for BLUES & FOLK . . .
. . . for NEW WAVE and MOD MUSIC

● LARGE STOCKS of NEW 45's NOW IN ●
YOUR No. 1 stockist for FANZINES

If you're into the music scene
get into us at:

Unit 1, Specialist Arcade
CENTRAL MILTON KEYNES
Tel.: MILTON KEYNES 660347

Figure 30 Pub and music shop advertisements: the essential backcloth for much of the local music (selected from advertisements in the local press)

free invitation ticket from MINNS MUSIC...' (*Milton Keynes Gazette*, 3 April 1980). Mr Music responded with a series of organ concerts in early 1981 ('Brian Sharp... playing the fabulous 4 manual KAWAI T30 concert organ') and in 1982 followed this up with a 'Lloyd Ryan drum clinic'. Other events drew on local performers. Archer's music shop was closely involved with the Milton Keynes rock contest, in which local as well as regional bands performed, while the city centre branch of Virgin Records put on a series of gigs in summer 1981 with local bands Fictitious, The Crew, and Kingsize Keen and his Rockin' Machine. Chappells funded local concerts by national or international celebrities, but they too sometimes drew on local performers, like the 1982 'Master Class' in the city centre with the Sherwood Sinfonia.

The music shops, then, played a significant role in local music in the early 1980s which went well beyond just the sale of musical materials, important though that itself was. They were also both formally and informally involved in the musical life of the area, providing skills and services as well as equipment, and they and their staff were part of local musical networks.

The same was true of that other musical resource in the locality, the small recording studios. Their proliferation depended on widespread social and technological developments in the distribution and publication of music, no longer dependent just on live performance on the one hand or written forms on the other, but also taking place through recorded media. The local studios offered a large range of technical equipment, so that making your own recording had become a practical possibility even for groups that in the past would have had little access to a public wider than their own immediate audiences. Just about all the local groups had made recordings of one kind or another. These were sometimes just 'home tapes' for their own use, while slightly grander versions and more specialised equipment were used for tapes or cassettes for demonstration purposes or as souvenirs of a special performance. What a number of groups wanted, though, was to make their own recording in a 'proper studio' and distribute it under their name.

There were several local centres that undertook to provide this. Some were set up for other purposes, like the BBC studios at the Open University or the local community radio (CRMK); recording local bands was not their prime concern, but because of the personal network of musicians associated with both these organisations it was often possible for a local group to draw on their facilities for recording. Most others were freelance, run by local enthusiasts prepared to put expert commitment as well as finance into the venture, such as Mikro, Whitetower, Pace or Peartree Bridge. They provided opportunities for recorded performances by local musicians and for the kind of outlet and self-expression independent of the large recording companies that was sought by many local bands. Like the shops these studios were also the focus for a great deal of musical interaction and expertise, and formed part of the complex of local musical activities in the city.

Thus even what at first sight might seem the purely economic question of the supply of material resources depended on a network of local groups and individuals which involved social, not just commercial relationships.

The same overlap of social and economic considerations was found in the general processes of support and reward for local musical practitioners. As has already been mentioned, most of the musicians in this study were amateurs in the sense of not relying mainly on their art for their income; their rewards were not primarily financial. There were a few exceptions in jobs connected with music (say in WAP, MKDC or music shops and studios) who still played some direct part in the local amateur music scene. There were the local school music teachers as well – in one sense professionals employed in music teaching and yet in another not regarded as 'professional musicians' (see chapter 2); in fact probably only the peripatetic instrumental teachers and the handful of secondary school music staff spent their whole time teaching music, since for most schoolteachers music was only one element in their work. These 'full-time' workers in music shaded into those who spent more, or less, of their time in paid or partly paid work to do with music, like the self-employed music teachers, independent instrument makers and repairers, piano tuners, owners and technicians in the small recording studios, local agents and disc jockeys, small-scale entrepreneurs hiring out PA equipment on a part-time basis, and many others. The same full-time/part-time ambiguity applied to many local free-lance performers, of whom a few reckoned to be professional in that they were not looking for any other job, but for whom it was often not clear how far music was a major, let alone sole, source of finance. For others again, performing was in addition to a separate full-time job, even in some bands who, like the Fenny Stompers, regularly put on several performances a week.

Despite this overlapping and confusing link between 'professional' and 'amateur', 'full time' and 'part time', most of the active musicians studied here certainly tended towards the 'amateur and part time' end of the continuum. So the questions arise of how they financed their music and what rewards they gained from it. The answers are complex and throw further light on the problems of simplified distinctions between amateur and professional in monetary terms alone – for the rewards were not always or only economic, and even cash payments were not always quite what they seemed.

For local amateurs within the classical tradition there was commonly no fee for performances in their own groups. Performers in local choirs and orchestras were seldom or never paid directly; indeed, to the initial surprise of outsiders, they *paid* to sing or play through membership fees of, say, £10 a year. Their rewards were non-financial and consisted more in the prestige and praise from their audiences, the satisfactions of musical performance itself, and, in some cases, the awareness of having contributed to some good cause (see below).

This basically non-monetised quality of classical performances must be qualified, however, even for local amateur performers (visiting professionals were of course regularly paid a fee). First, money *was* exchanged in relation to local performances in that, with few exceptions, the audience had to buy tickets for local concerts, at prices from around £1.50 to £3. Further some musicians did receive a fee if they appeared as support in a concert arranged by some other group. A scratch orchestra for a local Gilbert and Sullivan performance, for example, were paid £25 each for adults, £5 for juniors, in return for playing at six performances besides evening practices in the previous weeks. Soloists or small ensembles like quartets were quite often offered a fee, if only a token one, if they were giving all or most of a concert.

The ethos surrounding such payments was an interesting one, for the convention was to regard the transaction more as a kind of gift than as a direct market payment for services. Local classical performers preferred to see their musical activity as removed from any direct involvement with the market-place. Sometimes a barrier was set up by the sale of tickets through other channels than the performers themselves. They were thus sometimes sold through some local agency with a personal connection with some member of the group: the music shops, a travel agent, a bookshop, local stationer, general store, or, for the Amateur Operatic Society, the coal-desk at the Bletchley Co-op; the local music centres also sold tickets for concerts where their members were involved; and for concerts held in larger halls tickets were also sold through their box offices. This introduced a welcome divide between performers and money. In practice though, most tickets for local performances had to be sold personally, often by the performers themselves through their own personal networks. This could be embarrassing. So the sale was sometimes conducted in a roundabout way, with performers paying themselves and then presenting the tickets to their friends or relations. For a charity concert, they could stress the contribution to a 'good cause' rather than direct payment for performance. Even fees to supporting players or local soloists were often expressed as a mark of appreciation rather than direct payment negotiated in a market framework beforehand (indeed if judged by Musicians' Union rates, such fees *were* only token), and thanks were often given in a non-monetised form like a book-token, flowers or hospitality. Once more the rewards were represented as lying more in artistic satisfaction and acclaim than in financial profit.

The ideology in some other musical traditions was different. Take brass bands, for instance. Here expenses were often heavy, especially for bands with their own special uniforms or instruments, and it was regarded as acceptable to engage in direct fund-raising from their own playing. Brass bands were more likely than classical groups to set playing fees in advance and for their payment to be seen in more directly economic terms. Even in these cases, however, rewards were not just financial. Not only did brass bands frequently play for charity, but the more local or personal the occasion the smaller the fee and the less stress on its monetary quality.

The financial ethos was more marked among the small popular bands, above all the country and western and the rock bands. Here the ideal was that appearances in local clubs and pubs should be directly recompensed by money. The amount varied, but the basic expectations about money payment were shared by both local bands and those likely to engage them. The fee for a small local band in a pub was usually £25–£45, in social clubs £50–£100; a common pattern with youth clubs was for a proportion of the door takings to be divided among the players. Much the same applied to the duos and solo performers, like singer-guitarists in pubs and wine bars, or pianists or electronic organ players in lounge bars. Music was a marketable skill, with the performers rewarded in cash.

But some qualifications need to be made, this time in the opposite direction from classical music. There the overt ethos was non-monetary even though money was in fact involved, whereas with the more 'popular' performers the explicit monetary philosophy was partly contradicted by the implicit role of *non*-financial elements. This came out in various ways. Even in material terms, the payment was not just money, for players also often received rewards in kind – most commonly beer or other drink, sometimes food or complimentary tickets. Less usual rewards included a trout after a performance at an angling club social and (once) six straw hats. Financial profit was also often minimal or non-existent. Expenses were seldom paid, so that the heavy costs of transport or equipment hire had to be met out of the fee. Income was generally small in relation to overheads, especially in the pubs, and the local branch of the Musicians' Union with its relatively few members had little success in persuading performers and employers to raise their fees. A few bands could command fees at the top end of the scale and some did make some profit, even keeping formal accounts and declaring their proceeds for income tax. But even among the more admired and popular local bands, most made little or nothing from their music when their various expenses were totted up – though the ideal of making money from their music was so pervasive that they were unwilling to recognise this explicitly.

In practice bands quite often performed free. Sometimes this was because they had not yet reached what they regarded as the 'normal' state of getting paid, so if they wanted to play in public at all had to do so free – and often preferred not to say too much about this. A few admitted it: 'the band is usually so desperate for a gig that we'll take practically nothing' said one, and a few others, including extremely popular groups like the T-Bone

Boogie Band, made a point of saying that they were not in it for the money. There were acceptable reasons for playing without a fee (or for a reduced one). Performing for 'charity' was one, though there the overt principle of payment was sometimes kept to in the terminology that players 'hand the fees back'. Playing free or nearly free for special audiences like old people was another form, as was performing from friendship, either for a special low fee or, in the case of a friend's wedding, a party, or a memorial to a dead colleague, completely free.

When so many bands were not income-generating, why – and how – did they continue? As with the classical musicians, the answer lay partly in non-economic rewards like artistic satisfaction, self-esteem, sociability or the admiration of others. To be able to classify oneself as a 'musician' and play in public while others listened, applauded and (ideally) paid, certainly counted for something, and for some was taken as a mark that they were indeed on the way to fulfilling their aspirations to become professional performers (a less common ambition among classical players). Another aspect was the informal exchange of goods and services, so that resources did not just depend on money. Help with transport or phones or photo-copying was provided by parents or friends or (sometimes unwittingly) by employers. Equipment was lent between bands, and local contacts used to get goods 'in the trade'. Technical services were provided by friends with the necessary expertise or resources from their own jobs, and a whole series of otherwise costly skills were called on through a personal network – graphics work in designing and producing posters or record sleeves, mechanical help with the band van, the sewing of stage uniforms, recording, repair of instruments and equipment and so on. This could not totally overcome financial needs, but the non-monetary resources which were to a greater or lesser extent exploited by players helps to explain how small groups continued to function despite their lack of financial backing.

In many cases, then, such musicians ended up with little if any long-term financial advantage from their performance fees. In practice their rewards were not in the end so very different materially from those in the classical or folk traditions, with perhaps the greatest rewards, except for those few who played regularly for substantial fees, lying in the satisfaction and acclaim of participating in public musical performance. The prevailing *ethos*, though, that their efforts earned money, was part of this satisfaction, whatever the balance of the final bills. The fee was also regarded as a mark of their musical competence and seriousness – as one band member put it about their performance at an acquaintance's wedding, taking a fee was an earnest of their putting on a 'professional show' and not just 'clowning about'. The size of fee was also a sign of their position in the local pecking order, this being perhaps as important as the money itself.

Even though non-financial rewards for local performers thus turned out to be important in all the local musical traditions, their overt philosophies were different. The classical music tradition was mainly a non-monetised one, perhaps drawn in part from its 'high art' association with its history of a right to patronage by church, court and state and the assumption that material matters should be kept separate from the pure exercise of the music itself. In 'popular' music, by contrast, the common view was that music should be supported through the market-place, disseminated through establishments like pubs and clubs which should pay the price for the desired services – an over-simplified but powerful ideology among the small local bands and performers.

There were therefore various direct rewards for local musicians, fewer of them monetary than appeared at first sight: like most musicians they wanted to perform in public, and that, rather than any more tangible payment, was often the point of their activities. Nevertheless even amateur music had its conditions and costs, and in most cases musicians were actually paying out – 'dipping into their own pockets', as they often admitted – in order to practise their art.

This brings us to the question of the patronage and support of music more generally. This has of course taken many different forms in different cultures and historical eras. The major sources of patronage have generally been described as – at various times and to various extents – the church, the state, aristocratic or royal courts, leading families, business, the 'local community' or, finally, the mechanisms of the market. Where did local music in Milton Keynes in the early eighties fit? The quick answer is that almost all of these entered in and that reliance on just one main source of support was no longer the pattern (if it ever was). The overlap between the various sources of support was a complex one, however, and needs further elucidation. Though the basic system was in a sense a 'self-support' one by the amateur players themselves, there were also certain resources beyond the musicians' own pockets.

One was still government. A certain amount of money and assistance for local music was forthcoming from such national or regional bodies as the National Federation of Music Societies or the East Midland Arts Association (and later the Bucks Arts Association) which drew a proportion of their funds from the state via the Arts Council. They gave grants to some local music societies or otherwise subsidised their activities. This was practically all for classical music events and mainly went to support professional performers appearing at local concerts rather than the running costs of local amateurs. As one local society found to their cost, engaging artists not regarded as 'professional' or 'well known' was unlikely to attract funding, with the result that, as described below, they found themselves turning more and more to commercial sponsors to fund their concerts.

Grants were also made by government organisations functioning at the local level, through both the Milton Keynes Development Corporation and the Milton Keynes Borough Council. Small sums were given from 'the Minor Amenities Fund' to help set up new groups and continue established ones during 'new city' development, a valuable, sometimes essential, boost to local activities. The same general policy of giving small grants to support local musical activities of various kinds was continued later by the Milton Keynes Arts Association under the auspices of the Milton Keynes Borough Council.

Certain groups and events were specially patronised by the Milton Keynes Development Corporation (and sometimes later the Milton Keynes Borough Council) as part of their policy of developing the arts in the new city, among them the Milton Keynes Chamber Orchestra (professional) and Stantonbury Brass who, like the jazz band the Original Grand Union Syncopators, several times represented the new city both locally and in tours abroad. In addition the Milton Keynes Development Corporation and/or Borough of Milton Keynes helped to found musical events like the February Festival and the annual brass band competition, and various concerts by well-known professional musicians were also organised by BMK/MKDC Promotions. Regular concerts were also held by WAP at 'the Stables' in Wavendon which, though independent, was subsidised in its early years by the MKDC.

Public funding therefore played a part in the practice of local music. Indeed the Borough of Milton Keynes received regular awards from the National Music Council for their activity in music, including amateur music and music education in the wide sense of the term, and the MKDC's support for providing 'spaces' for recreation – for example in the building of public halls, recreation centres, and meeting places – was one valuable element in their development policy. Such support, in both money, physical resources and staff time, obviously had a significant role, especially in the pump-priming phases of the city. It would be misleading, though, to represent public funds as the only or even the main source of support for the detailed practices of local music. Even in the early stages of the new city, the support from 'the top' for apparently new musical ventures was probably not as crucial as it sometimes seemed to those involved (the pre-existence of local musical institutions has already been noted in chapter 3), while for continuing musical activities, the state-provided money had a limited role and had to be supplemented by other resources.

The schools have already been discussed (chapter 15) but should be mentioned again briefly: another form in which public funding indirectly assisted musical activity. They had the important role of socialising the younger generation into certain skills of musical performance and appreciation, and also employed staff with musical interests who often practised music outside as well as inside school; many of those active in local music were schoolteachers (not necessarily music teachers). In addition through their halls and material resources the schools provided facilities for local music more generally as well as regular musical events for friends and parents from the local community. The state thus took an indirect part through the schools in addition to the more overt ways in which it supported local music via the Arts Council and local government bodies.

The church is another well-known source of patronage, and, as explained earlier (chapter 16), local churches did indeed facilitate music in various ways even if they were no longer the major source of support for practising musicians. The churches did not employ musicians full time, though a few paid small honorariums for organists and choirmasters or let part-time organists earn small fees at church weddings. But the patronage of music goes beyond just the hiring of musicians, and local churches were responsible for facilitating much regular music throughout the year. Practically all had music in their services and most had special occasions such as carol services or concerts. Without much or any financial payment, they drew the loyalty of organists, pianists, choirmasters, singers and, at times, other instrumentalists, leading them to give of their time and enthusiasm to making music in a church context. The extent of this form of music-making will already be apparent from chapter 16, so it will suffice here merely to emphasise again that their extensive and often invisible provision of (heated) premises to perform and practise in, a meeting place of enthusiasts, the occasion and stimulus for musical performance, and the back-up of national organisations all meant that the churches still played an important role in supporting and promoting music at the local level.

Public funds and church assistance did not constitute the only sources of support. There was also patronage by leading citizens in the area and – sometimes the same thing under a different name – by business.

Many local musical societies appointed formal 'patrons' or honorary officials such as a 'President'. In a way these were empty titles: they were neither employers nor regular financial providers for local musicians. Nevertheless they did give support in a range of ways. In some cases they gave monetary donations or presented trophies for use in their society's activities. The annual Festival of Arts in Bletchley was a good example, with cups and other prizes named after their various donors, several of them listed as 'Vice-Presidents' and 'Patrons' on the official programme. Such figures also provided links into the local business community – valuable because of the sponsorship or other services they could lead to – or with members of national musical organisations, equally influential for access to information or funds. Some patrons and honorary officials took an active interest, attending concerts and rehearsals, bringing in a group of friends as audience, or laying on social activities for the members. Perhaps of equal importance was the status provided by the patronage of those regarded as leading personalities in the local community or wider musical world(s), and the sense of recognition for the society's musical activities that this brought.

The sources of support described so far often overlapped. However, it was noticeable that support from public funds, the churches or leading public figures tended to be limited to certain organisational forms (chiefly the formal associations) and to certain types of music (principally those regarded as the already well-established, and thus non-contentious, forms of classical, operatic and, up to a point, brass band music). There were other forms of local music, however, where neither church nor governmental patronage seemed at first sight to play much part but which nevertheless formed a large part of local musical activity: rock, country and western, and perhaps folk and jazz music, and in particular the activities of the many small bands. Where did they draw their resources? And did the groups patronised by church and state support have any additional sources? The answer here leads on to the very broad sphere variously termed 'the market', 'self-help' and 'private enterprise', all notions which are frequently invoked as alternative funding mechanisms to those of public bodies. This was certainly an important area in local music, but needs to be broken down into its different aspects.

One form was direct commercial sponsorship by local shops and firms. This was an increasingly common type of financial assistance for musical events, from the big prestige events organised by the Borough Council (Coca Cola, for example, which had a local base in the area, sponsored some of the big February Festival events) down to unpretentious recitals supported by grants of £50 or £60 from local shops.

One interesting case was the North Bucks Music Society (later renamed the Milton Keynes Music Society). This was a small non-performing society who put on concerts for their members drawing on both local (often amateur) performers and not-too-expensive younger professionals from the region. Such concerts cost money. In the 1970s their income came from members' subscriptions supplemented by small grants from such public bodies as the National Federation of Music Societies. There was a gradual change in the late seventies and early eighties, however. This was partly due to personal disagreements, partly to financial reasons, and partly to increasing dissatisfaction with the time-consuming demands of the National Federation, which local members regarded as dictatorial and unhelpful to their circumstances. The society began to draw more and more on commercial sponsorship, greatly aided by committee members with long business contacts in the area. Between 1980 and 1983, for example, they had concerts funded or partly funded by such local firms or branches as Telephone Rentals, Cowley and Wilson Ltd (a local garage), Chappells, Dickins and Jones, Marshalls Music, Terrapins Ltd, and several others in the local area, some keeping up their contributions from year to year. Some money still came from public funds (the Milton Keynes Arts Association in particular), as well as from members' subscriptions, personal donations, and fund-raising activities like jumble sales, raffles and socials, but the balance had shifted decisively from public funding to sponsorship. There were other similar examples, and it was clear that many local shops and firms were prepared to sponsor local activities, among them music of all kinds (not just classical), and that this was becoming one accepted source of support.

The music shops sometimes contributed directly by promoting and organising the kinds of concerts described earlier. In addition they supported musical events by lending equipment at no charge to the organisers: piano or harpsichord 'kindly provided by Chappells' became a common item in programmes and organisers' speeches of thanks, from classical concerts to jazz festivals.

Local music was also supported by the pubs and social clubs. To some in the classical musical tradition, the notion of 'entertainment' looked very different from the 'concert' devoted to music and supported (ideally) by non-commercial and high artistic resources. Yet for the facilitating of musical practice, there was no difference in principle between commercially run pub and publicly sponsored concert hall – they both provided the same end, a setting for artists to perform their music in public, and for audiences, within the conventions appropriate to their own musical world, to hear them. For most players of rock and of jazz, it was to the pubs and clubs they looked for opportunities to play and, perhaps, to earn.

Basically these establishments were run on commercial lines. There were a few exceptions, in the youth clubs (one locale for the local bands) and, for a time, the community radio (CRMK), where many local bands used to practise. But mainly these venues had to maintain themselves from their takings and music was one means to this end. The situation was complex, however, for though in a sense music was here supported through 'the market' rather than by church or state, it was not a case of purely economic mechanisms being paramount in all respects. In practice, as will be clear from the discussion of pubs in chapter 17, music did not always result in a profit; live music was something a club or pub *ought* to put on for its clients and its image, rather than a money-maker assessed in profit or loss terms. Once again, it is not easy to divide off the economic from the social dimensions. But whatever the precise finances, local pubs and social clubs had become accepted as among the main patrons of certain forms of local music – something which may not perhaps be as new as is sometimes assumed, but certainly provided a contrast and complement to other more discussed forms of patronage.

The specialist clubs also played a part. Local folk and jazz clubs, financed mainly by membership subscriptions, entrance fees and fund-raising such as raffles, provided occasions for people to meet and enjoy their chosen music.

Some clubs were ambitious affairs. The Milton Keynes Divided Country and Western Club has already been described (chapter 9): it met fortnightly in the local football club, and had developed from a small venture funded by a handful of friends to an established institution with 400 members and an annual turnover in the thousands. Another specialist club was Muzaks, founded in 1980 by two well-known local musicians (both in full-time non-musical jobs) to provide more musical mix than in other local clubs: 'folk, blues, jazz, rock, new wave, country and western'. It ran fortnightly for a couple of years at the New Inn in Bradwell, mainly relying on local bands such as Merlin's Isle, the bluegrass Hole-in-the-Head Gang, Kingsize Keen Band, T-Bone Boogie Band, Safety Valve, and the occasional appearances of other local groups such as the Woburn Silver Band playing carols at their 'Belated Christmas and New Year Party' in January. Later there was a change of policy and personnel leading to more ambitious programmes with professional 'big-name' performers – which the club did not survive.

All these specialist clubs, whether successful or not in commercial terms, depended on the enthusiasm and work of those who ran them, almost always on an unpaid voluntary basis. This leads into the general area of self-help – of music as essentially dependent not so much on outside support as on the efforts of the musicians themselves and their close associates and helpers.

Some local musicians were not in a position to draw on the kinds of support discussed so far to meet costs of materials and services. Small bands did not have grants or formal patrons but, within the opportunities afforded them by the pub and club 'circuits', financed their music partly from performance fees (if any), but mainly from their own incomes and efforts or help from parents, friends and supporters. Similarly the local choirs, orchestras, operatic groups, or brass bands were largely self-reliant. They might get the occasional grant, but for the bulk of their activity were dependent on their own fund-raising activities and membership subscriptions, aided by the personal network of members through which they gained access to a range of services and potential venues for performance. In all these groups money was certainly needed for premises, subscriptions, performers' fees, and concert expenses, and various money-making devices had to be sought to obtain this. But for much of what was involved the main need was people's *time* – time to practise, organise, and keep up the contacts necessary to arrange concerts, drum up audiences, and lay on the essential back-up. In this sense the local community itself was the main supporter of much local amateur music rather than any 'outside' patron, with the proviso that the 'local community' in each case was a differentiated and separate one: made up of the musically participating individuals each with his or her own network and resources rather than a homogeneous or single community shared by all. As so often, the main resource was *people*, and the work they put in. 'Self-help' meant individuals working hard within a small group to carry out their chosen musical activities, supporting these by their own resources both financial and through the input of that other equally valuable but usually uncounted commodity, their own time.

There was one additional form of support, one of great importance at both local (and more recently) national level yet seldom noticed in discussions of patronage. In Milton Keynes in the early eighties, a constantly recurring theme was 'charity'. This, it turned out, was one extremely pertinent – if unexpected – element in supporting local music. Just to mention a few local events, there was a 'charity cabaret show' at the local Gladiator Club held by the Milton Keynes Divided Country and Western Club for a Paraplegic Boys' Home; a concert by the local operatic societies for the British Heart Foundation; a concert at the United Reformed Church by the Milton Keynes Gilbert and Sullivan Society for the Friends of Willen Hospice attended by about 100 people and raising £50; the Woburn Silver Band at Woughton Centre in aid of the Samaritans; an entertainment at Springfield School with two live bands and a disco for victims of the Italian earthquake disaster; a concert by a class of first-school children at Holne Chase Combined School 'for Ethiopia'; a church organist sponsored to play in a local pub for church funds; a concert at Woughton for the Buy-a-Bed Fund for the Milton Keynes Hospital by the three local bands Dancing Counterparts, Fictitious and Young Parisiennes; an operatic evening at the Lord Grey Comprehensive School for their neighbours, the Queen's School for handicapped children; free playing by Unit Six at a Conservative Club for the Jimmy Savile Fund; a concert at St Andrew's Church for the church restoration fund; carol singing for a local playgroup and village friendship club; a first-school concert for the Save the Children Fund; the Tadige Singers, first in Willen Church for Willen Hospice, then in Whaddon Way Church for Playgroup Opportunities; two performances of the pantomime *Aladdin* by the Bishop Parker Combined School based on two months' work by more than ninety children in aid of the Milton Keynes Hospital Play Area; and many many others.

The list seemed endless – after a while I stopped noting down examples because there were so many. And each example, it must be remembered, probably represented hours of commitment for both performers and organisers, time and financial contributions by the audience, and in most cases a donation – substantial or otherwise depending on circumstances – to something regarded as a worthwhile cause. The instances listed here are only a minute proportion of the huge number of 'good cause' musical performances put on locally, for this was almost invariably one regular part of local groups' musical programmes.

These charity performances fell into various categories. There were those, first, where an established group themselves organised a concert whose proceeds were for charity. Usually only minimal expenses were taken out so that the whole income from the sale of tickets plus any other contributions during the evening went to the named charity, leaving the performers to pick up the overheads – costs of practising, hire of music, and sometimes the hall, publicity and printing. A variant was a group performing in a setting where few or no expenses were involved beyond people's time before and during the performance. Carol singing round the local streets was one common practice and there was also occasional instrumental busking in the shopping concourse for charity (not always viewed kindly by the police, to the indignation of some residents). In such cases the money collected could all go directly to the chosen charity, a low-key type of fund-raising chosen by many school groups.

On other occasions performers were invited by the organisers of a charity event to give their services free. The artists needed to take little part in the arrangements but had the satisfaction of contributing by their performance to some cause they too valued. The Canzonetta Singers, for example, used to give about fifteen concerts a year, almost all in aid of church occasions or fund-raising for some local cause. Here again the performers themselves were probably out of pocket over the year as a whole, but on the other hand were freed of direct concert expenses, which were dealt with by the organisers (and which might, or might not, be taken out before the profits were calculated); in any case expenses were often small when, for example, a local church group arranged a concert on their own premises and dealt with publicity by hand-made posters and word of mouth. Collections were sometimes taken on such occasions instead of selling tickets or programmes and resulted in quite large sums being donated even on small and unpretentious occasions. This was one very common form of 'charity concert', to be found in just about all forms of music.

One or more musicians agreeing to give their services free to a non-paying audience was a third form. This was usually to some category of people currently classified as particularly worth cherishing (like children) or somehow disadvantaged – old people, hospital patients, and the physically or mentally handicapped. The host institution made the arrangements, so the performers merely had to provide the musical entertainment and (usually) meet their own expenses, rewarded not only by the opportunity to perform and their sense of well-doing (not a negligible element) but also by hospitality from their audience. One local folk duo explained half-seriously that they never asked for a fee from 'old folks', just did it for 'the grub and the booze!'.

The causes supported by these three kinds of 'charity dos' were very varied indeed and depended on the particular interests and personal contacts of influential individuals among performers or organisers. There were some recurrent themes, however. Hospital and medical charities were particularly popular, especially those directed to local or near-local institutions. Concert after concert was held in aid of Jimmy Savile's Stoke Mandeville hospital appeal, and even more for Willen Hospice, for the highly successful 'Buy-a-Bed Fund' for Milton Keynes Hospital, and the local Scanner Appeal. Others were for organisations for the ill, the deprived or the handicapped. There were many performances in aid of such causes as the British Heart Foundation, the Arthritis Council, Dr Barnardo's, the Save the Children Fund, Christian Aid, Amnesty International, the Samaritans, the Red Cross, and the St John Ambulance Brigade. Local institutions for the handicapped or disadvantaged were also common causes: old people's homes, youth clubs, handicapped children's schools or hostels, either for their general funds or for some piece of equipment such as a wheel chair, a piano, or a computer for a handicapped child. Overseas aid was also thought particularly suitable for musical fund-raising, especially for appeals in the public eye after coverage on television, like the East African Emergency Appeal, the Cambodia Appeal, or food for Ethiopia. Local churches were another important category, and many concerts and festivals were to raise money for organ maintenance and the upkeep of the church roof – the most common needs – as well as for general restoration funds, financing an extension, the rebuilding of an ancient organ or purchase of a new one, or a replacement for the historic iron gates which had been vandalised over the years. Such concerts were especially common not just because of the 'good cause' element but also through the frequent close connections between churches and local choral singers and the free access to an appropriate and evocative venue for the concert, the church itself.

The notion of 'charity' is of course a loose one, and while most of the causes mentioned so far would be widely felt to be 'good' ones, there were also other more controversial or particularistic causes. Thus there were concerts for the local football club, a playgroup, uniforms for the brass band, a local music centre, a school PTA, or a district school music festival. Others drew on a particular political enthusiasm, like CND, March for Jobs, or the Right to Work Campaign. Amidst all these divergent interests, however, the same basic theme could be found – the concept of publicly contributing to some cause valued by the participants and their supporters through the local performance of music.

For the performers there were many rewards in playing for charity, and, since patronage of music is not just a matter of money but of providing the facilities and incentive for musical performance, these played an essential role in the support of local music. Most local musicians wanted to perform in any case, and the opportunity to supplement the artistic enjoyment by the awareness of contributing to a cause they held to be a good one added an extra dimension. They were doing it not just for their own pleasure or that of their audience but for a wider cause beyond the immediate event, whether it was a church choir singing 'for the glory of God', a brass band playing for the benefit of patients in a local hospital, or a rock concert for a handicapped children's school. People like to give, after all, and to know that they are contributing to something worth while; and here was an occasion for both.

These performances at the same time provided the occasion for audience, organisers and musicians alike to reaffirm values which they all shared – or were at least prepared to go along with – whether this was a set of commitments shared specifically within a small group (like some of the more political causes) or some widely held value like that of giving help to 'the less advantaged'. In some respects 'music', despite the many conflicts within and between the music worlds, is often held to be somehow inherently 'above the battle' and thus a particularly appropriate medium through which certain major values in the society can be expressed and supported.

Some performers were either not allowed to perform directly for money (schoolchildren, for example) or felt it not quite nice to do so, but at the same time thought it appropriate that some financial token should be recognised. So the idea of money going to charity but in a sense earned by their efforts was an appropriate solution to this dilemma. In fact this suited both types of ethos about performance reward. For bands who preferred to play for a direct money fee, there was the rationale that their 'fee' had been donated to charity (whether or not, that is, they normally *did* get paid at all!), whereas for those who preferred to separate the concept of perfor-mance from payment, the idea of 'charity' neatly interposed a barrier: it was all right to pressurise friends and relations to pay to hear you if it meant contributing to a good cause.

The charity concerts organised by people other than the musicians themselves were particularly advantageous from the performers' viewpoint. For it meant that others dealt with the publicity, sales, booking and preparing the hall, servicing the piano, juggling the accounts, providing the refreshments and programmes, drawing in the audience – all the performers had to think of was the musical side. They still had to get themselves to the concert on time and suitably dressed (which might cost money) and musically prepared (which would certainly have taken work and perhaps money), but the other requirements, not least the all-important and scarce commodity of *time*, were put in by others. As the secretary for one small group put it, they always tried to sing for some existing organisation like a church restoration fund, Help the Aged, a parish church, or the Friends of Willen Hospice – that way 'we're not involved in the slog of publicity, making programmes, getting an audience'; if they got enough expenses to cover the cost of travel and perhaps music, they felt they had done well and were happy to pay for rehearsal and dress expenses themselves. For them, as for so many others, 'charity' provided not just the means for contributing to worthy causes but support for their musical performances.

The funds raised through these performances was not symbolic only or just a matter of fine feelings, for the amounts were sometimes quite considerable. A police charity concert raised £750 for the Police Dependants' Trust, for example, carol singing organised by the Rotary Club in a Bletchley shopping centre brought in £750 to be distributed to various charities, and a whole series of 'beds' were 'bought' for the new general hospital (each in effect a donation of over £250) through concerts as well as other activities, while the parish church in Bletchley made £800 from their three-day 'Flower Festival with Music and Crafts' which included church choir and clarinettist on the Friday, recitals by six different artists throughout the Saturday, and a concert by the Canzonetta Singers and the organist on the Sunday. Even the sums like £50, £30, £20 or less which resulted from smaller performances still mounted up when the large number of such events is taken into account. Overall a huge amount of money must have been redistributed from such events, generated partly through direct audience collections, ticket payments, and purchase of associated items like refreshments, partly through hidden subsidies by performers or organisers, and partly through the time put into providing the necessary services by all those involved.

There are various occasions in our society where exchange takes place outside or parallel to the mechanisms of the formal market-place – a form of gift exchange, as it were – and musical performance is clearly one of them. There were no doubt both costs and benefits for all those who took part in these charity performances (even for the charities), but certainly an opportunity was provided by this system for people to achieve certain valued purposes of both musical artistry and economic redistribution. 'Charity' has become one of the major resources and occasions for the performance of local music.

Support for local music thus turned out to be a complex system in which many different institutions overlapped and complemented each other. There were public funds from central and local government, music shops, local firms, churches, pubs and social clubs, specialist music clubs, local performing societies and their organisers and audiences, a whole series of special interest groups. Finally there was what in a sense has become one of the leading patrons of local amateur music today: 'charity' and the organised activities carried out in its name.

Considering the overall support system for local amateur music has brought up a number of economic points. Musical activity, it must be remembered, is part of the economic nexus of production, distribution and exchange in our society, and not, as has sometimes been romantically pictured, some asocial and pure artistic activity divorced from the problems of material supply. The practice of music itself demands certain resources – and those who provide them – just as it itself can in turn be used to supply services. Music can be a marketable skill with its own rewards and requirements; it also has costs and conditions which have to be covered in one way or another if the activity is to continue. Hence the need to see how it is that these are met, and how the rewards are distributed and among whom.

That for local musicians the support system is not only a financial matter, however, should also be clear from the discussion here; analysing the resources for local music has had to consider far more than just economic elements. With amateur music, people's time and work are often as important as their money. So too are non-monetary rewards such as aesthetic enjoyment, the pleasure of performing, status, the sense of creativity, or even just the *symbol* of having earned 'a fee' irrespective of its actual monetary price. This in turn chimes in with a series of commonly held values: the high worth commonly attached to 'performance', to 'music' and to working for a 'good cause' as well as the view held by many people that 'doing your own thing' has something inherently valuable about it – or, at the least, that the various groups organised to pursue different ends are an acceptable part of modern urban life.

It would be too simple just to assert – as some do – that local music is supported by 'the community' or to speak of it as essentially 'community music-making'. There are too many different interests, sections, conflicts and unfamiliarities to take that rather romantic picture (a point to be elaborated further in the next chapter). Nevertheless there is a grain of truth in this view. For local musical activities only remain possible through the support of a complex network of institutions, many of them essentially realised by local participants at the local level whatever their wider links: not only the continuing moral, social and financial (as well as musical) input of local musicians, but also all the local music shops, studios, businesses, special interest groups, bands, performers, musical societies, pubs, personalities, fund-raising groups, schools, churches, and charities. In short music is interwoven with just about the whole complex of institutions, economic and non-economic, to be found in the locality: the warp and woof of English town life.

5

The significance of local music

Are there wider implications that can be drawn out from this system of local music-making? This part builds on the earlier ethnographic material to explore such questions as what local music practice and its pathways mean for those who live out their lives in the urban (perhaps impersonal?) setting of modern society or for the rituals and functioning of our society and culture more generally. Finally – and on a more speculative level – are the many many small acts and decisions which, however little recognised, lie behind the continuance of music-making of any wider significance for the fundamental experience and reality of humankind?

21

Pathways in urban living

This study has tried to uncover the system that lies behind the practices of music-making in a modern English town. Given the existence of this underlying structure, and the way that local music involves its practitioners in the locality they live in – the extensive interactions discussed in the last chapter, the many-sided work necessary for the enactment of music, and the local memberships and settings described earlier – one would therefore expect this far-reaching system to have implications for the way people live together locally, all the more so because local music is a matter of active collective practice rather than just passive mass-controlled consumption or the solitary contemplation of musical works. This expectation was indeed fulfilled, though not always in quite the ways I had anticipated. Contrary to many assumptions, the practice of local music turns out to be relevant for central questions about life in urban industrial society. It makes a difference, for example, to one's assessment of the significance or otherwise of 'community', or 'class', of how people's lives are ordered in space and time within a modern urban setting, and of the processes of continuity and change by which our culture is both maintained and developed.

Many commentators have given the impression that local amateur music is nowadays of little significance: if not 'dying out', then the concern of only a small minority, or, at best, merely marginal to serious concerns. So one preliminary question to touch on before turning to the more general queries is the *scale* of local music. What conclusions can we draw from the Milton Keynes evidence? Were the musical practitioners such as to draw serious attention in terms of their numbers, or only a small or specialised minority with little impact on the local life around them?

It was difficult to reach any exact quantitative measure – even more so than I had first supposed. Some rough preliminary indications can perhaps be attempted. Multiplying out from the known or estimated numbers of locally based music groups and clubs and taking some account of overlapping membership suggests that those adults and children actively practising as players or singers ran to several thousand individuals (possibly between 6,000 and 7,000). This number looked not unreasonable from the (partial) listings I drew up of named individuals engaged in music – i.e. maybe 5–6 per cent of the population.[1] That these figures were not wildly exaggerated (and might even be an under-estimate) was suggested by other quantitative measures: for example the 1,000 or so instrumental classical examinations held every year in local centres, the 3,000 plus entrants to the Milton Keynes Festival of Arts in the mid 1980s (80 per cent of them 'local'), the many school musical events involving 100 or more performers (chapter 15), or the 1985 grand 21st anniversary concert by the orchestras, wind bands and choirs based at the North Bucks Music Centre in Bletchley, at which there were about 400 performers,[2] mainly from the under-20s, and a capacity audience which (including performers) totalled over 1,500. I might add too – an observation rather than evidence – that I have practically never mentioned in informal conversation that I was studying local music to anyone either in Milton Keynes or elsewhere without getting the (usually unsolicited) response that either they themselves or some close relative or friend were actively engaged in music in such and such a way.

But the survey counting of heads or any conclusion claiming such and such a percentage participating in music would be misleading. For one thing it gives an atomistic and over-individualised picture of the essentially collective practices and institutions of local music-making. Equally important, it by-passes the key question of definitions. Who should be counted as a 'musician' or 'musical practitioner' turned out to be an elusive and relative matter. It was often part-time engagement in music, but how 'part time' could this be? What about the complex amateur/professional continuum? And which of several possible roles in relation to music should be included? Trying to make an exact count of an ill-defined and variegated field is not altogether productive. It also leaves out many other people who, as described in this volume, themselves played a necessary part in local music. There were the parents of children taking classical music lessons and exams; the part-time music teachers and home electronic organ players; the 400 or so members of the Milton Keynes Divided Country and Western Club and the committee who ran it; the whole series of supporters' networks and institutions which, as indicated in part 4, worked together to maintain local music; the 8,000–10,000 who participated in the music of local church services on any one Sunday; or the audiences without whose active participation the numerous performances could not have reached a successful enactment, from the runs of a week or more for operatic performances to the regular pub or social club musical evenings on which 100- or even 200-strong audiences were not unusual, or the tens of thousands attending school concerts over the year. These people too were participants in the various musical 'worlds' described in part 2. Many of them can be regarded as, to a greater or lesser degree, themselves musical practitioners, not least the regular audience members who played a skilled and essential part in forming musical performances (see chapter 12). This in itself vastly enlarged the numbers participating, in one way or another, in the practice of local music. So too did the presence of the more 'professional' musicians and organisations like WAP or the MKDC/BMK-arranged concerts (which, given the focus of this book, have been little mentioned but were part of the whole scene), as did the wider implications, to be discussed in the next chapter, by which music was one significant element in both 'public' and 'individual' rituals, a role with repercussions far beyond just 'music-making' in the narrow sense.

Thus there were indeed only a minority of people who were active musicians in the accepted sense of consistently deploying the recognised arts of singing or playing an instrument, but the widening circles of involvement in music meant that the practice of music was of much wider local significance. Far from being the kind of marginal and unstructured activity often suggested by the label 'leisure', with its implication of residual items somehow left over from 'real' life, these musical practices were upheld not by isolated individuals in an asocial vacuum or by people merely trying to fill in the time to 'solve' the 'problem of leisure', but through a series of socially recognised pathways which systematically linked into a wide variety of settings and institutions within the city.

In view of this wide spread, did the practice of music have any relevance for the overall life of the city, or at least for the way people structured and experienced urban life? The answer is, broadly, yes, but in a complex form which needs some further discussion.

Two familiar paradigms for understanding the place of music (or any regular set of practices) in urban life will immediately occur not just to the academic analysts but also to most people involved in urban life. First, the idea of the city as a large and heterogeneous arena inimical to personal control or warmth; and, second, that of 'community', in which people are bound by numerous ties, know each other, and have some consciousness of personal involvement in the locality of which they feel part.[3] Neither of these exactly fitted the practice of music as I found it in this study, but elements from both did enter in. Some examination of each can thus throw further light on local music and its wider implications.

Several people with whom I spoke quickly translated my mention of 'local music-making' into 'community music', often with the implication that I was thus rediscovering our 'lost community' in some nostalgic quasi-spiritual sense. But the city as a whole was not a 'community' in that sense if only for the obvious fact that its population was too large and in many cases too recent for people all to know each other, or even to have forged extensive indirect links, and there were many different occupations, interests and social contacts. Some city-wide institutions, certainly, did provide some central facilities, controls and perhaps definitions for the area, but for the most part neither these nor the concept of Milton Keynes as a *whole* were of direct concern to most people in the everyday conduct of their musical (or other) activities, nor were their musical pathways necessarily confined within the boundaries of the city.

What, then, about the various localities *within* the city? Looking at smaller groupings has been one way in which researchers have revealed the often close internal ties in, for instance, ethnic or single-occupation communities embedded within a wider urban framework. Though from the outset I felt it unlikely that Milton Keynes would turn out to contain 'urban villages' in this sense, I had still vaguely expected that I would end up focussing in the traditional anthropological mode on some local neighbourhood within which musical ties were closely intertwined with other social links. But this never happened. This was mainly because of the extra-neighbourhood pattern of much musical activity (elaborated below), but also because Milton Keynes simply was not made up of local 'communities' of that kind. There were areas in the city, it is true, where a longer-established population gave a greater sense of local attachment: Wolverton, with its long connection with the British Rail works, parts of Bletchley, and certain of the villages. Even there, however, one could scarcely speak of a close-knit, far less homogeneous, population by the 1980s, and close social ties were not necessarily neighbourhood-based if only because of the influx of new population, jobs and demands. Even the new planned neighbourhoods, each with its own type of housing, environment and likely social profile, could not easily be designated as 'communities' as far as music went – or perhaps for other purposes either (see Abrams 1980). Local music-making was not typically practised within a neighbourhood-based 'community' in the traditional sense (admittedly vague, but still with some meaning) of a collectivity of people living together in a specific territorial area bound together by interpersonal ties or a sense of belonging together.

Some musical groups did take their names from particular localities. There were the Stony Stratford Singers, the Wolverton Light Orchestra, the Newport Pagnell Choral Society, the Woburn Sands Band (indeed all the older brass bands), and the many church and school choirs. Such groups usually had a local practice place and gave at least some of their performances nearby; even when, as with the Woburn Sands Band, they were in demand elsewhere they had some feeling of responsibility to 'the local community' and made an effort to play there at Christmas or other special occasions. Insofar as such fluidly defined localities did at times present themselves as having some unity separate from others, this was partly defined precisely through local events like a carnival or a festival centred on a local church where the ritual element could be marked by a musical contribution from 'local' singers, brass band or instrumentalists. In this sense 'community' could be regarded as a situational and emergent aspect of localities (rather than some absolute property), a process in which music, and above all music by local performers, played its part.

But even in this relative sense, the significance of these groups for their 'own' neighbourhood was limited. Many of their members did not in fact live in the locality and even brass bands, with their strong local traditions, often contained a geographically diverse membership. The Woburn Sands Band, for example, did indeed draw nearly one-third of their players from Woburn Sands (ten in all) but the rest lived elsewhere – in Bletchley (five), Newport Pagnell (five), Simpson (three), Wolverton (two) and other places in and near Milton Keynes (one each); the conductor lived in Bletchley. So too in the 80-year-old Bradwell Silver Band: despite their practising in a local school and assuming some responsibility for playing 'for our own community, our own parish', by 1982 only one of the players actually lived in New Bradwell. Many people were members of more than one musical group – particularly in classical, operatic, brass and jazz contexts – so that it was difficult for any one musical association, whatever its base, to be made up predominantly of people from the same neighbourhood.

This absence of a 'local community' setting for music also resulted from the way most musical activities were organised. In any given locality only a minority were active musicians, and with the exception of home-based music and some school and church music-making they practised not on a neighbourhood basis but in groups, clubs or performance venues which were unlikely to be where they lived. People *travelled* to join with others in the practice of music, a pattern intensified by but also predating the establishment of the 'new city'.

As far as local music making goes, then, looking to small neighbourhood 'communities' for its generation or setting would be misleading. Local music is not produced by some traditional 'communal' culture, nor does it fit the romantic *Gemeinschaft* model of the amateur arts. It is fine for anthropologists and others to want to explore small-scale communities within larger urban settings but, as Hannerz rightly argued in his powerful call for an urban anthropology (1980), the 'urban' aspects of modern city life may be as important and interesting as smaller cohesive 'communities'. This is certainly so for the practice of local music, for Milton Keynes (probably like many British towns) is not an agglomeration of village communities but a *town* with the characteristics of a town: large, heterogeneous and complex.

But is it necessary then to go to the opposite picture of the city as a cold, market-dominated and anonymous setting for human activity? This view was indeed held by some Milton Keynes dwellers, as the trickle of letters to local newspapers from disillusioned settlers illustrated.

> What makes the bureaucrats think any sane person wants to live here anyway? They're much better off in London, or anywhere else for that matter. There isn't, nor is there likely to be, any form of community spirit. Milton Keynes is just a scar on the countryside of Britain – I can't see it changing, can anyone else? (*Milton Keynes Mirror*, 3 November 1983)

This kind of formulation would be taken as typical by commentators concerned to dispute the facile community-orientated view of harmonious urban life or perhaps depict local dwellers as the passive creatures of mass forces. Was it characteristic, though, of those participating in the musical activities described in this book?

There is certainly *something* in the picture of impersonality. Though Milton Keynes was not large by urban standards, relatively few of the 100,000 plus population could be known to each other in a sustained personal sense; few if any live musical occasions were genuinely accessible to everyone; and even in smaller neighbourhoods local performances were not necessarily widely recognised. Any given musical event was the direct personal concern of a relatively small number of people (different in each case), while others either failed to notice them consciously or regarded them as just part of the imposed environment within which they had to live. Even those keenly involved in music usually had little to do with other musical worlds and were often surprised that I was studying various forms of local music: they knew about their own, but was there really much else? Even *within* musical worlds people did not necessarily interact personally; I was constantly taken aback to find that, for example, members of different choirs did not know each other (sometimes were not even aware of the *existence* of other choirs), and that local musicians highly regarded by some local enthusiasts might be unknown even to those of the same musical 'world' living or working nearby.

There was also an element of anonymity even *within* musical groups. My original expectation had been that choirs, music clubs, instrumental groups, rock bands and so on would be made up of people who knew each other well and that their shared *musical* interest would be complemented by some rounded knowledge of other aspects of each others' lives.[4] I came to realise that this could not be assumed either for all groups or for all individuals within them. Some groups *were* close knit, especially the older brass bands, and members had other ties besides their joint music-making; some were friends or colleagues or members of the same church or school, while others were relatives. Even there, though, links between individuals differed – there was no *single* social life shared by the group – and some had little or no additional contact. Other groups had fewer personal links, and people knew little about their co-members' lives. In larger groups people did not always even know each other's names beyond their immediate partners and, even when they did, often had little knowledge of, for example, their jobs or domestic situations: such matters were unimportant for the purpose for which they had come together.

There was also an impersonal element in public performance. Audiences were often linked by personal ties to one or more of the performers – but they were not necessarily so linked among themselves. Indeed the whole concept of 'public' performance allied to the acceptance of anonymity as one element in urban living meant that musical events sometimes took place with relatively little direct social acknowledgment or personal acquaintance between most members of the audience apart from their joint participation in the event.

In some respects, then, local musical activity fitted with the impersonal model of city life: a point that needs emphasising to challenge the common but unjustified assumption that all special-interest groups are necessarily marked by strong personal solidarity. But this was not the whole truth either. One essential point here has already been mentioned – the *variety* of groupings, some with closer internal ties than others. The extent of close-knit interaction on the one hand, compared to more superficial single-faceted relationships on the other, would be hard to measure conclusively (and the balance was perhaps different in the developing context of Milton Keynes from that in some older towns). But it was clear at least that *both* processes could be found in local music and that close multi-faceted relationships were by no means exceptional; many groups had elements of both. To concentrate just on the impersonal and segmented processes would be misleading, however typically 'urban' they might appear in theoretical terms.

Furthermore, this was not how many participants themselves perceived their musical activity. People commonly did not know much about all their co-members in musical groups – but in the sense that mattered to them they knew *enough*. Individuals often joined because they knew one or more members already and their joint musical activity then reinforced and amplified that existing contact, if not through practicalities like sharing lifts or delivering messages then at least through supporting the same group and making music together. There was no felt need to know *everyone* in the round. New personal links could be created too. A break for refreshments and a chat was a normal part of the proceedings in the larger musical groups: a meagre gap, perhaps, but one defined as a social, not a musical one. These links were regularly repeated too and associated with an intense and deeply valued mode of activity: links in this context, even if not expressed through knowledge of names, ages or social backgrounds, brought people together in a way scarcely covered by the model of urban relationships as anonymous and superficial. For regular members of musical groups this could represent a constant theme, carried over week after week in the same order and with the same companions. The same feature was also evident in the smaller groups like the bands discussed in chapter 19; here again some players knew little about their colleagues or seldom met outside band occasions, but their intensive joint activity was, surely, of a different order from the utilitarian and fleeting relationships sometimes supposed characteristic of urban activity outside the home.

Thus the extreme anonymous model of urban life does not fit all aspects of local music-making either, at least as that is experienced by the participants. The fact that they conduct their lives within a town does not mean that they necessarily find their *own* engagement in town life cold and anonymous (even though for some individuals and in some situations this was undoubtedly the experience), nor are they merely the passive recipients of arts manufactured by others. The active practice of collective music-making is pre-eminently a sphere within which people can, and regularly do, experience a justified awareness of personal meaning and control.

It is of course nothing new to find that the theoretical models do not precisely fit specific cases while at the same time illuminating certain recurrent elements and revealing the complexity of differing processes. But if these opposed paradigms of all-embracing 'community' as against impersonal anonymity are of limited use, do any alternative social science perspectives help us to understand further the implications of local music within the town?

Many of the approaches in urban studies can indeed be brought to bear, and a number of their key terms have surfaced already – 'network', 'groups', 'associations' or (the central metaphor in parts 2–3) the less widely used but far-reaching concept of 'worlds'. Such terms illumine many aspects of this study and I certainly do not wish to challenge them as such. But I ultimately found that they were not as useful as I had expected for analysing local musical practice and its implications.

One has to start from the characteristics of the musical practices actually found on the ground. These are, first, the *part-time* nature of much musical involvement, second, the combination of a varied degree of individual participation with some clear habitual patterns, and, third, the relative and non-bounded nature of musical practice, in one sense locally based, in another extending more widely across the country.

These features make the more closed, integrated and concrete associations of terms like 'world' (see chapter 14) or 'community' (see above) for all their flexibility somewhat misleading for local musical activity. 'Group' is also a revealing concept to try. In one way it is clearly appropriate to the more specific units like the small bands discussed in chapter 19 or (in its extended sense) to the voluntary association form of many choirs, operatic societies or brass bands. But the term does not alert us to the wider pathways into which both these associations and the small bands ultimately fit: the established symbolic and habitual practices which made sense of the separate 'groups'. Nor do the extensions of the term into 'interest groups' or 'action groups' really capture the continuing artistic conventions and the institutional frameworks beyond and behind the specific local units. The vaguer 'grouping' perhaps brings us back once again to the 'community' concept, this time in the non-localised sense of being 'based on a subjective feeling of the parties...that they belong together' (Weber 1947, p. 136, cf. Neuwirth 1969, Wild 1981, pp. 35ff.), like the 'moral communities' associated with, say, churches, friendship groups and certain occupational groups (as in Abrams 1980), or Cohen's (1985a) 'symbolically constructed' communities marked out by their perceived boundaries from others. This conveys one aspect of local musical practitioners, reminding us of the sense of familiarity and shared symbols which often form part of their experience; but once again this approach can mislead both in its connotation of boundedness and the emphasis on subjective feeling. Local musicians are linked not just by shared views or emotions but by social *practices*. People may or may not feel a sense of closure or separation from others in specific situations, but what does define their habitual musical pathways are their shared and purposive collective *actions*.

Approaches in terms of 'networks' or 'quasi-groups'[5] are helpful in the opposite way: drawing attention to the *individual* element in musical practice, its relative openness, and the part-time and essentially non-neighbourhood nature of most local music. Personal networks and their significance for 'working at' music has been one main theme of the earlier discussion. But once again these terms do not quite comprehend local music, mainly because of their often atomistic and sociometric, even mechanistic, overtones. Local musical practices depend indeed on individuals' connections but also have a certain abiding structure over and above the links of particular individuals; so when one set of links – or bands or clubs – dissolve others can be forged in their place following the same tradition. This is something more rich and continuing than the two-dimensional picture suggested by the 'network' image.

No term is perfect, but the idea of 'pathways' seemed to me a better one to capture and summarise aspects of musical practice missed in other approaches. Let me explain how this can be used as one possible metaphor for illuminating certain features of local music and its implications for urban life.

The participants in local music described in this book followed a series of known and regular routes which people chose – or were led into – and which they both kept open and extended through their actions. These 'pathways' more or less coincided with the varying musical 'worlds' presented in part 2 but avoid the misleading overtones of concreteness, stability, boundedness and comprehensiveness associated with the term 'world'. 'Pathways' also reminds us of the *part-time* nature of much local music-making (people follow many pathways concurrently, and leave or return as they choose throughout their lives), of the overlapping and intersecting nature of different musical traditions, and of the purposive and dynamic nature of established musical practices. The many different forms of musical activity described in this study were not random or created from nothing each time by individual practitioners, but a series of familiar and – by their followers – taken-for-granted routes through what might otherwise have been the impersonal wildernesses of urban life, paths which people shared with others in a predictable yet personal fashion. They were not all-encompassing or always clearly known to outsiders, but settings in which relationships could be forged, interests shared, and a continuity of meaning achieved in the context of urban living.

These pathways did more than provide the established routines of musical practice which people could choose to follow: they also had symbolic depth. One common impression given by very many participants was that their musical pathways were of high value among the various paths within their lives. Of course, this varied among individuals and was scarcely susceptible to precise measurement. The several different pathways any individual followed were often not in direct competition so did not need to be explicitly ranked, and in any case assigning 'importance' is a notoriously tricky undertaking. But given the findings of this study on the time, commitment and personal investment so many people gave to music, and the kind of personal engagement manifest even in many of the photographs reproduced in this book, let alone to the first-hand observer of musical events and practice – given all this it would be uninformed to go on assuming without question, as is often done, that people's other pathways like job or household-maintaining were automatically of paramount importance in their scale of values. Indeed the impression given, not indeed by *everyone* involved in music, but by person after person in spontaneous comment, answers to questions, and, above all, action was that their music-making was one of the habitual routes by which they identified themselves as worthwhile members of society and which they regarded as of somehow deep-seated importance to them as human beings.

This leads on to a second point. These local musical pathways were established, already-trodden and, for the most part, abiding routes which many people had taken and were taking in company with others. To be sure, none were permanent in the sense of being changeless, nor could they survive without people treading and constantly re-forming them; new paths *were* hewn out, some to become established, others to fade or be only faintly followed, others again to be extended and developed through new routings by the individuals and groups who patronised them. But for any given individuals the established pathways were in a sense already there, as a route at least to begin on: they were part of the existing cultural forms rather than something that had to be calculated afresh each time. Such pathways furthermore needed more than just an odd few hours every week or so in some haphazard leisure activity; for those who followed them seriously, they were also a recognised channel for self-expression in many senses, for drawing on personal networks, for growing up through the various stages of life, for achieving a whole series of non-musical aims in the locality, for sharing with others, and, not least, for providing meaning for personal action and identity. These pathways included both personal networks and established groups, and were another way in which local musical 'worlds' were realised in practice. From the point of view of both individual participants and the localities through which they ran, they constituted one set of purposive actions – an invisible structure – actions through which people chose to conduct their lives.

Given the significance of these musical pathways for many people's lives and experience, it would be interesting for our understanding of modern urban life to know how people entered on to them. What made them choose – or avoid – certain pathways rather than, or as well as, others? This is all a bit of a mystery, as, perhaps, basic life choices usually are, whether they relate to job, love, religion or personality. But the often unnoticed but pervasive pathways which structure local music turn out to be more worth exploring than has usually been assumed by analysts of modern urban life, and, however elusive, to have something to tell us about the maintenance and continuity – or perhaps change – of our traditional cultural forms.

In commenting on this themselves, some musicians stressed the self-chosen nature of their music: they had put in the necessary work, had the requisite talent, and had continued to pursue this path alongside the other aspects of their lives like employment or education. The achieved rather than ascribed nature of musical competence was one major theme in local musical activity, when *what* you achieved musically was more important than *who* you were. This applied in a measure to all music performers, but the younger rock musicians in particular saw music as a channel for individual self-expression, for publicly acclaimed achievement, even for social mobility and economic advancement. An individual could make a mark free from the otherwise limiting constraints of occupation, bureau-cracy or education.

Another view was of music as an 'inborn gift'. This is a well-developed model in the classical music world, with its emphasis on individual 'talent' and 'the great artist' (a model that could also, cynically, be interpreted as a charter to rationalise the current ranking). But though this view was sometimes expressed by local practitioners as a full or partial explanation of their own interests it was less common than I expected and was mainly concentrated among those conscious of coming from 'non-musical back-grounds' and composers (where confidence in innate talent was perhaps especially important).

Neither 'achievement' nor 'inborn genius' was the whole story. An even more common reaction was to remark how parents or other relations had provided the initial stimulus, and how this had then grown into an established interest. In fact one of the most striking characteristics of local musicians was the high proportion who had grown up in families who were in some way or another musical. Exact figures are impossible without a far more extensive survey than I was able to conduct, but among the Milton Keynes musicians practising in the early 1980s whose names I was able to record a surprisingly high proportion had some family musical connection. This was borne out by looking at names over time. It was fascinating to scan the lists of entrants in the annual Festival of Arts over the years and see the same family names coming up again and again as first the older children, then their younger brothers and sisters moved through the graded musical classes. Similarly with the published lists of classical musical examinations, where successive members of the same family worked their way through the grades. Programmes of local concerts showed a similar pattern. The Bletchley Amateur Operatic Society, the Gilbert and Sullivan societies, and the local brass bands all contained multiple members of the same family, with new generations joining the older in their involvement in musical practice.

This hereditary feature could perhaps be explained by saying that there was a lot of music around, so some family connections were only to be expected. But I suspect there was more to it than that, not least because of the mechanisms by which this hereditary pattern was implemented. Given the way many kinds of music are currently practised it is difficult to see how music-making could emerge generation after generation *without* family influence.

To be sure, many children learnt a minimum of musical performance and appreciation at school, and were often much influenced by school peers in their attitudes to music. But even in the relatively undemanding activities of choir singing, ensemble playing, or recorder lessons in primary schools, it will be recalled that one crucial factor influencing *which* children partici-pated was parental interest (see chapter 15). If a schoolchild was to learn an instrument seriously either at school or privately then parental support was of the essence. Quite apart from the cost of lessons, parents had to provide facilities for practising (no light imposition on family living), and finance for sheet music, for equipment like music stands and, eventually, the instrument itself. Private music lessons in particular could be costly and, as was discussed earlier, made demands on parental support for facilitating progress through the years as part of the lengthy process of the child's gradual consolidating of interests and achievements. It was often initiated because of the parents' own musical experience. One or both had often themselves learnt instruments in childhood or perhaps wished their children to have opportunities in classical learning that they felt they had lost out on themselves. Either way, it was a common assumption that acquiring musical skills was part of a child's socialisation for which parents took responsibility. It was thus small wonder that so many families included *several* musicians: two or three children at different stages, often with parental participation too.

The hereditary emphasis in music was further consolidated by family leisure patterns. Parents were sometimes themselves active musicians in instrumental ensembles or choral groups, which often contained more than one generation, with parents gradually being joined by their children. Most audiences for local musical performances included a proportion of the performers' children, along with their other friends and relatives. Growing up in a musical family thus helped to set an individual's interests and skills in certain channels for the future – not ones followed through in every single instance, but accepted pathways which those from musical backgrounds were more likely to find themselves treading, and, whether on and off or consistently throughout their lives, recognising as a natural and self-evidently justifiable pattern of habitual action.

These hereditary patterns were most prominent in classical music, where the established learning system depended on parental support. *Singing* was a bit of an exception, for many choral singers had had little if any vocal tuition and had learnt from school or church choirs. It was not totally different, however, for singers in the classical choirs had to read music, something many choral singers had learnt through instrumental lessons, with the hereditary factor once again inclining them towards classical pathways. Learning through church choirs usually meant there was already some family involvement, and many local singers spoke of a family musical – sometimes specifically choral – interest which had awakened and reinforced their own. Here too, if in a less direct way, family background encouraged people on to certain musical paths.

Though this family basis was most evident in classical pathways, parallel processes also applied in other learning modes. Brass bands contained multiple members from the same families within and across the generations, and learning still sometimes took place *within* the family, supported by the quasi-apprentice system of brass bands; it also sometimes went along classical learning lines. It was thus common for these brass pathways to extend over several generations of the same family, a still-continuing tradition. Operatic societies too were partly hereditary as younger members of active families grew up with a set of interests, habits, and relationships which led them into similar pursuits. So too with country and western musical performances, at least in respect of the learned skill of expert audience participation: the flourishing local club was very much a family affair (sometimes a three-generation one), and many club evenings swarmed with younger children coming with their families to a familiar cultural occasion.

With jazz and folk music the hereditary pattern was not so marked, but there too musically inclined parents encouraged their children's interest, sometimes themselves teaching or providing opportunities for learning in one of their own bands. But the pathways were sometimes more musically diverse; many local jazz and folk performers did indeed come from musical families – but classical ones. Several had learnt an instrument (not necessarily their current one) in the classical mode, or had organised such lessons for their own children. There was family musical continuity, therefore, even if not in exactly the same pathways.

The rock world seemed different. There was particular stress on *self*-achievement through music, and the accepted mode of self-teaching made this feasible. In addition the relatively innovative nature of rock meant less opportunity for musical transmission through generations. For some rock players there was also conscious breaking away from patterns they saw as imposed on them by authority (parents as well as teachers or employers), so peer-influence and to some extent models set up in the mass media and jointly admired with those of their own generation outside the family or formal school context were often as important as *family* background. These differences should not be exaggerated, however. Many parents gave quiet support to local teenage bands through help with instruments or transport. A considerable proportion of rock players did come from musical families, some had learnt instruments in the classical tradition and, as in the folk or jazz worlds, several older rock musicians were encouraging their own children's interests across a range of musical modes. There were also earlier forms of popular music from which rock seemed a natural progression. Several local rock players came from families in which one or both parents had performed in pubs or working men's clubs; in such cases playing in a rock band was a kind of continuity.

With the only partial exception of rock, then, one of the most striking characteristics of musical transmission – of how people tended to enter on particular musical pathways – was its hereditary basis. Of course there were exceptions, and people were not programmed into pre-selected paths: but essentially the tendency was for people from musical families to themselves enter on musical pathways of some kind, often ones similar to those followed by one or both parents or grandparents, by siblings or by other relatives. This was evident through all the local musical pathways. There were the parents in a local brass band (one a bass player and librarian, the other secretary) with their two sons playing percussion and cornet/trumpet in local brass bands and orchestral groups and a third who had begun the tuba; the three rock band sons of a local jazz player; the many small popular bands centring on two or more brothers, themselves from a musical background; the stream of choir-singing mothers with all their children learning instruments; the music centre director and brass player tracing his Salvation Army band interest back to his grandfather, whose family had all sung tenor, and who had grown up in a background of 'old-fashioned Victorian family music-making'; and the typical comments, even from rock players, on the lines of 'Dad's a drummer, brother a guitarist', 'Father sings and used to be in a dance band in the thirties, mother a pianist and church organist', 'Dad sings, plays guitar, piano and drums; grandpa and aunt also musical', 'Father a clarinettist; both sisters play instruments', or 'Father very musical – bass, piano, trombone; last year was in jazz band with him; mother used to play piano' (quotations from band survey: see appendix).

It has often been observed that in some non-industrial cultures there are hereditary arts in which specific families provide experts for the society as a whole: specialists in, say, poetry, divination, drumming, smith-craft, or particular forms of dancing, singing or other musical performance. Such experts are usually not full-time professionals or totally determined by birth, but it is accepted that they are most likely to come from particular family lines. The English situation has often been contrasted with such cultures because of its greater division of labour, professionalisation of many tasks, and (it has often been assumed) overriding significance of paid employment and/or class as determinants of people's lives. But in the practice of amateur music, which bulks so large at the local level, the English form may not after all be so different. Certainly there tends to be little *explicit* ideology of a hereditary basis in England (unlike some other cultures); but the family-based transmission of music and its skills from generation to generation appears to be a much more wide-spread and important mechanism in our society than is usually realised.

One reason why the family basis of musical pathways has been little noticed may be the preoccupation of so many social scientists and others with 'class' as the paramount factor in western industrial society for transmitting life-styles from one generation to the next. Following this through in detail would need a whole further study, but, given common assumptions about the importance of socio-economic class in music as in everything else, something must be said here on its possible role in leading people into the various musical pathways in local music. It will turn out that certain widely assumed generalisations are in practice highly questionable.

In a *general* sense, people's entry on to particular musical pathways, dependent as this largely was on family membership, was partly related to that family's social and economic resources. Certain activities needed money, transport, or access to specific venues or networks, or were perhaps related to particular kinds of educational achievements, material possessions, cultural interests, or social aspirations. All these were thus likely to play some part in the selection of particular pathways – though differently in different contexts and for different individuals. One term under which this complex of factors is sometimes grouped together is of course 'class'. But just in what sense or in what precise directions this really did influence people's pathways, and to what extent these different factors *did* tend to coincide within one complex is obscure indeed, perhaps particularly so when it was not jobs, education or house-ownership but musical practice that was involved: something hard to measure and seldom investigated by researchers and government surveys.

Interpretation and evidence are thus elusive, but one point was clear. Contrary to some expectations, the findings on local musicians and their backgrounds in Milton Keynes in the early 1980s did *not* reveal any clear class-dominated patterns for involvement in music generally. Active music-making of any kind was a minority interest, mainly undertaken by part-timers, but within that minority were numbered people of many backgrounds in terms of education, wealth and – for many class analysts the crucial variable – occupation (or lack of it).

One of the striking features of local music was thus the overall *mixture* of people practising it. They included senior local government administrators, university academics, middle and junior and trainee managers, school-teachers, nurses and midwives, technicians, housewives and mothers, factory workers, bus, train and forklift drivers, railway workers, school-children, unemployed people, retired people, apprentices, shop assistants, self-employed decorators, plumbers and carpenters, mechanics, bankers, civil servants, engineers, clerks, insurance workers, farmers, hairdressers, graphic artists, youth and social workers, electricians and salesmen – to name only some. Local music was not self-evidently the monopoly of any one social category, nor was there any indication from the rather general findings available to me that the musical practices described in this study were heavily concentrated in one or another of the class strata into which sociologists and survey-takers often like to divide the English population.[6]

It could be argued that the financial costs mentioned several times in this volume made musical activity unaffordable for certain people. This was undoubtedly sometimes a factor, but did not translate unambiguously into class terms. Access to cash for musical instruments or entertainment was not necessarily the preserve just of those with 'middle-class' jobs or higher education. Type of housing or car ownership were perhaps equally important, affecting both mobility and places to meet and play. But here again it would be facile to link these directly with 'class' alone. Furthermore, musical access did not depend just on *ownership* of house or car, for another feature of some musical pathways was the sharing of resources to facilitate joint musical activities. All in all, whether or not individuals entered and stayed on musical pathways was not related in any simple way to the class to which they could be allocated by government statistics or sociological labels.

If local music was not in general class-dominated, were *specific* musical paths perhaps associated with specific classes? Many analysts would expect the answer 'yes' and go on to predict certain associations, linking classical music with middle- and upper-class culture, brass bands with the traditional working class, folk and country and western with 'the people' in some sense (rural, maybe), and perhaps jazz and certainly rock with the working class (or perhaps 'working-class youth culture').

It will be clear from the evidence in the earlier chapters that these predictions were not borne out by the local practice. Many of those engaged in classical music *were* from reasonably affluent, educated and privileged families, but certainly not all. Particularly in the choirs and the partially overlapping operatic societies, and among the children currently embarking on musical interests in Milton Keynes (the vast majority at local state schools), musicians came from a wide variety of backgrounds. The once-acceptable description of the piano as a 'middle-class instrument' (Weber 1958, pp. 120ff.) was no longer applicable, and though in the higher-status orchestral groups such as the Sherwood Sinfonia older players were said to come from a traditional 'middle-class pool', this did not cover all its younger entrants and other orchestral and choral groups in the town drew on mixed backgrounds, not least the many church choirs and their organists. It was true that a family on a low income found it harder to undertake regular instrumental lessons for their children, but families committed to music still tried to pursue it even from meagre resources (in some cases paying cash lesson by lesson rather than in advance for a series), while well-off families could be doubtful about the costs if music was not one of their priorities. For the question of who entered upon classical music pathways and how they did this, the 'middle-class' image did indeed have some counterpart in people's behaviour and perceptions – particularly with private instrumental lessons and classical examinations – but even then did not apply either to all families that could be termed 'middle class' or to all classical players practising or learning in the area. Overall, 'class' turned out to be both too general and too ambiguous a concept to provide much explanation for people's classical music pathways, especially given the minority of both individuals and families at all levels who were actively pursuing such interests.

The same complexity was evident in the other music worlds, with musical *family* seemingly of more immediate importance than class. The main evidence is summed up in the earlier chapters, so it will just be repeated briefly here that, contrary to prevailing expectations, neither rock music nor brass bands could be said to be exclusively or even primarily 'working class'; nor was folk music (indeed, if anything it was mainly favoured by highly educated practitioners); while jazz and operatic activities were particularly heterogeneous in terms of social and economic background. Country and western music was the one form apparently closely connected to the occupations and background traditionally labelled 'working class'; but even here there were exceptions (not least among the Wild Bunch, who frequented many country and western music occasions), and it might be rash to generalise beyond Milton Keynes. Class-based explanations about differing musical pathways are all the more difficult to uphold in view of the fact that a single family (one presumably belonging to a single 'class') could contain members involved in *different* musical worlds or entering on different musical paths at different stages of their lives: brass, classical and operatic, for example, or jazz, rock, folk and classical.

This is not to say that within particular groups (say, a given choir or jazz band) people were not in practice pulled together by shared social, economic or educational backgrounds; 'class' – if that is the term to sum up such similarities – was certainly not irrelevant. But as an overriding categorisation of individuals and families on particular musical pathways or an explanation of how and why they entered them, it proved unhelpful. It was seldom spontaneously mentioned by the musical participants themselves either (the main exception being musicians at the Open University, who were also academics). The nearest most people came was in the frequent comment that for them one of the benefits of music was that jobs or education became irrelevant in the context of music-making: 'you meet all kinds of people'. As one conductor summed it up, 'brass band players can come from any kind of background, and any kind of child – with physical infirmities, cowardly, brave, big, little; there are some incredible friendships between different ends of the social scale ... music is a great leveller'; or – from a brass band secretary – 'we're a common-interest group – that's what's important, not "class"'. This kind of thing is easy to say, of course, and actors' assumptions about lack of class constraint can always be interpreted as complacent naïvety rather than accurate insight. But in Milton Keynes musical practice there really did seem a basis of fact for such assertions. Both at the level of people's own awareness and from an objective examination, 'class' seemed to have little significance for people's choice of musical pathways.

There *were* constraints, of course, on how and why people chose and practised their music, but most related to less grandiose-sounding factors. The specific circumstances of individuals and families often seemed more significant than general patterns, so that there were usually a set of idiosyncratic factors, none in themselves of paramount significance, which influenced particular choices and problems, not least the values and interests held by an individual and his/her family and peers. The many and varied influences on people's musical pathways thus depended so much on individual circumstances that it would be impossible to give them all their due weight. But some recurrent patterns already touched on in earlier chapters are worth recalling again briefly.

First among these was gender – as indeed will be clear from the photographs reproduced in this book. Assumptions about 'natural' male and female activities go deep in our culture, as elsewhere, and often directly influenced musical activities. Growing up in the eighties, boys found it harder than girls to enter on classical music paths as active players and learners, while girls were less accepted than boys in teenage rock bands. On both sides individuals broke through such barriers – perhaps all the more determined having done so – but the barriers were there nevertheless. As one head teacher put it, sport for secondary-school boys was felt as semi-obligatory and music secondary: a boy 'can only have a violin in one hand if he has a rugby ball in the other'.

Gender could affect not just whether an individual got involved in music at all, but also the particular musical interest. Choirs of all kinds were chronically short of men, as if choral singing were somehow not so typically a male as a female activity; but then those men who did choose this pathway were often extremely committed – and in demand: some had been attending several different choirs every week for years. In brass bands, by contrast, there were fewer women than men in the older generation, reflecting the traditional view about the unsuitability of brass blowing for girls, a view currently under challenge, as the high proportion of girls in the younger bands demonstrated. Within groups too, gender often affected the actual roles taken up by participants. This applied partly to the way in which the difference between men's and women's voices was highlighted in the division into separate parts in four-part choirs, often symbolised by a joking relationship between the sexes at choir practices. But it also came out in less obvious ways. Girls were often (though not always) the singers in rock bands while boys were drummers, PA experts and drivers, and in all contexts men tended to take on public roles like those of chairman, dance-caller or conductor, with women called on for back-up typing, 'social secretary' tasks and, inevitably, the provision of refreshments at practices and concerts. None of this was at all surprising – or confined to just musical contexts – and there were also plenty of exceptions, demonstrating that these gender-influenced roles were general expectations rather than absolute requirements. It was interesting too that, apart from the important exception of most rock groups and some country and western bands, there were relatively few single-sex musical groups. Despite the imbalance of male and female in many groups and the gender constraints on certain activities, most musical pathways depended on the co-operation of both men and women.

Age was sometimes a second influential factor. A few groups were age-stratified. Notable among these were the teenage popular bands, often formed at a time when age group affiliation was of central influence, as made clear in many advertisements in the local press on the lines of: 'Static Blue require rhythm guitarist age 16–18 years' or 'Drummer wishes to join or form a band with other enthusiastic players. 17 to 19 years only'. Later, age became less important, and older rock bands had players of varied ages (sometimes a 15- or 20-year age range). In general, one characteristic of local musical activities was the wide age range of the participants: it was musical competence and commitment, not age that counted. Many choirs and orchestras contained members across several generations, brass bands fielded players from 10 to 70 years old, and most orchestral groups ranged from teenage learners right through to old age pensioners.

This pattern was, again, scarcely surprising given the near lifelong nature of many people's commitment to their chosen musical pathways. Even those who for a time withdrew at certain stages of their domestic or working life-cycle (especially women with young children) could return later. This mixed-age co-operation was something both taken for granted by most musical enthusiasts and also explicitly commented on by reflective partici-pants. Given the common association in our culture between age and authority, it is interesting that in local music this tended *not* to apply. Co-operation and competence bridged age divisions within a general ethic of musical equality irrespective of age.

Feeding into these patterns were many other associations through which individuals were drawn into their musical paths and into particular roles within these. Links with specific churches or schools or localities were influential for some, in turn facilitated or hindered by other experiences or ties, or by the particular opportunities or constraints to do with jobs, family links, local groupings or mobility patterns, access or otherwise to a car, or other competing demands on time. Often enough, it seemed partly to depend on accident, and, very important, on particular *individuals* who, as teachers or friends or models, exercised a far-reaching influence on future musical directions.

There seems, then, to be no *single* answer to why particular people find themselves on one or another of the established musical pathways, leading them in directions shared with many others but still favoured by only a minority of the population at large. A whole series of factors can come in – some seemingly just matters of individual accident – and those people perceiving their choices as unfettered and personal ones certainly have one part of the truth. Musical paths are voluntary, something essentially self-chosen not primarily for monetary reasons but in some sense for their own sake, something too which demands continual work and commitment to balance the undoubted satisfactions. But to this awareness of free choice must also be added the patterns of constraints and opportunities that – sometimes partly outside the actors' own awareness – help to draw individuals towards or away from particular paths, or shape the way they tread them, chief among these the influences of gender, of age, of stage in the life-cycle, the link to various other social groupings and – the point that recurs again and again – family musical background.

People's following of their particular musical pathways – however selected in the first place – involved more than just music. Some of these other aspects will be explored further in the next chapter, but two will be followed up here, since they are of particular relevance for the questions about urban living raised in this chapter. These concern the structuring of people's spatial and temporal experience.

As described earlier, participants in musical activities mostly moved outside their own homes and neighbourhoods to engage in music, travelling through what according to one model of the city might seem an alien and anonymous urban environment. But looking at this in terms of the familiar pathways established in musical practice throws a different light on people's experience. This is the more so when it is considered in conjunction with current approaches to 'space' in terms not of objective distance or direction but of people's 'cognitive maps' or the symbolic classifications of their spatial relationships.[7]

The musical pathways (like others) can be envisaged as stretching out and criss-crossing through the town. Physical distance was not in itself a barrier to local music-making (though social access could be), and people regularly moved out of their immediate localities by foot, cycle, car, bus or taxi to one or more regular meeting-places. This did not usually mean pioneering strange localities, though there were always first times and relative unfamiliarities on the way, but of following known and in the subjective sense 'near' pathways. To outsiders the 'back streets' in Fenny Stratford seemed out of the way, as did the complicated and 'remote' venue of the Gladiator Club (off the bus route and over the cramped canal bridge at the playing fields on the edge of Bletchley) – yet to the regular attenders of the Amateur Operatic Society's Wednesday evening practices on the one hand, or the frequenters of the fortnightly country and western music club on the other, they were near and familiar. Similarly, the journeys in turn to Aspley Guise in one direction and Stony Stratford in another were close paths for those in the jazz world, while the singers who went out every Wednesday evening to the Sherwood Choir in the sports pavilion beside the playing field, so hard to find for outsiders, followed a regular and familiar route. Subjectively they never travelled far, certainly not to 'alien' localities.

Travelling in and beyond the city did involve an element of moving through an unknown environment to reach the familiar destinations; but from the viewpoint of those with experience their pathways were punctuated by known landmarks. There were the houses of friends, colleagues and teachers, churches, schools or pubs where people had heard or given performances, halls where they had rehearsed, streets or squares where they had witnessed a brass band or a Morris group performance, shops where they had bought music or displayed their posters. A gang of young people meeting to travel to London for a concert might seem to be undertaking a lengthy journey; but if the participants were bound together by, for example, their shared passion for their local band the Crew, and rendez-voused at the White Hart, where the Crew had so often performed to their plaudits, then travelled together in their jointly hired coach to cheer on their band collectively in the national competition and return late at night in triumph, it was only a small extension of their already known paths. Even going to as yet unvisited localities for some familiar purpose meant some predictability in otherwise strange contexts. Think of a band going to play at an unknown pub, for example, an experienced choral singer joining a new choir, a folk enthusiast attending different clubs throughout the country: because of the known and established pathways, people could move through apparently wide spaces and not see them as presenting serious obstacles of either distance or of the cold impersonality sometimes assumed typical of urban life outside the home.

One feature of local musical activities is worth recalling again: their *regularity*. Most choirs, instrumental groups, operatic societies, music clubs, music teaching and popular bands met repeatedly in the same place. The routes were thus regular ones, pathways that telescoped what might be distant in other respects and that could be perceived as under the partici-pants' control. There was no single musical 'community', but neither were there merely alien bricks and mortar; rather, musical participants marked out their own social and spatial settings by the pathways they drew through the town and in the venues and actions which in a sense constituted and sanctified these paths. It is not only non-literate peoples who, as described in the standard anthropological work, develop a specific 'world view' through which their spatial classifications are structured in parallel to their dominant interests and values. The same could be seen in the activities and movements of late-twentieth-century musical practitioners in Milton Keynes.

In modern urban society, as elsewhere, people also order their lives in terms of 'time' – another well-known topic in social science, where the stress is now often on the social use and perception of time rather than its 'objective measurement'.[8] Going on from there, a contrast has also often been made between the 'rational' or 'clock'-dominated time resulting from industrialisation and the 'socially' or 'cyclically' orientated time held to be typical of non-industrial cultures.[9] This is a widely believed distinction about which the experience of local musical pathways raises some questions.

One pertinent example is the folk musician mentioned in chapter 6 who was also an electrical engineer in a local firm and whose time was ordered not just by his work – though this was one element – but by his evening commitments. For him the reality of his existence throughout time was, week after week after week, structured by his musical interests, for each day of the week was marked by the particular folk club he participated in that night: Monday, the Hogsty Folk Club, Tuesday, The Black Horse Folk Club... and so on through the week. Other folk musicians had similar cycles. These were extreme cases – people who 'lived for folk' – but they were not unparalleled. There were many individuals whose weekly cycle focussed on four, five or even more evenings or weekends at regular musical engagements on top of full-time employment during the day. There was the middle-school teacher who accompanied the local Gilbert and Sullivan group on Mondays and Thursdays and a choir on Wednesdays, played the cello in the Wolverton Light Orchestra on Tuesdays, and sometimes percussion in a youth wind band on Fridays; or the instrumental teacher who, not content with all-day musical work, spent Wednesday evenings conducting a choir, Thursdays in the Sherwood Sinfonia, Fridays and Saturday mornings conducting a wind band, and playing concerts with his own group most weekends; or the small band members, like those in Offbeat or the Memories, who met to practise three times or more in the week. It was not uncommon either for brass band players to belong to more than one band, each demanding two practices a week and frequent public performances, and many keen singers belonged to two, even three choirs, like the tenor who spent Tuesdays at the Fellowship Choir, Wednesdays at the Sherwood Choir, and Thursdays at the Canzonetta Singers.

The timing of musical events followed similar weekly patterning. Pubs normally arranged their live music on a named day (or days) of the week, trying to build up a habit among their clientele of classifying, say, every Friday night as the one to be spent at that pub. The local folk and jazz clubs were also organised on weekly cycles so that the real enthusiasts (like the folk musician above) could go to a different one all or most evenings in the week; thus a new club or venue trying to establish itself had to take account of other pulls on given nights of the week. When the popular Muzaks club was founded at a New Bradwell pub the organisers chose Mondays as 'a night when little was on', and the Blue Yodel fortnightly country music club started by the White Hart in 1981 quickly shifted from Thursdays to Fridays when they discovered that Thursdays already had other competing clubs. A group of local rock enthusiasts founded the Gap both to fill the hole in their kind of music and 'to bridge the gap' between Muzaks on Mondays and the Wednesday Woughton Rock Nites. Predictable weekly patterns of this kind were part of the agreed – if often unspoken – conventions of local musical practitioners, even of those who only spent one evening a week on music.

They formed one social mechanism by which people marked out the division of their time – and hence of their activities and their lives.

Cycles based on the *week* were the most prominent, and, indeed, seem to be important in structuring time in our culture generally. But there were also longer cycles. Some were multiples of the weekly unit and worked on the same principles, fitting in with the expected planning mechanisms of, for example, booking halls on named days of the week. Fortnightly timing was often interlocked to form weekly cycles and 'monthly' meetings arranged to fall on the same day each month (in effect a 4- or 5-weekly interval), like the local organ society on the last Thursday of every month, a predictable and regular date for its members.

Other time sequences were performance-related. Many larger musical groups like choirs, operatic societies, or orchestras gave two or three main concerts during the year, and each of these implied its own internal cycle in addition to the weekly timing of the regular rehearsals. Each planned performance had its known pattern of preparation, tension and climax which in itself provided a measure of the passing of time. So that familiar performance-oriented cycle was not an undifferentiated or unproductive continuum but a meaningful and, in the strict sense, significant ordering of activity. Parallels were to be found in just about all forms of musical performance, sometimes less regularly spaced or lengthy than in the larger concert-giving groups but still with recognisable preparation-to-performance cycles. Once again, the predictable sequence of events had implications for the control and, as it were, the creation of time divisions for both players and other participants.

Yearly occasions were also important, following the annual cycle once again apparently so basic in our culture. Several local events were expected to occur just once a year, and for those involved the preliminary planning, immediate run-up, execution and aftermath were often significant processes which imposed a meaningful structure on the passing months. For those participating, they were not one-off incidents but important occasions which depended on many months' anticipation and recollection. Every March, for example, the local middle school in Bletchley joined in the Bletchley and District Middle School Music Festival. Over 200 children from nine or more local middle schools had been practising separately for months ready to play and sing together for two evenings to hundreds of parents and friends, the highlight being a specially composed orchestral and choral work. Parallel primary-school festivals took place in other parts of Milton Keynes, as well as dance displays to music, like the Annual Folk Dance Festival held in Bletchley since 1953 (figure 31). Another yearly event that perhaps demanded even more planning and caused more of a general stir in the locality was the Milton Keynes (earlier Bletchley) Festival of Arts, which by the early eighties had grown to a festival lasting a week or more every

Figure 31 An annual celebration of music and dance: the 29th Bletchley Primary Schools Folk Dance Festival with sixteen schools and 800 children participating

February and attracting several thousand entrants and scores of helpers. Or again, there was the 'Folk on the Green' day every June – 'one of the family high spots of the local musical year', according to a local teacher and musician – which had come to be known by both the 3,000 or so participants and the local residents as once more the familiar time for the Stony Stratford celebrations. There was also the large-scale February Festival started by the BMK recreation department (creating much heart-burning for those committed to the often-conflicting Festival of Arts), the annual brass band festival, and a whole host of neighbourhood- and church-based festivals like the 'St Andrews Prom', the Spurgeon choir 'Carols for Everyone', the Cock and Bull Festival, the Black Horse Folk Day, the Milton Keynes Village Festival, the annual switching on of the Christmas lights (usually complete with bands) and the carnival in Newport Pagnell. Even their annual barn dances to a ceilidh band held by many local PTAs and sports clubs, though less visible to outsiders, formed a meaningful sign for those in the group that, once again, the due time of year had come round.

Some points in the year were marked by a special proliferation of musical – and other – celebrations, giving the lie to the common assumption that there is no longer an annual calendar in urban Britain. There were regularly special social and musical events in the pubs to mark such dates as St

Valentine's Day, Burns Night, St Patrick's Night, Easter, Midsummer, Bank Holiday weekends in May and August, Hallowe'en and New Year's Eve. Doubtless it suited the pubs and others to fix on such dates to draw in customers, but it was still significant that *those* were the ones used to mark out the passing of the year. Edmund Leach's comment is as applicable to English as to non-industrial culture: 'We talk of measuring time, as if time were a concrete thing waiting to be measured; but in fact we *create time* by creating intervals in social life. Until we have done this there is no time to be measured' (Leach 1966, p. 135).

For almost all kinds of music, Christmas was the high point of the musical year. That was the season when, all through December and with increasing intensity as Christmas Day itself approached, musical groups of all kinds were putting on concerts, appearing at parties, singing carols in the streets, the schools and the old people's homes, playing brass instruments out of doors, holding special carol services, and performing musical nativity plays. This was the time of year too when musicians were in demand, often bound into different performances for days or nights on end or torn between conflicting commitments. There was a festival quality at this season distinguished from the rest of the year by a series of ceremonial markers, but pre-eminently by music. To quote Leach again:

All over the world men mark out their calendars by means of festivals ... among the various functions which the holding of festivals may fulfil, one very important function is the ordering of time. The interval between two successive festivals of the same type is a 'period', usually a named period, e.g. 'week', 'year'. Without the festivals, such periods would not exist, and all order would go out of social life (Leach 1966, pp. 132, 134–5)

It was through the recurrent rituals of the year – Christmas above all, but also all the other musical celebrations observed in the locality, large or small – that people's consciousness of time was in part created and the intervals in social life marked out.

This leads back once more to the earlier discussion, for if we follow an emergent definition of 'community', then it could be argued that periodic musical festivals can indeed play a part in how – in a situational and relative way – people can experience a sense of 'community', musically defined and marked, at certain points in the unfolding of the year. As Roger Abrahams put it in his discussion of rituals in culture,

How may we even go about defining community for ourselves when there are so many conflicting claims on our loyalties?... Given the direction of society today, I suppose we must say simply that communities will define themselves as they organize into communities, and that the deepest part of this organization will be the establishment of rituals (1977, pp. 46–7).

Among the foundations for this emergent sense of community, however ephemeral and situational, must be included the work put by local musicians into forming the public rituals which themselves in turn help to create the festival realisation and cyclical shaping of the localities in which they practise.

The ordering of time, therefore – and hence of other shared symbols and practices – in and through local music is not after all so very different from the social and symbolic cycles so commonly described for non-industrial cultures. It seems that the theorists who see a radical divide in the social organisation of time after industrialisation have missed some of the characteristics of our continuing cultural reality.[10] In their regular music-making local musicians and their associates are dominated not by mathematically rational principles but by *socially* recognised and recurrent practices: the weekly, seasonal or yearly cycles set by and in the habitual musical pathways they jointly share with others.

One way of looking at people's musical activities is therefore to see them as taking place along a series of pathways which provide familiar directions for both personal choices and collective actions. Such pathways form one important – if often unstated – framework for people's participation in urban life, something overlapping with, but more permanent and structured than, the personal networks in which individuals also participate. They form broad routes set out, as it were, across and through the city. They tend to be invisible to others, but for those who follow them they constitute a clearly laid thoroughfare both for their activities and relationships and for the meaningful structuring of their actions in space and time. Some pathways are made up of the regular activities related to membership of particular local brass bands, for example, or – extending more broadly – to brass band activity on a regional or national basis; others to involvement in classical orchestral or choral groups and performances; others again to country and western music, to folk groups and clubs, to operatic or pantomime performances, or, more narrowly, to some specific musical or partly musical group like the local Irish society. Not all involve organised groups, for there are also the practices followed by individuals like the private instrumental teachers or the organists in local churches, where, once again, the pathway is a recognised one with accepted conventions about their roles and their musical, educational or religious functions. These many pathways, then, are culturally established ways through which people structure their activities on habitual patterns that – however unnoticed by outsiders – are known to and shared with others.

Such pathways are relative only and, despite their continuity over time, changing rather than absolute – unlike the picture conveyed by the more concrete-sounding and bounded concepts of 'world' or 'community'. People follow out their lives not from nothing but along a series of familiar paths from which they variously construct their own individual routes. Where people's own paths touch on and share with others – as so often in musical contexts – they find themselves on well-trodden pathways where, with all the openings to individual deviance and innovation, certain predictable conventions are already established. Some pathways are wider and better known (shared with large numbers of people and extending far beyond the immediate locality), others are narrower; some are well trodden and clearly marked out with few alternative routes, others larger with more room – indeed need – for variation and new starts; some are highly particularistic (the pathway followed perhaps by just one small idiosyncratic local group or by a band with a distinctive voice of its own); others, like the choirs with their own individual 'personalities', include some unique features, yet join in the broad stream of the widespread choral tradition in this country.

Individual participation in these pathways varies too, of course. For some people a particular pathway (brass bands, for example) is a lifelong commitment – a pilgrimage from cradle to grave; while for others that, or another, pathway is something they follow less continuously, perhaps leaving at certain points in their lives to return again later, perhaps only coming in at one stage. Even for the intermittent participants, though, the pathway of shared expectations still in a sense remains irrespective of their own absences and presences, a structured and predictable channel for their participation.

Note again, though, that the musical pathways form only one part of their participants' lives. Even the 'cradle-to-grave' follower may only spend a certain proportion of life in musical practice and is bound to have other interests and ties too: family obligations, other leisure activities, perhaps a series of jobs or other full- or part-time work commitments, and so on – in other words, many other pathways as well as the musical ones.

In this sense the multiplicity of pathways matches the heterogeneity often seen as characteristic of urban life, the overlap of many relatively distinct paths reflecting the many-sided, situational, often changing lives that people lead in towns today. But they bring, too, a sense of belonging and reality: travelling not in an alien environment but along familiar paths in time and space, in family continuity and habitual action. The pathways have their continuities too. They depend on regular sets of largely predictable and purposeful activities that it is easy to overlook if attention is focussed primarily on networks of individuals or the interaction of multiple special-interest groups. Not *everyone* follows these particular pathways, of course. But those who do are scarcely likely to agree either with the anonymous letter-writer complaining of the lack of 'community spirit' in Milton Keynes or with social theorists positing impersonality, alienation or calculation as the basis of urban life. For they are themselves forging and keeping open the routes which to them bring not just value and meaning but one framework for living in space and time. The *specific* conditions within Milton Keynes (or any locality) are likely to be unique, but I have no doubt that other towns too have their pathways which represent neither tight-knit 'community' nor alien anonymity but one established and habitual way in which people find their meaning in urban living.

These pathways, then, are one of the ways in which people within an urban environment organise their lives so as to manage, on the one hand, the heterogeneity and multiplicity of relationships characteristic of many aspects of modern society, and, on the other, that sense of both predictable familiarity and personally controlled meaning that is also part of human life. In our culture there are many pathways that people do, and must, follow – within employment, schooling, households, sport, church, child-rearing. Within these many paths, who is to say that the pathways to do with music are the least important, either for their participants or in the infinite mix of crossways that make up an urban locality and, ultimately, our culture?

There is one final point to re-emphasise. This is that the continuance of these pathways – so often either ignored or taken for granted as 'just there' – depends not on the existence in some abstract sphere of particular musical 'works', but on people's collective and active practice on the ground. The structure and extent of this work by the local grass-roots musicians and their supporters often goes unrecognised. Many examples have been given in earlier chapters, but the general point must be stressed again: these pathways of music-making are not 'natural' ones that cut their own way through the bush, but were opened up and kept trodden by those who worked them. This is very clear with innovative forms of music-making, where people are creating new pathways; but exactly the same point applies to keeping up the older established paths where even 'tradition' means active fosterage if it is to be maintained. Some people can drop out from time to time, but enough must continue to keep the paths clear so that when one group dissolves or one individual passes on their work is replaced or complemented by that of others. The old picture of blind tradition passing mechanically down the generations, as if irrespective of human act, is easily rejected once made explicit, but it still often influences us into assuming that our accepted cultural forms – classical music performances, church choirs, brass bands, rock groups in pubs, carol singing at Christmas – somehow carry on automatically. On the contrary. These paths may be trodden deep, but they only continue because thousands of people up and down the country put thousands of hours and an unmeasurable quantity of personal commitment into keeping them open. As Peter Burke put it of the classical culture of earlier centuries:

The classical tradition ... has often been described in terms of metaphors like 'survival' or 'inheritance' or 'legacy'; one needs to make an effort to remember that this inheritance was not automatic, that it depended on beating some knowledge of certain classical authors into generation after generation of schoolboys (1980, p. 4).

Exactly the same point could be made of the traditions of local music-making in modern towns and the manner in which they – among other pathways – constitute the structure and rituals through which people live out their lives. Some paths go out of use, others are kept trodden only with a struggle, some seem for a time effortlessly open. But all depend on the constant hidden cultivation by active participants of the musical practices that, with all their real (not imaginary) wealths and meanings, keep in being the old and new cultural traditions within our society.

22

Music, society, humanity

This study has focussed on the often unrecognised *practice* (rather than the more familiar works or theory) of music, and so has kept away from philosophical or aesthetic speculation. This has mainly been on the grounds that grander abstractions or evaluations bring little illumination without some appreciation of how music is in practice actualised by its practitioners. Are there, however, any more general conclusions which can be drawn from this investigation? And do the actions of local musicians in one city in the early 1980s have any wider implications for our understanding either of music or of the human realities and social processes of our culture? This chapter, in rather more abstract vein than the earlier ones, touches on some of these questions.

The difficulty, of course, is that it is dangerous – if tempting – to try to set up an ideal model of the functions or meaning of 'music'. For it will be clear that there are many *different* musics, and that how people practise music or what it means to them in particular contexts varies to an extent that can only be misrepresented by any abstract (and no doubt ethnocentrically based) theory about its once-for-all significance. Despite this, I want to end with some more general and speculative remarks: not to construct a theory of Music but to try to put the manifold musical practices in Milton Keynes at a particular period of history into some wider perspective.

The first point is very obvious. That is, that music whether in Milton Keynes or elsewhere has many *non*-musical implications. This has been touched on earlier and will in any case come as no surprise to most readers, but it is worth returning to briefly if only to confirm that local music is not just a purist and abstract contemplation of the arts but also has other more mundane associations.

The view of music as a timeless form divorced from everyday human concerns is not irrelevant; but to imply that local musical practitioners move, or ought to move, in some high rarefied atmosphere would be a laughable travesty. Enthusiastic about music they certainly are, but at the same time their musical activities are embedded in a whole series of other interests and commitments. The choirs, the orchestras, the small and large bands, the many clubs, and the accepted musical occasions all provide settings in which people can act in many different and quite down-to-earth ways – finding opportunities, for example, to make friends or enemies; meet potential mates; keep up with the Joneses; escape from domestic pressures one evening a week; assert themselves, throw their weight around, or impress their peers; make useful business or social contacts; enjoy the pleasures of working in a co-operative venture or of agitating for changes; enter competitions; please their families, peers, teachers, colleagues or friends; get acclamation from those whom they admire; earn money or the appearance of money; have an evening out with friends... The list is endless, for as with any other set of pathways in society people make use of the established institutions and symbols in an almost infinite number of directions to suit their own circumstances and aspirations.

Some patterns are especially prominent. One is the element of sociability. This runs through musical practice. People are moved not just by the love of music but also by the desire to be with their acquaintances, friends, teachers, peers, colleagues, relatives, and enjoy the whole social side of engaging in musical pursuits along with other people and with their approbation. A night out at band practice or choir rehearsal or concert is more than just a period of time allocated to the pursuit of music: it is also a *social* occasion. Nor do people first enter into such pursuits or keep them going over years so much because they have set out to become 'musicians' as through the social relationships and habits set up over time. The established musical pathways kept in being by hundreds and thousands of people are vehicles not just for music but for the powerful human desire for social intercourse.

Important too is the way in which music provides a channel to a socially recognised position in a relatively intimate setting – an aspect often pointed out in studies of grass-roots activities among minority groups. The sense of making a significant aesthetic contribution is perhaps particularly emotive for individuals regarded as in some way 'marginal': outside formal employment, say, or somehow at the bottom of the heap. But those 'advantaged' in material terms are often as keen as any to take part in something valued, perhaps balancing their 'profane' success by their intangible but perceptibly real contribution in music – that is, in a pursuit judged worthy not only by the practitioners and their peers but also, in a very real if elusive sense, profoundly valued by society more widely. The familiar patterns of achievement in a valued activity and a well-founded sense of identity are thus indeed to be found among local musicians and their supporters, a role for musical activity no less important because paralleled by similar functions in other special-interest groups.

The musical practices in which people find this sense of reality and value are not just a matter of arbitrary individual choices or unique events for, as described earlier, they are structured in recognised pathways which have wider implications for social relationships and for cultural continuity-and-change more generally. Such pathways are laid down by the purposeful actions of the participants rather than by the bureaucratic rules of wider bodies (though these play some part) but also have a real existence outside and, in a sense, independent of individuals, giving them, as it were, one road to live by with all the detailed expectations about behaviour, content, ritual, values, and social relationships that this implies. Such musical pathways – not so unlike those of religion – also constitute symbolic constructs within which people can create and control the world, providing a continuing thread, often taken up week after week after week, which both creates and differentiates social activity – one arena in which people thus manifest and experience their social reality.

It is also worth remembering that though music is not the only form of activity which brings people together, this *is* one of its common results (indeed often one of its conditions). Some of the traditional speculations on this subject – like music's role in upholding the 'harmony of the whole', or reflecting 'the inner truth of man' – are too ethereal to relate in any specific way to actual musical practice and can be left to the philosophers and aestheticians. But this collective element in music-making has certain wider implications for society more generally which are worth noting.

One aspect has already been touched on. The pathways of musical practice involve people in a series of cumulatively overlapping and criss-crossing social relationships. These in turn relate them both to each other and, through the series of personal networks, institutional links, and social ordering of space and time necessarily implicated in each of these pathways, to other elements in social life. This extends not just within a single town (the focus of chapter 21) but also much more broadly to national institutions and the many country-wide musical worlds and their pathways. To be involved in musical practice is not merely an individual matter or, indeed, asocial withdrawal (as it has sometimes been pictured) but *is* to be involved in social action and relations – in society.

Not that this involvement is either problem-free or consistently harmonious, for in music, as in any social process, there are all the usual struggles as well as agreements typical of human affairs. Some analysts would no doubt go further, to argue that, far from bringing people together, music should be seen as perpetuating divides, above all through class divisions. On this I would briefly repeat my earlier conclusion (chapter 21) that in the Milton Keynes study the concept of class turned out not to be of particular significance either for participants' own perceptions or for any overall analysis of local musical practice. Even its relevance for musical differentiation is elusive and at best only partial, and for people's musical choices and divisions many other factors besides socio-economic class as such come into play: gender, age, parents' preferences, school, peer group, colleagues at work, individual skills and properties, spouse's interests – a whole series of mixed personal influences. It seems to be as valid to regard music-making as a sphere in which people transcend divisions as in any general way perpetuating or symbolising overall divides between people.

Indeed, one of the characteristics of musical activities is the great *diversity* not just in the music itself but in the kind of people who take part – from both sexes, all ages, and just about every kind of occupational and educational background. This variety itself has wider social implications, for the interaction of groupings provides one means by which individuals and sections within society are bound together. This works at various levels – from the sense of identity held by innumerable individuals linked together through their engagement in recognised cultural pathways to the interaction of more articulate minority groups formed to pursue some specialist interest. These aspects are worth reverting to briefly here in the context of the overall effects of musical practice for wider social processes of cohesion and division in our society. Without the involvement of millions of individuals in thousands of musical groups and activities up and down the country, together with all the other comparable interest groups (whether dubbed 'leisure' or 'work', voluntary or paid), and the interaction, overlap, co-operation, cross-cutting links, and conflict between these many path- ways, British culture would not continue as it now does. One does not have to believe that the present order is necessarily fully beneficial or equitable, or that *every* aspect of life can be fully subsumed under the heading of the interest groups and their interactions, to accept that these kinds of pluralist processes play an important part in the current functioning of British society in a socio-cultural as well as political context.[1]

In this overall system, the many criss-crossing musical pathways discussed in the study join with other comparable pathways to make their essential contribution to the whole. Ultimately the macro-patterns of British life are cumulatively based on such apparently trivial commitments as Mrs Taylor putting on coffee for the interval, Jane being fetched from her music lesson and reminded each evening to practise, Don badgering his friends to come and work at a rock number in his garage, neighbours getting irritated by the noise of drumming next door, a couple of friends struggling to fix the band van in time for a gig that evening, a father bringing his son along to his brass band, a publican agreeing to have a live group on Thursday nights, the doctor's receptionist and music club treasurer filling in application forms for a grant from the National Federation of Music Societies, a band or choir breaking up and its members dispersing to bring their expertise to new groups, a whole series of people of every kind of background putting their hands in their pockets for new uniforms for the local brass band – and the thousand and one other things that can be imagined just from this one study of musical activities over a few years in a single not very large town in Britain. Seen within the wider picture, each and all of these actions make their contribution to the overall system of interacting and overlapping interests which – for good or ill – is one notable characteristic of modern British society.

This point needs stressing. Not that the local foundation of overall cultural patterns is particularly new or difficult to grasp; indeed it may seem too obvious to need elaboration. And yet, it *is* often overlooked, not just at the local level, but also in the wider studies of the functioning of our society in general. Too often the major focus is 'occupation' or 'economic' institutions, while activity that can be labelled as 'leisure' or even 'culture' is taken as peripheral, not a serious part of the 'real' social structure. Even those who do emphasise 'leisure' or, yet rarer, consider not just sport or planning but the arts tend to be interested in large-scale professional institutions rather than the relatively amateur and small-scale practices presented in this study. And yet, let me emphasise once more, the overall interaction of the many pathways which make up British society *cannot* be fully understood without some appreciation of the contribution of the local musical activities at the grass roots. In the overall system music is, it is true, only one part. But it *is* one part, and as emerges in this study, not a negligible one. It engages hundreds of thousands – probably millions – of people in this country. It is partly through the often-invisible work of such people along both established and innovative musical pathways that, ultimately, the institutions and traditions of our society are perpetuated and recreated.

So far in this chapter music has been treated as essentially sharing the same characteristics as other kinds of special interests at the local level. Indeed similar points about the functions for individual and society could equally well have been made for a whole range of other voluntary activities from flower-arranging, bridge, football, horse-riding, model railways or family-life-history associations, to more 'serious' pursuits like political parties, welfare societies or churches. Such functions have been well rehearsed in studies both of special-interest groups[2] and of 'leisure' and its role in society.[3] Because of the mystical character often exaggeratedly attributed to 'music', it is worth emphasising that its implications for individuals, communities, groups, even 'Society' at large, partially coincide with those of many other less apparently 'high' interests. In this context, then, music is indeed important because of its widespread distribution, but has no *special* position above all the other interests followed more, or less, ardently by various minorities among the people of Britain.

But perhaps music *is* also in some sense 'special'? Can we speculate that there may be something unique or additional about music-making which also gives it an additional quality beyond those it shares with other minority pursuits? Both the views of the musicians themselves and my own observations suggest that such questions are at least worth raising.

To the participants themselves, their musical experience *was* different in kind from other pursuits: others might prefer sport or politics or drama, but to the music-lovers it was music they were involved in. The elements out of which this musical experience was constructed did of course also appear in other activities, for the various combinations of aesthetic, intellectual, emotive, kinetic, visual, verbal, or acoustic – to mention just some ways such elements have been labelled – form the basis of many of the actions we term artistic. But the specific blend which was classified as *music* (differing, of course, on the differing musical pathways) was experienced as unique by its participants. Not that this was often verbalised, and in any case capturing it in any one definition is difficult, though the aesthetic and symbolic experience of the beauty of artistically controlled and created sound was something near it. What did seem unmistakable was an unspoken but shared assumption among the participants in local music that there was something *sui generis*, something unparalleled in quality and in kind about music which was not to be found in other activities of work or of play. This assessment was neither exactly measurable nor precisely definable, but was for all that itself part of the reality, one way in which music had indeed, as experienced by its local participants, its own inimitable meaning.

This experience must somehow enter into the explanation of why so many people chose to involve themselves in *music* rather than the numerous other pathways that they could have followed. Of course, there are also all the other factors discussed earlier – the diverse rewards people get out of any leisure interest, the effect of habit, of personal or family or group pressures, of sociability, of prestige, and so on. But it was *music* they turned to, with all the effort and commitment that have been described in this volume. Thus though the rewards lay partly in the 'social' sphere, there was also something about music which for the participants set it apart – rewards which must be sought in the aesthetic domain, something akin perhaps to the spiritual meaning in religion. It is easy for social analysts to ignore this aspect, concerned as they often are to question the asocial romantic picture sometimes painted of music and its participants. But the unique aesthetic basis of music is *not* just a creation of the theorists or an artefact foisted upon passive dupes by the elite or the mass media: it is part of the essence of what is meant by – experienced as – music in its various realisations by its active creators.

This perception of music as somehow irreducible is further reinforced by the special value that, however unspoken, seems to be attached to music in our culture. At a perhaps trivial but nonetheless significant level this comes out in the absence of the derogatory labels attached to some of our other part-time cultural pursuits: I have often heard 'horsey', 'hearty' and 'arty' – but never 'music-y'.[4] More seriously, there seems to be a widespread assumption that if something is described as 'music' it is, whatever the facts of the situation, by that very label somehow set above the battle, a suitable vehicle for 'charity', a life-enhancing expression of something rich and eternal in humanity. This is more than just the negative view that 'music' can occupy people in a harmless way, keeping them off the streets and away from reprehensible occupations; rather music is perceived as having positive value in some deeper sense. Just what that sense is, is often not precisely articulated, and in any case varies from traditional classical idealising to more robust though equally strongly felt views about the profound reso-nances of 'the beat' in rock music or deep back-to-the-roots overtones of folk. But however this comes out in detailed rationalisation or application, the idea of 'music' as something valuable in itself seems to be deeply embedded, further sanctioned by the vague but powerful High Art view of music. It forms the background that joins 'music' to such other concepts as 'religion' or 'the family' as among the unquestioned good things of our society. Such a basic value does not necessarily have to be fully explicit – published in sacred texts, for example – to be deeply influential on the lives and perceptions of the participants: on their views of themselves and of their place in the universe.

This is not to say that everyone is agreed about just what comes within these notions. As with religion, there can be bitter arguments about what counts as 'music' or as 'real' music, with accusations and counter-accusations of, say, 'romantic snobbery' or 'cultural degeneration'. And, in the same way as with 'the family', any apparent change may be seen as fundamentally threatening society itself and its basic values. But such anxieties and disputes are themselves the point, for they reflect the deep significance attached to 'music'. Thus the dire consequences that some have predicted will result from rock (or earlier jazz) suggest that music is envisaged not as a peripheral form of entertainment but as somehow fundamental to the social order. Any perceived changes in musical practice, whether the death of a particular institution or the enthusiasm of large numbers of people, can be feared as entailing almost cosmic results – for the moment, that is, until new groups or new practices are redefined as after all acceptable ones.[5] In this sense too, then, 'music' is represented as somehow holding a special place which sets it above and beyond more 'ordinary' leisure pursuits.

This is taken further in the commonly held idea that there is a specially close and intimate relationship to the self in musical experience. As Jim Obelkevich has commented (1985), this is evident in the long popularity of the radio programme *Desert Island Discs*: it is assumed not only that *everyone* can make informed selections within music (unlike, say, painting or poetry) but that these choices are uniquely revealing of the person interviewed. This came out in the local situation too. People took pride in being identified by the label 'musician' or in performing their *own* original compositions; and there were the poignant cases where favourite music was played to try to rouse a child or adult from coma, reinforced by the widely believed explanation, reported time after time in local papers, that it was indeed that music that had pulled them back from the depths.

The special quality attached to music is in one sense self-standing, a fundamental value in itself rather than measurable by its public uses or appearances. It does have a tangible realisation too, though, which sets it apart from pursuits like, say, chess or painting or even sport. For it would be difficult to imagine the public life of any community in Britain or the life-cycle rites of most individuals without the practice of music.

Consider, for example, the many ceremonies and public occasions in any English town (for Milton Keynes is only one example) and try to imagine them bereft of music. From Christmas festivities with their carolling, church services and brass bands, to summer outdoor fêtes, public processions, weddings, funerals, school performances for friends and parents, entertainments, parties, presentations, dances, not to speak of the specifically musical performances exemplified in this book – all of these receive their fame and definition at least in part through music. Publicly celebrated events, in one sense or another of the term, have somehow to be set apart as belonging not to everyday practice but to some special enhanced sphere. Among these various markers music seems to take not the sole but perhaps the leading part. It is almost as if a celebration cannot be classed as such without the framing of music.

How this works out in practice varies, and music can come in more, or less, and at a number of levels. One view – for the point is certainly not new – envisages music as an essential concomitant for the great symbolic events through which a community reinvigorates itself or marks transitions to new stages of life or new phases of the annual cycle. That traditional picture could not be applied wholesale to most modern English towns, certainly not to Milton Keynes, where, as discussed in the last chapter, there was not one single 'community' but a series of differentiated groupings bound together by overlapping ties at different levels and by the persistent pathways individuals trod through the town. 'City' ceremonies of a kind, of course, there were, including the 'civic' occasions organised or attended by the Mayor, together with Remembrance Day in November and certain Christmas festivities. Most ceremonies, however, were not meant to be city-wide but to fit in with the expectations of some specific group or locality within the area, and here too music regularly played an essential role. For those directly involved, these events could (as described in the last chapter) mark out the divisions of their year and the transitions in the life-cycles of them and theirs, whether in a local festivity or public musical event, the weddings or funerals arising from the circumstances of individuals, or the yearly socials and dances and entertainments put on by interest groups of all kinds.

For all such rituals music is among the prime signals that set them apart from everyday life and provide an essential framework for their validation and true celebration. Remembrance Day has to have its brass band, an organist has to play at funeral and wedding services, a local festival needs its singers or instrumentalists, the local PTA or tennis club secretary must find a ceilidh band for its annual barn dance, a pub's Christmas celebrations means hiring a musician to grace the occasion, the Christmas season is signalled by brass bands in the streets, a school puts on its presentation to parents and friends by calling on the skills of those who can sing, dance or play – and so on and so on.

In the broad sense of marking out a special space within the everyday flow of life and of defining certain moments and transitions as imbued with somehow transcendent significance, all these events are among the rituals of contemporary society.[6] Fragmented and disparate as they may seem compared to the idealised model of 'tribal rituals' or harmonious 'community', they still play a significant part in modern urban life. As Roger Abrahams put it in concluding his perceptive study of rituals in culture, 'rituals are built on the foundation of ... smaller acts and investments' (1977, p. 47); preeminent among these – and, it seems, somehow obligatory for the continued enactment of our modern-day rituals – are the kinds of musical activities presented in this book. The high place accorded to music in our culture and the continued coming-forward of countless individuals up and down the country prepared to train and define themselves as musicians are no accidents, but closely related to central values and practices in our social life.

Local musical practice thus turns out after all *not* to be just of minority interest, the specialised concern of musical purists or specialist leisure sociologists. Rather, it is of fundamental significance in our culture. As was mentioned in the last chapter, the existence of part-time experts who can be called on to support important ceremonial occasions has often been noted for non-industrial societies: though less often commented on, the same is true of our own. The division of labour in its broad sense must surely mean not just 'full-time work' (i.e. formal paid employment) but also the part-time – and essential – role of active workers outside the official labour market.[7] Musicians fulfil a crucial role here, recruited through the hereditary channels described in chapter 21, complemented by overlapping and partly unpredictable mechanisms like peer-group interest, personal skills or enthusiasm, individual achievement, church and school encouragement, or personal accident. The exact forms in which such experts are socialised and practise their music no doubt change over the years, as do the complex interactions along the amateur–professional continuum. But what remains constant is the existence of accepted roles for musical practitioners in a local and part-time rather than professionally 'employed' setting, and recognised social mechanisms for filling these roles. This is a long-standing feature, perhaps indeed a fundamental requirement, of our culture.

It has been said of music in nineteenth- and early twentieth-century England that 'all told no other form of English leisure ... was so all pervasive, so influential and so nationwide as the enjoyment of music' (Walvin 1978, p. 112). In view of the significance of music as revealed in this study, it becomes a serious question whether the same assessment might not equally apply to late-twentieth-century English culture, not just in the more superficial senses of the amount of 'leisure' activity and the commitment of its participants, but also the more profound role of music and musicians in the functioning of our society.

Music and musicians are thus recognised as having the special role of creating a space in social life and framing events as 'rituals' – a responsibility of deep and essential significance for our society. But there is also more to be said. For music does more than just frame this space: it also *fills* it. This brings us to the quality of musical enactment in itself – an elusive subject about which it is only too easy to romanticise. Let me, however, make some attempt at comment, however speculative.

People are involved in local music at several different and often overlapping levels. Some are back-up supporters (though not without their own culturally learned appreciation of the music along one or more purposive pathways), some take the role of active and knowledgeable audience, and some actively play or sing for their own pleasure or exercise their skills in performances of the kinds defined and discussed in this volume. At all these levels, but most intensely in the active performance modes, people are *practising* music, not just passively 'consuming' or theorising about it; they are engaged in the actively realised and purposeful enacting of a widely recognised form of human experience and action.

The cluster of ideas centring round such notions as 'performance', 'enactment' and 'practice' runs through our social life. Taken in an extended sense 'performance' can even be seen, as Vic Turner among others has so perceptively argued (1982), as one basic process in the way we live together, a metaphor which reminds us of the continuum among all kinds of performances from the most official and public to the informal interactions of every day. Here, however, I want to focus not on this extended meaning, but on explicit performed enactment in music. This is the prerogative of musicians at every level, especially in the prototypical form which imbues all musical action with a special aura: the specific events differentiated as public musical performances in the direct meaning of the term – concerts, gigs, bookings, recitals, the kind of audience-directed musical events described in this book.

Music, society, humanity

This again is something accorded high value in our society. Preparing for and partaking in them is also, as will have become clear from earlier discussions, of central concern to local musical groups; and the number of public musical performances in any one year is likely to be enormous, from choir concerts, school entertainments, or amateur operatic performances to rock bands playing in pubs, folk musicians singing in clubs, singer-guitarists in wine bars, brass bands in the streets, and jazz bands performing in fortnightly pub jazz clubs, to mention only some. The concept of 'performance' is, of course, a relative one; as explained earlier (chapter 12), what precisely counts as 'public' is partly situational, and some 'performances' are more 'special' or more formalised than others. But that there is some notion of 'performance' as a set-piece event with an audience, representing in some sense the epitome of musical enactment, and that such a notion is central to the consciousness and operation of most local musicians was quite clear from the explicit comments and continued actions of the musicians in this study.

These events take many different forms, but in all cases their musical performance quality sets them apart from everyday life in an even more intense sense than the more general ceremonials discussed earlier. Once again, there is a ritual quality, the aura of raising the activity to another sphere of existence – 'they enable us to project our valued vitality into transcendent realms', as Roger Abrahams puts it. 'In fact, they guarantee the transcendence' (1977, p. 46). Vic Turner expresses the same point in more general terms:

In a sense, every type of cultural performance, including ritual, ceremony, carnival, theatre, and poetry, is explanation and explication of life itself... Through the performance process itself, what is normally sealed up, inaccessible to everyday observation and reasoning, in the depth of sociocultural life, is drawn forth (Turner 1982, p. 13).

If this seems overblown of the small-scale and sometimes ragged or fractious performances that can doubtless be recalled by every reader, it is worth remembering too the special quality that, *despite* all this, is yet somehow attached to the whole notion and experience of a musical performance, the way that, small or large, brilliant or indifferent, classical or folk or jazz, it creates and expresses experience as a special enactment.

Classical musicians might object that while they can recognise this quasi-cosmic quality in classical performances, in many rock and some jazz or folk performances, the audience are treating the music just as pleasant background rather than true musical 'performance'. But *all* musical performances are to a degree relative, and even in the grandest of performances other more 'mundane' activities and distractions are going on at the same time (among the performers too), without necessarily changing the quality of the essential enactment. The classical convention of audience behaviour is in any case not the only one, and needs to be revised (along the lines suggested in chapter 12) to take fuller account of kinaesthetic and visual elements which constitute an essential part of many multi-faceted musical performances. We need to remind ourselves again, perhaps, to be more sensitive to the mix of playful and serious which, as anthropologists and others have well reminded us, forms one recurrent theme in ritual (e.g. Turner 1982, pp. 32ff., Abrahams 1977, Martin 1981, p. 184). This kind of mix does not undermine the special quality in public musical performance, a form of purposeful enactment uniquely accomplished and expressed in music.

Such performances, furthermore, are not just any ritual or any artistic experience, but specifically *musical* ones. They take place in public, characteristically through a co-operating group of enactors (in notable contrast to the relatively solitary acts of some other artistic experiences), and are made up of the joint participation of a number of people in the combined visual, kinaesthetic and acoustic experience which, in its various manifestations, is in our culture defined as live musical performance. This special crystallisation of musical experience created by the interaction of both performers and audience represents somehow a shared symbolic dimension which removes it above and beyond ordinary experience. It is tempting to write in facile mystical terms, but there does seem to be a sense in which the process of joining together in music, with all its problems and conflicts, really does unite people 'in harmony' – to follow the significantly common musical metaphor – in some unique and profound way which, except perhaps in religious enactment, is seldom found in other contexts.[8] Given this, some of the speculative theorising about music does not seem so out of place, such as Schutz's analysis of the mutual 'tuning-in' relationship between performers and listeners established by 'the reciprocal sharing of the... flux of experience in inner time, by living through a vivid present together, by experiencing this togetherness as "we"' (Schutz 1977, pp. 116, 118). Or perhaps the Milton Keynes plumber summed it up better still in speaking of his own discovery of music: 'it's sad and happy... and just *everything*'.

In this context the often-cited connection between music and religion no longer looks absurd. They are not the *same*, at any rate in our culture. But with all the differences and complexities there is something akin in the way that musical – not so different from religious – enactment both characterises and constitutes some form of ritual, that musicians like priests and seers bear their necessary part in public events, and that the participants in musical rituals can achieve a self-fulfilment conjointly with a loss of self and of the everyday mundane affairs of life in a somehow transcendent and symbolic enactment. The concept of 'performance' has sometimes been used to throw a metaphorical light on the nature of religious action (Tambiah

1973, 1979, Finnegan 1969, Ray 1973). The overtones of religious ritual can equally aptly be applied to musical enactment: the quality of being not a 'mere' performance but of transmuting action to a new dimension in which the participants both lose themselves and at the same time create and control their own experience and the world around them.

The musical practices along the various pathways described in this book all, at a greater or lesser remove, touch somehow on this quality of performance. Musical enactment is at once a symbol of something *outside* and above the usual routines of ordinary life and at the same time a continuing thread of habitual action running *in* and through the lives of its many local practitioners.

This study has revealed the system underlying the practice of music in our society: the invisible organisation – fragile, changing, but continuing, imbued with both everyday practicality and transcendent overtones – which in late-twentieth-century Britain is maintained by, and depends upon, people's active engagement along their local pathways. But one further question is irresistible. Is there also something more fundamental behind this, of which the specific conventions of a particular time and place are only one realisation?

Why do we have music? This is a more puzzling question than it seems, and one we seldom ask ourselves. There is no easy utilitarian answer, for despite its profound social functions – of linking people, giving them identity and status, and marking out and constituting the rituals of our time – music of itself has no essential *use*. Why after all should people engage in music? If we follow the analysis above, we would have to say that in the last analysis and beyond all the manifold ways in which we clearly do use it, musical enactment is not an essentially utilitarian practice at all but one form of celebratory and non-useful artistic action, one unparalleled mode to realise and create the age-old blend of the fantasy and reality, ritual and ordinariness, sacred and profane of our human existence. Musical practice is essentially *of* society, dependent on and expressed in all the kinds of activities and settings described in this book; but it is also perhaps a unique and distinctive mode through which people both realise and transcend their social existence.

If this line of speculation has anything to it, is there perhaps something inherently both universal and unique about music itself? It has often been said that language is one of the fundamental – perhaps even defining – characteristics of humanity, and further suggested that there is somehow some inherent propensity for linguistic formulation deep in the structure of the human mind. Might the same two points not equally apply to music?

Certainly musical practice in one form or another seems to be widespread, probably universal, in human cultures. Despite their many diversities, language, music and perhaps religion are so widely found that, as John Blacking has argued, we may well regard them as species-specific capabilities of mankind.[9] Music, furthermore, does not just occur as a specialist art form but also seems to be one distinctively human mode through which human beings express and formulate their experience. The elitist theory that only certain highly gifted people can 'really' become musicians is an influential one in our society but has also misled us about the widespread potential to make and to use music. In many cultures it is taken for granted that everyone can learn musical skills of performance and appreciation even though only some become experts. Despite the conventional wisdom, the situation in our own culture may not be so very different when, as here, *all* forms of music are considered. Perhaps only a small proportion actually take this very far, but that far more are capable of and committed to musical practice than is often supposed was certainly for me one of the main findings of this study. Music is by no means the preserve of a favoured few or of peripheral minority groups but one mode of action – one set of pathways – potentially open to all, pervading many events in our society, and actively practised more, or less, fully by large numbers of people from every kind of background.

If music is indeed one unique modality of human experience, it is hardly surprising that, like language, it should be embodied in a number of different manifestations and social practices, and that musical enactment can be used, again like language, to achieve a whole series of ends. In this view 'music' is not to be identified or defined in abstract or ideal terms – for there can be many different musics – but rather, as has been the emphasis in this book, found in the activities ordered and classified as the musical pathways of a given culture. Certainly there are shared conventions about music-making at any point in time, and to understand musical practice one must also take cognisance of these (often unnoticed) conventions: another basic theme in this book. But perhaps the background to all this is a universally shared propensity of human beings to realise themselves and their culture through the medium of musical action.

If this is so then music is both similar to and different from language as a basic characteristic of humanity. Language is usually seen as a fundamentally *cognitive* mode, the capacity for it deep in the human *mind*. To be sure, it is in social interaction and the full flow of human life that language is developed in practice; but there is nevertheless often held to be something intellectual, mental, propositional about language. Music, by contrast, is not essentially a *cognitive* code, and extends beyond the 'mind' to the 'body'. It is associated not primarily with words, but with rhythm, movement, and overt physical enactment, a context in which it is perhaps scarcely surprising that participants experience a particular sense of active control and of personal creativity. Perhaps this dimension of life does indeed share some of the characteristics of language and maybe of religion, but at the same time represents a different and unique modality of human action *sui generis*.

Such questions cannot be settled just by the findings from one smallish town in one country in the late twentieth century. Yet this study of the grass-roots practice of local music certainly reveals that music may play a far larger part in the experience and fulfilment of human beings and the patternings of society than is usually allowed by social scientists, musicologists or the conventional wisdom on the topic. To ignore this modality of human action may be to miss something fundamental to our human experience. It leads me further to query once again not only the still-fashionable view that human beings somehow gain their central social reality from their *economic* involvement in society (usually based on the 'man as paid worker' model) but even the richer and, in my opinion, more realistic 'man as symboliser' approach (current in some social science, specially anthropology), with its overtones of an ideational and ultimately linguistically modelled view of humanity. It is surely equally valid to picture human beings essentially as practitioners and performers: artistic and moral enactors rather than symbolic perceivers or paid workers. And for the musicians of the kind described in this study – most of all the expert musical exponents, but also the whole range of active listeners as well as players, skilled audiences as well as performers – it is in no small part in virtue of their engagement in the recognised pathways of music that they are realising their essential human reality and are implicated in the society in which they live out their lives.

Perhaps we now need to forget some of the 'industrialisation'-based theorising of both social science and much popular wisdom. It might be better to go back to Huizinga or, even better, to Aristotle (if we can shed their more elitist implications) and remind ourselves once more of certain truths about our humanity. These have perhaps been with us all the time, even if recent fashions have combined to make us conceal them from ourselves; they became very evident in this study of a late-twentieth-century English town. That is, that the reality of human beings is to be found not only (maybe not mainly) in their paid employment or even their thought but also in their engagement in recognised cultural practices. It is here that, as Alasdair MacIntyre so wisely argues, they exercise and exhibit human virtue in the full sense of the term.[10] Among the most valued and, it may be, most profoundly human of such practices in our society is that of music. And far from being either 'marginal' to society or confined to a small elite of specialists, this deeply social and deeply human practice of music is engaged in and fought over and created and maintained by the many many unacclaimed local musicians whose work both reveals them as creative and active human beings and serves to uphold the cultural traditions we take for granted.

Appendix

A note on methods and presentation

The study was mainly carried out in 1980–4, but I had lived in the area since 1969 (apart from three years abroad, 1975–8), so I also drew on recollections from earlier years. I used a mixture of methods, as described below.

(1) Participant observation.

By this I mean the kind of first-hand fieldwork which takes the form of personally participating in the events and processes being studied, including informal observation and conversations, contact with regular (if informal) informants, and focussing on intensive case studies rather than quantitative surveys. This method was suitable both for the kinds of questions I wanted to investigate and for my personal circumstances (since I had lived in Bletchley for many years and taken part in local music both as a performer and an audience member and also had three children learning music and attending local schools).

However, though participant observation is one recognised method in social science research,[1] it has variants and ambiguities, as well as some specific problems when applied to research in an urban context. A full discussion of methodological issues is not appropriate here, but some points should be mentioned briefly.

'Participation' in a large urban setting is different from the 'traditional' anthropological setting where one can see or take part in a large proportion of what is going on, as in a small-scale rural society (not that it is as problem-free or unselective as sometimes assumed even there). I had to select either explicitly or implicitly which of the huge number of possible events I should observe or take part in, and in what capacity. Should it be just one small locality and the people there, say in the street I lived in? But then many forms of music-making would have escaped me, and even those that *did* take place there or were organised by musicians from that locality had many ramifications outside the locality. Should it be across the whole city? But then I could only observe a very small proportion of musical events and would not get to know any properly. Should it be of just one or two musical worlds or of a few specific musical groups so as to give some deeper understanding 'from the inside' (as in many traditional anthropological accounts)? But then I would miss out on the comparisons between different musical traditions and their interactions.

In the end I adopted a mixed and perhaps rather haphazard strategy, participating much more directly and deeply in some worlds and activities than others but trying to gain some appreciation of them all through a (varied) mix of methods. In all cases *some* of my understanding was drawn from personal observation, but particularly in the rock and pop chapter and for the account of social clubs, pubs and the small bands generally I relied more heavily on non-observational methods than in my descriptions of the classical world or of school and church settings. Even in the latter cases, though, I supplemented personal observation by at least some of the other methods mentioned later so as to gain some city-wide understanding.

'Participation' can take a number of forms, related among other things to what part the participant is playing. In the musical activities I studied, there were accepted roles which I could take up, but it was not possible to adopt all of them at once, and there were also some that I was not willing to assume; doing fieldwork in one's own locality where one *already* has established roles (wife, mother, middle-aged woman, full-time professional worker) brings its personal as well as research dilemmas. In some cases I participated as a full member of musical groups in the sense of taking an active performing role (especially in a local choir, church congregation, and home music-making), in others as joint organiser (in a classical music society), in others as a genuine admirer but not performer (folk or brass band music), in others as parent of musical children, in yet others in the accepted role of audience. Even this last setting had its variety, ranging from the membership of a relatively small and skilled group jointly appreciating a familiar performance in a well-known setting to the more anonymous reception (another accepted form of participation) where the performers and most of the audience were not personally known. The role of fan, admirer or potential client was also a recognised one, so that it was not difficult to approach even unfamiliar performers with questions or comments. There were thus a number of roles into which I could fit – indeed in some ways already fitted – but at the same time there were others I was not prepared or able to undertake; in contrast to some popular music researchers, I did not learn skills like drumming or guitar-playing, nor did I make the least attempt to become a performing member of local jazz, rock or folk bands.[2]

I did not conceal the fact that I was doing research on local music (and with the methods discussed later made a point of making this explicit), and in a vague way it was fairly generally known; but at the same time I did not keep reminding people about it during the ordinary course of my life or in the many off-hand conversations which turned out to be illuminating. The observation was therefore not covert, but neither was it constantly obvious throughout (as it must be when a stranger comes to study a foreign community), for I was *already* an established person with her own responsibilities and interests which even by those who remembered that studying local music was one of them were rightly assumed to extend more widely than just her research.

Participant observation in my own locality thus had its ambiguities and problems. Most were probably inevitable for an anthropologist studying a familiar culture: the well-known issue of how far one should or should not 'become a native' looks rather different, if still pressing, in one's own community. Being *too* much of an insider (and so ceasing to be a detached observer) was always a danger, partly balanced by the need to move between different musical worlds in some of which I was more of an outsider than others – an additional reason for valuing comparisons which provided the kind of detachment which would have been impossible if I had immersed myself completely in just one world. The problems were both intensified and diminished by the further fact that during most of the research I was only participating and observing on a part-time basis, for I consistently had other academic and personal responsibilities which consumed much of my time. Such part-time commitment to 'the field' will doubtless make many anthropologists shudder. In a way I do too, but would also comment that I *was* living in the locality ('the field') for over a decade and that if I had waited to be wholly 'free' in the way one is in fieldwork away from home, the study would never have been done at all. If it was not possible to follow through many of the local actors' lives in all their settings – 'in the round' as it is often put in anthropological contexts – it might also be said on the other hand that people's musical activities themselves were often part time and yet formed a continuous and arguably autonomous thread in their lives, with its own coherence independent of their other engagements. Much local amateur music was therefore practised on precisely the same lines of *non*-full-time involvement. Perhaps my part-time commitment was after all one form of typical urban participation in the practice I was studying.

I have focussed on problems, but must add finally that without the measure of participant observation that, with all its unsatisfactoriness, I *did* achieve, I do not feel I could have begun to understand what was involved in the meaningful practice of local music and its pathways. The other methods were essential as a supplement – and it will be obvious that in some cases I relied on them extensively – but participant observation was central to the study.

(2) Extended personal interviews.

Beside the many informal conversations already mentioned, deliberate interviews of around one to two hours each were held with a few key individuals. These were normally arranged in advance, but were then conducted on a very free basis, mainly just encouraging people to talk about their experiences and views ('interview' is perhaps too formal a word for these friendly conversations). I usually took rapid notes at the time (with permission) and wrote them up more fully later.

(3) Documentary sources.

Though inevitably somewhat patchy, these represented a most valuable source. They included both published sources (for example, local newspapers and publications by the MKDC or BMK) and unpublished material (for instance, records of certain music clubs and groups, compilations about clubs in the local library, and some BMK and MKDC files, especially those relating to the 'Minor Amenities Fund' which I am grateful to the MKDC Recreation Unit for allowing me to consult).

The local newspapers were particularly useful – needing to be used with care, of course, but overall a valuable and much under-rated source in social research. There were four main ones (not all published throughout the full period of the research): the long-established *Milton Keynes Gazette* and (until late 1982) *Milton Keynes Express*, and the free papers *Milton Keynes Mirror*, *Milton Keynes Sunday Mirror* and *Milton Keynes Citizen*. Items to do with music were systematically cut out from

A note on methods and presentation

1981–4 (plus a selection from 1980 and 1985). These included advertisements and notices as well as news items and feature articles, and by the end filled eight hefty files.

(4) School postal questionnaire.

This was sent out to teachers responsible for music in all 92 schools (including 6 independent schools) in the Milton Keynes Educational Division in the 1982 summer term, concentrating especially on extra-curricular musical activities. Fifty-one schools sent usable replies (a 55.4 per cent response rate); information for those not replying was in many cases obtained from other sources.

(5) Face-to-face and telephone interviews.

These were a series of interviews carried out on my behalf in 1982–3 by Liz Close, to whose energy and enthusiasm I am extremely indebted. They gave some quantitative background to the personal observations I had been able to carry out on just a few groups and venues, and also, on account of both Liz Close's effective interviewing and informants' preparedness to provide often extensive comments, added greatly to my understanding of their views and activities, particularly in the lengthy band interviews. These interviews fell into four categories:

(a) Pubs. From a total of 85 pubs, 29 publicans/landlords were interviewed personally, followed up by 47 on the telephone, all in the autumn and winter of 1982–3 (9 refused or could not be contacted). This covered all the local pubs in the main area of the Milton Keynes 'new city' and some beyond (as listed in such sources as the *Milton Keynes Business & Buying Directory*, the Milton Keynes Development Corporation's *Where to Buy in Milton Keynes & District*, telephone directories, *Yellow Pages* and local newspapers).

(b) Small bands. Fifty-two bands were interviewed between August 1982 and February 1983, all face to face (33 in the general area of pop and rock, 9 jazz, 3 country and western, 6 folk and one school classical/carol group). This was neither the full number nor a systematic sample (impossible since no comprehensive list of local bands was available; there were perhaps 200 in all at that period, though that is only an estimate). Names and contacts were gathered from various sources: partly through 'snowball' (one contact leading to another), partly from mentions in local newspapers and background knowledge. An attempt was made to get a spread both of different forms of music and of different kinds of bands in terms of newer and older bands, more or less 'successful' (in terms of fees and numbers of bookings), and varying types of venue.

(c) Churches. All the churches and formal religious groups in the Milton Keynes area were contacted (their names drawn both from MKDC information guides and from records of the Milton Keynes Christian Council, whose ecumenical officer, the Reverend Gethin Abraham-Williams, provided much-valued help), amounting to something over 70 in all, including 4 non-Christian groups. Of these, representatives from 39 churches (usually one of the clergy) were interviewed face to face, followed by briefer telephone interviews with 32 others in late 1983. Given the combination of some churches under one minister and the often informal development of others as new population moved into the area, exact counting and delimitation of 'a church' was not easy, but certainly the vast majority were covered.

(d) Social clubs. Representatives of 34 social clubs (including 10 youth clubs) were interviewed in the spring and summer of 1983, 22 face to face followed by 12 on the telephone. The sampling was not systematic (partly because there turned out to be many more such clubs than had appeared on the original list from local sources), but again some attempt was made to include a number of different categories: youth clubs (10), general sports and social clubs (4), firms' social clubs (9), working men's clubs (6) and a few special association clubs such as Conservative Clubs. The end result was interesting but not necessarily representative and, as with the other survey material, was supplemented from other sources.

These quantitative sources were useful in giving some numerical background, but it should also be remarked that the areas they variously covered were not uniform since administrative and other boundaries did not always coincide (the education division, for example, was not precisely the same as that used in church organisations, and the boundaries of the Milton Keynes Borough Council were wider than those of the 'designated new city' area (see figure 1)). This raises the more general question of just what was covered by the term 'Milton Keynes'. There is clearly no one answer to this. In this volume the majority of the examples are in practice drawn from the designated new city area (which also included the older towns of Bletchley, Wolverton and Stony Stratford) given that that was where the majority of the population was located, but the overall scope of the study also extends to the Borough of Milton Keynes (thus including Newport Pagnell, Woburn Sands and the various associated villages as well as the central 'new city' area), and in some cases (which ones should be obvious if the map is consulted) refers to relevant material from further afield. It must be remembered too that the population was growing and changing over the four years or so of the research and the surveys were not all conducted at the same time. Numerical conclusions, therefore (even if fully representative of one area at a given time), cannot be compared precisely against each other, though the amount of overlap in the central areas was extensive. Here, as throughout the research, what *exactly* was meant by 'Milton Keynes' was in part a relative and variable matter.

One final point concerns names versus anonymity. It is common in social scientific research either to avoid proper names altogether or to use pseudonyms in contexts where publication could result in the recognition of individuals or (sometimes) of organisations and places. This both protects people's privacy and gives the research an air of scientific detachment. I decided, however, to follow what is also an accepted research tradition[3] and *not* try to mask the locale or the names. I was unlikely to be able to conceal them successfully in any case, but also, more important, people took pride in their musical achievements (some were already well known as composers or performers), most local groups craved rather than feared publicity, and the imaginative names of many musical groups were themselves part of the findings and could not possibly be represented by made-up substitutes. I have not included many names of *individuals* (though a few had to appear), and have avoided attaching certain information such as that of a financial kind to specific named groups. In the end, however, since I consider that local musicians, both individuals and groups, have much to be proud of, I see no reason to try to give the impression of spurious generality or objectivity by concealing their names or their locality.

Notes

1 The existence and study of local music

1 I speak of 'English' and 'England' because this was the main context of the research, but many of the general patterns (with differences in detail) can no doubt also be found elsewhere in the United Kingdom.

2 There has been much discussion (as well as exemplification) of the merits of case studies in social science writings: for recent discussion see, e.g., Mitchell 1983 and Pahl 1984, pp. 146–7.

3 E.g. Nettel 1944, 1956 etc., Sutcliffe 1945, Walvin 1978 (esp. chapter 8 and references given there), Temperley 1981; for urban musical research elsewhere see e.g. Wustman 1909, Schering 1926, 1941, Fellerer 1935, Malm 1971, Weber 1975, Nettl 1978, Hanson 1985.

4 E.g. White 1983, Dunn 1980, Willis 1978, Hebdige 1979, Harker 1980, Woods 1979, Mackenzie 1977, Taylor 1979. Sarah Cohen's exemplary study of rock bands in Liverpool (1987) became available just as this book went to press, as did White (1987) and Pickering and Green (1987), unfortunately too late to be drawn on here.

5 See e.g. Frith 1978, 1981b, 1983, the various issues of *Popular Music* (ed. Middleton & Horn), plus a great deal of ephemera.

6 Some exceptions are noted in the relevant chapters later; among the few general works on contemporary English music which include such topics are Cole 1978, Lee 1970.

7 For a useful critique of this and similar views in relation to music see Frith 1981b.

8 In this and later points I follow many earlier ethnomusicologists, anthropologists and sociologists of music, e.g. Becker 1982, Bennett 1980, Stone 1982, Blacking 1976 etc., Merriam 1964, Basso 1985; see also Fish 1980, pp. 108–9, whose comments on literature I have here adapted to music.

9 The term 'popular' holds similar ambiguities in music as in other aspects of culture. It has sometimes been used of specific *forms* assumed at any one time to contrast with 'high art' (thus often applied just now to rock, pop, country and western, and sometimes jazz, but *not* to classical music), sometimes of the social process involved (created by 'ordinary' people as against the highly trained or selective professionals), sometimes of what has been excluded from traditional academic study, sometimes of the dispersal of particular practices or tastes in

numerical or sometimes class terms (for discussion of the concept of 'popular' see especially Bigsby 1976, esp. pp. 16ff, Burke 1978, esp. prologue, Middleton and Horn 1981, pp. 1ff, Scribner 1981, pp. 59ff, Yeo 1981, pp. xif, IASPM 1985, pp. 3ff, Briggs et al. 1985, Kaplan 1984, esp. introduction by D. Hall). I mostly use the term roughly in the first or, more often, the second of these senses – which, should be clear from the context – and certainly take it that, in the second sense at least, all the musical activities focussed on in this book (*including* the 'classical') form part of our contemporary popular culture.

10 This book follows the same lines as my earlier analyses of oral literature as social process and not just 'text' (e.g. 1977, 1982, 1987) and also relates to the American 'performance-centred' and 'ethnography of speaking' analyses of such writers as Hymes, Sherzer or Bauman, and to Howard Becker's approach to 'art worlds' (1982). Since this study is not primarily one of social theory, no great theoretical import should be attached to the term 'practice' beyond the obvious – but important – contrasts sketched in the text and exemplified in the later discussion. However, I find it interesting that the term has played a key part in recent influential works across several of the social sciences (e.g. Bourdieu 1977, Scribner & Cole 1981, MacIntyre 1981; see also Hymes 1974, p. 5, quoted in Ostendorf 1983, p. 5); despite their differing, but arguably related, views, I interpret this as a welcome change from both intellectualist and product-based approaches towards a greater interest in human action and social processes in the context of 'naturalistic' social reality.

11 A point illustrated both in Becker's recent book on art worlds (1982: see especially p. ix) and in Temperley's fascinating history of English parish church music (1979, see especially preface); see also Graña 1971, p. 66, Cole 1978, Raynor 1972, Stevens 1979.

12 That there are some notable exceptions whose work I have found of the greatest importance – above all Howard Becker and John Blacking – will, I hope, be clear in the various notes and references throughout this volume.

13 A general point effectively discussed by Cato Wadel in the context of the anthropology of work (1979).

14 The standard books tend to focus either on specific primary or secondary 'groups' and associations, or on wider terms like 'class', 'networks', 'family', 'neighbourhood' or 'community' or (if they are more adventurous) 'ethnic groups' or specific occupations; amidst this the kinds of pathways followed by local part-time musicians (and other committed but amateur practitioners) often seem not to be captured (discussed further in chapter 21).

15 A standard problem, of course, in the sociology of art (discussed, e.g., in Wolf 1983).

2 'Amateur' and 'professional' musicians

1 Some interesting exceptions are Cole 1978, Stebbins 1977, 1979, Ehrlich 1985 and (for some historical background) Donakowski 1977 chap. 8, Burke 1978, Rosselli 1984.

2 This blurring is particularly striking in music, but it may be that we now in any

case need to question the once self-evident divide between full-time employment on the one hand and 'leisure' on the other, with its assumed corollary that activities must be divided into *either* those by full-time specialists ('work') *or* those by amateurs ('leisure'). This model is certainly misleading in music and may be now in other contexts too (a general point raised by recent sociological and anthropological work on the division of labour and/or informal economic activities, e.g. Pahl 1984, Wadel 1979, Davis 1985).

3 A point particularly well made by John Blacking (e.g. 1971).

3 Introduction to Milton Keynes and its music

1 Further discussed in the appendix. On the lack of clear-cut boundaries for 'local' musical practice see also chapters 14, pp. 183ff. and 21.

2 The term 'city' was used by the early planners and has become accepted in the area, even though by some criteria Milton Keynes may not qualify for the title. Since I do not think the term of any great moment in the context of this study I use 'town' and 'city' more or less interchangeably.

3 Letter from Teresa Collard, *Milton Keynes Express*, 18 February 1982.

Part 2 Musical worlds in Milton Keynes

1 See for example Ellen 1984, pp. 31ff.; also the general emphasis in the 'Chicago school' of sociology on the differing 'social worlds' in urban life such as the taxi dance hall (Cressey 1932), hoboes (Anderson 1923), or gangs (Thrasher 1927) (see also Hannerz 1980, chap. 2). Hugo Cole also uses the term in a similar way in his perceptive study of music in England (1978).

2 For some further assessment of this concept, see chapter 14.

4 The classical music world at the local level

1 Since this chapter, like the following, is based on local study rather than library research, it is not appropriate to produce lengthy academic references in ostensible validation of my own conclusions. However, works I have found particularly stimulating (not that I necessarily agree with them all) are Shepherd et al 1977, Becker 1982, Blacking 1976, 1982, Martin 1980 (esp. chap. 9), Middleton 1981, Geertz 1975, Eades 1982 and Weber 1958.

2 'Classical' is being used here in the familiar (though admittedly inexact) sense of 'serious' or 'art' music in contrast to the more 'popular' forms discussed in later chapters, rather than in the more limited sense in which it is opposed to, say, 'romantic' or 'baroque' music.

5 The brass band world

1 Here, as elsewhere, my account is based on local rather than library research, but I have found the following sources particularly useful: Russell & Elliott 1936, Taylor 1979, 1983, Russell 1985, Brand 1979, Jackson 1972 (chap. 3), Roberts 1981, and Boon 1978.

2 Brass band players in classical orchestras may not be part of the traditional brass band mythology, but the practice probably goes back a long way (Russell 1985).

6 The folk music world

1 This is not the place for a detailed account of this complex subject, for which see, e.g., Woods 1979, Harker 1980 (chap. 9), 1985, Finnegan 1977, pp. 30ff, Laing 1975, and further references in these works.

8 Jazz

1 Background works on jazz and blues that I have found particularly useful include Dankworth 1968, Berendt 1976, Middleton 1979, Collier 1978.
2 One exception was John Dankworth, a professional musician with international connections based at WAP who also occasionally played locally; there were also a couple of local players regarded as 'ex-professionals' but currently playing in local groups.

9 The country and western world

1 See e.g. Wilgus and Greenaway 1965, Malone 1968, 1980, *Western Folklore* 1971, Shestack 1977, Carr 1980.
2 The local Hole in the Head Gang, playing 'Bluegrass and American country music', were often more assimilated to folk music: they performed at folk clubs and festivals, mixed with folk performers, had the high educational background typical of local 'folk' musicians, and used a range of instruments regarded as acceptable within folk music in Milton Keynes but rather less favoured by most local country and western venues (banjo, mandolin, guitar, fiddle and vocals).

10 Rock and pop

1 For useful critiques of some of this literature, see Frith 1981b, 1983, Ostendorf 1983.
2 This will be clear from my sources: interviews with about 33 bands in Milton Keynes in late 1982/early 1983, together with personal observation, extended interviews with individual players, and information from local newspapers, 1980–4. My relatively limited aim should also be clear from the broad sense of rock/pop I am accepting: any full coverage of the historical/social development of such music(s) or its detailed musicological features and changes would demand more differentiated and precise terms (not that all the more general works are themselves all that consistent in their terminology and definitions). My basic sources were thus local, but I also found the following useful as background (not necessarily addressing the same questions or reaching the same answers as I did): Frith 1978, 1981a and b, Hebdige 1979, Vulliamy & Lee 1980, Middleton

1981, Middleton & Muncie 1981, Elliott 1982, Martin 1981, chap. 8, Laing 1985. (See also the excellent study in Cohen 1987, only available after this chapter was completed.)

3 Not all these bands would describe themselves precisely as either 'rock' or 'pop', but they generally fell within the broad area of music discussed in this chapter.

4 For a succinct and perceptive account of these and subsequent approaches see Frith 1981b, especially chap. 3.

5 For a general critique of this youth (or working-class youth) sub-cultural interpretation developed by the influential Birmingham Centre for Contemporary Cultural Studies (expressed in such works as Hebdige 1979, Muncie 1981, Mungham and Pearson 1976, Brake 1980), see Frith 1981b, 1983, Hustwitt 1986.

6 CSEs (19), one or more O levels (18), A levels (13), music diploma (1), ONC in business studies (1), part-way through HNC courses etc., studying part-time by day release etc. (3), various City and Guilds (6) or professional qualifications (MBIM/MIM 1), teacher training qualifications (3) or degrees (4).

7 Of the players who gave their band roles 27 played guitars, 18 drums/percussion and 16 bass, with 30 in all also singing; there were also 8 keyboard and 3 synthesiser players and occasionally other instruments.

8 Further examined in chapter 19.

12 Performances and their conditions

1 The stress on the centrality of 'performance' and 'performance event' draws particularly on the writings of 'performance centred' folklorists, anthropologists and ethnomusicologists (mainly American), such as Abrahams 1968 and 1977, Bauman and Sherzer 1974, Ben-Amos and Goldstein 1975, Hymes 1974, 1975, Stewart and Philipsen 1984, Bauman 1977, Stone 1982; see also Finnegan 1977 (esp. pp. 88ff., 118ff.) and 1982, Basso 1985, Spencer 1985, Kapferer 1986.

2 They are not perfect examples, but have been selected because they happen to be ones that I attended within a short time of each other, so that the contrasts struck me particularly strongly: the main lines of difference were confirmed by parallel performances at other times.

3 The importance of learning to participate appropriately in performance whether as audience member or performer is well discussed in Stone 1982, pp. 29–30; see also Blacking 1971, 1973.

4 I employ the term 'ritual' of these events following the lead of such writers as Moore and Meyerhoff 1977, Bocock 1974, La Fontaine 1972 (esp. pp. xvii and 159ff.) and, on artistic and musical performance, Martin 1980, pp. 140ff., Kapferer 1986, Abrahams 1977, and Spencer 1985, who are prepared to use the word of non-religious as well as 'religious' enactments in modern life. Though I have never seen an undisputed definition of 'ritual', the kinds of elements which in one way or another appear in most usages of the term seem equally applicable to musical performance: some quality of being an end in itself rather than utilitarian or technological; somehow set apart from (everyday) routines; in some sense obligatory and repeated, with some kind of set and expected programme; a collective and jointly stated enactment; and some symbolic, religious or at any

rate deeply evaluative or in some sense externally validated meaning.
5 The total numbers of such events over two sample months (November 1981 and May 1982) were 96 and 130, but this certainly did not cover even all those often publicised in this form, let alone the others. (This can be compared with the Leicester survey (a town of about two and a half times the Milton Keynes population), which over 1981 as a whole counted 281 productions (703 performances) by both professionals and amateurs, reported in Nissel 1983, p. 177 – again I guess an under-estimate.)
6 Comments from band interviews (see appendix).

13 Composition, creativity and performance

1 This account is based on personal observation and discussion, and on the 1982–3 band survey in which nearly four-fifths of the 33 bands questioned said their repertoire consisted mostly or (in over one-third of the cases) solely of original material. The other fifth varied: some used a minimal amount of their own (say one or two songs), others up to 25 per cent original material or 'three or four songs a night'. Only two bands performed *no* material of their own, and of these one went out of their way to explain that they had only given up playing their own music because of the large turnover in players.
2 Out of the 33 questioned the only group using notated music was Unit Six, one of the only two *not* performing their own compositions.
3 For discussion of this assumption, see Finnegan 1977, chap. 3, 1985.
4 Well exemplified in a recent account of Bob Dylan's lyrics, to take just one example (Bowden 1982).

14 Plural worlds

1 About 57 in all in the Milton Keynes area in 1982 (figures from the Social Development Section of MKDC).
2 For example the National Federation of Music Societies, the British Federation of Brass Bands, the National Operatic and Dramatic Association, the Royal School of Church Music, the (national) Society of Recorder Players, the English Folk Dance and Song Society, the British Federation of Music Festivals and the various regional Arts Associations.
3 The much-discussed topic of the general influence of the 'mass media' is not covered as such in this study. This may seem a large gap, but I believe that their influence on musical experience has often been exaggerated precisely because the role of *local* activities and perceptions has been ignored. This study attempts to redress the balance by emphasising the *local* experiences which provided not only the foundation of the performance modes presented in the broadcasts and print media but also the framework within which local participants experienced and classified those performances.
4 Estimate by committee member at the Green Grass Social Club, June 1983.
5 Because of the particular examples treated in Becker's work, I do not think he can be accused of confusion on this point himself, even though pressing his

theoretical framework too hard, perhaps for examples which he did not intend, could be misleading. (Despite my qualifications here I have found his work in every way illuminating – a marvellous eye-opener to the social reality of artistic practice.)

15 Music in the home and school

1 This was based on local documentary sources and personal observation over several years, with some quantitative background provided by a survey of Milton Keynes schools carried out in 1982 (details in appendix). The survey and most of my research on the schools was in 1982; later school activities had probably been somewhat affected by disruptions in schools in the mid 1980s.
2 The number depends on various assumptions, but is based mainly on multiplying out the figures for the size of groups and the length and frequency of practices given in the questionnaire. Figures from the additional forty or so schools which did not respond to the questionnaire (but at least some of which certainly had similar groups) would also need to be added to the total.
3 The full question ran: 'Have you noticed any particular pattern about what kinds of children usually take part in extra-curricular musical activities (e.g. in terms of age, sex, academic achievement, parental background etc.)? If so, could you comment briefly?'

16 The churches and music

1 My description is based on participant observation (fairly frequent attendance at one local church, some visits to others, and many informal contacts with church members over some years), supplemented by a survey of all local churches near the end of 1983 carried out by Liz Close (see appendix).
2 These figures are based on a number of calculations and assumptions, drawing mainly (though not exclusively) on the estimates given by the churches in the 1983 survey.

17 Club and pub music

1 The information in this chapter is mainly based on local documentary sources and on interviews with representatives of 34 clubs carried out by Liz Close in 1983 (further details in appendix). Unattributed quotations are from responses in this survey.
2 They thus followed the general trend in these clubs away from the earlier stress on political and intellectual radicalism to more emphasis on the 'social' and entertainment side, well expounded in Taylor's illuminating history of working men's clubs (1972).
3 The few exceptions are relatively little known or difficult to obtain, e.g. Wilders [1975], Jackson 1976, Gorman 1978, chap. 3, Mass Observation 1943, Rowntree and Lavers 1951, pp. 174–81, Wilson 1980, Hunt 1983, and Hunt and Saterlee 1986.

4 This account is based on personal observation and interviews, local documentary
sources (mainly newspapers), and the survey of Milton Keynes pubs in 1982–3
carried out by Liz Close (see appendix). The term 'pub' has no precise definition,
for though it is used primarily of a licensed house for the sale of alcoholic drink
(mainly beer) to be consumed on the premises, popular usage also includes an inn
or tavern which provides accommodation as well as drink, and several Milton
Keynes 'hotels' and 'inns' advertised themselves as 'pubs'. In the discussion here,
'pub' is thus used to refer to all those establishments appearing under that term
(or as 'public houses') in official sources, local newspapers, and common speech –
a total of nearly 100 in all (85 in the central area surveyed, plus around a dozen in
the general locality).

5 Forty-two out of the 76 responses gave details of their current live music events,
and of the 9 further pubs which were uncontactable or unwilling to respond, at
least 4 were known from other sources to put on live music in 1982; of those not
currently providing music at the time of the survey, about 12 had had live music
within the previous two to three years, sometimes very frequently. About a
quarter only had juke boxes, taped background music or radio music, while
several of those without live music were intending to try it in the near future (see
appendix for a general account of the pub survey).

21 Pathways in urban living

1 The population during the period of the study was of the order of 100,000–
140,000 (varying at different periods). Five to 6 per cent of the population sounds
not so very different from the findings of the Medical Research Council National
Survey of Health and Development, in which 135 (4.1 per cent) of a sample of
3,313 36-year-olds said they played musical instruments with others and had
done so in the last 2 weeks (*singing* was not included) (thanks to Dr Mike
Wadsworth for supplying me with this information); but direct comparison is
difficult, partly because of age differences (the Milton Keynes population figures
of course covered the full age range, i.e. included the under-fives and the very
elderly); there is also the problem of deciding just who counts as 'local': some
members of Milton Keynes-based groups worked or travelled into Milton Keynes
rather than *residing* there, while some residents travelled elsewhere for their
musical activities. There are few comparative figures available on participation in
amateur, part-time or local music: the ESRC Data Archive did not have any data
sets on this in mid 1985, and Nissel's authoritative survey of statistics on the arts
concludes that 'the full extent of participation in amateur music-making remains
uncharted ground' (Nissel 1983, p. 90). So even if the figures here are an accurate
guide to local practice it is not possible to conclude how typical this is.

2 Practically all drawn from Milton Keynes players and singers apart from a small
contingent from the Buckingham 'Swan' and 'Cygnet' junior orchestras. The
North Bucks Music Centre in Bletchley was one of two music centres serving
Milton Keynes; the other – with its own clutch of music groups – was based at
Stantonbury.

3 These are well-worn themes in social science, with a long history of discussion

and controversy. I have found the following particularly illuminating (not that their authors would necessarily approve my approach): Pahl 1966, 1975, Stacey 1969, Neuwirth 1969, Spradley 1970, Bell and Newby 1971, Fischer 1977, Hannerz 1980, Abrams 1980, Wild 1981, 1984, Wright 1984, Lloyd 1984, Cohen 1985a, Bulmer 1986. A full theoretical analysis would no doubt rehearse the different senses of, for example, 'community', but neither space nor the general balance of this study permits more than a general discussion in relation to the specific implications of local musical practice in Milton Keynes.

4 An expectation reinforced by such common conclusions as that in Tomlinson's authoritative survey of leisure clubs and associations that such 'essentially primary groups...usually exhibit high degrees of sociability; interpersonal contact and purely social activity are often as important as the activity itself' (1979, p. 39).

5 See, e.g., Mitchell 1969, 1974, Boissevain and Mitchell 1973, Hannerz 1980, chap. 5, Abrams 1980 and (on quasi-groups) Mayer 1966.

6 A detailed quantitative survey of the Milton Keynes population as a whole, which I did not have the opportunity to undertake, *might* lead to a modification of this conclusion, but I doubt it.

7 E.g. the overlapping (if slightly differing) approaches in Hall 1959, chap. 10, Spradley 1970, Downs and Stea 1977, Thornton 1980, Ardener 1981 (I would modify some of these approaches to focus more on habitual *practice* than on the cognitive elements, but in other respects their insights are extremely pertinent for local musical practice).

8 Influential treatments include, among others, Evans-Pritchard 1939, Gurvitch 1958, Hall 1959, Fraisse 1963, Bourdieu 1963, Leach 1966; see also Finnegan 1982 (and further references there) and following note.

9 See e.g. Eliade 1965, Thompson 1967, Hearn 1975, Jahoda 1982, pp. 22ff.

10 A parallel critique to that presented here is found in May McCann's account of 'the past in the present' in some Northern Irish music (McCann 1985, esp. chap. 11); cf. also Finnegan 1982.

22 Music, society, humanity

1 The standard discussion and critiques of the so-called 'pluralist' approach (e.g. Playford 1968, McGrew and Wilson 1982, section 4) tend to focus on pressure groups and political power rather than (as here) cultural interests, but there has been some parallel discussion of recreational and leisure groups: e.g. Roberts 1978, chap. 7, Newton 1976 (see also n. 2 below).

2 There are now a number of relevant studies of voluntary interest groups and clubs in recent Britain (mostly, unfortunately, not very widely known), e.g. Tomlinson 1979, Kew 1979, Boothby and Tungatt 1977, Weinberger [1975], Hutson 1979, Khan 1976, and Newton 1976, which supplement earlier classic studies from elsewhere.

3 E.g. Parker 1976, Roberts 1978, Stebbins 1979, and Kelly 1983.

4 Thanks to Sheila Fieldhouse for drawing this to my attention.

5 The supposed consequences of rock are curiously similar to the crime, barbarism

and social collapse predicted to result from jazz in the 1920s and 1930s (see Merriam 1964, pp. 241–4, Cole 1978, p. 146, Rogers 1982, pp. 17ff.).

6 On the term 'ritual' see chap. 12, n. 4.

7 Something of which social scientists are now showing themselves more aware – notably Pahl 1984 and Bulmer 1986.

8 For some psychological work on the empirical study of processes in the practice (rather than theory) of music, including 'popular' as well as 'elite' music, see Deutsch 1982 (esp. essays by Sloboda and Konecni), Davies 1978, and Sloboda 1985 (such aspects seem to have been rather underplayed in psychology, however, and have not been drawn on directly here).

9 Blacking 1976, pp. 7, 100, 111, and 1982, pp. 40ff. Blacking's writings have been especially drawn on throughout this final section.

10 MacIntyre 1981, esp. chap. 14.

Appendix

1 See, for example, Whyte 1955 (esp. appendix), Pelto and Pelto 1973, Agar 1980, Hammersley and Atkinson 1983, Ellen 1984 (esp. chap. 2).

2 The problems of doing participant observation in one's own cultural setting, in particular when retaining one's *own* existing role, have received less attention than that of participating in foreign societies or unfamiliar 'social worlds'. There is some pertinent discussion, however, in Ellen 1984, 129ff., Messerschmidt 1981, Becker and Geer 1957, and in papers at the 1985 ASA Conference on 'Anthropology at home' (especially those by Callan, Cohen and Kelly), some published in Jackson 1987. Personal fieldwork in specifically urban settings is discussed in several of the sources above, also in Hannerz 1976 and 1980, Wallman et al 1980, Agar 1980 (esp. chap. 6), Wild 1981.

3 See, e.g., the discussion by Anne Akeroyd and John Davis in Ellen 1984, pp. 151–2, 317–18.

References

References include only those heavily relied on or directly cited, and do not therefore constitute a comprehensive bibliography of any of the topics touched on in this volume.

Abrahams, Roger D. 1968. Introductory remarks to a rhetorical theory of folklore. *Journal of American Folklore,* 81, 143–58
    1977. *Rituals in culture,* Folklore Preprint Series, 5, 1, Bloomington, Folklore Institute
Abrams, Philip. 1980. Social change, social networks and neighbourhood care. *Social Work Service,* 22, 12–23
Agar, Michael H. 1980. *The professional stranger: an informal introduction to ethnography.* New York, Academic Press
Anderson, Nels. 1923. *The hobo: the sociology of the homeless man.* Chicago, University of Chicago Press
Ardener, Shirley (ed.). 1981. *Women and space: ground rules and social maps.* London, Croom Helm
Baker, David. 1969. *Jazz improvisation.* Chicago, Maher
Banton, Michael (ed.). 1966. *The social anthropology of complex societies.* London, Tavistock
Barbu, Zev. 1976. Popular culture: a sociological approach. In Bigsby 1976
Barzun, Jacques. 1969. *Music in American life.* Bloomington, Indiana University Press (first pub. 1956)
Basso, Ellen B. 1985. *A musical view of the universe.* Philadelphia, University of Pennsylvania Press
Bauman, Richard. 1977. *Verbal art as performance.* Rowley, Mass., Newbury House
Bauman, Richard and Joel Sherzer (eds.). 1974. *Explorations in the ethnography of speaking.* London, Cambridge University Press
Becker, Howard S. 1951. The professional dance musician and his audience. *American Journal of Sociology,* 57, 136–44
    1960. Notes on the concept of commitment. *American Journal of Sociology,* 66, 32–40
    1974. Art as collective action. *American Sociological Review,* 39, 767–76
    1982. *Art worlds.* Berkeley, University of California Press

References

Becker, Howard S. and Blanche Geer. 1957. Participant observation and inter-viewing: a comparison. *Human Organization*, 3, 28–32

Bell, Colin and Howard Newby. 1971. *Community studies: an introduction to the sociology of the local community*. London, Allen and Unwin

Ben-Amos, Dan and Kenneth S. Goldstein (eds.). 1975. *Folklore: performance and communication*. The Hague, Mouton

Benamou, Michael and Charles Caramello (eds.). 1977. *Performance in post-modern culture*. Milwaukee, Center for Twentieth-Century Studies, University of Wisconsin, and Madison, Coda Press

Bennett, H. Stith. 1980. *On becoming a rock musician*. Amherst, University of Massachusetts Press

Berendt, Joachim. 1976. *The jazz book*. St Albans, Paladin

Bigsby, C. W. E. (ed.). 1976. *Approaches to popular culture*. London, Arnold

Blacking, John. 1971. Towards a theory of musical competence. In E. J. De Jager (ed.), *Man: anthropological essays presented to O. F. Raum*. Cape Town, C. Struik, 19–34

  1973. Fieldwork in African music. *Review of Ethnology*, 3, 23, 177–84

  1976. *How musical is man?* London, Faber

  1982. A case for higher education in the arts. In Ken Robinson (ed.), *The arts and higher education*, Research into Higher Education Monographs 48, Guildford, Society for Research into Higher Education, University of Surrey

Blacking, John and Joann W. Kealiinohomoku (eds.). 1979. *The performing arts: music and dance*. The Hague, Mouton

Bloch, Maurice. 1974. Symbols, song, dance and features of articulation or is religion an extreme form of traditional authority? *Archives européennes de sociologie*, 15, 55–81

Bocock, Robert. 1974. *Ritual in industrial society: a sociological analysis of ritualism in modern England*. London, Allen and Unwin

Boissevain, Jeremy and J. Clyde Mitchell (eds.). 1973. *Network analysis*. The Hague, Mouton

Boon, Brindley. 1978. *Play the music, play!*. London, Salvationist Publishing

Boothby, John and Malcolm Tungatt. 1977. *Clubs for sports and arts: results of a survey of facilities, members and activities in Cleveland County*. North-East Area Study Working Paper 46, University of Durham

Bourdieu, Pierre. 1963. The attitude of the Algerian peasant towards time. In J. Pitt-Rivers (ed.), *Mediterranean countrymen*. Paris, Mouton

  1977. *Outline of a theory of practice*. Eng. trans., Cambridge, Cambridge University Press

Bowden, Betsy. 1982. *Performed literature: words and music by Bob Dylan*. Bloomington, Indiana University Press

Brake, M. 1980. *The sociology of youth culture and youth subcultures*. London, Routledge and Kegan Paul

Brand, Violet and Geoffrey (eds.). 1979. *Brass bands in the twentieth century*, Letchworth, Egon

Briggs, Asa et al. 1985. What is the history of popular culture? *History Today*, December, 39–45

References

Bulmer, Martin. 1986. *Neighbours: the work of Philip Abrams*. Cambridge, Cambridge University Press

Burke, Peter. 1978. *Popular culture in early modern Europe*. London, Temple Smith

Burke, Thomas. 1947. *The English inn*. London, Jenkins

Callan, H. 1985. Ethnography of the personal: some problems and observations. Paper at ASA Conference 'Anthropology at home', Keele

Carr, Patrick (ed.). 1980. *The illustrated history of country music*. Garden City, Doubleday

Castells, Manuel. 1983. *The city and the grassroots: a cross-cultural theory of urban social movements*. London, Arnold

Chadwick, H. M. and N. K. 1932–40. *The growth of literature*, 3 vols., Cambridge, Cambridge University Press

Chambers, Iain. 1985. *Urban rhythms: pop music and popular culture*. Basingstoke, Macmillan

Clarke, Michael. 1982. *The politics of pop festivals*. London, Junction

Cohen, Anthony P. 1985a. *The symbolic construction of community*. London, Tavistock

    1985b. The symbolic construction of social boundaries: a soliloquy, on confusion. Paper at ASA Conference 'Anthropology at home', Keele

Cohen, Sara. 1987. Society and culture in the making of rock music in Liverpool. Unpublished doctoral thesis, University of Oxford

Cole, Hugo. 1978. *The changing face of music*. London, Gollancz

Collier, James L. 1978. *The making of jazz: a comprehensive history*. London, Granada

Corrigan, Paul and Simon Frith. 1975. The politics of youth culture. *Working Papers in Cultural Studies*, 7/8, 231–9

Cressey, Paul G. 1932. *The taxi-dance hall: a sociological study in commercialized recreation and city life*. Chicago, University of Chicago Press

Croft, R. H. (ed.). 1984. *Victorian and Edwardian Milton Keynes: a photographic collection*. Luton, White Crescent Press

Dankworth, Avril. 1968. *Jazz: an introduction to its musical basis*. London, Oxford University Press

Darbellay, Etienne. 1986. Tradition et notation dans la musique baroque. In Tokumaru and Yamaguti 1986

Dasilva, Fabio, Anthony Blasi and David Dees. 1984. *The sociology of music*. Notre Dame, Indiana, University of Notre Dame Press

Davies, John Booth. 1978. *The psychology of music*. London, Hutchinson

Davis, John. 1985. Rules not laws: outline of an ethnographic approach to economics. In Roberts et al. 1985

Deutsch, Diana (ed.). 1982. *The psychology of music*. New York, Academic Press

Donakowski, Conrad L. 1977. *A muse for the masses: ritual and music in an age of democratic revolution 1770–1870*. Chicago, Chicago University Press

Downs, Roger M. and David Stea. 1977. *Maps in minds: reflections on cognitive mapping*. London and New York, Harper and Row

References

Dunn, Ginnette. 1980. *The fellowship of song: popular singing traditions in East Suffolk*. London, Croom Helm

Eades, J. S. 1982. Dimensions of meaning, western music and the anthropological study of symbolism. In J. Davis (ed.). *Religious organization and religious experience*. London, Academic Press

Eames, Edwin and Judith Granich Goode. 1977. *Anthropology of the city: an introduction to urban anthropology*. Englewood Cliffs, Prentice-Hall.

Ehrlich, Cyril. 1976. *The piano: a history*. London, Dent

1985. *The music profession in Britain since the eighteenth century: a social history*. Oxford, Clarendon Press

Eliade, Mircea. 1965. *The myth of the eternal return*. Princeton, Princeton University Press

Ellen, Roy F. (ed.). 1984. *Ethnographic research: a guide to general conduct*. ASA Research Methods in Social Anthropology, 1, London, Academic Press

Elliott, Dave. 1982. The rock music industry. Unit 24 in Open University Course *Popular culture* (U203), Milton Keynes, Open University Press

Evans-Pritchard, E. E. 1939. Nuer time-reckoning. *Africa*, 12, 189–216

Feld, Steven. 1974. Linguistic models in ethnomusicology. *Ethnomusicology*, 18, 197–217

Fellerer, Carl Gustav. 1935. *Mittelalterliches Musikleben der Stadt Freiburg im Uechtland*. Freiburger Studien zur Musikwissenschaft, 3, Regensburg

Finkelstein, Sidney. 1975. *Jazz: a people's music*. New York, Da Capo Press

Finnegan, R. 1969. How to do things with words: performative utterances among the Limba of Sierra Leone. *Man*, 4, 537–52

1977. *Oral poetry: its nature, significance and social context*. Cambridge, Cambridge University Press

1982. '*Short time to stay*': comments on time, literature and oral performance. Hans Wolff Memorial Lecture, African Studies Program, Bloomington, Indiana University

1985. Oral composition and oral literature in the Pacific. In Bruno Gentili and Giuseppe Paione (eds.), *Oralità: cultura, letteratura, discorso*. Roma, Edizioni dell'Ateneo

1986. The relations between composition and performance: three alternative modes. In Tokumaru and Yamaguti 1986

Fischer, Claude S. 1977. *Networks and places: social relations in the urban setting*. New York, Free Press

Fish, Stanley. 1980. *Is there a text in this class? The authority of interpretive communities*. Cambridge, Mass., Harvard University Press

Foley, John Miles. 1985. *Oral-formulaic theory and research: an introduction and annotated bibliography*. New York, Garland

Fraisse, Paul. 1963. *The psychology of time*. Eng. trans., New York, Harper and Row

Frith, Simon. 1978. *The sociology of rock*. London, Constable

1981a. 'The magic that can set you free': the ideology of folk and the myth of the rock community. In Middleton and Horn, 1981– (*Popular Music*, 1)

References

1981b. *Sound effects: youth, leisure, and the politics of rock 'n' roll*. New York, Pantheon

1983. *British popular music research*. UK Working paper 1 [Exeter], IASPM

Gammond, Peter and Raymond Horricks (eds.). 1980. *Brass bands*. Cambridge, Stephens

Gans, Herbert J. 1974. *Popular culture and high culture*. New York, Basic Books

Geertz, Clifford. 1975. *The interpretation of cultures*. London, Hutchinson

Gluckman, Max. 1962. Les Rites de passage. In M. Gluckman (ed.), *Essays on the ritual of social relations*, Manchester, Manchester University Press

Goffman, Erving. 1967. *Interaction ritual: essays on face-to-face behavior*. Chicago, Aldine

1974. *Frame analysis: an essay on the organization of experience*. New York, Harper and Row

Goody, Jack. 1977. Against 'ritual': loosely structured thoughts on a loosely defined topic. In Moore and Meyerhoff 1977

Gorman, Clem. 1978. *Backstage rock*. London, Pan

Graña, Cesar. 1971. *Fact and symbol: essays in the sociology of art and literature*. New York, Oxford University Press

Grossman, Loyd. 1976. *A social history of rock music*. New York, McKay

Gurvitch, Georges. 1958. Structures sociales et multiplicité des temps. *Bulletin de la société française de philosophie*, 50, 99–142

Hall, Edward T. 1959. *The silent language*. New York, Doubleday

Hall, Stuart and Paddy Whannel. 1964. *The popular arts*. London, Hutchinson

Hammersley, Martyn and Paul Atkinson. 1983. *Ethnography: principles in practice*. London, Tavistock

Hannerz, Ulf. 1976. Methods in an African urban study. *Ethnos*, 41, 68–98

1980. *Exploring the city: inquiries toward an urban anthropology*. New York, Columbia University Press

Hanson, Alice M. 1985. *Musical life in Biedermeier Vienna*. Cambridge, Cambridge University Press

Harker, Dave. 1980. *One for the money: politics and popular song*. London, Hutchinson

1985. *Fakesong: the manufacture of British 'folksong' 1700 to the present day*. Milton Keynes, Open University Press

Harrison, Max. 1980. Jazz. In Sadie 1980

Hearn, Frank. 1975. Remembrance and critique: the uses of the past for discrediting the present and anticipating the future. *Politics and Society*, 5, 201–27

Hebdige, Dick. 1979. *Subculture: the meaning of style*. London, Methuen

Hendler, Herb. 1983. *Year by year in the rock era*. Westport and London, Greenwood

Holoman, D. Kern and Claude V. Palisca (eds.). 1982. *Musicology in the 1980's*. New York, Da Capo

Horton, Robin and Ruth Finnegan (eds.). 1973. *Modes of thought: essays on thinking in western and non-western societies*. London, Faber

Huizinga, Johan. 1970. *Homo ludens: a study of the play element in culture*. Eng. trans., London, Paladin

References

Hunt, G. P. 1983. The culture of drinking: an anthropological analysis of alcohol use. Paper at Scottish ethnography workshop, Edinburgh

Hunt, G. P. and S. Saterlee. 1986. The pub, the village and the people. *Human Organization*, 45, 62–74

Hustwitt, Mark. 1986. Cultural studies and pop. Unpublished paper at Kent Popular Culture Group Conference on 'A limited number of interpretations: the making of popular music studies', Canterbury, University of Kent

Hutson, Susan. 1979. *A review of the role of clubs and voluntary associations based on a study of two areas in Swansea*. London, Sports Council and Social Science Research Council

Hymes, Dell. 1974. *Foundations in socio-linguistics: an ethnographic approach*. Philadelphia, University of Pennsylvania Press

1975. Breakthrough into performance. In Ben-Amos and Goldstein 1975

IASPM. 1985. *Popular music perspectives*, 2. Göteborg, Exeter, Ottawa and Reggio Emilia, International Association for the Study of Popular Music

Jackson, Anthony. 1968. Sound and ritual. *Man*, 3, 293–9

Jackson, Anthony (ed.). 1987. *Anthropology at home*. London, Tavistock

Jackson, Brian. 1972. *Working class community*. Harmondsworth, Penguin

Jackson, Michael. 1976. *The English pub*. London, Collins

Jahoda, Marie. 1982. *Employment and unemployment: a social-psychological analysis*. Cambridge, Cambridge University Press

Jewell, Derek. 1980. *The popular voice: a musical record of the 60s and 70s*. London, Deutsch

Jones, Bryn. 1972. A bibliography of rock. *Working Papers in Cultural Studies*, 2, 129–37

Kapferer, Bruce. 1986. Performance and the structuring of meaning and experience. In Turner and Bruner 1986

Kaplan, Steven L. (ed.). 1984. *Understanding popular culture: Europe from the Middle Ages to the nineteenth century*. Berlin, Mouton

Kelly, E. 1985. Studying the city: what should the social anthropologist do when there is no community?. Paper at ASA Conference, 'Anthropology at home', Keele

Kelly, John R. 1983. *Leisure identities and interactions*. London, Allen and Unwin

Kew, Stephen. 1979. *Ethnic groups and leisure*. London, Sports Council and Social Science Research Council

Khan, Naseem. 1976. *The arts Britain ignores: the arts of ethnic minorities in Britain*. London, Arts Council, Gulbenkian Foundation and Community Relations Committee

La Fontaine, Jean (ed.). 1972. *The interpretation of ritual*. London, Tavistock

Laing, Dave. 1985. *One chord wonders: power and meaning in punk rock*. Milton Keynes, Open University Press

Laing, Dave et al. 1975. *The electric muse: the story of folk into rock*. London, Eyre Methuen

Lamb, Andrew. 1981. Music of the popular theatre. In Temperley 1981

Leach, Edmund. 1966. Time and false noses. In Two essays concerning the symbolic representation of time, *Rethinking anthropology*. London, Athlone Press

References

Lee, Edward. 1970. *Music of the people: a study of popular music in Great Britain*. London, Barrie and Jenkins
Lloyd, A. L. 1967. *Folk song in England*. London, Lawrence and Wishart
1974. Popular music. *Encyclopaedia Britannica*
Lloyd, Peter. 1984. Community action: panacea or placebo. *Royal Anthropological Institute News*, 63, 13–15
Lord, Albert. 1960. *The singer of tales*. Cambridge, Mass., Harvard University Press
MacIntyre, Alasdair. 1981. *After virtue: a study in moral theory*. London, Duckworth
MacKenzie, Justin R. A. 1977. Contemporary English folk music: the social context of stylistic change. MA thesis, University of Keele
Malm, William P. 1971. The modern music of Meiji Japan. In Donald H. Shively (ed.), *Tradition and modernization in Japanese culture*, Princeton, Princeton University Press
Malone, Bill C. 1968. *Country music U.S.A.: a fifty-year history*. American Folklore Society, Austin and London, University of Texas Press
1980. Country music. In Sadie 1980
Martin, Bernice. 1981. *A sociology of contemporary cultural change*. Oxford, Blackwell
Martin, David. 1980. *The breaking of the image: a sociology of Christian theory and practice*. Oxford, Blackwell
1984. Music and religion: ambivalence towards 'the aesthetic'. *Religion*, 14, 269–92
Mass Observation. 1943. *The pub and the people: a work town study*. London, Gollancz
Mayer, Adrian C. 1966. The significance of quasi-groups in the study of complex societies. In Banton 1966
McCann, May. 1985. The past in the present: a study of some aspects of the politics of music in Belfast. Unpublished Ph.D. thesis, Queen's University, Belfast
McGrew, Anthony G. and M. J. Wilson (eds.). 1982. *Decision making: approaches and analyses*. Manchester, Manchester University Press
McGuinness, Rosamund. 1985. The music business in early eighteenth-century London. *Quarterly Journal of Social Affairs*, 1, 249–59
Merriam, Alan P. 1964. *The anthropology of music*. Evanston, Northwestern University Press
Messerschmidt, Donald A. (ed.). 1981. *Anthropologists at home in North America: methods and issues in the study of one's own society*. New York, Cambridge University Press
Middleton, Richard. 1972. *Pop music and the blues*. London, Gollancz
1979. The rise of jazz. Units 25–7 in Open University course *The rise of modernism in music 1890–1935* (A308), Milton Keynes, Open University Press
1981. 'Reading' popular music. Unit 16 in Open University course *Popular culture* (U203), Milton Keynes, Open University Press

364

References

Middleton, Richard and David Horn (eds.). 1981–. *Popular music* (yearbook). Cambridge, Cambridge University Press
   1981. *Folk or popular? Distinctions, influences, continuities, Popular music*, 1, Cambridge, Cambridge University Press
Middleton, Richard and John Muncie. 1981. Pop culture, pop music and post-war youth: countercultures. Unit 20 in Open University course *Popular culture* (U203), Milton Keynes, Open University Press
Milton Keynes household survey 1983. 1985. Milton Keynes, Milton Keynes Development Corporation
Milton Keynes postal survey 1979. 1981. Milton Keynes, Milton Keynes Development Corporation
Mitchell, J. Clyde. 1974. Social networks. *Annual review of anthropology*, 3, 279–99
   1983. Case and situation analysis. *Sociological Review*, 31, 187–211
Mitchell, J. Clyde (ed.). 1969. *Social networks in urban situations*. Manchester, Manchester University Press
Moore, Sally Falk and Barbara G. Meyerhoff (eds.). 1977. *Secular ritual*. Assen, Van Gorcum
Muncie, John. 1981. Pop culture, pop music and post-war youth: subcultures. Unit 19 in Open University course *Popular culture* (U203), Milton Keynes, Open University Press
Mungham, Geoff and Geoff Pearson (eds.). 1976. *Working class youth culture*. London, Routledge and Kegan Paul
Needham, Rodney. 1967. Percussion and transition. *Man*, 2, 606–14
Nettel, Reginald. 1944. *Music in the five towns 1840–1914*. London, Oxford University Press
   1956. *Seven centuries of popular song*. Phoenix House, London
Nettl, Bruno (ed.). 1978. *Eight urban musical cultures: tradition and change*. Urbana, University of Illinois Press
Neuwirth, Gertrud. 1969. A Weberian outline of a theory of community: its application to the 'Dark Ghetto'. *British Journal of Sociology*, 20, 148–63
Newton, Kenneth. 1976. *Second city politics: democratic processes and decision-making in Birmingham*. Oxford, Clarendon Press
Nissel, Muriel (ed.). 1983. *Facts about the arts: a summary of available statistics*. London, Policy Studies Institute
Obelkevich, Jim. 1985. Introduction. In workshop on 'Music and society in England since 1850', Coventry, University of Warwick
Ohmiya, Makoto. 1986. The lost performance tradition: the notated and the unnotated in European classic music. In Tokumaru and Yamaguti 1986
Ostendorf, Berndt. 1983. *Ethnicity and popular music*. Working paper 2, IASPM
Pacey, Betty. n.d. Musical memories. Four-page unpublished typescript
Pahl, R. E. 1966. The rural–urban continuum. *Sociologia Ruralis*, 6, 299–329
   1975. *Whose city? and other essays on sociology and planning*. Harmondsworth, Penguin
   1984. *Divisions of labour*. Oxford, Blackwell
Paredes, Americo and Richard Bauman (eds.). 1972. *Toward new perspectives in*

folklore. American Folklore Society, Austin and London, University of Texas Press

Parker, Charles. 1975. Popsong, the manipulated ritual. In Peter Abbs (ed.), *The black rainbow: essays on the present breakdown of culture*. London, Heinemann

Parker, Stanley. 1976. *The sociology of leisure*. London, Allen and Unwin

Pearson, Lynn F. 1978. *Non work time: a review of the literature*. Research Memorandum 65, Centre for Urban and Regional Studies, University of Birmingham

Pelto, P. J. and G. H. 1973. Ethnography: the fieldwork enterprise. In J. J. Honigman (ed.), *Handbook of social and cultural anthropology*, Chicago, Rand-McNally

Pickering, Michael and Tony Green (eds.). 1987. *Everyday culture: popular song and the vernacular milieu*. Milton Keynes, Open University Press

Playford, J. 1968. The myth of pluralism. *Arena*, 15, 34–47

Ray, Benjamin. 1973. 'Performative utterances' in African rituals. *History of religions*, 13, 16–35

Raynor, Henry. 1972. *A social history of music from the Middle Ages to Beethoven*. London, Barrie and Jenkins

Roberts, Carrie. 1981. Brass bands: a case study. Appendix in 'Leisure activities: home and neighbourhood', Unit 10 in Open University course *Popular culture* (U203), Milton Keynes, Open University Press

Roberts, Bryan, Ruth Finnegan and Duncan Gallie (eds.). 1985. *New approaches to economic life: economic restructuring, unemployment and the social division of labour*. Manchester, Manchester University Press

Roberts, Kenneth. 1978. *Contemporary society and the growth of leisure*. London, Longman

Rogers, Dave. 1982. *Rock 'n' roll*. London, Routledge and Kegan Paul

Rosselli, John. 1984. *The opera industry in Italy from Cimarosa to Verdi: the role of the impresario*. Cambridge, Cambridge University Press

Rowntree, B. Seebohm and G. R. Lavers. 1951. *English life and leisure: a social study*. London, Longmans, Green

Russell, Dave. 1985. The brass band movement 1850–1914. Paper at workshop on 'Music and society in England since 1850', Coventry, University of Warwick

Russell, John F. and J. H. Elliott. 1936. *The brass band movement*. London, Dent

Sadie, Stanley (ed.). 1980. *The new Grove dictionary of music and musicians*. 20 vols., London, Macmillan

Schering, Arnold. 1926, 1941. *Musikgeschichte Leipzigs*. Vols. 2–3, Leipzig, Kistner und Siegel

Schutz, Alfred. 1951. Making music together: a study in social relationship. *Social Research*, 18, 76–97 (reprinted in J. L. Dolgin et al. (eds.), *Symbolic anthropology*, New York, Columbia University Press, 1977)

Scribner, R. W. 1981. *For the sake of simple folk: popular propaganda for the German Reformation*. Cambridge, Cambridge University Press

Scribner, Sylvia and Michael Cole. 1981. *The psychology of literacy*. Cambridge, Mass. and London, Harvard University Press

References

Shepherd, John et al. 1977. *Whose music? A sociology of musical languages.*
London, Latimer

Shestack, Melvin. 1977. *The country music encyclopaedia.* London, Omnibus
Press

Silbermann, Alphons. 1963. *The sociology of music.* Eng. trans., London, Routledge and Kegan Paul

Simmel, Georg. 1950. The metropolis and mental life. In K. F. Wolff (ed.). *The
sociology of Georg Simmel.* New York, Free Press

Sloboda, John A. 1985. *The musical mind: the cognitive psychology of music.*
Oxford, Clarendon Press

Smith, J. Sutcliffe. 1945. *The story of music in Birmingham.* Birmingham, Cornish
Brothers

Sparshot, F. E. 1980. Aesthetics of music. In Sadie 1980

Spencer, Paul (ed.). 1985. *Society and the dance: the social anthropology of
process and performance.* Cambridge, Cambridge University Press

Spradley, James P. 1970. *You owe yourself a drunk: an ethnography of urban
nomads.* Boston, Little, Brown

Stacey, Margaret. 1969. The myth of community studies. *British Journal of
Sociology*, 20, 134–47

Stebbins, Robert A. 1964. The jazz community: the sociology of a musical sub-
culture. Ph.D. thesis, University of Minnesota

  1977. The amateur: two sociological definitions. *Pacific Sociological Review*, 20,
  582–606

  1979. *Amateurs: on the margin between work and leisure.* Beverley Hills, Sage

Stevens, John. 1979. *Music and poetry in the early Tudor Court.* Cambridge,
Cambridge University Press

Stewart, John and Gerry Philipsen. 1984. Communication as situated accomplish-
ment: the cases of hermeneutics and ethnography. *Progress in Communication Sciences*, 5, 177–217

Stone, Ruth M. 1982. *Let the inside be sweet: the interpretation of music event
among the Kpelle of Liberia.* Bloomington, Indiana University Press

Tambiah, S. J. 1973. Form and meaning of magical acts: a point of view. In
Horton and Finnegan 1973

  1979. A performative approach to ritual. *Proceedings of the British Academy*,
  65, 113–69

Taylor, Arthur R. 1979. *Brass band.* London, Hart-Davis MacGibbon

  1983. *Labour and love: an oral history of the brass band movement.* London,
  Elm Tree

Taylor, John. 1972. *From self-help to glamour: the working man's club, 1860–
1972.* History workshop pamphlets, 7, Oxford

Temperley, Nicholas. 1979. *The music of the English parish church.* 2 vols.,
Cambridge, Cambridge University Press

Temperley, Nicholas (ed.). 1981. *The romantic age 1800–1914.* Athlone History of
Music in Britain, vol. 5, London, Athlone Press

Thompson, E. P. 1967. Time, work-discipline, and industrial capitalism. *Past and
Present*, 38, 56–97

References

Thornton, Robert J. 1980. *Space, time and culture among the Iraqw of Tanzania.* New York, Academic Press

Thrasher, Frederic M. 1927. *The gang.* Chicago, University of Chicago Press

Tokumaru, Yosihiko and Yamaguti Osamu (eds.). 1986. *The oral and the literate in music.* Tokyo, Academia Music

Tomlinson, Alan. 1979. *Leisure and the role of clubs and voluntary groups.* London, Sports Council and Social Science Research Council

Treitler, Leo. 1982. Structural and critical analysis. In Holoman and Palisca 1982

Turner, Victor. 1982. *From ritual to theatre: the human seriousness of play.* New York City, Performing Arts Journal Publications

Turner, Victor and Edward M. Bruner (eds.). 1986. *The anthropology of experience.* Urbana, University of Illinois Press

Vaughan Williams, Ralph and A. L. Lloyd (eds.). 1959. *The Penguin book of English folk songs.* Harmondsworth, Penguin

Veal, A. J. 1975. *Recreation planning in new communities: a review of British experience.* Research Memorandum 46, Centre for Urban and Regional Studies, University of Birmingham

Vulliamy, Graham and Edward Lee (eds.). 1980. *Pop music in school.* 2nd edn, Cambridge, Cambridge University Press

  1982. *Popular music: a teacher's guide.* London, Routledge

Wadel, Cato. 1979. The hidden work of everyday life. In Wallman 1979

Wallman, Sandra (ed.). 1979. *Social anthropology of work.* London, Academic Press

Wallman, Sandra et al. 1980. Ethnography by proxy: strategies for research in the inner city. *Ethnos,* 45

Walvin, James. 1978. *Leisure and society 1830–1950.* London, Longman

Ware, Kenneth L. 1976. The Parry–Lord oral formulaic theory applied to the Afro-American jazz tradition. MA thesis, Indiana University

Weber, Max. 1947. *The theory of social and economic organization.* Eng. trans., New York, Oxford University Press

  1958. *The rational and social foundations of music,* trans. and ed. by D. Martindale et al., Carbondale, Southern Illinois University Press

Weber, William. 1975. *Music and the middle class: the social structure of concert life in London, Paris and Vienna.* London, Croom Helm

Weinberger, Barbara. [1975.] *Leisure and the arts in Birmingham: a pilot investigation.* Research Memorandum 47, Centre for Urban and Regional Studies, University of Birmingham

Western Folklore, 30, 3, July 1971 (special issue on hillbilly music)

White, Avron. 1983. 'Convention and constraint in the operation of musical groups: two case studies'. Unpublished Ph.D. thesis, Keele University, 1983

White, Avron (ed.). 1987. *Lost in music: culture, style and the musical event.* Sociological Review Monograph 34, London, Routledge and Kegan Paul

Whyte, William F. 1955. *Street corner society: the social structure of an Italian slum.* 2nd edn, Chicago, University of Chicago Press

Wild, R. A. 1981. *Australian community studies and beyond.* Sydney, Allen and Unwin

References

1984. Community studies: an overview. Paper at SSRC Community Studies Workshop, Aston University

Wilders, Malcolm G. [1975.] Some preliminary discussions on the sociology of the public house. In Stanley Parker et al. (eds.), *Sport and leisure in contemporary society*, School of the Environment, Polytechnic of Central London

Wilgus, D. K. 1970. Country-western music and the urban hillbilly. *Journal of American Folklore*, 83, 157–79

Wilgus, D. K. and John Greenaway (eds.). 1965. Hillbilly issue, *Journal of American Folklore*, 78, 309, July–Sept.

Willis, Paul E. 1978. *Profane culture*. London, Routledge and Kegan Paul

Wilson, Paul. 1980. *Drinking in England and Wales: an enquiry carried out on behalf of the Department of Health and Social Security*. London, HMSO

Wirth, Louis. 1938. Urbanism as a way of life. *American Journal of Sociology*, 44, 1–24

Wolf, Janet. 1983. *Aesthetics and the sociology of art*. Controversies in sociology, 14, London, Allen and Unwin

Woods, Frederick. 1979. *Folk revival: the rediscovery of a national music*. Poole, Blandford Press

Wright, Kenneth et al. (compilers). 1979. *Fenny Stratford album*. Wolverton, People's Press of Milton Keynes

Wright, Susan. 1984. Rural communities and decision makers. *Royal Anthropological Institute News*, 63, 9–13

Wustman, Rudolf. 1909. *Musikgeschichte Leipzigs*, vol. 1. Leipzig and Berlin, Teubner

Yeo, E. and S. (eds.) 1981. *Popular culture and class conflict 1590–1914: explorations in the history of labour and leisure*. Brighton, Harvester Press

Index

Index

Boys' Brigade Bugle Band, 28, 48
Brackley Morris Men, 65
Bradwell, New Inn, 287
Bradwell Monk, 234
Bradwell Silver Band, 47, 48, 51, 52, 301
Branchette, Ken, 73
brass bands *and see* name of band, 18, 27, 47–57
  and classical music, 49–50
  and the community, 56–7
  competitions, 51–2
  composition, 161
  conductors, 51
  family tradition, 48–9, 54
  finances of, 53, 279–80
  music libraries, 53–4
  organisation of, 50–1
  performances, 51–3
  size of, 47
  and social class, 48–50
  social tradition of, 56–7
  teachers, 50
  venues, 231
Broseley Brass, 47, 51
Buckingham Parish Church, 245
Bucks Arts Association, 282
Buddhist community and music, 186, 216
Bull, Newport Pagnell, 230
Bull, Stony Stratford, 228
Bull and Butcher Singers' Club, 250

Canzonetta Singers, 39, 289
careers in music, 17–18, 136, 140
Cavatina Strings, 37
ceilidh bands *and see* Irish music, 62, 65, 256, 266
Chappells, 274, 275, 277
charity and local music, 288–92
Chinese community and music, 186, 186
choirs *and see* name of choir
  church, 211–14, 218
  classical, 38–40
  finances of, 249, 278–9
  membership, 40, 238–9
  organisation of, 38–9, 236–49
choral tradition, 27
'Christians Awake', 52
church attendance, 219–20
church music *and see* religion and music, 207–21
  choirs, 211–14, 218
  classical, 35
  composition, 162–3
  and education, 218–19
  instrumental groups, 215–16
  non-Christian religions, 216–17
  patronage, 207, 284

performance conventions, 150
repertoires, 213–14, 216
research method, 345
and social class, 220
venues, 217–18
Clark, Paul, 165
classical music *and see* name of group, 33–46
  audiences, 146–8
  and brass bands, 49–50
  choirs, 38–40
  and churches, 35
  composition, 160–1
  conductors, 242
  and education, 133–6, 140–1
  experience of, 41–2
  finances, 278–9, 282
  and folk music, 62, 69
  local influences, 43–4
  music libraries, 43–4
  and musicianship, 17–18
  orchestras, 27, 35–9, 278–9
  participants, 44–5
  performance of, 146–8, 174–5
  repertoire, 39, 42–4
  and rock music, 44
  and schools, 33–5
  and social class, 44–5
  teachers and teaching, 33–5, 133–6
clubs *and see* social clubs, 222–6, 251–2
  country and western, 90–3
  folk, 58–61, 286–7
  jazz, 286–7
Co-operative Choral Society, 27
Cock and Bull Band, 61–2
Cock and Bull Folk Festival, 62, 228
Cock Inn, Stony Stratford, 228, 230, 233
Colin James Trio, 84
community music *and see* local music, 299–302, 304
Compass Youth Club, 105, 224–5
competitions, 183–4
  brass band, 51–2
composition, 160–179, 267–8
  brass bands, 161
  church music, 162–3
  classical, 160–1
  folk, 176
  jazz, 166–7, 178, 267–8
  opera, 161
  rock and pop music, 103–7, 167–71, 176–8, 267–8
composition-in-performance, 165–7
Concorde Jazz Band, 84
Concrete Cow Folk Club, 250
Concrete Cows, The, 265
conductors

Index

MUSIC/CULTURE

A series from Wesleyan University Press
Edited by Harris M. Berger and Annie J. Randall
Originating editors: George Lipsitz, Susan McClary, and Robert Walser

The Other Side of Nowhere:
Jazz, Improvisation and
Communities in Dialogue
edited by Daniel Fischlin
and Ajay Heble

Empire of Dirt:
The Aesthetics and Rituals of
British Indie Music
by Wendy Fonarow

The 'Hood Comes First:
Race, Space, and Place in Rap and
Hip-Hop
by Murray Forman

Wired for Sound: Engineering and
Technologies in Sonic Cultures
edited by Paul D. Greene and
Thomas Porcello

Sensational Knowledge:
Embodying Culture Through
Japanese Dance
by Tomie Hahn

Voices in Bali:
Energies and Perceptions in
Vocal Music and Dance Theater
by Edward Herbst

Traveling Spirit Masters:
Moroccan Gnawa Trance and
Music in the Global Marketplace
by Deborah Kapchan

Symphonic Metamorphoses:
Subjectivity and Alienation in
Mahler's Re-Cycled Songs
by Raymond Knapp

Music and Technoculture
edited by René T.A. Lysloff and
Leslie C. Gay, Jr.

A Thousand Honey Creeks Later:
My Life in Music from Basie to
Motown—and Beyond
by Preston Love

Songs, Dreamings, and Ghosts:
The Wangga of North Australia
by Allan Marett

Phat Beats, Dope Rhymes: Hip Hop
Down Under Comin' Upper
by Ian Maxwell

Carriacou String Band Serenade:
Performing Identity in the
Eastern Caribbean
by Rebecca S. Miller

Global Noise:
Rap and Hip-Hop outside the USA
edited by Tony Mitchell

Popular Music in Theory:
An Introduction
by Keith Negus

Upside Your Head! Rhythm and
Blues on Central Avenue
by Johnny Otis

Singing Archaeology:
Philip Glass's Akhnaten
by John Richardson

Black Noise:
Rap Music and Black Culture in
Contemporary America
by Tricia Rose

The Book of Music and Nature:
An Anthology of Sounds, Words,
Thoughts
edited by David Rothenberg and
Marta Ulvaeus

Angora Matta:
Fatal Acts of North-South
Translation
by Marta Elena Savigliano

Making Beats:
The Art of Sample-Based Hip-Hop
by Joseph G. Schloss

Dissonant Identities: The Rock 'n'
Roll Scene in Austin, Texas
by Barry Shank

Among the Jasmine Trees:
Music and Modernity in
Contemporary Syria
by Jonathan Holt Shannon

Banda: Mexican Musical Life
across Borders
by Helena Simonett

Subcultural Sounds:
Micromusics of the West
by Mark Slobin

Music, Society, Education
by Christopher Small

Musicking: The Meanings of
Performing and Listening
by Christopher Small

Music of the Common Tongue:
Survival and Celebration in
African American Music
by Christopher Small

Singing Our Way to Victory:
French Cultural Politics and Music
During the Great War
by Regina M. Sweeney

Setting the Record Straight:
A Material History of Classical
Recording
by Colin Symes

False Prophet:
Fieldnotes from the Punk
Underground
by Steven Taylor

Any Sound You Can Imagine:
Making Music/Consuming
Technology
by Paul Théberge

Club Cultures:
Music, Media and
Sub-cultural Capital
by Sarah Thornton

Dub: Songscape and Shattered
Songs in Jamaican Reggae
by Michael E. Veal

Running with the Devil:
Power, Gender, and Madness in
Heavy Metal Music
by Robert Walser

Manufacturing the Muse:
Estey Organs and Consumer
Culture in Victorian America
by Dennis Waring

The City of Musical Memory:
Salsa, Record Grooves, and
Popular Culture in Cali, Colombia
by Lise A. Waxer

About the author

Ruth Finnegan is Professor Emeritus at the Open University in the UK, where she studies the comparative sociology and anthropology of artistic activity. Her previous publications include *Communicating: The Multiple Modes of Human Interconnection* (Routledge, 2002), *Tales of the City: A Study of Narrative and Urban Life* (Cambridge University Press, 1998), *South Pacific Oral Traditions,* edited with Margaret Orbell (Indiana University Press, 1995), and *Oral Poetry: Its Nature, Significance, and Social Context* (Cambridge University Press, 1977; second edition, Indiana University Press, 1992).